# Lecture Notes in Computer Science 5824

Commenced Publication in 1973
Founding and Former Series Editors:
Gerhard Goos, Juris Hartmanis, and Jan van Leeuwen

T0223386

Tsuyoshi Takagi    Masahiro Mambo (Eds.)

# Advances in Information and Computer Security

4th International Workshop on Security, IWSEC 2009
Toyama, Japan, October 28-30, 2009
Proceedings

Springer

Volume Editors

Tsuyoshi Takagi
Future University Hakodate
School of Systems Information Science
116-2 Kamedanakano-cho, Hakodate, Hokkaido 041-8655, Japan
E-mail: takagi@fun.ac.jp

Masahiro Mambo
University of Tsukuba
Graduate School of Systems and Information Engineering
1-1-1 Tennodai, Tsukuba, Ibaraki 305-8573, Japan
E-mail: mambo@cs.tsukuba.ac.jp

Library of Congress Control Number: 2009935384

CR Subject Classification (1998): E.3, G.2.1, D.4.6, K.6.5, K.4.1, F.2.1, C.2

LNCS Sublibrary: SL 4 – Security and Cryptology

ISSN       0302-9743
ISBN-10    3-642-04845-5 Springer Berlin Heidelberg New York
ISBN-13    978-3-642-04845-6 Springer Berlin Heidelberg New York

springer.com

© Springer-Verlag Berlin Heidelberg 2009
Printed in Germany

Typesetting: Camera-ready by author, data conversion by Scientific Publishing Services, Chennai, India
Printed on acid-free paper       SPIN: 12772520       06/3180       5 4 3 2 1 0

# Preface

The Fourth International Workshop on Security (IWSEC 2009) was held at Toyama International Conference Center, Toyama, Japan, October 28–30, 2009. The workshop was co-organized by CSEC, a special interest group on computer security of the IPSJ (Information Processing Society of Japan) and ISEC, a technical group on information security of IEICE (The Institute of Electronics, Information and Communication Engineers). The excellent Local Organizing Committee was led by the IWSEC 2009 General Co-chairs, Kazuo Takaragi and Hiroaki Kikuchi.

IWSEC 2009 received 46 paper submissions from all over the world. We would like to thank all the authors who submitted papers. Each paper was reviewed by at least three reviewers. In addition to the Program Committee members, many external reviewers joined the review process in their particular areas of expertise. We were fortunate to have this energetic team of experts, and are grateful to all of them for their hard work. The hard work includes very active discussion; the discussion phase was almost as long as the initial individual reviewing. The review and discussion were supported by a very nice Web-based system, iChair. We thank its developers.

Following the review phases, 13 papers were accepted for publication in this volume of Advances in Information and Computer Security. Together with the contributed papers, the workshop featured an invited talk and a hash function panel both of which were respectively given and chaired by eminent researcher, Bart Preneel (Katholieke Universiteit Leuven). An abstract of the talk, titled "The Future of Cryptographic Algorithms," is included in this volume. We deeply appreciate his contribution.

Many people contributed to the success of IWSEC 2009. We wish to express our deep appreciation for their contribution to information and computer security.

October 2009

Tsuyoshi Takagi
Masahiro Mambo

Madison, 19xx
Madison Indiana

# IWSEC 2009
# Fourth International Workshop on Security

Co-organized by

CSEC (Special Interest Group on Computer Security of the Information
Processing Society of Japan)
and
ISEC (Technical Group on Information Security, Engineering Sciences Society,
of the Institute of Electronics, Information and Communication Engineers,
Japan)

## General Co-chairs

| | |
|---|---|
| Kazuo Takaragi | Hitachi Ltd., Japan |
| Hiroaki Kikuchi | Tokai University, Japan |

## Advisory Committee

| | |
|---|---|
| Norihisa Doi | Chuo University, Japan |
| Akira Hayashi | Kanazawa Institute of Technology, Japan |
| Hideki Imai | Chuo University, Japan |
| Günter Müller | University of Freiburg, Germany |
| Yuko Murayama | Iwate Prefectural University, Japan |
| Eiji Okamoto | University of Tsukuba, Japan |
| Ryoichi Sasaki | Tokyo Denki University, Japan |
| Shigeo Tsujii | Chuo University, Japan |
| Doug Tygar | University of California, Berkeley, USA |

## Program Committee Co-chairs

| | |
|---|---|
| Tsuyoshi Takagi | Future University Hakodate, Japan |
| Masahiro Mambo | University of Tsukuba, Japan |

## Local Organizing Committee

| | |
|---|---|
| Venue and Excursion Co-chairs | Takao Okubo (Fujitsu Laboratories Ltd., Japan) |
| | Koutarou Suzuki (NTT Corp., Japan) |
| Award Co-chairs | Hiroshi Doi (Institute of Information Security, Japan) |
| | Mitsuru Tada (Chiba University, Japan) |

Finance, Registration,
and Liaison Co-chairs          Ryuya Uda (Tokyo University of Technology,
                                   Japan)
                               Hisao Sakazaki (Hitachi Ltd., Japan)
                               Kazuhisa Sekine (NTT DoCoMo, Inc., Japan)
Publicity Co-chairs            Kunihiko Miyazaki (Hitachi Ltd., Japan)
                               Noboru Kunihiro (The University of Tokyo,
                                   Japan)
System Co-chairs               Toshihiro Tabata (Okayama University, Japan)
                               Yasuharu Katsuno (IBM Tokyo Research
                                   Laboratory, Japan)
Publication Co-chairs          Isao Echizen (National Institute of Infomatics,
                                   Japan)
                               Toru Nakanishi (Okayama University, Japan)

## Program Committee

| | |
|---|---|
| Toru Akishita | Sony Corporation, Japan |
| Gergei Bana | Technical University of Lisbon, Portugal |
| Alexandra Boldyreva | Georgia Institute of Technology, USA |
| Zhenfu Cao | Shanghai Jiao Tong University, China |
| Christian S. Collberg | University of Arizona, USA |
| Bart De Decker | K.U.Leuven, Belgium |
| Chang Ee-Chien | National University of Singapore, Singapore |
| Eiichiro Fujisaki | NTT, Japan |
| Steven Furnell | University of Plymouth, UK |
| Juan A. Garay | AT&T Labs - Research, USA |
| Philippe Golle | Palo Alto Research Center, USA |
| Dieter Gollmann | TU Hamburg, Germany |
| Tetsu Iwata | Nagoya University, Japan |
| Mariusz H. Jakubowski | Microsoft, USA |
| Marc Joye | Thomson R&D, France |
| Angelos D. Keromytis | Columbia University, USA and Symantec |
| | Research Labs, France |
| Seungjoo Kim | Sungkyunkwan University, Korea |
| Takeshi Koshiba | Saitama University, Japan |
| Michiharu Kudo | IBM Japan, Japan |
| Noboru Kunihiro | University of Tokyo, Japan |
| Dong Hoon Lee | Korea University, Korea |
| Javier Lopez | University of Malaga, Spain |
| Mark Manulis | TU Darmstadt, Germany |
| Kanta Matsuura | University of Tokyo, Japan |
| Alfred Menezes | University of Waterloo, Canada |
| Atsuko Miyaji | JAIST, Japan |
| Hirofumi Muratani | Toshiba, Japan |
| David Naccache | ENS, France |

# Table of Contents

## Authentication

# The Future of Cryptographic Algorithms

## (Extended Abstract)

Bart Preneel[1,2]

[1] Katholieke Universiteit Leuven, Dept. Electrical Engineering-ESAT/COSIC,
Kasteelpark Arenberg 10, bus 2446, B-3001 Leuven, Belgium
[2] IBBT, Van Crommenlaan, B-9000 Gent
bart.preneel@esat.kuleuven.be

Until the early 1970s, cryptology was restricted to closed government and military applications; commercial applications of cryptology were very rare. Cryptographic devices were expensive and they were mostly used for the protection of communications at the data link layer. The invention of public key cryptography in 1975 and the publication of the DES (Data Encryption Standard) in 1977 by the US government formed the start of open academic research in cryptology; these developments were also essential contributions towards the deployment of cryptography in large scale systems.

The explosion of information and communication technologies at the beginning of the 1990s created applications with important security needs such as electronic payments, e-commerce and e-government. At the same time, the progress in technology opened the door to a massive deployment of cryptographic technologies in both software and hardware. Today, cryptography has become a commodity: almost all wireless communication devices use cryptographic protection (e.g., GSM and 3GSM, Bluetooth, WLAN, and Zigbee); hundreds of million of users have banking cards with public key cryptography; an increasing number of countries issues electronic identity cards and passports with public key cryptography; computers use cryptographic libraries for secure VPNs (IPsec), secure web access (SSL/TLS), file encryption, hard disk encryption, secure software updates and DRM. Cryptology has become an established scientific discipline: the IACR (International Association for Cryptologic Research) has close to 1500 members, and in addition to the seven IACR annual conferences and workshops there is a growing number of conferences with at least one session on cryptology.

In this talk we discuss the state of the art and future of cryptographic algorithms. We revisit progress on block ciphers, stream ciphers, hash functions, MAC algorithms, public-key encryption and digital signatures. For each of these we will assess the maturity of the primitive and discuss challenges for future research. The main challenge is to create better trade-offs between performance, cost and security. More concretely, the following topics can be identified:

**Extremely low cost solutions** are essential to get cryptography everywhere, that is, for applications such as ambient intelligence, sensor networks and RFIDs. A specific target is encryption with less than 1500 gates or an entity authentication protocol that consumes less than 50 mJoules.

**Extremely fast solutions** for applications such as bus encryption, and authenticated encryption for Petabyte storage devices and Terabit networks.

T. Takagi and M. Mambo (Eds.): IWSEC 2009, LNCS 5824, pp. 1–2, 2009.

**Long term security solutions:** for applications such as e-voting, e-health and national security we need cryptographic algorithms that provide guaranteed protection for 50 years or more. While this is conceivable for symmetric cryptography, this goal is currently a major challenge for public key cryptography, in view of progress in research to attack hard mathematical problems and the anticipated development of quantum computers.

Even if cryptographic algorithms are mathematically secure, attackers can break applications by exploiting side channel attacks. Passive attacks try to recover key information by measuring physical parameters such as execution time, power consumption, or electromagnetic radiation. Active attacks include attacks that probe the memory or processor bus and attacks that introduce faults during the calculation. Experience during the last decade has taught us that developing implementations that remain secure under these powerful attacks is a very challenging problem. Another challenge is that applications need to be developed in a way that key lengths can be upgraded and algorithms can be replaced. Finally, an important decision for each application is whether we adopt open standards, use proprietary algorithms or even algorithms that are kept secret. This decision has important implications on security aspects, but it has also an economic and strategic dimension.

**Acknowledgements.** This author's work was supported in part by the IAP Programme P6/26 BCRYPT of the Belgian State (Belgian Science Policy) and by the European Commission through the IST Programme under contract number ICT-2007-216676 ECRYPT II.

# Bit-Free Collision: Application to APOP Attack

Lei Wang[1], Yu Sasaki[1,2], Kazuo Sakiyama[1], and Kazuo Ohta[1]

[1] The University of Electro-Communications,
1-5-1 Chofugaoka, Chofu-shi, Tokyo, 182-8585, Japan
{wanglei,yu339,saki,ota}@ice.uec.ac.jp
[2] NTT Information Sharing Platform Laboratories, NTT Corporation
sasaki.yu@lab.ntt.co.jp

**Abstract.** This paper proposes a new variant of collisions on hash functions named *bit-free collision*, which can be applied to reduce the number of chosen challenges in password recovery attacks on hash-based challenge and response protocols, such as APOP (Authentication Post Office Protocol). In all previous APOP attacks, the attacker needs to impersonate the server and to send poisoned chosen challenges to the user. Impersonating the server takes a risk that the user may find out he is being attacked. Hence, it is important for the attacker to reduce the number of impersonation in order to lower the probability that the attack will be detected. To achieve this, reducing the number of chosen challenges is necessary. This paper is the first approach to improve previous APOP attacks based on this observation to our best knowledge. With $t$-bit-free collisions presented in this paper, the number of chosen challenges to recover each password character can be reduced by approximately a factor of $2^t$. Though our attack utilizing $t$-bit-free collisions needs higher offline complexity than previous attacks, the offline computation can be finished in practical time if the attacker can obtain reasonable computation power. In this research, we generate 1-bit-free collisions on MD5 practically. As a result, the number of challenges for password recovery attacks on real APOP is approximately *half* reduced. Of independent interest, we apply the bit-free-collision attack on a simpler hash function MD4, and show that 3-bit-free collisions can be generated practically.

**Keywords:** hash function, bit-free collision, APOP, MD5, MD4.

## 1 Introduction

With the development of internet, challenge and response password authentication protocols have become popular. In the communication through internet, the user may face several threats: (a) a third party may impersonate the server, and (b) a third party may eavesdrop on the communication channel. Accordingly, it is dangerous for the user to send the password itself directly to the server to get authenticated. As a countermeasure to protect the password, challenge and response password authentication protocols have been adopted. The crucial idea is, in every authentication round, randomly generating challenges and computing responses based on challenges and the password. One popular approach to

T. Takagi and M. Mambo (Eds.): IWSEC 2009, LNCS 5824, pp. 3–21, 2009.
© Springer-Verlag Berlin Heidelberg 2009

generate responses is hashing challenges and the password, which will base the security of the protocols on the underlying hash functions. As far as the hash function is secure, the protocol is secure.

APOP (Authentication Post Office Protocol) [8] is a challenge and response password authentication protocol based on MD5 [10], which has been *practically* utilized in real mail systems. The responses are generated by hashing the challenges concatenated with the password. Recently password recovery attacks on APOP have been proposed [6] [11] [12], which originated from collision attacks on MD5 [15]. All previous APOP attacks are *chosen* challenge attacks. The attacker impersonates the server and sends chosen challenges to the user to make the user provide corresponding responses. The attack scenario is as follows.

1. the user sends access requests to the attacker (impersonating the server).
2. the attacker sends poisoned chosen challenges to the user.
3. the user sends the corresponding responses to the attacker.
4. the attacker responds "No new email" to the user.

Impersonating the server takes a risk that the user may suspect to have being attacked in the following situations:

(a) the user does not get a new email for a long time if the attacker continuously impersonates the server.
(b) the user gets a new email delayed even if the attacker impersonates the server from time to time. Suppose the user accesses to the server once an hour. The user may get a new email delayed an hour even though the attacker only impersonates once.

From this observation, the attacker should reduce the times of impersonating in order to lower the probability that the attack will be detected. This means that the number of necessary chosen challenges should be reduced. So far, no result has been published to improve previous APOP attacks on reducing the number of chosen challenges to our best knowledge.

## 1.1 Our Results

We will propose the first approach to reduce the number of challenges of APOP attacks, by presenting a new variant of collisions on hash functions named *bit-free collision*.

Conceptually, bit-free collision is a pair of partially-fixed messages, which will collide regardless of the value of the unfixed bits. The unfixed bits are denoted as *free bits* in this paper. We denote by $t$-bit-free collision a bit-free collision with $t$-free bits for simplicity. For example, suppose $(M, M')$ is a 1-bit-free collision. By setting the free bit to 0, we can obtain a pair of messages $(M_0, M_0')$ from $(M, M')$. By setting the free bit to 1, we can obtain another pair of messages $(M_1, M_1')$ from $(M, M')$. Both $(M_0, M_0')$ and $(M_1, M_1')$ are collisions. So $(M, M')$ will be a collision no matter what the value of the free bit is. Similarly, for $t$-bit-free collision, a set of $2^t$ pairs of messages can be derived by setting the values of the $t$-free bits, and each pair of messages from this set is a collision. Here we will roughly point out the difference between free bit in this paper and neutral bit proposed by Biham and Chen in [1]. The usage of free bit is mainly allowing the attacker to freely determine several bit-values of the colliding messages without affecting the collision, while the usage of neutral bit is mainly speeding up collision search. Refer to Section 3 for more details.

Bit-free collisions can be utilized to reduce the number of chosen challenges of APOP attacks. Previous APOP attacks recover the password characters one by one. One character is 8-bit long, so there are $2^8$ possible candidates for one password character. The attacker adopts *guess-then-verify* approach to exhaustively check the correctness of all possible candidates for one password character. In order to check one possible candidate, the attacker needs to generate a pair of challenges. If a possible candidate is the *true* password character, the responses of the corresponding pair of challenges will collide. There are in total $2^8$ candidates for a password character, and each candidate needs a pair of challenges. As a result, $(2^8 - 1)$ pairs of challenges[1] are necessary in the worst case.

On the other hand, our attack utilizes bit-free collisions to reduce the number of chosen challenges. Our attack will also recover password characters one by one. *The main novelty of our attack is recovering one password character part by part, which will reduce the number of necessary chosen challenges.* The high-level description of our attack to recover one password character is as follows. More details are explained in Section 5.2.

1. Locate $t$-free bits in the targeted password character, which divides the password character into $(8 - t)$-non-free bits and $t$-free bits.
2. Recover the $(8 - t)$-non-free bits first. The attacker adopts exhaustive guess-then-verify approach: guess the value of $(8 - t)$-non-free bits, then generate a pair of challenges, which will lead to a $t$-bit-free collision after being concatenated with the guess value, and finally send the pair of challenges to the user to check whether the responses collide or not. If the responses collide, the guess value is true. Otherwise, the guess value is wrong. There are in total $(2^{8-t})$ possible candidates for the $(8 - t)$-non-free bits, so $(2^{8-t} - 1)$ pairs of challenges are necessary in the worst case.
3. Recover the $t$-free bits also by guess-then-verify approach. The attacker can recover the $t$-free bits one bit by one bit. For example, the attacker sets the value of the first target bit to 0, then generates a pair of challenges that leads to a $(t - 1)$-bit-free collision, and finally sends the pair of challenges to check whether the responses collide or not. If the responses collide, then the guess is correct and the value of the first target bit is 0. Otherwise, the value of the first target bit is 1. Similarly, the attacker can recover the second bit until the whole $t$-free bits are obtained. So $t$ pairs of challenges are necessary in the worst case.

In the above procedure of recovering one password character, the attacker will first exhaustively guess and recover the values of $(8 - t)$-non-free bits without

---

[1] The attacker does not need to check the last possible candidate if the attacker has confirmed all other candidates are not correct.

the knowledge of the $t$-free bits, and then recover the value of the $t$-free bits. As shown above, $(2^{8-t} - 1 + t)$ pairs of challenges are necessary in the worst case. The total number of necessary challenges has been reduced by approximately a factor of $2^t$ compared to previous APOP attacks. Consequently following our attack strategy, the probability that the user will detect the attack has become lower, which makes the attack become more realistic.

We will analyze the complexity of generating bit-free collisions. In general, such bit-free collisions are harder to be found than regular collisions, but can provide more serious damages to hash-based protocols. We believe that bit-free collisions have more applications besides APOP attacks. We will use one compression function computation as a unit to count the complexity. The complexity of generating $t$-bit-free collisions on a general Merkle-Damgård hash function is $\left(\frac{n}{2}\right)^{2^t} \times 2^{\frac{n}{2}+t}$ computations. Here we omit the descriptions. Refer to Section 3.1 for more details. The complexity of $t$-bit-free collisions on a general compression function is $2^{2^{t-1} \times n + t}$ computations. Refer to Section 3.2 for more details. Moreover, we apply bit-free-collision attacks on MD5 [10] and MD4 [9] by utilizing previous collision attacks on MD5 and MD4 [2] [15] [14]. We show that 1-bit-free-collision attacks on MD5 and 3-bit-free-collision attacks on MD4 are practical.

Finally, we show the effect of applying 1-bit-free collisions on MD5 to password recovery attacks on APOP in a real environment. The previous paper [6] assumes that each password character has 6 bits of entropy (they consider a kind of password most people use). Under this assumption, a password character is recovered by generating $2^5$ colliding challenge pairs, and asking $2^6$ queries impersonating the server. Previous paper [6] assumes that a user runs the authentication protocol once per minute, and estimates that asking $2^6$ queries takes about 1 hour. In our attack, with the same assumption, we need to generate $2^4$ 1-bit-free collisions for recovering non-free bits and a single collision for recovering the free bit. Hence, our attack needs to ask $2^5 + 2$ queries in the online phase, which can be finished in roughly 30 minutes[2]. Another our concern is the validity of the assumption that the attacker can ask chosen challenges once per minute. This assumption is not always true. It is typical that a user checks new mails only several times per day. Let us consider the case that the impersonation can be done only once per day. Clearly, the previous attack takes roughly 60 days to recover a password character while our attack takes only 30 days. We therefore can say that reducing the number of queries is important in a real environment.

## 1.2  Organization of the Paper

Section 2 explains background and related works. Section 3 defines bit-free collision and analyzes the complexity of generating bit-free collisions. Section 4 shows practical bit-free-collision attacks on MD5 and MD4 based on previous differential collision attacks. Section 5 applies bit-free collisions to APOP attack. Section 6 gives the conclusion and discussion of future work.

---

[2]  We ignore the offline complexity of generating 1-bit-free collisions. Actually, this can be finished quickly, e.g. 36 seconds with 14400 PCs (details are discussed in Section 4.2). Hence, the assumption is reasonable.

## 2 Background and Related Works

### 2.1 Merkle-Damgård Hash Function

Many hash functions such as MD5 [10] and MD4 [9] have been designed following the well-known framework *Merkle-Damgård* [7] [3]. A Merkle-Damgård hash function map arbitrary-length messages to short hash digests by iterating a fixed-input-length component usually described as *compression function*. Denote by $H$, $F$ and $M$ a Merkle-Damgård hash function, underlying compression function and an input message respectively. The hash procedure is as follows:

1. $M$ will be padded and divided into fixed-length blocks $m_1$, $m_2$, $\cdots$, $m_l$: $pad(M) = m_1 \| m_2 \| \cdots \| m_l$, where $\|$ means concatenation.
2. $F$ takes a public constant $IV$ and $m_1$ as input and outputs an intermediate value $h_1$. Then $F$ takes $h_1$ and $m_2$ as input and outputs $h_2$. Similarly, the calculation will be carried out until all the message blocks are used.
3. Finally $H$ outputs $h_l$ as the hash digest.

We will describe one property of Merkle-Damgård hash functions, which has been adopted by APOP attacks.

**One property of Merkle-Damgård hash function**
Denote by $M$ and $M'$ two messages. $pad(M) = m_1 \| m_2 \| \cdots \| m_l$ and $pad(M') = m'_1 \| m'_2 \| \cdots \| m'_l$. Moreover there is some $t$ ($1 \leq t \leq l$) such that $m_i = m'_i$ ($\forall i : t \leq i \leq l$). According to the above hash procedure, the following relation holds:

$$h_t = h'_t \implies h_l = h'_l.$$

### 2.2 APOP

APOP is a hash-based challenge and response authentication protocol [8], which is used in mail system by servers to authenticate users. The procedure of APOP is detailed as follows. A mail server and a user share one common password.

1. The user sends one access request to the mail server.
2. The mail server generates a random challenge, and sends it to the user.
3. The user calculates one hash digest MD5(challenge||password), and sends the digest to the mail server.
4. The mail server itself carries out the same calculation, gets another hash digest, and compares it with the user's response.
5. If the two digests are the same, authentication succeeds. Otherwise, authentication fails.

### 2.3 Previous Password Recovery Attacks on APOP

Password recovery attacks on APOP [6] [11] [12] are chosen challenge attacks. The attacker impersonates the server and sends chosen challenges to the user. Briefly speaking, the attacker will recover the password characters one by one based on the property of MD5 (Merkle-Damgård hash function), which has been shown in Section 2.1. Consequently, the complexity of recovering the whole password will be reduced significantly from the expected complexity. Denote the password by $P_1||P_2||\ldots||P_l$. Suppose the attacker has recovered the values of $P_1$, $P_2$, $\ldots$, $P_{i-2}$ and $P_{i-1}$ ($i \leq l$). The high-level description of the procedure of recovering $P_i$ is as follows.

1. Guess the value of $P_i$.
2. Generate a pair of challenges $(C, C')$ satisfying three conditions: $C$ and $C'$ have the same length; the length of $C||P_1||P_2||\cdots||P_i$ is multiple of block-length; and $H(C||P_1||P_2||\cdots||P_i) = H(C'||P_1||P_2||\cdots||P_i)$.
3. Send $C$ to the user to obtain the response $R$.
4. Send $C'$ to the user to obtain the response $R'$.
5. If $R = R'$, then the current guess value is the true $P_i$.
6. If $R \neq R'$, change the guess value, and go to step 2.

Suppose $P_i$ has $n$ bits. There are $2^n$ possible candidates for $P_i$. As a result, steps 2-6 will be repeated $2^n$ times in the worst case. So the bit-length of $P_i$ should be as short as possible. From the specification of APOP [8], the length of challenges must be a multiple of 8 bits. Therefore, the minimum length of $P_i$ is 8 bits, namely, one character. So, the previous APOP attacks [6] [11] [12] recover the password characters one by one. A password character is 8-bit long, so there are in total $2^8$ possible candidates for one password character. Following the above previous APOP attack procedure, $2^8 - 1$ pairs of challenges are necessary in the worst case. This paper will mainly deal with how to reduce the number of necessary challenges.

## 3   Bit-Free Collision

**Definition 1.** *If a pair of partially-fixed messages $(M, M')$ satisfies the following conditions[3], it is denoted as a bit-free collision on a hash function $H$:*

1. *$M$ and $M'$ have the same bit-length.*
2. *$M$ and $M'$ have the unfixed bits at the same bit positions.*
3. *the unfixed bits of $M$ and the unfixed bits of $M'$ are equal.*
4. *any pair of messages, derived by setting the value of the unfixed-bits of $M$ and $M'$, will be a collision on $H$.*

*where the unfixed bits are denoted as free bits.*

Denote by $t$-bit-free collision a bit-free collision with $t$-free bits for simplicity. $2^t$ pairs of colliding messages can be derived from a $t$-bit-free collision. So a $t$-bit-free collision is a set of $2^t$ independent colliding message pairs.

   Picking 1-bit-free collision, denoted as $(M, M')$, as an example. $M$ and $M'$ have the same bit-length, and have one same bit position (the free bit), where the value is not fixed. By setting the free bit to 0, a pair of messages $(M_0, M_0')$ is

---

[3] The conditions are restrictive. In fact we can give more general definition for bit-free collision. For example, conditions 1, 2 and 3 are not necessary. Since this paper deals with application to APOP attacks, we define the bit-free collision according to this application for consistency.

derived from $(M, M')$. By setting the free bit to 1, a pair of messages $(M_1, M_1')$ is derived from $(M, M')$. Both $(M_0, M_0')$ and $(M_1, M_1')$ are collisions on $H$.

This paper will deal with bit-free-collision attacks on the compression function of MD5, which makes this concept similar to the neutral bit concept proposed by Biham and Chen [1]. The concept of the neutral bit has been detailed in Appendix A. Free bit can be regarded as neutral bit up to the last step of MD5 compression function. Previous works never consider neutral bit up to the last step. This is because the usage of neutral bits is mainly speeding up the collision search. So the previous works are interested in finding neutral bits up to *some* intermediate step of hash computation. Free bit does not speed up the collision search. However, it has the following potential advantage: the attacker has the power to freely control *some* bit-values of the colliding messages without affecting the collision. We believe the concept bit-free collision has many applications.

In the following two sections, we will analyze the complexity of generating a $t$-bit-free collision on a general iterated hash function and a general compression function.

### 3.1   Bit-Free Collisions on a General Merkle-Damgård Hash Function

Denote by $H$ a general Merkle-Damgård hash function. Denote by $n$ the bit-length of hash values of $H$. We will utilize Joux's multi-collisions [4] to generate bit-free collisions on $H$. The format of generated bit-free-colliding messages with $l$-block length is as follows: $(M = m_0 || m_1 || \ldots || m_{l-1}, M' = m_0 || m_1' || \ldots || m_{l-1}')$, and the free bits locate in the $m_0$.

To warm up, we first show how to generate 1-bit-free collisions. We will locate the free bits in the first message block $m_0$. $m_0^0$ and $m_0^1$ are derived by setting the 1-free bit of $m_0$ to 0 and 1, respectively.

1. Determine the bit position of the 1-free bit.
2. Set the 1-free bit to 0, and adopt Joux's multi-collision technique [4] to obtain $2^{\frac{n}{2}}$ multi-collisions on $H$ as shown in Fig. 1 with $l = \frac{n}{2}$. The colliding messages will be denoted as $m_0^0 || m_{1,k_1} || \ldots || m_{\frac{n}{2}, k_{\frac{n}{2}}}$, where $k_1, k_2, \ldots, k_{\frac{n}{2}} \in \{0, 1\}$.
3. Calculate the hash values of messages $m_0^1 || m_{1,k_1} || m_{2,k_2} || \ldots || m_{\frac{n}{2}, k_{\frac{n}{2}}}$, for all $k_1, k_2, \ldots, k_{\frac{n}{2}}$.

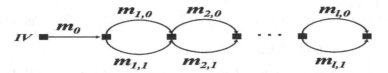

**Fig. 1.** Joux's multi-collision

4. If a pair of colliding messages is found: $(m_0^1||m_{1,k_1}||m_{2,k_2}||\ldots||m_{\frac{n}{2},k_{\frac{n}{2}}},$ $m_0^1||m_{1,k_1'}||m_{2,k_2'}||\ldots||m_{\frac{n}{2},k_{\frac{n}{2}}'})$, where $k_1, k_1', \ldots, k_{\frac{n}{2}}, k_{\frac{n}{2}}' \in \{0,1\}$, then $(m_0||m_{1,k_1}||\ldots||m_{\frac{n}{2},k_{\frac{n}{2}}}, m_0||m_{1,k_1'}||\ldots||m_{\frac{n}{2},k_{\frac{n}{2}}'})$ is 1-bit-free collision.

Similarly, we can utilize Joux's multi-collision technique to generate $t$-bit-free collisions. The high-level description is as follows:

1. Determine the bit positions for the $t$-free bits in $m_0$. There are $2^t$ possible values for the $t$-free bits, which will be denoted as $\{0, 1, \ldots, 2^t - 1\}$ for simplicity.
2. Set the values of the $t$-free bits to 0.
3. Generate multi-collisions on $H$ as shown in Fig. 1 with $l = (\frac{n}{2})^{2^t}$. The complexity is $(\frac{n}{2})^{2^t} \times 2^{\frac{n}{2}}$, counting one compression function computation as a unit.
4. Change the free bits to 1. Denote the new derived first message block as $m_0^1$.
5. First calculate the intermediate hash value at $(\frac{n}{2} + 1)$-th block of new messages (starting with $m_0^1$) to find a collision $(M_{1,0}, M_{1,1})$. Denote the colliding intermediate hash value as $h$. Then fix the intermediate hash value at $(\frac{n}{2}+1)$-th block as $h$, and calculate the intermediate hash values at $(n+1)$-th block to find a collision $(M_{2,0}, M_{2,1})$. Similar calculation will be carried out until the last message block. Finally we obtain $m_0||M_{1,k_1}||M_{2,k_2}||\ldots||M_{(\frac{n}{2})^{2^t}-1,k_{(\frac{n}{2})^{2^t}-1}}$ $(k_i \in \{0,1\})$, which will collide when the value of the free bits are 0 or 1.
6. Repeat steps 4 and 5 setting the free bits to the rest possible values.
7. Finally we will obtain a pair of messages, which can collide for any possible value of the free bits. This pair of message is a $t$-bit-free collision on $H$.

The complexity of generating a $t$-bit-free collision on $H$ is roughly $(\frac{n}{2})^{2^t} \times 2^{\frac{n}{2}+t}$.

### 3.2  Bit-Free Collisions on a General Compression Function

Denote by $F$ a general compression function. Denote by $n$ the bit-length of the outputs of $F$. We will assume that the message space is always large enough to carry out the exhaustive $t$-bit-free collision search. We will analyze the complexity of generating a $t$-bit-free collision on $F$ by the exhaustive search. The exhaustive search is as follows:

1. Determine the bit positions for the $t$-free bits. There are in total $2^t$ possible values for the whole $t$-free bits, which will be denoted as $\{0, 1, \ldots, 2^t - 1\}$.
2. Randomly select a message $M$, and expand $M$ to a set of messages $\{M_0, \ldots, M_{2^t-1}\}$, where $M_i$ differs from $M$ only at the $t$-free bits and the value of the $t$-free bits is $i$.
3. Search a pair of messages $(M, M')$ such that $F(M_i) = F(M_i')$ for any $i \in \{0, 1, \ldots 2^t - 1\}$.
4. $(M, M')$ is a pair of $t$-bit-free collision on $F$.

Denote by $F^*$ a compression function $F^*(M) = F(M_0)||F(M_1)||\ldots||F(M_{2^t-1})$. The exhaustive search can be regarded as searching a collision on $F^*$. The bit-length of $F^*$ is $2^t \times n$. So the complexity of generating a $t$-bit-free collision on a general compression function $F$ with $n$ bit-length hash digests is $2^{(2^t \times n)/2}$ $F^*$ computations. One $F^*$ computation consists of $2^t$ $F$ computations. As a result, $t$-bit-free-collision attacks on $F$ is with a complexity $2^{2^{t-1} \times n + t}$ $F$ computations.

# 4 Bit-Free-Collision Attacks Based on Differential Collision Attacks on Hash Functions

This section will deal with how to find bit-free collisions based on Wang *et al.*'s differential collision attacks.

In 2005, Wang *et al.* published their differential collision attacks on hash functions from MD4 family [14] [15]. Here we will briefly recall Wang *et al.*'s collision attacks. Refer to Appendix C.1 for more details. The attack procedure is as follows: first determine a message difference $\Delta$, then determine how the $\Delta$ will propagate during hash computation, which is usually denoted as *differential path*, then derive sufficient conditions that make sure the difference propagation will follow the differential path, and finally search a message $M$ satisfying all sufficient conditions, which leads to a collision $(M, M + \Delta)$.

## 4.1 Crucial Ideas

We first show a 1-bit-free collision as an example in Fig. 2. Denote by $\Delta$ the message difference of the chosen collision attack on $H$ in Fig. 2. Following Wang *et al.*'s collision attacks, if $M^0$ can satisfy all the sufficient conditions, $(M^0, M^0 + \Delta)$ is a collision. Similarly, if $M^1$ can satisfy all the sufficient conditions, $(M^1, M^1 + \Delta)$ is a collision. So, as long as both $M^0$ and $M^1$ can satisfy all the sufficient conditions, $(M, M + \Delta)$ will collide no matter what the value of the free bit is. Consequently, 1-bit-free-collision search can be transformed to search a pair of messages $(M^0, M^1)$ satisfying two conditions: $M^0$ and $M^1$ only differ at the free bit, and both $M^0$ and

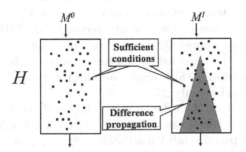

**Fig. 2.** a 1-bit-free-collision based on a collision attack

Sufficient conditions are from a collision attack on $H$. $M^0$ and $M^1$ are derived by setting a bit-value of $M$ to 0 and 1, respectively. Difference propagation describes how the 1-bit difference between $M^0$ and $M^1$ propagates during the hash computation.

$M^1$ can satisfy all sufficient conditions of a differential path for collision attack. Usually the difference propagation in Fig. 2 starts from *some* intermediate step of hash computation depending on the bit position of the free bit. So after the bit positions of the free bits are determined, a suitable differential path should have the minimum number of sufficient conditions, which might be affected by the difference propagation in Fig. 2.

A high-level description of $t$-bit-free-collision attack based on Wang *et al.*'s collision attacks is as follows.

1. Pre-determine the bit positions of $t$-free bits.
2. Choose a differential path of a collision attack with the minimum number of sufficient conditions, which might be affected by changing the values of the free bits. Denote by $\Delta$ the message difference of the collision attack.
3. Search a message $M$ that can satisfy all the sufficient conditions no matter what the value of the $t$-free bits is.
4. $(M, M + \Delta)$ is a $t$-bit-free collision.

## 4.2    Bit-Free-Collision Attacks on MD5

This section deals with bit-free-collision attacks on MD5. For specification of MD5, refer to Appendix B.

**Pre-determine the bit position of the free bits:**
   Since we will apply bit-free-collision attacks on MD5 to improve APOP attacks, we locate the free bits in the last 8-bit positions of messages.
**Well-suited differential path for collision attacks on MD5:**
   We adopt a differential path obtained from previous attacks on MD5 as follows:
   -Pseudo-collision attack on the compression function of MD5 proposed by Den Boer and Bosselaers in [2] has been shown in Appendix C.2. The differential path for the pseudo-collision attack on MD5 has the least number of sufficient conditions to our best knowledge. Moreover, Klima in [5] proposes a fast collision search technique on MD5 named *Tunnel*. By using Klima's tunnel Q9 detailed in Appendix C.3, the bit-free collision search can be regarded as starting from step 25. So the number of sufficient conditions, which might be affected by changing the value of the free bits, will be only 23.
   -A so-called technique *IV bridge* proposed by Sasaki *et al.* in [12] provides a pair of messages which can link public constant IV of MD5 to necessary differences for pseudo-collision attacks in [2]. The pair of messages in [12] is shown in Table 1: $(M_0||M_1, M_0||M_1')$, which provides a pair of intermediate hash values $(h, h')$ well-suited for pseudo-collision attacks in [2].

Finally there are roughly 23 sufficient conditions that might be affected by changing the value of the free bits. For one collision on MD5, roughly $2^{23}$ MD5 computations are necessary. Hence, for $t$-bit-free collisions, $2^{23 \times 2^t}$ MD5 computations are necessary. It seems that 1-bit-free collision with a complexity $2^{46}$ is practical.

**Table 1.** One example of 1-bit-free collision on MD5

$(M_0||M_1||M_2, M_0||M_1'||M_2)$ is a 1-bit-free collision, where the free bit locates at the 24-th bit of $m_{15}$ of $M_2$. Denote by $md5$ the compression function of MD5. $h = md5(md5(IV, M_0), M_1)$ and $h' = md5(md5(IV, M_0), M_1')$. $h$ and $h'$ is well-suited for pseudo-collision attacks on MD5 [2]: $md5(h, M_2) = md5(h', M_2)$.

| | | | | |
|---|---|---|---|---|
| $M_0$ | $m_4$=0x37373936 | $m_5$=0x3433302d | $m_6$=0x38312d35 | $m_7$=0x61704035 |
| | $m_8$=0x6f777373 | $m_9$=0x645f6472 | $m_{10}$=0x63657465 | $m_{11}$=0x5f726f74 |
| | $m_{12}$=0x2e636264 | $m_{13}$=0x6976746d | $m_{14}$=0x632e7765 | $m_{15}$=0x73752e61 |
| $M_1$ | $m_0$=0x986e1da4 | $m_1$=0x83707d06 | $m_2$=0xa86e1ddd | $m_3$=0xe264eedb |
| | $m_4$=0xff68e19f | $m_5$=0x120ea5b3 | $m_6$=0x7437d3e2 | $m_7$=0x600f543d |
| | $m_8$=0x7c63c5ab | $m_9$=0xe9ead9d9 | $m_{10}$=0xa9b5c51e | $m_{11}$=0xc309f623 |
| | $m_{12}$=0xfd534f1e | $m_{13}$=0xad33c7ad | $m_{14}$=0xfd0380c6 | $m_{15}$=0x7745f36a |
| $M_1'$ | $m_0'$=0x986e1da4 | $m_1'$=0x83707d06 | $m_2'$=0xa86e1ddd | $m_3'$=0xe264eedb |
| | $m_4'$=0xff68e19f | $m_5'$=0x120ea5b3 | $m_6'$=0x7437d3e2 | $m_7'$=0x600f543d |
| | $m_8'$=0x7c63c5ab | $m_9'$=0xe9ead9d9 | $m_{10}'$=0xa9b5c51e | $m_{11}'$=0x4309f623 |
| | $m_{12}'$=0xfd534f1e | $m_{13}'$=0xad33c7ad | $m_{14}'$=0xfd0380c6 | $m_{15}'$=0x7745f36a |
| $h$ | $h[a]$ = 0xbd7ade50; | $h[b]$ = 0xe17a619d; | $h[c]$ = 0x8e940937; | $h[d]$ = 0xfd4af95f; |
| $h'$ | $h'[a]$ = 0x3d7ade50; | $h'[b]$ = 0x617a619d; | $h'[c]$ = 0x0e940937; | $h'[d]$ = 0x7d4af95f; |
| $M_2$ | $m_0$ = 0xc0797ae2; | $m_1$ = 0xe95d42e6; | $m_2$ = 0x49fe29af; | $m_3$ = 0x3329c9a9; |
| | $m_4$ = 0xa790a55d; | $m_5$ = 0x783e6d3; | $m_6$ = 0xb906c7b1; | $m_7$ = 0x2d63e951; |
| | $m_8$ = 0x9edac296; | $m_9$ = 0x26afe101; | $m_{10}$ = 0xd4cfc4fb; | $m_{11}$ = 0xcb0d1667; |
| | $m_{12}$ = 0x77b75eab; | $m_{13}$ = 0xea993a34; | $m_{14}$ = 0x8c9868ae; | $m_{15}$ = 0x7effffff; |
| | 24-th bit of $m_{15}$ of $M_2$ is free bit: $m_{15} = $ 0x7effffff or 0x7fffffff. | | | |

We implement 1-bit-free collision search. Surprisingly, it takes only 12 hours by 12 computers on average to generate 1-bit-free collision, which is much faster than the usual time for $2^{46}$ computations. One reason is that the complexity calculated by counting the number of sufficient conditions is greater than the precise complexity. Moreover, due to the biased bit position of sufficient conditions, since all sufficient conditions are located in only MSB of intermediate values, the complexity should be less than $2^{46}$.

One example of generated 1-bit-free collision is shown in Table 1.

### 4.3   Bit-Free-Collision Attacks on MD4

We will also apply bit-free-collision attacks on MD4 [9]. For the specification of MD4, refer to Appendix B.

**Pre-determine the bit position of the free bits:**
   Similarly with MD5 case, considering the application to APOP attack, we set the free bits at the last 8-bit positions of messages.

**A well-suited differential path for collision attacks on MD4:**
   We determine to use the differential path on MD4 in [13] detailed in Appendix C.4, since it has the minimum number of sufficient conditions which might be affected by changing the value of the free bits to the best of our knowledge.

**Table 2.** One example of 3-bit-free collision on MD4

| | |
|---|---|
| $M_0$ | $m_0$ = 0x3938313c; $m_1$ = 0xbfdc10ea; $m_2$ = 0xc5708671; $m_3$ = 0xa0196be0; <br> $m_4$ = 0xa8d2a83a; $m_5$ = 0xfd15dd85; $m_6$ = 0x992e75bc; $m_7$ = 0xabc6ccb8; <br> $m_8$ = 0x6f6fd206; $m_9$ = 0xfd303797; $m_{10}$ = 0x764081f6; $m_{11}$ = 0xd6821ee2; <br> $m_{12}$ = 0xcc7e0ed5; $m_{13}$ = 0x53c72d75; $m_{14}$ = 0x446d4fe9; $m_{15}$ = 0x1854dfdc; |
| $M_1$ | $m_0$ = 0x182994f8; $m_1$ = 0xc989fe5e; $m_2$ = 0xe3e086f0; $m_3$ = 0x17eb1082; <br> $m_4$ = 0x562a7af6; $m_5$ = 0xa6f0e339; $m_6$ = 0xc46682a8; $m_7$ = 0xb817cfa4; <br> $m_8$ = 0xe5a24a72; $m_9$ = 0x8eca35be; $m_{10}$ = 0x12c6229e; $m_{11}$ = 0xaf84be49; <br> $m_{12}$ = 0x1a94a2a5; $m_{13}$ = 0x8a2386b0; $m_{14}$ = 0x76d2a8b1; $m_{15}$ = 0x003effff; |
| | 27-th, 28-th and 29-th bits of $m_{15}$ of $M_1$ are the 3-free bits: <br> $m_{15}$=0x003effff, 0x083effff, 0x103effff, 0x183effff, 0x203effff, <br> 0x283effff, 0x303effff, 0x383effff |

Here we will show one 3-bit-free collision example $(M_0||M_1, M_0||(M_1 + \Delta))$, where $M_0$ and $M_1$ have been shown in Table 2. The message difference $\Delta M$ ($M_1' - M_1$) is ($\Delta m_0 = 2^{28}$, $\Delta m_2 = 2^{31}$, $\Delta m_4 = 2^{31}$, $\Delta m_8 = 2^{31}$, $\Delta m_{12} = 2^{31}$). No matter what the value of the 3-free bits (27, 28, 29-th bits of $m_{15}$ of $M_1$) is, MD4($M_0||M_1$) = MD4($M_0||(M_1 + \Delta M)$).

# 5    Application to APOP Attacks

## 5.1    Overview of Our Contribution

Previous APOP attacks [6] [11] [12] are *chosen* challenge attacks. The attacker will impersonate the server and send chosen challenges to the user. Impersonating the server takes a risk that the user may suspect being attacked by the following situation: (a) the user does not get a new email for a long time if the attacker continuously impersonates the server; (b) the user get a new email delayed even when the attacker impersonates the server from time to time. To lower the probability that the attack will be detected, the number of impersonation should be reduced. To achieve this, the number of necessary challenges has to be reduced. This section will utilize bit-free collisions on MD5 to reduce the number of necessary chosen challenges. As shown in Section 4.2, 1-bit-free-collision attack on MD5 is practical. We will adopt 1-bit-free-collisions on MD5 to improve previous APOP attacks. The number of necessary challenges is almost *half*-reduced. For one password character, our attack needs $2^7$ pairs of challenges in the worst case, while previous APOP attack needs ($2^8 - 1$) pairs of challenges.

## 5.2    Improved APOP Attack

In this section, we will detail how to improve previous APOP attacks utilizing bit-free-collisions. Our attacks will also recover the password characters one by one, following previous attacks. Our attack procedure with a comparison with previous attacks has been shown in Table 3.

**Table 3.** Comparison between our attack and previous attacks

Denote by $p_r$ the password characters which have been recovered. Denote by $p$ a password character which is going to be recovered. Note that the online work and offline work are *parallel* and *independent*.

| Our procedure | Previous procedure |
|---|---|
| Our attack utilizes 1-bit-free collision. Set the bit position of the free bit in $p$, which will divide the $p$ into two parts: 1-free bit and 7-non-free bits denoted as $p_f$ and $p_{nf}$, respectively. For simplicity, we assume that the 1-free bit locates at MSB of $p$. | -Chosen challenge collection (offline)<br>1. For $p$=00000000 to 11111111 (8 bits)<br>2. Generate a pair of challenges $(C, C')$: $(C\|p_r\|p,\ C'\|p_r\|p)$ is a collision.<br>3. Store $(C, C', p)$ to Table $\mathcal{T}$.<br>4. End For<br>-Impersonating as server (online)<br>If $\mathcal{T}$ is not NULL, then<br>1. Pick an element $(C, C', p)$ from $\mathcal{T}$.<br>2. Erase $(C, C', p)$ from $\mathcal{T}$<br>3. Send $C$ to the user to obtain the response $R$.<br>4. Send $C'$ to the user to obtain the response $R'$.<br>5. If $R = R'$, then the current value $p$ is the target password character. Halt the program.<br>6. If $R \neq R'$, continue to run the program.<br>Else, the attacker does not impersonate. Continue to run the program. |
| Stage 1: recover the value of $p_{nf}$.<br>-Chosen challenge collection (offline)<br>  1. For $p_{nf} = 0000000$ to $1111111$ (7-non-free bits)<br>  2. Generate a pair of challenges $(C, C')$: $(C\|p_r\|p_f\|p_{nf},\ C'\|p_r\|p_f\|p_{nf})$ is a 1-bit-free collision.<br>  3. Store $(C, C', p_{nf})$ to Table $\mathcal{T}$.<br>  4. End For<br>-Impersonating as server (online)<br>If $\mathcal{T}$ is not NULL, then<br>  1. Pick an element $(C, C', p_{nf})$ from $\mathcal{T}$.<br>  2. Erase $(C, C', p_{nf})$ from $\mathcal{T}$.<br>  3. Send $C$ to the user to obtain the response $R$.<br>  4. Send $C'$ to the user to obtain the response $R'$.<br>  5. If $R = R'$, then the current value $p_{nf}$ is the true 7-non-free bits of $p$. Goto Stage 2.<br>  6. If $R \neq R'$, continue to run Stage 1.<br>Else, the attacker does not impersonate. Continue to run Stage 1.<br>Stage 2: recover the value of $p_f$.<br>  1. Guess the 1-free bit is 0.<br>  2. Generate a pair of challenges $(C, C')$ such that $(C\|p_r\|0\|p_{nf}, C'\|p_r\|0\|p_{nf})$ is a collision.<br>  3. Send $C$ to the user to obtain the response $R$.<br>  4. Send $C'$ to the user to obtain the response $R'$.<br>  5. If $R = R'$, the value of $p_f$ is 0. Otherwise, the value is 1.<br>  6. Halt the program. | |

As shown in Table 3, our procedure generates $2^7$ chosen challenge pairs at Step 1 of the offline phase and 1 chosen challenge pair at Step 2 of Stage 2, whereas, the previous procedure generates $2^8$ chosen challenge pairs at Step 1 of the offline phase. Hence, the number of chosen challenges in our attack is roughly half of the previous attack. Note our attack needs to generate 1-bit-free collisions. This requires higher complexity than generating collisions, but can be computed at offline. In the real protocol, it is typical that the protocol is triggered by the user, not by the server (or the attacker impersonating the server). Therefore, to make the user provide the responses of chosen challenges, the attacker needs to wait for the user's access requests. Such a waiting time might be long, e.g., half day. During this time, the attacker can process the offline part in parallel. Since 1-bit-free collisions of MD5 can be generated in 12 hours with 12 PCs as described in Section 4.2, we can conclude that the extra cost of offline complexity has less impact than reducing the number of chosen challenges in the real environment.

**Application to APOP-MD4**
Suppose APOP utilizes MD4 instead of MD5. As shown in Section 4.3, 3-bit-free collisions on MD4 can be found practically. For APOP-MD4 case, the attacker can adopt similar attack procedure with Table 3: first recover the non-free bits and then recover the free bits. So for one password character (8-bit long) in the worst case, $(2^{8-3} - 1)$ pairs of challenges are necessary to recover the $(8 - 3)$-non-free bits, and $2^3$ pairs of challenges are necessary to recover the 3-free bits. In total, the number of necessary challenges is 71 for one password character in the worst case, while previous attacks need 510 challenges. So the number of necessary challenges has been reduced by a factor of 7.2 compared with previous attacks.

# 6   Conclusion and Discussion

In this paper, we presented the first approach of reducing the number of chosen challenges in the APOP attacks. The newly proposed variant of collision "bit-free collision" enabled us to achieve this. Roughly speaking, when $t$-bit-free collisions are available, the number of chosen challenges becomes $1/2^t$ compared to the previous attacks. We showed how to generate $t$-bit-free collisions in general case, 1-bit-free collisions on MD5, and 3-bit-free collisions on MD4 with giving examples of generated bit-free collisions on MD5 and MD4. We applied bit-free collisions to APOP attacks, and proposed the improved attack procedure.

Finally we would like to discuss potential applications of bit-free collisions, which will be our future work. Here we will give one application on distinguishing a compression function family from a random function family. Moreover, all the elements of the compression function family share the same structure but differ in $IV$ values. During interacting with the distinguisher, each of the two families changes its element to calculate responses from time to time. Suppose the attacker has enough offline computational power. The distinguishing attack procedure is as follows.

1. Locate the free bits in $IV$, then guess the bit-values of non-free bits of $IV$, and finally generate a $t$-bit-free collision $(M, M')$ on the compression function.

2. Send $M$ and $M'$ to a oracle to obtain responses $R$ and $R'$ respectively.
3. If $R$ is equal to $R'$, then the oracle is the compression function family.

Denote by $n$ the bit-length of $IV$. Suppose the distinguisher uses $t$-bit-free collisions. The bit-length of non-free bits is $(n-t)$, so if the oracle is the compression function family, after $2^{n-t}$ pairs of messages are queries, a pair of colliding responses will be obtained with non-negligible probability. On the other hand, a pair of colliding responses will be obtained after roughly $2^n$ pairs of messages are queried. Consequently, utilizing bit-free collisions, the distinguisher can succeed with non-negligible probability with an online rough complexity $2^{n-t+1}$ queries.

We expect more applications of bit-free collisions can be found in future.

# References

1. Biham, E., Chen, R.: Near-collisions of SHA-0. In: Franklin, M. (ed.) CRYPTO 2004. LNCS, vol. 3152, pp. 290–305. Springer, Heidelberg (2004)
2. den Boer, B., Bosselaers, A.: Collisions for the Compression Function of MD-5. In: Helleseth, T. (ed.) EUROCRYPT 1993. LNCS, vol. 765, pp. 293–304. Springer, Heidelberg (1994)
3. Damgård, I.: A design principle for hash functions. In: Brassard, G. (ed.) CRYPTO 1989. LNCS, vol. 435, pp. 416–427. Springer, Heidelberg (1990)
4. Joux, A.: Multicollisions in iterated hash functions. Application to cascaded constructions. In: Franklin, M. (ed.) CRYPTO 2004. LNCS, vol. 3152, pp. 306–316. Springer, Heidelberg (2004)
5. Klima, V.: Tunnels in Hash Functions: MD5 Collisions Within a Minute. Cryptology ePrint Archive, Report 2006 /105, http://eprint.iacr.org/2006/105.pdf
6. Leurent, G.: Message freedom in MD4 and MD5 collisions: Application to APOP. In: Biryukov, A. (ed.) FSE 2007. LNCS, vol. 4593, pp. 309–328. Springer, Heidelberg (2007)
7. Merkle, R.C.: One Way Hash Functions and DES. In: Brassard, G. (ed.) CRYPTO 1989. LNCS, vol. 435, pp. 428–446. Springer, Heidelberg (1990)
8. Myers, J., Rose, M.: Post Office Protocol - Version 3. RFC 1939 (Standard), Updated by RFCs 1957, 2449 (May 1996), ftp://ftp.isi.edu/in-notes/rfc1939.txt
9. Rivest, R.L.: The MD4 Message Digest Algorithm. Request for Comments (RFC 1320), Network Working Group (1992)
10. Rivest, R.L.: The MD5 Message Digest Algorithm. Request for Comments (RFC 1321), Network Working Group (1992)
11. Sasaki, Y., Yamamoto, G., Aoki, K.: Practical Password Recovery on an MD5 Challenge and Response. Cryptology ePrint Archive, Report 2007/101
12. Sasaki, Y., Wang, L., Ohta, K., Kunihiro, N.: Security of MD5 challenge and response: Extension of APOP password recovery attack. In: Malkin, T.G. (ed.) CT-RSA 2008. LNCS, vol. 4964, pp. 1–18. Springer, Heidelberg (2008)
13. Sasaki, Y., Wang, L., Ohta, K., Kunihiro, N.: New message difference for MD4. In: Biryukov, A. (ed.) FSE 2007. LNCS, vol. 4593, pp. 329–348. Springer, Heidelberg (2007)
14. Wang, X., Lai, X., Feng, D., Chen, H., Yu, X.: Cryptanalysis of the hash functions MD4 and RIPEMD. In: Cramer, R. (ed.) EUROCRYPT 2005. LNCS, vol. 3494, pp. 1–18. Springer, Heidelberg (2005)
15. Wang, X., Yu, H.: How to break MD5 and other hash functions. In: Cramer, R. (ed.) EUROCRYPT 2005. LNCS, vol. 3494, pp. 19–35. Springer, Heidelberg (2005)

# A     Definition of Neutral Bits [1]

Biham and Chen proposed a concept *neutral bit* to speed up the collision search on hash functions. Here we will give a brief description. For more detailed description, refer to [1].

**Definition 2.** *[1] For a pair message $M_0$ and $M_1$, denote by $\Delta_i$ the difference of intermediate chaining variables at $i$-th step during hash computations. The $j$-th bit of $M_0$ and $M_1$ is a neutral bit with respect to $M_0$ and $M_1$ up to $i$-th step if it can satisfy the following property: $M_0'$ and $M_1'$ are obtained by flipping the $j$-th bit of $M_0$ and $M_1$, respectively, and the $\Delta_i'$ of $M_0'$ and $M_1'$ is equal to $\Delta_i$ of $M_0$ and $M_1$.*

# B     Specification of MD5 and MD4

MD5 [10] and MD4 [9] map arbitrary length messages to 128 bit-length hash digests. At first, the input message is padded and divided into 512-bit blocks. Here we will omit the description of padding rule. Then the message blocks will be sent to a primitive called *compression function* sequentially and hashed. A fixed 128-bit constant *initial value (IV)* and $M_1$ will be hashed by the compression function, which outputs a 128 bit-length $H_1$. Then $H_1$ and $M_2$ will be hashed by the compression function. After the last message block is hashed, the output of the compression function will be the hash digest.

In the following, we will briefly describe the compression functions of MD5 and MD4 respectively.

**Compression function of MD5**
The message block $M$ and the intermediate value $H$ will be divided into 32-bit values denoted as $(m_0, \ldots, m_{15})$ and $(a_0, b_0, c_0, d_0)$ respectively. The compression function consists of 64 steps, regrouped into four 16-step rounds. Each step is defined as follows:

$$a_i = d_{i-1}, c_i = b_{i-1}, d_i = c_{i-1},$$
$$b_i = b_{i-1} + (a_{i-1} + f(b_{i-1}, c_{i-1}, d_{i-1}) + m_k + t) \lll s_i,$$

where $m_k$ is one of $(m_0, \ldots, m_{15})$, the index $k$ being given by a permutation of $\{0, \ldots, 15\}$ depending on the round, $t$ is a constant defined in each round, $\lll s_i$ means a left-rotation by $s_i$ bits, and $f$ is a Boolean function depending on the round.

$$1R: f(X, Y, Z) = (X \wedge Y) \vee (\neg X \wedge Z)$$
$$2R: f(X, Y, Z) = (X \wedge Z) \vee (Y \wedge \neg Z)$$
$$3R: f(X, Y, Z) = X \oplus Y \oplus Z$$
$$4R: f(X, Y, Z) = (X \vee \neg Z) \oplus Y$$

The final output is $(a_0 + a_{64}, b_0 + b_{64}, c_0 + c_{64}, d_0 + d_{64})$.

**Compression function of MD4**
The differences between MD5 and MD4 are the following:

- MD4 consists of 48 steps regrouped into three 16-step rounds.
- Each step is defined as: $b_i = (a_{i-1} + f(b_{i-1}, c_{i-1}, d_{i-1}) + m_k + t) \lll s_i$, where $m_k$ is given by different round permutations.
- In the 2nd round: $f(X, Y, Z) = (X \wedge Y) \vee (Y \wedge Z) \vee (X \wedge Z)$.

# C   Previous Related Collision Attacks on MD5 and MD4

## C.1   Wang *et al.*'s Differential Collision Attack

Current popular collision attack on hash functions are mainly differential attacks following the strategy proposed by Wang *et al.* [15] [14]. Here we will describe the procedure of collision attacks.

1. Find the "Message Difference ($\Delta M$)" that yields a collision with high probability. Let $M$ and $M'$ be a pair of messages that yield a collision. Difference $\Delta M$ is defined to be the value yielded by subtracting $M$ from $M'$: $\Delta M = M' - M$.
2. Determine how the impact of $\Delta M$ propagates. The propagation of the message difference at all intermediate statements is fixed and called the "Differential Path (DP)."
3. Derive "Sufficient Conditions (SC)" from differential path to guarantee that the message difference will propagate following the differential path at all intermediate statements.
4. Apply the technique called "Message Modification (MM)" such that a randomly selected message can be modified to make several sufficient conditions be satisfied.
5. Search a message that satisfies all SCs as follows: first randomly select a message, then modify it by message modification to make several sufficient conditions satisfied, and finally check whether the other sufficient conditions are satisfied or not. Denote the obtained message as $M$.
6. Calculate $M' = M + \Delta M$. $M$ and $M'$ will be a collision pair.

**Complexity of collision attacks**
In the above attack procedure, the first three steps are pre-stage works before searching collisions, and they are carried out only once. So the complexity of these three steps is not counted into the complexity of the collision attack. In steps 4 and 5, based on the technique MM, the SCs are divided into two cases: 1) the SCs can be satisfied by applying MM to any randomly selected message; 2) the SCs have to be satisfied by testing randomly selected messages, that is the exhaustive search. So the current popular approach of calculating the complexity of collision attacks is counting the number of the SCs of the second case. Denote the hash function as $H$. Suppose there are $q$ SCs of the second case. Then the complexity of the collision attack is roughly regarded as $2^q$ $H$ computations.

## C.2   Pseudo-Collision Attacks on MD5

A pseudo-collision on the compression function of MD5 has been proposed by Den Boer and Bosselaers in [2], where the differences exist in the intermediate hash values instead of the message blocks. Denote the intermediate hash value as $(a_0, b_0, c_0, d_0)$. The XOR differences are

$$(\Delta a_0, \Delta b_0, \Delta c_0, \Delta d_0) = (0x80000000, 0x80000000, 0x80000000, 0x80000000).$$

Moreover, An extra condition is that the MSBs of $b_0$, $c_0$ and $d_0$ should be equal. The sufficient conditions are as follows:

$$1R \text{ and } 2R: b_{i,31} = b_{i-1,31} \ (1 \le i \le 31);$$
$$4R: b_{i,31} = b_{i-2,31} \ (48 \le i \le 63).$$

In total, there are 46 sufficient conditions.

## C.3   Tunnel Technique

We used "Q9 tunnel" in [5], which are based the local collision from step 8 until step 12. The details are shown in Table 4. The crucial idea of Q9 tunnel is that for any message $m_8$, the chaining variables after the first round will remain the same by modifying only $m_9$ and $m_{12}$. $m_8$, $m_9$ and $m_{12}$ are used at steps 25, 28 and 32 in the second round, respectively. So the exhaustive search can start from step 25 in the second round. The number of sufficient conditions from step 25 is 23.

**Table 4.** Tunnel Q9

| step index | message | fixed chaining variables |
|:---:|:---:|:---:|
| 7 | $m_7$ | $b_8 = b_7$; |
| 8 | $m_8$ | |
| 9 | $m_9$ | $b_{10} = 0xffffffff$; |
| 10 | $m_{10}$ | $b_{11} = 0x00000000$; |
| 11 | $m_{11}$ | |

## C.4  Collision Attacks on MD4

Sasaki *et al.* [13] published a differential path on MD4 with only 1 sufficient condition located in the third round, which can not be satisfied by the message modification. Here we will only show the sufficient conditions. The message differences are ($\Delta m_0 = 2^{28}$, $\Delta m_2 = 2^{31}$, $\Delta m_4 = 2^{31}$, $\Delta m_8 = 2^{31}$, $\Delta m_{12} = 2^{31}$).

**Table 5.** Sufficient conditions

| Chaining variables | Conditions on bits | | | |
|---|---|---|---|---|
| | 31 - 24 | 23 - 16 | 15 - 8 | 7 - 0 |
| $b_1$ | 1 - - - - - - - | - - - - - - - - | - - - - - - a - | a - - - - - 0 1 |
| $b_2$ | 1 - - - - - - - | - - - - 0 - - - | - - - - a - 1 - | 0 - - - - - 0 1 |
| $b_3$ | 1 - - - - - - 0 | - - a a 1 - - - | - - - - 1 - 0 - | 0 - - - - - 1 0 |
| $b_4$ | 1 - - - - - - 1 | a a 1 0 0 - - - | - - - - 0 - 1 a | 1 a a a a - - - |
| $b_5$ | a - - - - - - 0 | 1 1 0 0 0 a - - | - - - - 0 - 0 1 | 1 1 1 1 1 - - - |
| $b_6$ | 0 - - - - - - 1 | 1 1 1 1 0 0 - - | - - - - - - 0 0 | 0 0 0 0 0 a a - |
| $b_7$ | 0 - - - - - 1 1 | 0 0 - 0 1 0 - - | - - - - - - 0 1 | 1 1 1 1 1 1 1 - |
| $b_8$ | 1 - - - - - a 0 | 0 0 - 1 0 1 - - | - - - 0 - - 0 0 | 0 0 0 0 1 0 0 - |
| $b_9$ | 0 a a - a a 0 1 | 0 1 - - - - - - | - - - a - - 1 1 | 1 1 0 1 1 1 1 - |
| $b_{10}$ | 0 1 1 - 1 0 0 - | 1 1 - - - - - - | - - - 1 - - - - | - - - - - - - - |
| $b_{11}$ | 0 0 0 - 1 1 0 - | 1 1 - - - - - - | - - - 0 - - - - | - - - - - - - - |
| $b_{12}$ | 0 1 1 a 0 0 1 - | - - - - - - - - | - - - 1 - - - - | - - - - - - - - |
| $b_{13}$ | - - 1 0 - - 0 - | - - - - - - - - | - - - 0 - - - - | - - - - - - - - |
| $b_{14}$ | - - 0 0 - - 0 - | - - - - - - - - | - - - 0 - - - - | - - - - - - - - |
| $b_{15}$ | a - 1 1 - - 1 - | - - - - - - - - | - - - - - - - - | - - - - - - - - |
| $b_{16}$ | 1 - - a - - - - | - - - - - - - - | - - - - - - - - | - - - - - - - - |
| $b_{17}$ | b - - 0 - - - - | - - - - - - - - | - - - - - - - - | - - - - - - - - |
| $b_{18}$ | b - - c - - - - | - - - - - - - - | - - - - - - - - | - - - - - - - - |
| $b_{19}$ | - - - a - - - - | - - - - - - - - | - - - - - - - - | - - - - - - - - |
| $b_{20}$ | a - - - - - - - | - - - - - - - - | - - - - - - - - | - - - - - - - - |
| $b_{21}$ | 0 - - - - - - - | - - - - - - - - | - - - - - - - - | - - - - - - - - |
| $b_{22}$ | c - - - - - - - | - - - - - - - - | - - - - - - - - | - - - - - - - - |
| $b_{23}$ | a - - - - - - - | - - - - - - - - | - - - - - - - - | - - - - - - - - |
| $b_{24}$ | - - - - - - - - | - - - - - - - - | - - - - - - - - | - - - - - - - - |
| $\cdots$ | | | | |
| $b_{33}$ | 0 - - - - - - - | - - - - - - - - | - - - - - - - - | - - - - - - - - |
| $\cdots$ | | | | |

The notation '0' stands for the conditions $b_{i,j} = 0$, the notation '1' stands for the conditions $b_{i,j} = 1$, the notation 'a' stands for the conditions $b_{i,j} = b_{i-1,j}$, 'b' stands for the condition $b_{i,j} \neq b_{i-1,j}$ and 'c' stands for the condition $b_{i,j} = b_{i-2,j}$.

# Impossible Boomerang Attack for Block Cipher Structures

Jiali Choy and Huihui Yap

DSO National Laboratories
20 Science Park Drive, Singapore 118230
{cjiali,yhuihui}@dso.org.sg

**Abstract.** Impossible boomerang attack [5] (IBA) is a new variant of differential cryptanalysis against block ciphers. Evident from its name, it combines the ideas of both impossible differential cryptanalysis and boomerang attack. Though such an attack might not be the best attack available, its complexity is still less than that of the exhaustive search. In impossible boomerang attack, impossible boomerang distinguishers are used to retrieve some of the subkeys. Thus the security of a block cipher against IBA can be evaluated by impossible boomerang distinguishers. In this paper, we study the impossible boomerang distinguishers for block cipher structures whose round functions are bijective. Inspired by the $\mathcal{U}$-method in [3], we provide an algorithm to compute the maximum length of impossible boomerang distinguishers for general block cipher structures, and apply the algorithm to known block cipher structures such as Nyberg's generalized Feistel network, a generalized CAST256-like structure, a generalized MARS-like structure, a generalized RC6-like structure, etc.

**Keywords:** Block Ciphers, Impossible Boomerang Attack, Impossible Boomerang Distinguishers.

## 1 Introduction

Differential and linear cryptanalysis are the most common cryptanalytic tools against block ciphers. Provable security against differential and linear cryptanalysis has been an important consideration in the design of block ciphers. However, this is not sufficient to guarantee the security of the block ciphers as they may be vulnerable to other types of cryptanalysis. Analysis of new cryptanalytic techniques is thus always desirable since it enhances the evaluation of the security of a block cipher and the design of more secure ciphers.

Impossible differential cryptanalysis and boomerang-type attacks (including the boomerang, amplified boomerang and rectangle attacks as well as their related-key variants) have been used in the cryptanalysis of many block ciphers. For instance, a 6-round impossible differential attack was mounted on MISTY1 in [2] recently while a full-round related-key rectangle attack was applied to the KASUMI cipher [1]. Hence the importance of these cryptanalytic techniques cannot be undermined.

T. Takagi and M. Mambo (Eds.): IWSEC 2009, LNCS 5824, pp. 22–37, 2009.
© Springer-Verlag Berlin Heidelberg 2009

In [5], a new extension of differential cryptanalysis, which J. Lu calls the impossible boomerang attack, was proposed. This attack combines the ideas of impossible differential cryptanalysis and boomerang attack, and makes use of an impossible boomerang distinguisher. Similar to a boomerang attack, a block cipher $\mathbf{E}$ is treated as two sub-ciphers $\mathbf{E}^0 \circ \mathbf{E}^1$. Two (or more) differentials with probability 1 for $\mathbf{E}^0$ and two (or more) differentials with probability 1 for $\mathbf{E}^1$ are used, where the XOR of the intermediate differences of these differentials is not equal to zero. In [5], the impossible boomerang attack was used to break 6-round AES-128, 7-round AES-192 and 7-round AES-256 in a single key attack scenario, and 8-round AES-192 and 9-round AES-256 in a related-key attack scenario involving two keys.

As mentioned in [5], the advantages of the IBA over the boomerang attacks are analogous to those of impossible differential cryptanalysis over differential cryptanalysis. A block cipher resistant to boomerang-type attack will not necessarily be resistant against an IBA. In boomerang-type distinguishers, one generally assumes that the output of one intermediate round of the cipher is uniformly distributed and is independent from that of the previous rounds. On the other hand, an impossible boomerang distinguisher does not require this assumption, which is often not the case. Therefore, an impossible boomerang distinguisher seems more reasonable than boomerang-type distinguishers [5].

Though we can always obtain an impossible differential from an impossible boomerang distinguisher for the same number of rounds, this is not true for their variants in a related-key attack scenario. As explained in [5], the flexibilities in choosing the key differences may enable more rounds of a block cipher to be broken using a related-key impossible boomerang attack. Since related-key IBA is a variant of the basic IBA, we will be concentrating on the study of impossible boomerang distinguishers which form the core of IBA.

Inspired by the $\mathcal{U}$-method in [3], we introduce the $\mathcal{UB}$-method and provide an algorithm to compute the maximum length of impossible boomerang distinguishers and implement it on some selected block ciphers. As we shall see later on, the maximum length for impossible boomerang distinguishers are equal to that for impossible differential distinguishers for certain ciphers, increasing the likelihood that IBA will be a feasible attack on them. Although the impossible boomerang attack may not be the best known attack for some of the block ciphers, we believe that the results are important and useful, since the attack can be applied to other block ciphers not mentioned here, and the technique introduced in this paper can be modified and used in other works as well.

The rest of the paper is organized as follows. In Section 2, we briefly describe the impossible boomerang attack proposed by J. Lu in [5]. Section 3 introduces some notions, including the $\mathcal{UB}$-method, for the impossible boomerang attack. In Section 4, we present some additional definitions related to the $\mathcal{UB}$-method and use them to determine an expression for the maximum length of impossible boomerang characteristics. An algorithm is proposed in Section 5 to compute the maximum length of impossible boomerang distinguishers for any general block cipher structure with bijective round functions. The algorithm is then applied to various block ciphers and the results are summarized in Section 6.

## 2   The Impossible Boomerang Attack

The attack, described in [5], combines the boomerang attack with impossible differential cryptanalysis, and is called the impossible boomerang attack (IBA).

### 2.1   Impossible Boomerang Distinguisher

Similar to a boomerang distinguisher, an impossible boomerang distinguisher, as depicted in Figure 1, treats a block cipher $\mathbf{E}$: $\{0,1\}^k \times \{0,1\}^B \to \{0,1\}^B$ as two sub-ciphers $\mathbf{E}^0 \circ \mathbf{E}^1$ and consists of

- a differential $w \to x$ with probability 1 for $\mathbf{E}^0$,
- a differential $w' \to x'$ with probability 1 for $\mathbf{E}^0$,
- a differential $y \to z$ with probability 1 for $(\mathbf{E}^1)^{-1}$,
- a differential $y' \to z'$ with probability 1 for $(\mathbf{E}^1)^{-1}$,

where $w, w', x, x', y, y', z$ and $z'$ are all $B$-bit blocks, and the condition $x \oplus x' \oplus z \oplus z' \neq 0$ holds.

We state the following theorem from [5], which provides the theoretical basis for our proposed algorithm to compute the maximum length of impossible boomerang distinguishers.

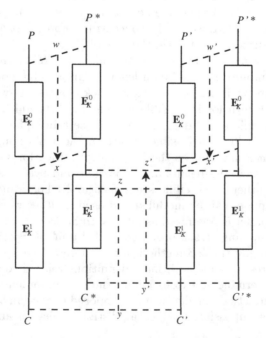

**Fig. 1.** An impossible boomerang distinguisher

**Theorem 1.** *[5] Suppose that $P$ and $P'$ are B-bit blocks and $K$ is a key for a B-bit block cipher $\boldsymbol{E}$, where $\boldsymbol{E} = \boldsymbol{E}^0 \circ \boldsymbol{E}^1$ for some $\boldsymbol{E}^0$ and $\boldsymbol{E}^1$. Let $w \rightarrow x$ and $w' \rightarrow x'$ be differentials with probability 1 for $\boldsymbol{E}_K^0$, and, $y \rightarrow z$ and $y' \rightarrow z'$ be differentials with probability 1 for $(\boldsymbol{E}_K^1)^{-1}$, where $x \oplus x' \oplus z \oplus z' \neq 0$. Then the following pairs of equations cannot hold at the same time:*

$$\boldsymbol{E}_K(P) \oplus \boldsymbol{E}_K(P') = y,$$

$$\boldsymbol{E}_K(P \oplus w) \oplus \boldsymbol{E}_K(P' \oplus w') = y'.$$

The impossible boomerang distinguisher can be written as $(w, w') \nrightarrow (y, y')$. Note that the two differentials for $\boldsymbol{E}^0$ or $\boldsymbol{E}^1$ may be identical as long as the condition $x \oplus x' \oplus z \oplus z' \neq 0$ holds.

## 2.2    A Key Recovery Attack

IBA is a chosen plaintext attack. Let the block cipher $\boldsymbol{E}: \{0,1\}^k \times \{0,1\}^B \rightarrow \{0,1\}^B$ be a cascade of four sub-ciphers $\boldsymbol{E} = \boldsymbol{E}^\lambda \circ \boldsymbol{E}^0 \circ \boldsymbol{E}^1 \circ \boldsymbol{E}^\mu$. Suppose $K_\lambda$ and $K_\mu$ are the guesses for the subkey used in $\boldsymbol{E}^\lambda$ and $\boldsymbol{E}^\mu$ respectively. The basic idea of IBA is as follows:

(1) Find an impossible boomerang distinguisher, $(w, w') \nrightarrow (y, y')$ for $\boldsymbol{E}^0 \circ \boldsymbol{E}^1$.
(2) For a guess of $K_\lambda$ and $K_\mu$, compute and check whether a candidate quartet of plaintext/ciphertext pairs $((P, C), (P^*, C^*)), ((P', C'), (P'^*, C'^*))$ satisfies the following four conditions:

$$\boldsymbol{E}_{K_\lambda}^\lambda(P) \oplus \boldsymbol{E}_{K_\lambda}^\lambda(P^*) = w,$$

$$\boldsymbol{E}_{K_\lambda}^\lambda(P') \oplus \boldsymbol{E}_{K_\lambda}^\lambda(P'^*) = w',$$

$$(\boldsymbol{E}_{K_\mu}^\mu)^{-1}(C) \oplus (\boldsymbol{E}_{K_\mu}^\mu)^{-1}(C') = y,$$

$$(\boldsymbol{E}_{K_\mu}^\mu)^{-1}(C^*) \oplus (\boldsymbol{E}_{K_\mu}^\mu)^{-1}(C'^*) = y'.$$

(3) If the quartet does satisfy the above conditions, then discard the subkey guess $(K_\lambda, K_\mu)$. Go to the previous step until the number of remaining subkeys is almost one.

As a concluding remark for this section, the basic impossible boomerang attack can be extended to a related-key impossible boomerang attack. Readers may refer to [5] for more details.

## 3    Basic Notions for IBA

In this section, we introduce and establish notions for IBA by modifying and extending those used in [3].

For a block cipher structure $S$, let the input and output of one round be $(X_1, X_2, \ldots, X_n)$ and $(Y_1, Y_2, \ldots, Y_n)$ respectively. Throughout this paper, we consider $S$ whose round function $F$ is bijective.

## 3.1   Basic Definitions and Operations

**Definition 1.** *[3] The $n \times n$ Encryption Characteristic Matrix $\mathcal{E} = (\mathcal{E}_{ij})_{n \times n}$ and $n \times n$ Decryption Characteristic Matrix $\mathcal{D} = (\mathcal{D}_{ij})_{n \times n}$ are defined as follows.*

$$\mathcal{E}_{i,j} = \begin{cases} 0, & \text{if } Y_j \text{ is not affected by } X_i, \\ 1, & \text{if } Y_j \text{ is affected by } X_i, \\ 1_F, & \text{if } Y_j \text{ is affected by } F(X_i). \end{cases}$$

$$\mathcal{D}_{i,j} = \begin{cases} 0, & \text{if } X_j \text{ is not affected by } Y_i, \\ 1, & \text{if } X_j \text{ is affected by } Y_i, \\ 1_F, & \text{if } X_j \text{ is affected by } F(Y_i) \text{ or } F^{-1}(Y_i). \end{cases}$$

**Definition 2.** *[3] A matrix is a 1-property matrix if the number of entries 1 ($\neq 1_F$) in each column of the matrix is zero or one.*

**Example.** Consider the CLEFIA-like block cipher structure whereby one $F$-function is used for two consecutive subblocks. The transformation can be described by

$$(Y_1, Y_2, Y_3, Y_4) = (F(X_1) + X_2, X_3, F(X_3) + X_4, X_1).$$

Then the encryption and decryption characteristics matrices for CLEFIA-like block cipher structure are given by

$$\mathcal{E} = \begin{pmatrix} 1_F & 0 & 0 & 1 \\ 1 & 0 & 0 & 0 \\ 0 & 1 & 1_F & 0 \\ 0 & 0 & 1 & 0 \end{pmatrix}, \mathcal{D} = \begin{pmatrix} 0 & 1 & 0 & 0 \\ 0 & 0 & 1 & 1_F \\ 0 & 0 & 0 & 1 \\ 1 & 1_F & 0 & 0 \end{pmatrix}.$$

Note that the matrices are 1-property matrices.

**Definition 3.** *[3] Given an input difference $\alpha = (\alpha_1, \alpha_2, \ldots, \alpha_n)$, the input difference vector $\mathbf{a} = (a_1, a_2, \ldots, a_n)$ corresponding to $\alpha$ is defined as follows.*

$$a_i = \begin{cases} 0, & \text{if } \alpha_i = 0, \\ 1^*, & \text{otherwise.} \end{cases}$$

The output difference after $r$ rounds for $\alpha$ is denoted by $\alpha^r$ and the value of the $i^{th}$ subblock of $\alpha^r$ is written as $\alpha_i^r$. The corresponding difference vector after $r$ rounds is denoted by $\mathbf{a}^r$, and its $i$th entry is denoted by $a_i^r$. For the decryption process, we use the notations $\beta, \beta^r, \beta_i^r, \mathbf{b}, \mathbf{b}^r$ and $b_i^r$ instead.

Given an input difference, the possible output differences of each subblock after $r$ rounds can be classified by five types of differences: zero difference, a nonzero nonfixed difference, a nonzero fixed difference, exclusive-or of a nonzero fixed difference and a nonzero nonfixed difference, and a nonfixed difference. This is summarized in Table 1.

**Table 1.** Entries of difference vectors and corresponding type of differences

| $a_i^r$ or $b_i^r$ | Corresponding type of difference |
|---|---|
| 0 | zero difference, denoted by 0 |
| 1 | nonzero nonfixed difference, denoted by $\delta$ |
| 1* | nonzero fixed difference, denoted by $\gamma$ |
| 2* | nonzero fixed difference $\oplus$ nonzero nonfixed difference, denoted by $\gamma \oplus \delta$ |
| $t(\geq 2)$ | nonfixed difference, denoted by ? |

The set $\{0, 1, 1^*, 2^*\}$ is denoted by $\mathcal{U}$.

Computation of $\mathbf{a}^r$ (similar for $\mathbf{b}^r$) is as follows:

$$\mathbf{a}^1 = \mathbf{a} \cdot \mathcal{E},$$
$$\mathbf{a}^2 = \mathbf{a}^1 \cdot \mathcal{E},$$
$$\vdots$$
$$\mathbf{a}^r = \mathbf{a}^{r-1} \cdot \mathcal{E}.$$

A multiplication of $\mathbf{a}$ and $\mathcal{E}$ (similar for $\mathbf{b}$ and $\mathcal{D}$) is defined by

$$\mathbf{a} \cdot \mathcal{E} = (a_i)_{1 \times n} \cdot (\mathcal{E}_{i,j})_{n \times n}$$
$$= (\sum_i a_i \cdot \mathcal{E}_{i,j})_{1 \times n}$$

Table 2 lists all the possible cases of multiplication between an entry of the difference vector $\mathbf{a}$ and an entry of the matrix $\mathcal{E}$; and addition of $a_i \cdot \mathcal{E}_{i,j}$ and $a_{i'} \cdot \mathcal{E}_{i',j}$.

**Table 2.** Multiplication (left) and addition (right)$(k \in \{0, 1, 1^*, 2^*, t\}, t, t' \geq 2)$

| Multiplication $(a_i \cdot \mathcal{E}_{i,j})$ | Addition $(a_i \cdot \mathcal{E}_{i,j} + a_{i'} \cdot \mathcal{E}_{i',j})$ |
|---|---|
| $k \cdot 0 = 0$ | $0 + k = k$ |
| $k \cdot 1 = k$ | $1 + 1 = 2$ |
| $0 \cdot 1_F = 0$ | $1 + 1^* = 2^*$ |
| $1^* \cdot 1_F = 1$ | $1 + 2^* = 3$ |
| $1 \cdot 1_F = 1$ | $1 + t = 1 + t$ |
| $2^* \cdot 1_F = 2$ | $1^* + t = 1 + t$ |
| $t \cdot 1_F = t$ | $2^* + t = 2 + t$ |
| | $t + t' = t + t'$ |

In this paper, although we concentrate mainly on block ciphers with 1-property encryption and decryption characteristics matrices, the algorithm proposed in Section 5 can be modified for block ciphers with non 1-property matrices. We leave the modification of the algorithm to interested readers. Here, we will just list down the additional operations required for block ciphers with non 1-property matrices.

(1) Since $\gamma \oplus \gamma = 0$, we have two possible cases:

$$1^* + 1^* = \begin{cases} 0, & \text{if } \gamma = \gamma', \\ 1^*, & \text{if } \gamma \neq \gamma'. \end{cases}$$

(2) Since $\gamma' \oplus (\gamma \oplus \delta) = (\gamma' \oplus \gamma) \oplus \delta$, we have

$$1^* + 2^* = \begin{cases} 1, & \text{if } \gamma = \gamma', \\ 2^*, & \text{if } \gamma \neq \gamma'. \end{cases}$$

(3) $2^* + 2^* = 4$.

With these new definitions, the addition operation is still always associative except for certain special cases. For example, for the sum $1 + 1^* + 2^*$, $(1 + 1^*) + 2^*$ gives 4 whereas $1 + (1^* + 2^*)$ gives 2 or 3. However, in these special cases, the sum evaluated both ways always results in a value $\geq 2$ and $x^{(*)} + t = x + t$ (where $t \geq 2$) which always corresponds to a ?. Furthermore, one may check that the operation is also commutative save for a case where the resulting values derived both ways are always $\geq 2$. Therefore, to sum three or more entries, always perform the addition from left to right. For example, $1 + 1^* + 1^* = 1$ or $2^*$ since $(1 + 1^*) + 1^* = 2^* + 1^*$.

## 3.2    Finding Impossible Boomerang Distinguishers

To find impossible boomerang distinguishers, from Theorem 1, we need four differentials with probability 1 and the XOR of the output difference of each differential must be non-zero. Also note that the two differentials for $\mathbf{E}^0$ or $\mathbf{E}^1$ may be identical.

Let $\mathcal{UB} = \{0, 1, 1^*\} \subset \mathcal{U}$. Adopting a similar approach to [3], we may use the elements of $\mathcal{UB}$ to find impossible boomerang characteristics. We call this method related to the impossible boomerang attack the $\mathcal{UB}$-method. In Table 3, we summarize all possible cases that satisfy the necessary conditions stated above.

Therefore, any of the 16 cases above gives us an impossible boomerang characteristic for $r + r'$ rounds, $(\Delta\alpha, \Delta\alpha') \nrightarrow_{r+r'} (\Delta\beta, \Delta\beta')$.

**Example.** Consider the CLEFIA-like block cipher structure. Let $\alpha = (0, 0, 0, \gamma)$, $\alpha' = (0, 0, 0, \gamma')$, $\beta = (\gamma'', 0, 0, 0)$ and $\beta' = (\gamma''', 0, 0, 0)$, where $\gamma \oplus \gamma' \neq \gamma'' \oplus \gamma'''$. It can be checked that $\alpha_1^3 = \gamma$, $\alpha_1'^3 = \gamma'$, $\beta_1^4 = \gamma'$ and $\beta_1'^4 = \gamma''$. Hence, corresponding to Case $\gamma\gamma\gamma\gamma$ in Table 3,

$$((0, 0, 0, \gamma), (0, 0, 0, \gamma')) \nrightarrow_7 ((\gamma'', 0, 0, 0), (\gamma''', 0, 0, 0)),$$

is an impossible boomerang distinguisher with length 7 for CLEFIA.

**Table 3.** Possible output differences $(\alpha_i^r, \alpha_i'^r)$ for encryption and $(\beta_i^{r'}, \beta_i'^{r'})$ for decryption

| Case | Value of $(\alpha_i^r, \alpha_i'^r)$ | Value of $(\beta_i^{r'}, \beta_i'^{r'})$ | Condition |
|------|------|------|------|
| $\delta000$ | $(\delta, 0)$ | $(0, 0)$ | - |
| $00\delta0$ | $(0, 0)$ | $(\delta, 0)$ | - |
| $\gamma000$ | $(\gamma, 0)$ | $(0, 0)$ | - |
| $00\gamma0$ | $(0, 0)$ | $(\gamma, 0)$ | - |
| $\gamma\gamma00$ | $(\gamma, \gamma')$ | $(0, 0)$ | $\gamma \neq \gamma'$ |
| $00\gamma\gamma$ | $(0, 0)$ | $(\gamma, \gamma')$ | $\gamma \neq \gamma'$ |
| $\gamma0\gamma0$ | $(\gamma, 0)$ | $(\gamma', 0)$ | $\gamma \neq \gamma'$ |
| $\gamma\gamma\gamma0$ | $(\gamma, \gamma')$ | $(\gamma'', 0)$ | $\gamma \oplus \gamma' \oplus \gamma'' \neq 0$ |
| $0\gamma\gamma\gamma$ | $(0, \gamma)$ | $(\gamma', \gamma'')$ | $\gamma \oplus \gamma' \oplus \gamma'' \neq 0$ |
| $\gamma\gamma\gamma\gamma$ | $(\gamma, \gamma')$ | $(\gamma'', \gamma''')$ | $\gamma \oplus \gamma' \neq \gamma'' \oplus \gamma'''$ |
| $\gamma\gamma\delta0$ | $(\gamma, \gamma')$ | $(\delta, 0)$ | $\gamma \oplus \gamma' = 0$ |
| $\delta0\gamma\gamma$ | $(\delta, 0)$ | $(\gamma, \gamma')$ | $\gamma \oplus \gamma' = 0$ |
| $\gamma\delta\gamma0$ | $(\gamma, \delta)$ | $(\gamma', 0)$ | $\gamma \oplus \gamma' = 0$ |
| $\gamma0\gamma\delta$ | $(\gamma, 0)$ | $(\gamma', \delta)$ | $\gamma \oplus \gamma' = 0$ |
| $\gamma\gamma\gamma\delta$ | $(\gamma, \gamma')$ | $(\gamma'', \delta)$ | $\gamma \oplus \gamma' \oplus \gamma'' = 0$ |
| $\gamma\delta\gamma\gamma$ | $(\gamma, \delta)$ | $(\gamma', \gamma'')$ | $\gamma \oplus \gamma' \oplus \gamma'' = 0$ |

# 4    Finding the Maximum Length of Impossible Boomerang Distinguishers

In this section, we introduce more definitions and concepts that will help us compute the maximum length of impossible boomerang characteristics that can be found by the $\mathcal{UB}$-method.

**Definition 4.** *[3] Let $m \in \mathcal{UB}$. Given an input difference vector $\mathbf{a}$ and output difference vector $\mathbf{b}$, the maximum number of encryption and decryption rounds with respect to $\mathbf{a}$ and $\mathbf{b}$ respectively are defined by*

$$\mathcal{ME}_i(\mathbf{a}, m) = \max_r\{r | a_i^r = m\},$$

*and*

$$\mathcal{MD}_i(\mathbf{b}, m) = \max_r\{r | b_i^r = m\}.$$

*The maximum number of encryption and decryption rounds with respect to $m$ are defined as*

$$\mathcal{ME}_i(m) = \max_{\mathbf{a} \neq 0}\{\mathcal{ME}_i(\mathbf{a}, m)\},$$

*and*

$$\mathcal{MD}_i(m) = \max_{\mathbf{b} \neq 0}\{\mathcal{MD}_i(\mathbf{b}, m)\}.$$

For the purpose of finding the maximum length of impossible boomerang distinguishers, we introduce the following definition.

**Definition 5.** *Let* $m \in \mathcal{UB}$. *The maximum number of encryption rounds with respect to $m$ and $m'$, denoted by $\mathcal{ME}_i(m, m')$, is defined as the maximum number of rounds, $r$, such that there exist input difference vectors $a$ and $a'$ with $a_i^r = m$ and $a_i'^r = m'$. Similarly, the maximum number of decryption rounds with respect to $m$ and $m'$, denoted by $\mathcal{MD}_i(m, m')$, is defined as the maximum number of rounds, $r'$, such that there exist input difference vectors $b$ and $b'$ with $b_i^{r'} = m$ and $b_i'^{r'} = m'$.*

Based on these definitions and the previous section, we may establish the following theorem.

**Theorem 2.** *Consider the round function of a block cipher structure as a bijective black box. If we use the notation*

$$\mathcal{M}_1 = \max_{1 \leq i \leq n} \{\mathcal{ME}_i(1, 0) + \mathcal{MD}_i(0)\},$$

$$\mathcal{M}_2 = \max_{1 \leq i \leq n} \{\mathcal{ME}_i(0) + \mathcal{MD}_i(1, 0)\},$$

$$\mathcal{M}_3 = \max_{1 \leq i \leq n} \{\mathcal{ME}_i(1^*) + \mathcal{MD}_i(0)\},$$

$$\mathcal{M}_4 = \max_{1 \leq i \leq n} \{\mathcal{ME}_i(0) + \mathcal{MD}_i(1^*)\},$$

$$\mathcal{M}_5 = \max_{1 \leq i \leq n} \{\mathcal{ME}_i(1^*) + \mathcal{MD}_i(1^*)\},$$

*then the maximum length of impossible boomerang distinguishers, $\mathcal{M}$, is given by*

$$\mathcal{M} = \max_{1 \leq i \leq 5} \{\mathcal{M}_i\},$$

*Proof.* Referring to Table 3, we know that $\mathcal{M}$ is the maximum length considering all 16 cases.

Case $\delta 000$: $\mathcal{M}_{\delta 000} = \mathcal{M}_1$.

Case $00\delta 0$: $\mathcal{M}_{00\delta 0} = \mathcal{M}_2$.

Case $\gamma 000$: $\mathcal{M}_{\gamma 000} = \max_{1 \leq i \leq n} \{\mathcal{ME}_i(1^*, 0) + \mathcal{MD}_i(0)\}$. Since $\mathcal{ME}_i(1^*, 0) \leq \min\{\mathcal{ME}_i(1^*), \mathcal{ME}_i(0)\}$,

$$\mathcal{M}_{\gamma 000} \leq \max_{1 \leq i \leq n} \{\mathcal{ME}_i(1^*) + \mathcal{MD}_i(0)\} = \mathcal{M}_3.$$

Case $00\gamma 0$: $\mathcal{M}_{00\gamma 0} = \max_{1 \leq i \leq n} \{\mathcal{ME}_i(0) + \mathcal{MD}_i(1^*, 0)\}$. Since $\mathcal{MD}_i(1^*, 0) \leq \min\{\mathcal{MD}_i(1^*), \mathcal{MD}_i(0)\}$,

$$\mathcal{M}_{00\gamma 0} \leq \max_{1 \leq i \leq n} \{\mathcal{ME}_i(0) + \mathcal{MD}_i(1^*)\} = \mathcal{M}_4.$$

Case $\gamma\gamma 00$: $\mathcal{M}_{\gamma\gamma 00} = \mathcal{M}_3$.

Case $00\gamma\gamma$: $\mathcal{M}_{00\gamma\gamma} = \mathcal{M}_4$.

Case $\gamma 0\gamma 0$: $\mathcal{M}_{\gamma 0\gamma 0} = \max_{1 \leq i \leq n} \{\mathcal{ME}_i(1^*, 0) + \mathcal{MD}_i(1^*, 0)\}$. Since $\mathcal{ME}_i(1^*, 0) \leq \min\{\mathcal{ME}_i(1^*), \mathcal{ME}_i(0)\}$      and $\mathcal{MD}_i(1^*, 0) \leq \min\{\mathcal{MD}_i(1^*), \mathcal{MD}_i(0)\}$,

$$\mathcal{M}_{\gamma 0 \gamma 0} \le \max_{1 \le i \le n} \{\mathcal{ME}_i(1^*) + \mathcal{MD}_i(1^*)\} = \mathcal{M}_5.$$

Case $\gamma\gamma\gamma 0$: $\mathcal{M}_{\gamma\gamma\gamma 0} = \max_{1 \le i \le n}\{\mathcal{ME}_i(1^*) + \mathcal{MD}_i(1^*,0)\}$. Since $\mathcal{MD}_i(1^*,0) \le \min\{\mathcal{MD}_i(1^*), \mathcal{MD}_i(0)\}$,

$$\mathcal{M}_{\gamma\gamma\gamma 0} \le \max_{1 \le i \le n} \{\mathcal{ME}_i(1^*) + \mathcal{MD}_i(1^*)\} = \mathcal{M}_5.$$

Case $0\gamma\gamma\gamma$: $\mathcal{M}_{0\gamma\gamma\gamma} = \max_{1 \le i \le n}\{\mathcal{ME}_i(1^*,0) + \mathcal{MD}_i(1^*)\}$. Since $\mathcal{ME}_i(1^*,0) \le \min\{\mathcal{ME}_i(1^*), \mathcal{ME}_i(0)\}$,

$$\mathcal{M}_{0\gamma\gamma\gamma} \le \max_{1 \le i \le n} \{\mathcal{ME}_i(1^*) + \mathcal{MD}_i(1^*)\} = \mathcal{M}_5.$$

Case $\gamma\gamma\gamma\gamma$: $\mathcal{M}_{\gamma\gamma\gamma\gamma} = \mathcal{M}_5.$

Case $\gamma\gamma\delta 0$: $\mathcal{M}_{\gamma\gamma\delta 0} = \max_{1 \le i \le n}\{\mathcal{ME}_i(1^*) + \mathcal{MD}_i(1,0)\}$. Since $\mathcal{MD}_i(1,0) \le \min\{\mathcal{MD}_i(1), \mathcal{MD}_i(0)\}$,

$$\mathcal{M}_{\gamma\gamma\delta 0} \le \max_{1 \le i \le n} \{\mathcal{ME}_i(1^*) + \mathcal{MD}_i(0)\} = \mathcal{M}_3.$$

Case $\delta 0\gamma\gamma$: $\mathcal{M}_{\delta 0\gamma\gamma} - \max_{1 \le i \le n}\{\mathcal{ME}_i(1,0) + \mathcal{MD}_i(1^*)\}$. Since $\mathcal{ME}_i(1,0) \le \min\{\mathcal{ME}_i(1), \mathcal{ME}_i(0)\}$,

$$\mathcal{M}_{\delta 0\gamma\gamma} \le \max_{1 \le i \le n} \{\mathcal{ME}_i(0) + \mathcal{MD}_i(1^*)\} = \mathcal{M}_4.$$

Case $\gamma\delta\gamma 0$: $\mathcal{M}_{\gamma\delta\gamma 0} = \max_{1 \le i \le n}\{\mathcal{ME}_i(1^*,1) + \mathcal{MD}_i(1^*,0)\}$. Since $\mathcal{ME}_i(1^*,1) \le \min\{\mathcal{ME}_i(1^*), \mathcal{ME}_i(1)\}$ and $\mathcal{MD}_i(1^*,0) < \min\{\mathcal{MD}_i(1^*), \mathcal{MD}_i(0)\}$,

$$\mathcal{M}_{\gamma\delta\gamma 0} \le \max_{1 \le i \le n} \{\mathcal{ME}_i(1^*) + \mathcal{MD}_i(1^*)\} = \mathcal{M}_5.$$

Case $\gamma 0\gamma\delta$: $\mathcal{M}_{\gamma 0\gamma\delta} = \max_{1 \le i \le n}\{\mathcal{ME}_i(1^*,0) + \mathcal{MD}_i(1^*,1)\}$. Since $\mathcal{ME}_i(1^*,0) \le \min\{\mathcal{ME}_i(1^*), \mathcal{ME}_i(0)\}$ and $\mathcal{MD}_i(1^*,1) \le \min\{\mathcal{MD}_i(1^*), \mathcal{MD}_i(1)\}$,

$$\mathcal{M}_{\gamma 0\gamma\delta} \le \max_{1 \le i \le n} \{\mathcal{ME}_i(1^*) + \mathcal{MD}_i(1^*)\} = \mathcal{M}_5.$$

Case $\gamma\gamma\gamma\delta$: $\mathcal{M}_{\gamma\gamma\gamma\delta} = \max_{1 \le i \le n}\{\mathcal{ME}_i(1^*) + \mathcal{MD}_i(1^*,1)\}$. Since $\mathcal{MD}_i(1^*,1) \le \min\{\mathcal{MD}_i(1^*), \mathcal{MD}_i(1)\}$,

$$\mathcal{M}_{\gamma\gamma\gamma\delta} \le \max_{1 \le i \le n} \{\mathcal{ME}_i(1^*) + \mathcal{MD}_i(1^*)\} = \mathcal{M}_5.$$

Case $\gamma\delta\gamma\gamma$: $\mathcal{M}_{\gamma\delta\gamma\gamma} = \max_{1 \le i \le n}\{\mathcal{ME}_i(1^*,1) + \mathcal{MD}_i(1^*)\}$. Since $\mathcal{ME}_i(1^*,1) \le \min\{\mathcal{ME}_i(1^*), \mathcal{ME}_i(1)\}$,

$$\mathcal{M}_{\gamma\gamma\gamma\delta} \leq \max_{1\leq i\leq n} \{\mathcal{ME}_i(1^*) + \mathcal{MD}_i(1^*)\} = \mathcal{M}_5.$$

The result now follows immediately. □

**Example.** For CLEFIA, we computed $\mathcal{ME}_1((0,0,0,1^*),1^*) = 3$ and $\mathcal{MD}_1((1^*,0,0,0),1^*) = 4$. By running through all possible difference vectors **a** and **b**, it can be verified that $\mathcal{ME}_1(1^*) = 3$ and $\mathcal{MD}_1(1^*) = 4$. Checking through all values of $i$ where $1 \leq i \leq 4$, we have

$$\begin{aligned}
\mathcal{M}_5 &= \max_{1\leq i\leq 4} \{\mathcal{ME}_i(1^*) + \mathcal{MD}_i(1^*)\} \\
&= \mathcal{ME}_1(1^*) + \mathcal{MD}_1(1^*) \\
&= 7.
\end{aligned}$$

By computing the values of $\mathcal{M}_1$ to $\mathcal{M}_4$, we obtain $\mathcal{M}_1 = \mathcal{M}_2 = 5$ and $\mathcal{M}_3 = \mathcal{M}_4 = 6$. These imply that $\mathcal{M} = \mathcal{M}_5 = 7$. Hence, for CLEFIA, the maximum length of impossible boomerang distinguishers that can be found in the $\mathcal{UB}$ method is 7, and a corresponding 7-round impossible boomerang characteristic is $((0,0,0,\gamma),(0,0,0,\gamma)) \nrightarrow_7 ((\gamma',0,0,0),(\gamma'',0,0,0))$, where $\gamma' \neq \gamma''$.

## 5  An Algorithm to Compute the Length of Impossible Boomerang Distinguishers

In this section, we present an algorithm to compute the maximum number of rounds, $\mathcal{M}$, for the impossible boomerang characteristics which can be found by the $\mathcal{UB}$-method. By modifying this algorithm, we may also identify the specific forms of impossible boomerang distinguishers.

At the outset, we shall assume that the block cipher structure that the algorithm is applied to has round functions which are bijective. Furthermore, the encryption and decryption characteristic matrices, $\mathcal{E}$ and $\mathcal{D}$ are assumed to be 1-property matrices. We employ the same variables as in Tables 6 and 7 of [3]. They are summarized in Tables 4 and 5 below.

**Table 4.** The meaning of variables used in Algorithm 1. $(y \geq 0)$

| Variables | Meanings |
|---|---|
| $e_{i,j} = 0$ | $\mathcal{E}_{i,j} = 0$ |
| $e_{i,j} = 1$ | $\mathcal{E}_{i,j} = 1$ or $1_F$ |
| $\tilde{e}_{i,j} = 0$ | $\mathcal{E}_{i,j} = 1$ $(x^* \cdot \mathcal{E}_{i,j} = x^*$ preserves $*$.$)$ |
| $\tilde{e}_{i,j} = 1$ | $\mathcal{E}_{i,j} = 0$ $(x^* \cdot \mathcal{E}_{i,j} = 0)$ or $\mathcal{E}_{i,j} = 1_F$ $(x^* \cdot \mathcal{E}_{i,j} = x)$ |
| $a_i^r = y$ (resp. $x$) | The $i^{th}$ entry of difference vector $\mathbf{a}^r$ is $y$ (resp. $x^*$) |
| $\hat{a}_i^r = 0$ | The $i^{th}$ entry of difference vector $\mathbf{a}^r$ has no $*$ |
| $\hat{a}_i^r = -1$ | The $i^{th}$ entry of difference vector $\mathbf{a}^r$ has $*$ |

**Table 5.** Multiplication between an entry of difference vector and an entry of matrix in Algorithm 1

| An entry $c$, $(\hat{a}_i^r)$ of difference vectors | An entry $d$, $(\tilde{e}_{i,j})$ of $\mathcal{E}$ | $c \cdot d$ | $\hat{a}_i^r + \tilde{e}_{i,j} = s_i$ if $(s_i = 1)$ $s_i \leftarrow 0$ |
|---|---|---|---|
| $x^*$, $(-1)$ | $0$, $(1)$ | $0$ | $0$ |
| $x^*$, $(-1)$ | $1_F$, $(1)$ | $x$ | $0$ |
| $x^*$, $(-1)$ | $1$, $(0)$ | $x^*$ | $-1$ |
| $x$, $(0)$ | $0$, $(1)$ | $0$ | $0$ |
| $x$, $(0)$ | $1_F$, $(1)$ | $x$ | $0$ |
| $x$, $(0)$ | $1$, $(1)$ | $x$ | $0$ |

---

*Step 1 : Input the encryption characteristic matrix $\mathcal{E} = (\mathcal{E}_{ij})_{n \times n}$*

for $i = 0$ to $n - 1$
    for $j = 0$ to $n - 1$
        if $\mathcal{E}_{i,j} = 0$, then $e_{i,j} \leftarrow 0$ and $\tilde{e}_{i,j} \leftarrow 1$
        if $\mathcal{E}_{i,j} = 1$, then $e_{i,j} \leftarrow 1$ and $\tilde{e}_{i,j} \leftarrow 0$
        if $\mathcal{E}_{i,j} = 1_F$, then $e_{i,j} \leftarrow 1$ and $\tilde{e}_{i,j} \leftarrow 1$

*Step 2 : Compute the values of $\mathcal{ME}_i(m)$ where $0 \leq i \leq n - 1$ and $m \in \{0, 1^*\}$.*

$\mathcal{ME}_i(0) \leftarrow 0$, $\mathcal{ME}_i(2) \leftarrow 0$, for $0 \leq i \leq n - 1$

/* The $m$'s values $0$, $1$, and $2$ indicate the entries $0$, $1$, and $1^*$ respectively. */

For each input difference vector $\mathbf{x}$      /* $\mathbf{x}$ represents $\mathbf{x}^0$. */
    for $i = 0$ to $n - 1$
        if $(x_i^0 = 0)$ $\hat{x}_i \leftarrow 0$
        else if $(x_i^0 = 1)$ $\hat{x}_i \leftarrow -1$
        $\mathcal{ME}_i(\mathbf{x}, 0) \leftarrow 0$, $\mathcal{ME}_i(\mathbf{x}, 2) \leftarrow 0$
    $r \leftarrow 0$
    while (there exists some index $l$ such that $x_l^r \leq 2$)
        for $j = 0$ to $n - 1$
            $t_j \leftarrow 0$, $\hat{t}_j \leftarrow 0$
            /* $t_j$ and $\hat{t}_j$ are the temporary parameters to compute $\mathbf{x}^{r+1}$ and $\hat{\mathbf{x}}^{r+1}$. */
            for $i = 0$ to $n - 1$
                $t_j \leftarrow t_j + x_i^r \cdot e_{i,j}$
                $s_i \leftarrow \hat{x}_i^r + \tilde{e}_{i,j}$
                if $(s_i = 1)$ $s_i \leftarrow 0$
                $\hat{t}_j \leftarrow \hat{t}_j + s_i$
        $r \leftarrow r + 1$
        $x_i^r \leftarrow t_i$, $\hat{x}_i^r \leftarrow \hat{t}_i$, for $0 \leq i \leq n - 1$

        for $i = 0$ to $n - 1$
            if $(x_i^r = 0)$ $\mathcal{ME}_i(\mathbf{x}, 0) \leftarrow r$
            if $(x_i^r = 1$ and $\hat{x}_i^r = -1)$ $\mathcal{ME}_i(\mathbf{x}, 2) \leftarrow r$

    for $i = 0$ to $n - 1$
        if $(\mathcal{ME}_i(0) \leq \mathcal{ME}_i(\mathbf{x}, 0))$ $\mathcal{ME}_i(0) \leftarrow \mathcal{ME}_i(\mathbf{x}, 0)$
        if $(\mathcal{ME}_i(2) \leq \mathcal{ME}_i(\mathbf{x}, 2))$ $\mathcal{ME}_i(2) \leftarrow \mathcal{ME}_i(\mathbf{x}, 2)$

*Step 3 : Compute the values of $\mathcal{MD}_i(m)$ where $0 \leq i \leq n - 1$ and $m \in \{0, 1^*\}$.*

Insert the matrix $\mathcal{D}$ into steps 1 and 2.

*Step 4 : Compute the values of $\mathcal{ME}_i(1, 0)$ where $0 \leq i \leq n - 1$*

$\mathcal{ME}_i(1, 0) \leftarrow 0$, for $0 \leq i \leq n - 1$

For each input difference vector **x** and each input difference vector **y**
  for $i = 0$ to $n - 1$
    if $(x_i^0 = 0)$ $\hat{x}_i \leftarrow 0$
    else if $(x_i^0 = 1)$ $\hat{x}_i \leftarrow -1$
    if $(y_i^0 = 0)$ $\hat{y}_i \leftarrow 0$
    else if $(y_i^0 = 1)$ $\hat{y}_i \leftarrow -1$
    $\mathcal{ME}_i(\mathbf{x}, \mathbf{y}, 1, 0) \leftarrow 0$

  $r \leftarrow 0$
  while (there exists some index $l$ such that $x_l^r \leq 2$ or $y_l^r \leq 2$ )
    for $j = 0$ to $n - 1$
      $tx_j \leftarrow 0,\ \hat{tx}_j \leftarrow 0$
      $ty_j \leftarrow 0,\ \hat{ty}_j \leftarrow 0$
      for $i = 0$ to $n - 1$
        $tx_j \leftarrow tx_j + x_i^r \cdot e_{i,j}$
        $sx_i \leftarrow \hat{x}_i^r + \tilde{e}_{i,j}$
        if $(sx_i = 1)$ $sx_i \leftarrow 0$
        $\hat{tx}_j \leftarrow \hat{tx}_j + sx_i$

        $ty_j \leftarrow ty_j + y_i^r \cdot e_{i,j}$
        $sy_i \leftarrow \hat{y}_i^r + \tilde{e}_{i,j}$
        if $(sy_i = 1)$ $sy_i \leftarrow 0$
        $\hat{ty}_j \leftarrow \hat{ty}_j + sy_i$

      $r \leftarrow r + 1$
      $x_i^r \leftarrow tx_i,\ \tilde{x}_i^r \leftarrow \hat{tx}_i,$ for $0 \leq i \leq n - 1$
      $y_i^r \leftarrow ty_i,\ \tilde{y}_i^r \leftarrow \hat{ty}_i,$ for $0 \leq i \leq n - 1$

  for $i = 0$ to $n - 1$
    for $j = 0$ to $r$
      if $(x_i^j = 1$ and $\tilde{x}_i^j = 0$ and $y_i^j = 0$ and $\tilde{y}_i^j = 0)$ $\mathcal{ME}_i(\mathbf{x}, \mathbf{y}, 1, 0) \leftarrow j$

  if $(\mathcal{ME}_i(\mathbf{x}, \mathbf{y}, 1, 0) \leq \mathcal{ME}_i(1, 0))$ $\mathcal{ME}_i(1, 0) \leftarrow \mathcal{ME}_i(\mathbf{x}, \mathbf{y}, 1, 0)$

*Step 5 : Compute the values of* $\mathcal{MD}_i(1, 0)$ *where* $0 \leq i \leq n - 1$.

Insert the matrix $\mathcal{D}$ into step 4.

*Step 6 : Compute the length* $\mathcal{M}_1$.

Output $\max_{0 \leq i \leq n-1}\{\mathcal{ME}_i(1, 0) + \mathcal{MD}_i(0)\}$.

*Step 7 : Compute the length* $\mathcal{M}_2$.

Output $\max_{0 \leq i \leq n-1}\{\mathcal{ME}_i(0) + \mathcal{MD}_i(1, 0)\}$.

*Step 8 : Compute the length* $\mathcal{M}_3$.

Output $\max_{0 \leq i \leq n-1}\{\mathcal{ME}_i(2) + \mathcal{MD}_i(0)\}$.

*Step 9 : Compute the length* $\mathcal{M}_4$.

Output $\max_{0 \leq i \leq n-1}\{\mathcal{ME}_i(0) + \mathcal{MD}_i(2)\}$.

*Step 10 : Compute the length* $\mathcal{M}_5$.

Output $\max_{0 \leq i \leq n-1}\{\mathcal{ME}_i(2) + \mathcal{MD}_i(2)\}$.

*Step 11 : Output the length* $\mathcal{M}$.

Output $\max_{1 \leq i \leq 5}(\mathcal{M}_i)$.

**Algorithm 1.** To compute the length $\mathcal{M}$

# 6 Results for Some Block Cipher Structures

We applied Algorithm 1 to several block cipher structures such as a generalized Feistel network, a generalized CAST256-like structure, a generalized MARS-like structure, a generalized RC6-like structure, CLEFIA, a generalized Feistel scheme with an substitution-permutation round function, SMS4, as well as a Skipjack-like structure. All of them have 1-property matrices $\mathcal{E}$ and $\mathcal{D}$. The reader may refer to [7,9,10,4,8] for the details of these cipher structures. We also found the specific forms of impossible boomerang characteristics which give the maximum lengths for each structure. Even though the computer simulation was only tested on a finite number of subblocks, we are able to generalize the results due to the regular structural feature.

Table 6 gives the specific forms of various impossible boomerang characteristics for each structure. Table 7 summarizes our cryptanalytic results. In both tables, $n$ denotes the number of subblocks and in the case of $n$ always even, we let $n = 2m$. In Table 7, we also compare the maximum lengths for the impossible differential cryptanalysis (IDC) with that for the impossible boomerang attack (IBA). As can be observed, these two maximum lengths are equal for the generalized MARS structure.

**Table 6.** Impossible boomerang characteristics for some generalized Feistel networks (All $\alpha$'s, $\beta$'s non-zero, $i$ odd, $\alpha \neq \alpha'$, $\beta \neq \beta'$)

| Structure | Case | Impossible Boomerang Characteristics |
|---|---|---|
| $GFN_m$ | $\gamma\gamma\gamma\gamma$ | $((0,\ldots,0,\alpha_n),(0,\ldots,0,\alpha_n)) \not\rightarrow_{3m} ((\beta_1,0,\ldots,0),(\beta_1',0,\ldots,0))$ |
| | $\delta 000$ | Many |
| | | E.g. For $GFN_3$, $((0,0,0,\alpha_4,0,0),(0,\ldots,0,\alpha_6)) \not\rightarrow_9 ((0,0,\beta_3,0,0,0),(0,0,\beta_3',0,0,0))$ |
| | $000\delta$ | Many |
| | | E.g. For $GFN_3$, $((0,\ldots,0,\alpha_6),(0,\ldots,0,\alpha_6')) \not\rightarrow_9 ((0,\beta_2,0,\ldots,0),(\beta_1,0,\ldots,0))$ |
| Generalized CAST256 | $\gamma\gamma\gamma\gamma$ | $((0,\ldots,0,\alpha_n),(0,\ldots,0,\alpha_n)) \not\rightarrow_{n^2-1} ((\beta_1,0,\ldots,0),(\beta_1',0,\ldots,0))$ |
| Generalized MARS | $\gamma\gamma\gamma\gamma$ | $((0,\ldots,0,\alpha_n),(0,\ldots,0,\alpha_n)) \not\rightarrow_{2n-1} ((\beta_1,0,\ldots,0),(\beta_1',0,\ldots,0))$ |
| Generalized RC6 | $\gamma\gamma\gamma\gamma$ | $((0,\ldots,0,\alpha_i,0,\ldots,0),(0,\ldots,0,\alpha_i,0,\ldots,0)) \not\rightarrow_{4m-1}$ |
| | | $\phantom{xxxxxxxx}((0,\ldots,0,\beta_{i+1},0,\ldots,0),(0,\ldots,0,\beta_{i+1}',0,\ldots,0))$ |
| CLEFIA | $\gamma\gamma\gamma\gamma$ | $((0,0,0,\alpha_4),(0,0,0,\alpha_4)) \not\rightarrow_7 ((\beta_1,0,0,0),(\beta_1',0,0,0))$ |
| $GFSP_4$ | $\gamma\gamma\gamma\gamma$ | $((\alpha_1,0,0,0),(\alpha_1,0,0,0)) \not\rightarrow_{15} ((0,0,0,\beta_4),(0,0,0,\beta_4'))$ |
| $SMS4$ | $\gamma\gamma\gamma\gamma$ | $((\alpha_1,0,0,0),(\alpha_1,0,0,0)) \not\rightarrow_5 ((0,0,0,\beta_4),(0,0,0,\beta_4'))$ |
| Skipjack-like | $00\gamma\gamma$ | Many |
| | | E.g. $((0,0,0,\alpha_4),(0,0,0,\alpha_4)) \not\rightarrow_{12} ((0,\beta_2,0,0),(0,\beta_2',0,0))$ |

## 6.1 Additional Comments

**Generalized CAST256 :** In [3] and [8], the authors conjectured that the maximum length of the impossible differential distinguisher for generalized CAST256 is $n^2 - 1$. This value was derived based on Figure 3 in [8]. In contrast, we looked at the structure shown in Figure 1 of [7]. Based on this diagram, we found the maximum length of the impossible differential distinguisher to be $n^2 + n - 1$ instead.

**GFSP$_4$ :** In [10], the authors only gave the upper bounds of the maximum differential/linear probabilities of 16-round $GFSP_4$. However, in the light of our

**Table 7.** Summary of our results. (*A*: The maximum number ($r$) of rounds for impossible differential characteristics. *B*: The maximum number ($r$) of rounds for impossible boomerang characteristics.)

| Block Cipher Structure | IDC | | IBA | |
|---|---|---|---|---|
| | *A* | Comment | *B* | Comment |
| $GFN_m$ | $r = 3m + 2$ $(m \geq 3)$ | [3] | $r = 3m$ $(m \geq 2)$ | This paper |
| Generalized CAST256 | $r = n^2 + n - 1$ $(n \geq 3)$ | This paper | $r = n^2 - 1$ $(n \geq 3)$ | This paper |
| Generalized MARS | $r = 2n - 1$ $(n \geq 3)$ | [3] | $r = 2n - 1$ $(n \geq 3)$ | This paper |
| Generalized RC6 | $r = 4m + 1$ $(m \geq 2)$ | [3] | $r = 4m - 1$ $(m \geq 2)$ | This paper |
| CLEFIA | 9 | [9] | 7 | This paper |
| $GFSP_4$ | 19 | This paper | 15 | This paper |
| SMS4 | 6 | This paper | 5 | This paper |
| Skipjack-like | 15 | [8] | 12 | This paper |

results, both for IDC and IBA, we recommend the use of at least 25 rounds for this scheme.

**SMS4 :** While the maximum lengths of the distinguishers found for IDC and IBA are quite small, note that this analysis only considers the general structure of the ciphers without taking into account the specific properties of the round functions. For example, for SMS4, a 12-round impossible differential characteristic was published in [6], formed by combining two 6-round differentials. Our results, however, give a definite lower bound for the number of rounds that can be attacked with an impossible differential or impossible boomerang distinguisher.

**Skipjack-like structure :** Our approach also works for the truncated case. With reference to Figure 1 of [8], a 15-round impossible truncated differential was found in [8], which agrees with the result which we found by the $\mathcal{U}$-method. By applying our Algorithm 1, we unveiled a 12-round impossible truncated boomerang distinguisher.

# 7   Conclusion

In this paper, we introduced a widely applicable method, called the $\mathcal{UB}$-method, to find various impossible boomerang characteristics for general block cipher structures. We presented Algorithm 1 which is used to determine the maximum length of impossible boomerang distinguishers that can be found by the $\mathcal{UB}$-method. Algorithm 1 was then applied to find the maximum length of impossible boomerang distinguishers for several known block cipher structures. By modifying Algorithm 1, we found the specific forms of impossible boomerang characteristics for each structure.

While our research presented in this paper only considers the general structure of the ciphers, it provides a definite lower bound for the maximum length of an impossible boomerang distinguisher. It is likely that longer ones may be found when the specific properties of the round functions are taken into account.

Furthermore, we saw that the lower bound for the maximum length of an impossible boomerang distinguisher is comparable to that of an impossible differential characteristic for some block ciphers. Since impossible boomerang attack may be a feasible attack on certain ciphers, our results will be useful in the study of the latter, which will in turn shed more light on variants of the attack such as the related-key version.

## Acknowledgements

The authors would like to thank Khoongming Khoo for his helpful comments and suggestions, and also the anonymous reviewers for their valuable comments.

## References

1. Biham, E., Dunkelman, O., Keller, N.: A related-key rectangle attack on the full KASUMI. In: Roy, B. (ed.) ASIACRYPT 2005. LNCS, vol. 3788, pp. 443–461. Springer, Heidelberg (2005)
2. Dunkelman, O., Keller, N.: An improved impossible differential attack on MISTY1. In: Pieprzyk, J. (ed.) ASIACRYPT 2008. LNCS, vol. 5350, pp. 441–454. Springer, Heidelberg (2008)
3. Kim, J., Hong, S., Sung, J., Lee, S., Lim, J., Sung, S.: Impossible Differential Cryptanalysis for Block Cipher Structures. In: Johansson, T., Maitra, S. (eds.) INDOCRYPT 2003. LNCS, vol. 2904, pp. 97–106. Springer, Heidelberg (2003)
4. Liu, F., Ji, W., Hu, L., Ding, J., Lv, S., Pyshkin, A., Weinmann, R.: Analysis of the SMS4 block cipher. In: Pieprzyk, J., Ghodosi, H., Dawson, E. (eds.) ACISP 2007. LNCS, vol. 4586, pp. 158–170. Springer, Heidelberg (2007)
5. Lu, J.: Cryptanalysis of Block Ciphers., Technical Report RHUL-MA-2008-19 ) (July 30, 2008) http://www.rhul.ac.uk/mathematics/techreports
6. Lu, J.: Attacking reduced-round versions of the SMS4 block cipher in the chinese WAPI standard. In: Qing, S., Imai, H., Wang, G. (eds.) ICICS 2007. LNCS, vol. 4861, pp. 306–318. Springer, Heidelberg (2007)
7. Moriai, S., Vaudenay, S.: On the Pseudorandomness of Top-Level Schemes of Block Ciphers. In: Okamoto, T. (ed.) ASIACRYPT 2000. LNCS, vol. 1976, pp. 289–302. Springer, Heidelberg (2000)
8. Sung, J., Lee, S.-J., Lim, J.-I., Hong, S.H., Park, S.-J.: Provable Security for the Skipjack-like Structure Against Differential Cryptanalysis and Linear Cryptanalysis. In: Okamoto, T. (ed.) ASIACRYPT 2000. LNCS, vol. 1976, pp. 274–288. Springer, Heidelberg (2000)
9. Tsunoo, Y., Tsujihara, E., Shigeri, M., Saito, T., Suzaki, T., Kubo, H.: Impossible Differential Cryptanalysis of CLEFIA. In: Nyberg, K. (ed.) FSE 2008. LNCS, vol. 5086, pp. 398–411. Springer, Heidelberg (2008)
10. Wu, W., Zhang, W., Lin, D.: On the Security of Generalized Feistel Scheme with SP Round Function. International Journal of Network Security 3(3), 215–224 (2006)

# Improved Distinguishing Attacks on HC-256*

Gautham Sekar[1,2,**] and Bart Preneel[1,2]

[1] Department of Electrical Engineering ESAT/SCD-COSIC,
Katholieke Universiteit Leuven, Kasteelpark Arenberg 10,
B-3001 Leuven-Heverlee, Belgium
[2] Interdisciplinary Institute for BroadBand Technology (IBBT), Belgium
{Gautham.Sekar,Bart.Preneel}@esat.kuleuven.be

**Abstract.** The software-efficient stream cipher HC-256 was proposed
by Wu at FSE 2004. Due to its impressive performance, the cipher was
also a well-received entrant to the ECRYPT eSTREAM competition.
The closely related stream cipher HC-128, also designed by Wu, went on
to find a place in the final portfolio of the eSTREAM contest. The cipher
HC-256 is word-oriented, with 32 bits in each word, and uses a 256-bit key
and a 256-bit *IV*. Since HC-256 was published in 2004, barring a cache-
timing analysis of unprotected implementations, there has not been any
attack on the cipher. This paper makes two contributions. First, we build
a class of distinguishers on HC-256, each of which requires testing the
validity of about $2^{276.8}$ linear equations involving binary keystream variables. Thereby, our attacks improve the data complexity of the hitherto
best-known distinguisher (presented by the designer along with the specifications of the cipher) by a factor of about 12. We also present another
observation that, we believe, can be further exploited to build more efficient distinguishing attacks on the cipher. It is hoped that the results
of this paper would also find use in future security evaluations of the
closely-related ciphers HC-128 and HC-256'.

## 1 Introduction

HC-128 and HC-256 are software-oriented synchronous stream ciphers designed
by Wu [15,16]. HC-256 was published in 2004. The ciphers were also submitted to the ECRYPT eSTREAM competition [5] in 2005. On the Pentium M
processor, the speed of HC-128 reaches 3.05 cycles/byte, while HC-256 requires
about 4.15 cycles/byte on the Pentium 4. Due to these impressive performance
figures, the ciphers were seen as forerunners in the stream cipher contest. In the
absence of attacks, both HC-256 and HC-128 were advanced to Phase III of the
competition as 'focus' ciphers. Since the main focus of eSTREAM was 128-bit
security, HC-128 was recently selected for the final eSTREAM portfolio under

* This work was supported in part by the IAP Programme P6/26 BCRYPT of the
Belgian State (Belgian Science Policy), and in part by the European Commission
through the ICT programme under contract ICT-2007-216676 ECRYPT II.
** This author is supported by an FWO project.

T. Takagi and M. Mambo (Eds.): IWSEC 2009, LNCS 5824, pp. 38–52, 2009.
© Springer-Verlag Berlin Heidelberg 2009

Profile 1 (software-based stream ciphers). The ciphers belong to the family of array-based stream ciphers that include, among others, the RC4, ISAAC and Py [2,7].

Barring a few interesting observations, HC-128 and HC-256 have not yet witnessed any serious attacks. The designer himself has presented distinguishers along with the specifications in [15,16]. In the case of HC-256, each distinguisher requires testing the validity of $2^{280}$ equations (where each equation involves 10 keystream output bits). Another observation, made by Dunkelman in [4], shows that the keystream words of HC-128 leak information on the internal states. However, this observation has not yet been exploited to construct distinguishers or to recover the key. Zenner has presented cache-timing attacks on unprotected implementations of HC-256 that allow reconstruction of the inner state and also the key [17]. This attack requires 6148 precise cache-timing measurements, $2^{16}$ known plaintext bits, 3 MBytes of memory and a computational effort equivalent to testing about $2^{55}$ keys. However, the attack uses very strong assumptions - under these assumptions any unprotected implementation of a cipher based on lookup tables such as AES or RC4 could be broken easily. Recently, Maitra *et al.* presented some observations on HC-128 in [8]. There they exploit the results of [14] (on linear approximation of modular addition of three integers) to show that the output generation of HC-128 can be well-approximated by linear functions. Using this they show that for HC-128, the distinguisher presented in [16] for the least significant bit can be extended for the other bits. Their paper also studies the aforementioned observation due to Dunkelman [4]. Yet, their paper does not show any improvement over the existing attacks (i.e., those presented by the designer along with the specifications of the cipher).

## 1.1   Contribution of This Paper

The main idea behind our distinguishers is to note that the keystream output word generation of HC-256 involves two elements of the state array directly which are 10 places apart. We exploit this to improve the distinguisher presented in [15]. Our attacks do not work immediately for HC-128 as in the keystream output generation no two elements of the state array are involved directly, but they are used with some rotation.

For the least significant bit, our analysis is similar to that in [15], but a more careful analysis shows that the bias probability was underestimated and thus the requirement of the keystream bits was overestimated in [15]. Our analysis improves the probability and thus our distinguishers require fewer keystream words. Each of our distinguishers requires examining about $2^{276.8}$ equations where each equation involves 8 keystream output bits.

This paper is organised as follows. Section 2 lists the notations used in the paper. Section 3 details the specifications of HC-256. Our main observation and the resulting distinguishing attack are presented in Sect. 4 and Sect. 5, respectively. Our second observation is presented in Sect. 6. Finally, Sect. 7 concludes the paper and presents a few interesting open problems.

## 2   Notation and Convention

We use the following notations and conventions.

The set of natural numbers is denoted by $\mathbb{N}$.

The $+$ operator denotes addition modulo $2^{32}$.

The $-$ operator denotes subtraction modulo $2^{32}$.

The symbol $\boxminus$ denotes subtraction modulo 1024.

The symbol $\oplus$ denotes bitwise exclusive-OR.

Concatenation is denoted by $\|$.

The complement of event $E$ is denoted by $E^c$.

$x \gg y$: $x$ is shifted to the right by $y$ bit-positions.

$x \ll y$: $x$ is shifted to the left by $y$ bit-positions.

$x \ggg y$: $((x \gg y) \oplus (x \ll (32 - y))$, where $y \in \{0, \ldots, 31\}$, $x \in \{0, \ldots, 2^{32} - 1\}$.

$x \lll y$: $((x \ll y) \oplus (x \gg (32 - y))$, where $y \in \{0, \ldots, 31\}$, $x \in \{0, \ldots, 2^{32} - 1\}$.

PRBG denotes the pseudorandom bit generation algorithm of the cipher.

The keystream word generated at round $i$ (i.e., the $(i + 1)$-th iteration of the PRBG) is denoted by $s_i$.

The terms $s_{i(j)}$, $(h_1(x))_j$, $(h_2(x))_j$, $r_{i(j)}$ and $(Q[r])_j$ denote the $j$-th bits ($j = 0$ for the least significant bit) of $s_i$, $h_1(x)$, $h_2(x)$, $r_i$ and $Q[r]$, respectively.

The term *word* denotes a 32-bit integer.

If $x$ is a word, then $x^{(i)}$ denotes the $i$-th byte of $x$, where $x^{(0)}$ is the least significant byte and $x^{(3)}$ is the most significant byte.

## 3   Specifications of HC-256

The cipher uses a 256-bit key $K$ and a 256-bit $IV$. Let $K = K[0]\| \ldots \| K[7]$ and $IV = IV[0]\| \ldots \| IV[7]$, where each $K[i]$ and $IV[i]$ ($i = 0, \ldots, 7$) is 32 bits in length. The internal state of HC-256 consists of two tables $P$ and $Q$, each with 1024 32-bit elements. The following functions are used in the specifications.

$$f_1(x) = (x \ggg 7) \oplus (x \ggg 18) \oplus (x \gg 3),$$
$$f_2(x) = (x \ggg 17) \oplus (x \ggg 19) \oplus (x \gg 10),$$
$$g_1(x,y) = ((x \ggg 10) \oplus (y \ggg 23)) + Q[(x \oplus y) \bmod 1024],$$
$$g_2(x,y) = ((x \ggg 10) \oplus (y \ggg 23)) + P[(x \oplus y) \bmod 1024],$$
$$h_1(x) = Q[x^{(0)}] + Q[256 + x^{(1)}] + Q[512 + x^{(2)}] + Q[768 + x^{(3)}],$$
$$h_2(x) = P[x^{(0)}] + P[256 + x^{(1)}] + P[512 + x^{(2)}] + P[768 + x^{(3)}].$$

### 3.1   *K/IV* Setup Algorithm

1. The $K$ and the $IV$ are expanded into an array $W[0, \ldots, 2559]$ as follows.

$$W[i] = \begin{cases} K[i] & 0 \leq i \leq 7; \\ IV[i - 8] & 8 \leq i \leq 15; \\ f_2(W[i - 2]) + W[i - 7] + f_1(W[i - 15]) \\ \quad + W[i - 16] + i & 16 \leq i \leq 2559. \end{cases}$$

2. Update the tables $P$ and $Q$ with the array $W$ as follows.

$$P[i] = W[i + 512], \text{for } 0 \leq i \leq 1023,$$
$$Q[i] = W[i + 1536], \text{for } 0 \leq i \leq 1023.$$

3. Run the cipher (i.e., the keystream generation algorithm provided in Sect. 3.2) 4096 steps without generating output.

## 3.2   The PRBG

The PRBG of HC-256 updates only one of the two tables $P$ and $Q$ in each round and outputs one word.

$i = 0$;
repeat until enough keystream bits are generated.
{
   $k = i \bmod 1024$;
   if $(i \bmod 2048) < 1024$
   {
      $P[k] = P[k] + P[k \boxminus 10] + g_1(P[k \boxminus 3], P[k \boxminus 1023])$;
      $s_i = h_1(P[k \boxminus 12]) \oplus P[k]$;
   }
   else
   {
      $Q[k] = Q[k] + Q[k \boxminus 10] + g_2(Q[k \boxminus 3], Q[k \boxminus 1023])$;
      $s_i = h_2(Q[k \boxminus 12]) \oplus Q[k]$;
   }
   end-if
   $i = i + 1$;
}
end-repeat

# 4   Motivational Observation

First, we recall the analysis provided by the designer in [15]. The analysis exploits weaknesses in the PRBG and is based on the assumption of a flawless $K/IV$ setup. At the $i$-th step, if $(i \bmod 2048) < 1024$, the S-box $P$ is updated as

$$P[i \bmod 1024] \leftarrow P[i \bmod 1024] + P[i \boxminus 10] + g_1(P[i \boxminus 3], P[i \boxminus 1023]).$$

Also, $s_i = h_1(P[i \boxminus 12]) \oplus P[i \bmod 1024]$. For $10 \leq (i \bmod 2048) < 1023$, this can also be written as

$$s_i \oplus h_1(z_i) = (s_{i-2048} \oplus h_1'(z_{i-2048})) + (s_{i-10} \oplus h_1(z_{i-10})) +$$
$$g_1(s_{i-3} \oplus h_1(z_{i-3}), s_{i-2047} \oplus h_1'(z_{i-2047})), \tag{1}$$

where $h_1(x)$ and $h_1'(x)$ are different functions since they are related to different S-boxes (see Sect. 3.2) and $z_i$ denotes the array element $P[i \boxminus 12]$ at the $i$-th step.

Since addition and exclusive-OR are the same at the least significant bit-position[1], from (1) we get:

$$s_{i(0)} \oplus s_{i-2048(0)} \oplus s_{i-10(0)} \oplus s_{i-3(10)} \oplus s_{i-2047(23)}$$
$$= (h_1(z_i))_0 \oplus (h_1'(z_{i-2048}))_0 \oplus (h_1(z_{i-10}))_0$$
$$\oplus (h_1(z_{i-3}))_{10} \oplus (h_1'(z_{i-2047}))_{23} \oplus (Q[r_i])_0, \qquad (2)$$

where $10 \le (i \bmod 2048) < 1023$, $r_i = (s_{i-3} \oplus h_1(z_{i-3}) \oplus s_{i-2047} \oplus h_1'(z_{i-2047}))$ mod 1024. Similarly, when $2048 \cdot \alpha + 10 \le i, j < 2048 \cdot \alpha + 1023$,[2] and $i \ne j$,

$$s_{j(0)} \oplus s_{j-2048(0)} \oplus s_{j-10(0)} \oplus s_{j-3(10)} \oplus s_{j-2047(23)}$$
$$= (h_1(z_j))_0 \oplus (h_1'(z_{j-2048}))_0 \oplus (h_1(z_{j-10}))_0$$
$$\oplus (h_1(z_{j-3}))_{10} \oplus (h_1'(z_{j-2047}))_{23} \oplus (Q[r_j])_0. \qquad (3)$$

For the LHS of (2) and (3) to be equal, i.e., for

$$s_{i(0)} \oplus s_{i-2048(0)} \oplus s_{i-10(0)} \oplus s_{i-3(10)} \oplus s_{i-2047(23)} =$$
$$s_{j(0)} \oplus s_{j-2048(0)} \oplus s_{j-10(0)} \oplus s_{j-3(10)} \oplus s_{j-2047(23)} \qquad (4)$$

to hold for $2048 \cdot \alpha + 10 \le i, j < 2048 \cdot \alpha + 1023$ ($i \ne j$), we require that

$$(h_1(z_i))_0 \oplus (h_1'(z_{i-2048}))_0 \oplus (h_1(z_{i-10}))_0$$
$$\oplus (h_1(z_{i-3}))_{10} \oplus (h_1'(z_{i-2047}))_{23} \oplus (Q[r_i])_0 =$$
$$(h_1(z_j))_0 \oplus (h_1'(z_{j-2048}))_0 \oplus (h_1(z_{j-10}))_0$$
$$\oplus (h_1(z_{j-3}))_{10} \oplus (h_1'(z_{j-2047}))_{23} \oplus (Q[r_j])_0. \qquad (5)$$

Using the fact that $z_i = z_{i-2048} + z_{i-10} + g_1(z_{i-3}, z_{i-2047})$ and $z_j = z_{j-2048} + z_{j-10} + g_1(z_{j-3}, z_{j-2047})$, we approximate (5) as

$$H(x_1) = H(x_2), \qquad (6)$$

where $H$ denotes a random secret 138-bit-to-1-bit S-box, $x_1$ and $x_2$ are two 138-bit random inputs, $x_1 = z_{i-3} \| z_{i-10} \| z_{i-2047} \| z_{i-2048} \| r_i$ and $x_2 = z_{j-3} \| z_{j-10} \| z_{j-2047} \| z_{j-2048} \| r_j$.

We now restate Theorem 1 and its proof from [15].

**Theorem 1.** *Let $H$ be an $m$-bit-to-$n$-bit S-box and all those $n$-bit elements are randomly generated, where $m \ge n$. Let $x_1$ and $x_2$ be two $m$-bit random inputs to $H$. Then $H(x_1) = H(x_2)$ with probability $2^{-m} + 2^{-n} + 2^{-m-n}$.*

*Proof.* Given $x_1 = x_2$, $H(x_1) = H(x_2)$. If $x_1 \ne x_2$, then $H(x_1) = H(x_2)$ with probability $2^{-n}$. Since the probability that $x_1 = x_2$ is $2^{-m}$, then $x_1 \ne x_2$ with probability $1 - 2^{-m}$. The probability that $H(x_1) = H(x_2)$ is, therefore, $2^{-m} + 2^{-n} - 2^{-m-n}$. □

---

[1] For more significant bits, addition may be approximated by exclusive-OR with some biased probability.

[2] $\alpha$ is an element in $\mathbb{N}$ such that $2048 \cdot \alpha + 1023 < 2^{123}$ (since HC-256 generates a maximum of $2^{123}$ outputs or $2^{128}$ output bits from a single $(K, IV)$ pair).

From Theorem 1, (6) and hence (4) holds with probability $1/2 + 2^{-139}$ given $2048 \cdot \alpha + 10 \leq i, j < 2048 \cdot \alpha + 1023$ and $i \neq j$. In Sect. 4.1, we show that (4) holds with a marginally higher probability when $i = j + 10$.

## 4.1  Our Improvement

Similar to the analysis above, our analysis is also based on the assumption of a perfect $K/IV$ setup. When $2048 \cdot \alpha + 10 \leq i, j < 2048 \cdot \alpha + 1023$ and $i = j + 10$, (4) and (5) respectively become:

$$s_{j-2038}(0) \oplus s_{j+10}(0) \oplus s_{j+7}(10) \oplus s_{j-2037}(23) =$$
$$s_{j-2048}(0) \oplus s_{j-10}(0) \oplus s_{j-3}(10) \oplus s_{j-2047}(23) \tag{7}$$

$$(h_1(z_{j+10}))_0 \oplus (h'_1(z_{j-2038}))_0 \oplus (h_1(z_{j+7}))_{10} \oplus (h'_1(z_{j-2037}))_{23} \oplus (Q[r_{j+10}])_0 =$$
$$(h_1(z_{j-10}))_0 \oplus (h'_1(z_{j-2048}))_0 \oplus (h_1(z_{j-3}))_{10} \oplus (h'_1(z_{j-2047}))_{23} \oplus (Q[r_j])_0. \tag{8}$$

Let $L$ denote the event that (8) is satisfied. We now examine the following cases under the assumption of a perfect $K/IV$ setup.

**Case 1:**

Let $E$ denote the event $z_{j-2038} \| z_{j+7} \| z_{j-2037} = z_{j-2048} \| z_{j-3} \| z_{j-2047}$. Since each $z$-term is a 32-bit variable distributed uniformly at random, the probability that $E$ occurs $Pr[E] = 2^{-96}$. When $E$ occurs, (8) reduces to:

$$(h_1(z_{j+10}))_0 \oplus (Q[r_{j+10}])_0 = (h_1(z_{j-10}))_0 \oplus (Q[r_j])_0. \tag{9}$$

We know that,

$$(h_1(z_{j+10}))_0 = (Q[z^{(0)}_{j+10}])_0 \oplus (Q[256 + z^{(1)}_{j+10}])_0$$
$$\oplus (Q[512 + z^{(2)}_{j+10}])_0 \oplus (Q[768 + z^{(3)}_{j+10}])_0. \tag{10}$$

Similarly,

$$(h_1(z_{j-10}))_0 = (Q[z^{(0)}_{j-10}])_0 \oplus (Q[256 + z^{(1)}_{j-10}])_0$$
$$\oplus (Q[512 + z^{(2)}_{j-10}])_0 \oplus (Q[768 + z^{(3)}_{j-10}])_0. \tag{11}$$

Let $z = z^{(3)} \| z^{(2)} \| z^{(1)} \| z^{(0)}$, where $z$ is a 32-bit integer, $z^{(0)}$ is the least significant byte of $z$, and $z^{(3)}$ is the most significant byte of $z$. Let $F$ denote the event $z^{(2)}_{j+10} \| z^{(1)}_{j+10} \| z^{(0)}_{j+10} = z^{(2)}_{j-10} \| z^{(1)}_{j-10} \| z^{(0)}_{j-10}$. Now, recall that

$$z_j = z_{j-2048} + z_{j-10} + g_1(z_{j-3}, z_{j-2047}). \tag{12}$$

Therefore,

$$z_{j+10} = z_{j-2038} + z_j + g_1(z_{j+7}, z_{j-2037}). \tag{13}$$

**Observation 1:** When event $E$ occurs, it follows from (12) and (13) that $z_{j+10}$ and $z_{j-10}$ take the forms $z_{j+10} = A + B + C \bmod 2^{32}$ and $z_{j-10} = -A + B - C \bmod 2^{32}$, respectively. Therefore, the least significant bits of $z_{j+10}$ and $z_{j-10}$ are identical and hence $Pr[F] = 2^{-23}$. Besides, the most significant bits of $z_{j+10}$ and $z_{j-10}$ are equal if and only if $z_{j+10} = z_{j-10}$ (which, in turn, happens with probability $2^{-31}$ since their least significant bits are identical). In other words, $Pr[z_{j+10} = z_{j-10}] = 2^{-31} = Pr[z_{j+10(31)} = z_{j-10(31)}]$,[3] where $z_{j(k)}$ denotes the $k$-th significant bit of $z_j$ ($k = 0$ denotes the least significant bit). We use this observation throughout the paper.

When $F$ occurs, (9) reduces to

$$(Q[768 + z^{(3)}_{j+10}])_0 \oplus (Q[r_{j+10}])_0 = (Q[768 + z^{(3)}_{j-10}])_0 \oplus (Q[r_j])_0. \qquad (14)$$

Now, if $z^{(3)}_{j+10(7)} \neq z^{(3)}_{j-10(7)}$, that is, $z_{j+10(31)} \neq z_{j+10(31)}$ (this is because $z^{(3)}_{j+10(7)}$ is the most significant bit of $z_{j+10}$, i.e., $z_{j+10(31)}$), then $768 + z^{(3)}_{j+10} \neq 768 + z^{(3)}_{j-10}$. Given this, if $r_{j+10} \| r_j = 768 + z^{(3)}_{j+10} \| 768 + z^{(3)}_{j-10}$ (probability is $2^{-20}$ since $r_j$ is a 10-bit variable) or $r_{j+10} \| r_j = 768 + z^{(3)}_{j-10} \| 768 + z^{(3)}_{j+10}$, then (14) holds. Note that we cannot have both the relations $r_{j+10} \| r_j = 768 + z^{(3)}_{j+10} \| 768 + z^{(3)}_{j-10}$ and $r_{j+10} \| r_j = 768 + z^{(3)}_{j-10} \| 768 + z^{(3)}_{j+10}$ to be satisfied; otherwise, $z^{(3)}_{j+10(7)} \neq z^{(3)}_{j-10(7)}$ is violated.

Summarising the above results, we have (8) to be satisfied when the following set of conditions (say $S_1$) simultaneously occur:

1. $z_{j-2048} \| z_{j+7} \| z_{j-2037} = z_{j-2038} \| z_{j-3} \| z_{j-2047}$ (probability $2^{-96}$),
2. $z^{(2)}_{j+10} \| z^{(1)}_{j+10} \| z^{(0)}_{j+10} = z^{(2)}_{j-10} \| z^{(1)}_{j-10} \| z^{(0)}_{j-10}$ (from Observation 1, this probability is $2^{-23}$ given condition 1),
3. $z^{(3)}_{j+10(7)} \neq z^{(3)}_{j-10(7)}$, i.e., $z_{j+10(31)} \neq z_{j+10(31)}$ (from Observation 1, this probability is $1 - 2^{-8}$ given condition 1 and condition 2),
4. $r_{j+10} \| r_j = 768 + z^{(3)}_{j+10} \| 768 + z^{(3)}_{j-10}$ (probability $2^{-20}$) or $r_{j+10} \| r_j = 768 + z^{(3)}_{j-10} \| 768 + z^{(3)}_{j+10}$ (we have just observed that the two events are mutually exclusive given condition 3; their combined probability is therefore $2^{-20} + 2^{-20} = 2^{-19}$).

Therefore, $Pr[S_1] = 2^{-96} \cdot 2^{-23} \cdot (1 - 2^{-8}) \cdot 2^{-19} \approx 2^{-138}$.

---

[3] This is confirmed by our simple experiments with 8-bit and 16-bit integers. We first considered the equations $X = A + B + C \bmod 256$, $Y = -A + B - C \bmod 256$, and evaluated $Pr[X = Y]$, $Pr[X_{(7)} = Y_{(7)}]$ varying $A$, $B$, $C$ over all possible 8-bit values. We obtained $Pr[X = Y] = Pr[X_{(7)} = Y_{(7)}] = 2^{-7}$. With 16-bit values, when $X = A + B + C \bmod 2^{16}$ and $Y = -A + B - C \bmod 2^{16}$, we obtained $Pr[X = Y] = Pr[X_{(15)} = Y_{(15)}] = 2^{-15}$. We performed several similar experiments and the results are tabulated in Appendix A.

**Case 2:**

Proceeding along the lines of the above arguments, we define $S_2$ as follows:

1. $z_{j-2038}\|z_{j+7}\|z_{j-2037} = z_{j-2048}\|z_{j-3}\|z_{j-2047}$ (probability $2^{-96}$),
2. $z_{j+10}^{(3)}\|z_{j+10}^{(2)}\|z_{j+10}^{(1)}\|z_{j+10}^{(0)} = z_{j-10}^{(3)}\|z_{j-10}^{(2)}\|z_{j-10}^{(1)}\|z_{j-10}^{(0)}$, i.e., $z_{j+10} = z_{j-10}$
   (from Observation 1, this probability is $2^{-31}$ given condition 1),
3. $r_{j+10} = r_j$ (probability $2^{-10}$).

From (9), (10) and (11), it is easy to see that the event $L$ occurs when $S_2$ occurs. The probability that $S_2$ occurs $Pr[S_2] = 2^{-96} \cdot 2^{-31} \cdot 2^{-10} = 2^{-137}$. From condition 3 of $S_1$ and condition 2 of $S_2$, we have $S_1$ and $S_2$ to be mutually exclusive. Therefore, $Pr[S_1 \cup S_2] = 2^{-138} + 2^{-137} = 2^{-136.4}$.

Actually, there are a few other such favourable events which result in the occurrence of $L$. However, from a large number of experiments we found that each of them occurs with much lesser probability when compared to $Pr[S_1]$ or $Pr[S_2]$. The combined probability of these mutually exclusive events was found to be approximately $2^{-136.35}$; therefore, the gain over $Pr[S_1 \cup S_2]$ is negligible. When none of these events occur, it follows that we will have at least two terms of one of the following forms in (8):

(a) $(Q[X])_m$, $(Q[Y])_m$ (where $X \neq Y$).
(b) $(Q[X])_m$, $(Q[Y])_n$ (where $m \neq n$).

In each case, it is easy to see that the two terms do not cancel out with biased probability. Besides, at least one of the two terms does not cancel out with any other term in (8) with biased probability. In other words, when $Q$ is a random S-box, if $X = Y$ with probability $p \neq 0$, then $(Q[X])_m = (Q[Y])_m$ holds with probability $1/2 + p/2$ by Theorem 1. When none of the $S$-like events occurs, we find that Theorem 1 may, even in the best case, be applied in the same way to all pairs of terms in (8) except one. We also illustrate it with an example in Appendix B.

Therefore, when $(S_1 \cup S_2)^c$ occurs, (8) and hence (7) holds with uniform probability $1/2$ under the assumption of a perfect $K/IV$ setup (also confirmed by a large number of experiments). Applying Bayes' rule, we obtain:

$$Pr[L] = Pr[L|(S_1 \cup S_2)] \cdot Pr[S_1 \cup S_2] + Pr[L|(S_1 \cup S_2)^c] \cdot Pr[(S_1 \cup S_2)^c]$$
$$= 1 \cdot 2^{-136.4} + 0.5 \cdot (1 - 2^{-136.4}) = 1/2 + 2^{-137.4}. \tag{15}$$

Note that:
(i) had HC-256 been an ideal cipher, this probability would have been $1/2$,
(ii) in [15], this bias was $1/2 + 2^{-139}$.

## 5   The Distinguisher

A distinguisher is an algorithm that distinguishes one probability distribution from another. In cryptography, it is an algorithm that distinguishes a stream of bits from a stream of bits uniformly distributed at random (i.e., bitstream generated by an ideal stream cipher). In this section we build a distinguishing attack on HC-256 using the results of Sect. 4. Let $N$ denote the total number of equations (7). Let $p$ and $p'$ respectively denote the probability that (7) holds given the outputs are collected from HC-256 and the probability that (7) holds given the outputs are generated by an ideal cipher. That is, $p = 0.5 + 2^{-137.4}$ (from (15)) and $p' = 0.5$. Let $D$ and $D'$ denote the distributions of the XOR-sum of the 8 output bits in (7) from HC-256 and an ideal cipher, respectively. Then, $\mu = Np$ and $\mu' = Np'$ are the respective means of $D$ and $D'$. Similarly, $\sigma = \sqrt{Np(1-p)}$ and $\sigma' = \sqrt{Np'(1-p')}$ denote the respective standard deviations of $D$ and $D'$. When $N$ is large, both these binomial distributions can be approximated with the normal distribution. Now, if $|\mu - \mu'| > 2(\sigma + \sigma')$, i.e., $N > 2^{276.8}$, the cipher can be distinguished from random signal with success rate 0.9772 (since the cumulative distribution function gives the value 0.9772 at $\mu + 2\sigma$). In [15], $N > 2^{280}$ for the same success rate. In [15], there was one advantage though. Every 1024 consecutive output words, there are many more equations (4) when compared to equations (7) and therefore more number of equations (4) per $(K, IV)$ pair.

Now, each equation (4) has 10 keystream bits, whereas each equation (7) has only 8 output bits. Therefore, for our distinguisher, $8 \cdot 2^{276.8} = 2^{279.8}$ keystream bits are required. Whereas, in [15], $10 \cdot 2^{280} = 2^{283.3}$ keystream bits are needed to build the distinguisher. Thus our attacks require about 12 times fewer keystream bits. We like to point out one issue here. It is actually possible to mount the distinguishing attack with fewer keystream bits. For example, if the adversary has $2^{106}$ sets of keystream bits $(s_{j-2038(0)}, s_{j+10(0)}, s_{j+7(10)}, s_{j-2037(23)}, s_{j-2048(0)}, s_{j-10(0)}, s_{j-3(10)}, s_{j-2047(23)})$ from $2^{170.8}$ random $(K, IV)$ pairs, then a total $2^{279.8}$ output bits are available and the distinguishing attack can be mounted.

Thus the conjecture [15] that HC-256 will require more than $2^{174}$ keystream output words (or, equivalently $2^{179}$ output bits) for distinguishing attack should be restated.

## 6    Another Observation

In this section, we present another observation on the cipher that stems from Observation 1 (see Sect. 4.1) and the following relation.

$$r_j = (s_{j-3} \oplus h_1(z_{j-3}) \oplus s_{j-2047} \oplus h'_1(z_{j-2047})) \bmod 1024. \qquad (16)$$

Hence, for the following equation to hold:

$$s_{j-2038(0)} \oplus s_{j+10(0)} \oplus s_{j+7(10)} \oplus s_{j-2037(23)} \oplus s_{j+7(7)} \oplus s_{j-2037(7)} =$$
$$s_{j-2048(0)} \oplus s_{j-10(0)} \oplus s_{j-3(10)} \oplus s_{j-2047(23)} \oplus s_{j-3(7)} \oplus s_{j-2047(7)}, \qquad (17)$$

we require that,

$$(h_1(z_{j+10}))_0 \oplus (h_1'(z_{j-2038}))_0 \oplus (h_1(z_{j+7}))_{10} \oplus (h_1'(z_{j-2037}))_{23}$$
$$\oplus (Q[r_{j+10}])_0 \oplus (h_1(z_{j+7}))_7 \oplus (h_1'(z_{j-2037}))_7 \oplus r_{j+10(7)}$$
$$= (h_1(z_{j-10}))_0 \oplus (h_1'(z_{j-2048}))_0 \oplus (h_1(z_{j-3}))_{10} \oplus (h_1'(z_{j-2047}))_{23}$$
$$\oplus (Q[r_j])_0 \oplus (h_1(z_{j-3}))_7 \oplus (h_1'(z_{j-2047}))_7 \oplus r_{j(7)}, \tag{18}$$

is satisfied. When event $E$ occurs, (18) reduces to:

$$(h_1(z_{j+10}))_0 \oplus (Q[r_{j+10}])_0 \oplus r_{j+10(7)} = (h_1(z_{j-10}))_0 \oplus (Q[r_j])_0 \oplus r_{j(7)}. \tag{19}$$

Now, we have the following four possibilities.

1. $r_{j+10(7)} = z_{j+10(7)}^{(3)}$ and $r_{j(7)} = z_{j-10(7)}^{(3)}$.
2. $r_{j+10(7)} \neq z_{j+10(7)}^{(3)}$ and $r_{j(7)} = z_{j-10(7)}^{(3)}$.
3. $r_{j+10(7)} = z_{j+10(7)}^{(3)}$ and $r_{j(7)} \neq z_{j-10(7)}^{(3)}$.
4. $r_{j+10(7)} \neq z_{j+10(7)}^{(3)}$ and $r_{j(7)} \neq z_{j-10(7)}^{(3)}$.

Let $G$ denote the event $z_{j+10(7)}^{(3)} = z_{j-10(7)}^{(3)}$ (note that $z_{j+10(7)}^{(3)}$ is the most significant bit of $z_{j+10}$, i.e., $z_{j+10(31)}$). When $E$ occurs, from Observation 1 in Sect. 4.1, we get $Pr[G] = 2^{-31}$ and when $G$ occurs we have $z_{j+10} = z_{j-10}$. Given $E$ occurs, we examine the above cases one by one.

**Case 1:** $r_{j+10(7)} = z_{j+10(7)}^{(3)}$ and $r_{j(7)} = z_{j-10(7)}^{(3)}$.

(a) When $G$ occurs: we get $r_{j+10(7)} = r_{j(7)} \Rightarrow s_{j+7(7)} \oplus s_{j-2037(7)} \oplus s_{j-3(7)} \oplus s_{j-2047(7)} = 0$. Besides, (19) reduces to:

$$(Q[r_{j+10}])_0 \oplus r_{j+10(7)} = (Q[r_j])_0 \oplus r_{j(7)}. \tag{20}$$

Given this, if $r_{j+10} = r_j$ (probability $2^{-9}$), then (20) and hence (17) holds with probability 1. Else, in (20), we will have two terms $(Q[r_{j+10}])_0$ and $(Q[r_j])_0$ from two different positions in the $Q$ array. Under the assumption that the elements of $Q$ are uniformly distributed at random, equation (20), therefore, holds with probability 1/2. This implies that (17) holds with probability 1/2.

(b) When $G^c$ occurs: we get $r_{j+10(7)} \neq r_{j(7)} \Rightarrow s_{j+7(7)} \oplus s_{j-2037(7)} \oplus s_{j-3(7)} \oplus s_{j-2047(7)} = 1$.

**Case 2:** $r_{j+10(7)} \neq z_{j+10(7)}^{(3)}$ and $r_{j(7)} = z_{j-10(7)}^{(3)}$.

(a) When $G$ occurs: we get $r_{j+10(7)} \neq r_{j(7)}$, that is, $s_{j+7(7)} \oplus s_{j-2037(7)} \oplus s_{j-3(7)} \oplus s_{j-2047(7)} = 1$.

(b) When $G^c$ occurs: we get $r_{j+10(7)} = r_{j(7)} \Rightarrow s_{j+7(7)} \oplus s_{j-2037(7)} \oplus s_{j-3(7)} \oplus s_{j-2047(7)} = 0$.

**Case 3:** $r_{j+10(7)} = z_{j+10(7)}^{(3)}$ and $r_{j(7)} \neq z_{j-10(7)}^{(3)}$.

(a) When $G$ occurs: we get $r_{j+10(7)} \neq r_{j(7)} \Rightarrow s_{j+7(7)} \oplus s_{j-2037(7)} \oplus s_{j-3(7)} \oplus s_{j-2047(7)} = 1$.

(b) When $G^c$ occurs: we get $r_{j+10(7)} = r_{j(7)}$, i.e., $s_{j+7(7)} \oplus s_{j-2037(7)} \oplus s_{j-3(7)} \oplus s_{j-2047(7)} = 0$.

**Case 4:** $r_{j+10(7)} \neq z_{j+10(7)}^{(3)}$ and $r_{j(7)} \neq z_{j-10(7)}^{(3)}$.

(a) When $G$ occurs: we get $r_{j+10(7)} = r_{j(7)} \Rightarrow s_{j+7(7)} \oplus s_{j-2037(7)} \oplus s_{j-3(7)} \oplus s_{j-2047(7)} = 0$. Given this, if $r_{j+10} = r_j$ (probability $2^{-9}$), then (20) and hence (17) holds with probability 1. Else, using similar arguments as in Case 1(a), it follows that (17) holds with probability $1/2$.

(b) When $G^c$ occurs: we get $r_{j+10(7)} \neq r_{j(7)}$, i.e., $s_{j+7(7)} \oplus s_{j-2037(7)} \oplus s_{j-3(7)} \oplus s_{j-2047(7)} = 1$.

Suppose $r_{j+10(b)} = r_{j(b)}$ for $b \in \{0,\dots,9\}$, $b \neq 7$ and (17) does not hold. Then, given $E$ occurs, $s_{j+7(7)} \oplus s_{j-2037(7)} \oplus s_{j-3(7)} \oplus s_{j-2047(7)} = 0$ is satisfied only in Case 2(b) and Case 3(b). In Case 2(b), $r_{j+10(7)} \neq z_{j+10(7)}^{(3)}$ (probability 0.5), $r_{j(7)} = z_{j-10(7)}^{(3)}$ (probability 0.5) and $G^c$ occurs (probability is $1 - 2^{-31}$ given $E$ occurs). Therefore, given the occurrence of event $E$, Case 2(b) happens with probability $0.5 \cdot 0.5 \cdot (1 - 2^{-31}) = 2^{-2} \cdot (1 - 2^{-31})$ and Case 3(b) also happens with the same probability. Thereby, we have the following observation.

**Observation 2:** When the following relations exist among keystream bits:

$$s_{j+7(b)} \oplus s_{j-2037(b)} = s_{j-3(b)} \oplus s_{j-2047(b)}, \text{ for all } b \in \{0,\dots,9\}, b \neq 7, \text{ and}$$

$$s_{j-2038(0)} \oplus s_{j+10(0)} \oplus s_{j+7(10)} \oplus s_{j-2037(23)} \oplus s_{j+7(7)} \oplus s_{j-2037(7)} \neq$$
$$s_{j-2048(0)} \oplus s_{j-10(0)} \oplus s_{j-3(10)} \oplus s_{j-2047(23)} \oplus s_{j-3(7)} \oplus s_{j-2047(7)},$$

and event $E$ occurs, then $s_{j+7(7)} \oplus s_{j-2037(7)} \oplus s_{j-3(7)} \oplus s_{j-2047(7)} = 0$ holds with probability $1/2 \cdot (1 - 2^{-31})$. We believe this observation can be further exploited to construct more efficient distinguishers on the HC-256. Before we conclude, we make one final remark.

**Remark:** Suppose the following relations exist among keystream bits:

$$s_{j+7(b)} \oplus s_{j-2037(b)} = s_{j-3(b)} \oplus s_{j-2047(b)}, \tag{21}$$

for all $b \in \{0,\dots,9\}$. Then, from (16), we observe that when the conditions 1 and 2 of $S_2$ (see Sect. 4.1) are satisfied, condition 4 is also satisfied. Therefore, in this case, $Pr[S_2] = 2^{-96} \cdot 2^{-31} = 2^{-127}$ and $Pr[S_1 \cup S_2] = 2^{-138} + 2^{-127} \approx 2^{-127}$. Therefore, $Pr[L] = 1/2 + 2^{-128}$. This is a notable improvement over the probability obtained in (15). The relation (21) was also exploited in [15], but resulting in a comparatively smaller bias of $2^{-129}$ and hence a distinguisher requiring about $2^{261}$ output words (for 0.9772 success rate).

# 7 Conclusions and Future Work

In this paper, we have presented distinguishing attacks on the stream cipher HC-256. The hitherto best-known distinguisher on the cipher has been presented in [15] and requires $2^{280}$ equations (each involving 10 keystream output bits) to be tested for a success rate of 0.9772. Each of our distinguishers requires $2^{276.8}$ equations (with 8 keystream bits in every equation) to be examined for the same success probability. Thereby, we have improved the data requirement in [15] by a factor of about 12. We have also provided leads for further cryptanalysis of the cipher.

In [3], Crowley employs a Hidden Markov Model to combine several biases in the keystream of the cipher Py and improves the attacks described in [11]. Given the structural similarities between Py and HC-256, it may be possible to apply similar techniques here to construct a more efficient distinguisher. We leave it as an open problem.

A variant of HC-256, named HC-256', was also proposed by Wu in [15, Section 6] but without any accompanying cryptanalysis. Investigating whether our attacks could also applied to HC-256' is another interesting open problem.

# Acknowledgments

It is a great pleasure to thank Hongjun Wu for valuable discussions. We also thank the anonymous reviewers of IWSEC2009 for their constructive comments on our work.

# References

1. Baignères, T., Junod, P., Vaudenay, S.: How far can we go beyond linear cryptanalysis? In: Lee, P.J. (ed.) ASIACRYPT 2004. LNCS, vol. 3329, pp. 432–450. Springer, Heidelberg (2004)
2. Biham, E., Seberry, J.: Py (Roo): A Fast and Secure Stream Cipher using Rolling Arrays. eSTREAM, ECRYPT Stream Cipher Project, Report 2005/023 (2005)
3. Crowley, P.: Improved Cryptanalysis of Py. In: Workshop Record of SASC 2006 – Stream Ciphers Revisited, ECRYPT Network of Excellence in Cryptology, Leuven, Belgium, February 2006, pp. 52–60 (2006)
4. Dunkelman, O.: A Small Observation on HC-128. November 14 (2007), http://www.ecrypt.eu.org/stream/phorum/read.php?1,1143
5. The eSTREAM Project, http://www.ecrypt.eu.org/stream/
6. Goldreich, O. (ed.): Lecture Notes on Pseudorandomness–Part-I. Department of Computer Science. Weizmann Institute of Science, Rehovot, Israel (January 2001)
7. Jenkins Jr., R.J.: ISAAC. In: Gollmann, D. (ed.) FSE 1996. LNCS, vol. 1039, pp. 41–49. Springer, Heidelberg (1996)

8. Maitra, S., Paul, G., Raizada, S.: Some Observations on HC-128. In: Workshop on Coding Theory and Cryptography, (to appear, 2009), http://eprint.iacr.org/2008/499.pdf

9. Mantin, I., Shamir, A.: A practical attack on broadcast RC4. In: Matsui, M. (ed.) FSE 2001. LNCS, vol. 2355, pp. 152–164. Springer, Heidelberg (2002)

10. Paul, S., Preneel, B.: On the (In)security of Stream Ciphers Based on Arrays and Modular Addition. In: Lai, X., Chen, K. (eds.) ASIACRYPT 2006. LNCS, vol. 4284, pp. 69–83. Springer, Heidelberg (2006)

11. Paul, S., Preneel, B., Sekar, G.: Distinguishing Attacks on the Stream Cipher Py. In: Robshaw, M.J.B. (ed.) FSE 2006. LNCS, vol. 4047, pp. 405–421. Springer, Heidelberg (2006)

12. Sarkar, P.: On Approximating Addition by Exclusive OR, http://eprint.iacr.org/2009/047.pdf

13. Sekar, G., Paul, S., Preneel, B.: New Weaknesses in the Keystream Generation Algorithms of the Stream Ciphers TPy and Py. In: Garay, J.A., Lenstra, A.K., Mambo, M., Peralta, R. (eds.) ISC 2007. LNCS, vol. 4779, pp. 249–262. Springer, Heidelberg (2007)

14. Staffelbach, O., Meier, W.: Cryptographic Significance of the Carry for Ciphers Based on Integer Addition. In: Menezes, A., Vanstone, S.A. (eds.) CRYPTO 1990. LNCS, vol. 537, pp. 601–613. Springer, Heidelberg (1991)

15. Wu, H.: A New Stream Cipher HC-256. In: Roy, B., Meier, W. (eds.) FSE 2004. LNCS, vol. 3017, pp. 226–244. Springer, Heidelberg (2004), http://eprint.iacr.org/2004/092.pdf

16. Wu, H.: The Stream Cipher HC-128. In: Robshaw, M.J.B., Billet, O. (eds.) New Stream Cipher Designs. LNCS, vol. 4986, pp. 39–47. Springer, Heidelberg (2008)

17. Zenner, E.: A Cache Timing Analysis of HC-256. Selected Areas in Cryptography (2008)(to appear)

# A    Experimental Results

Here, we elaborate on footnote 4 in Sect. 4.1. Consider the equations:

$$X = A + B + C \bmod 2^k, \qquad (22)$$
$$Y = -A + B - C \bmod 2^k, \qquad (23)$$

where $X$, $Y$, $A$, $B$, $C$ are $k$-bit random variables. Let $X_{(b)}$ denote the $b$-th bit of $X$ ($b = 0$ denotes the least significant bit and $b = k - 1$ denotes the most significant bit). Since the '+' and '-' operators are the same as the exclusive-OR for the least significant bit position, we have from (22) and (23):

$$X_{(0)} = A_{(0)} \oplus B_{(0)} \oplus C_{(0)},$$
$$Y_{(0)} = A_{(0)} \oplus B_{(0)} \oplus C_{(0)}.$$

Therefore, $X_{(0)} = Y_{(0)} \Rightarrow Pr[X = Y] = 2^{-(k-1)}$. Now, we ran simulations to evaluate $Pr[X_{(k-1)} = Y_{(k-1)}]$ and $Pr[X \neq Y | X_{(k-1)} = Y_{(k-1)}]$ for different values of $k$. As there was no need to vary $B$, we fixed it to zero and varied $A$ and $C$ over all possible $k$-bit values. The results are provided in Table 1. Following this trend, we obtain that for $k = 32$, $Pr[X_{(31)} = Y_{(31)}] = 2^{-31}$ and $Pr[X \neq Y | X_{(31)} = Y_{(31)}] = 0$.

**Table 1.**

| $k$ | $Pr[X_{(k-1)} = Y_{(k-1)}]$ | $Pr[X \neq Y \mid X_{(k-1)} = Y_{(k-1)}]$ |
|---|---|---|
| 4 | $2^{-3}$ | 0 |
| 5 | $2^{-4}$ | 0 |
| 6 | $2^{-5}$ | 0 |
| 7 | $2^{-6}$ | 0 |
| 8 | $2^{-7}$ | 0 |
| 9 | $2^{-8}$ | 0 |
| 10 | $2^{-9}$ | 0 |
| 11 | $2^{-10}$ | 0 |
| 12 | $2^{-11}$ | 0 |
| 13 | $2^{-12}$ | 0 |
| 14 | $2^{-13}$ | 0 |
| 15 | $2^{-14}$ | 0 |
| 16 | $2^{-15}$ | 0 |
| 17 | $2^{-16}$ | 0 |
| 18 | $2^{-17}$ | 0 |
| 19 | $2^{-18}$ | 0 |

# B    A Note on the Randomness of Keystream Bits When $S_2$ Does Not Occur

We restate (7) and (8) here:

$$s_{j-2038}(0) \oplus s_{j+10}(0) \oplus s_{j+7}(10) \oplus s_{j-2037}(23) =$$
$$s_{j-2048}(0) \oplus s_{j-10}(0) \oplus s_{j-3}(10) \oplus s_{j-2047}(23),$$

$$(h_1(z_{j+10}))_0 \oplus (h_1'(z_{j-2038}))_0 \oplus (h_1(z_{j+7}))_{10} \oplus (h_1'(z_{j-2037}))_{23} \oplus (Q[r_{j+10}])_0 =$$
$$(h_1(z_{j-10}))_0 \oplus (h_1'(z_{j-2048}))_0 \oplus (h_1(z_{j-3}))_{10} \oplus (h_1'(z_{j-2047}))_{23} \oplus (Q[r_j])_0.$$

Suppose the 1024 elements of $Q$ are uniformly distributed at random; same with the elements of $Q'$. We now examine the case when $z_{j-2037}\|z_{j+7}\|z_{j+10} = z_{j-2047}\|z_{j-3}\|z_{j-10}$, $r_{j+10} = r_j$, but $z_{j-2038} \neq z_{j-2048}$, i.e., one of the events comprising $S_2^c$. When $z_{j-2037}\|z_{j+7}\|z_{j+10} = z_{j-2047}\|z_{j-3}\|z_{j-10}$ and $r_{j+10} = r_j$, (8) reduces to:

$$(h_1'(z_{j-2038}))_0 = (h_1'(z_{j-2048}))_0. \qquad (24)$$

Similar to (10) and (11), we have:

$$(h_1'(z_{j-2038}))_0 = (Q'[z^{(0)}_{j-2038}])_0 \oplus (Q'[256 + z^{(1)}_{j-2038}])_0$$
$$\oplus (Q'[512 + z^{(2)}_{j-2038}])_0 \oplus (Q'[768 + z^{(3)}_{j-2038}])_0, \qquad (25)$$

$$(h_1'(z_{j-2048}))_0 = (Q'[z^{(0)}_{j-2048}])_0 \oplus (Q'[256 + z^{(1)}_{j-2048}])_0$$
$$\oplus (Q'[512 + z^{(2)}_{j-2048}])_0 \oplus (Q'[768 + z^{(3)}_{j-2048}])_0. \qquad (26)$$

Note that on the right-hand side of (25), we have four distinct array indices. That is, we access four elements of $Q'$ from four different positions; similarly in (23). If $z_{j-2038} \neq z_{j-2048}$, then at least one of the following holds:

1. $z_{j-2038}^{(0)} \neq z_{j-2048}^{(0)}$,
2. $z_{j-2038}^{(1)} \neq z_{j-2048}^{(1)}$,
3. $z_{j-2038}^{(2)} \neq z_{j-2048}^{(2)}$,
4. $z_{j-2038}^{(3)} \neq z_{j-2048}^{(3)}$.

If the first case alone happens, from (25) and (26), we get:

$$(h_1'(z_{j-2038}))_0 \oplus (h_1'(z_{j-2038}))_0 = (Q'[z_{j-2038}^{(0)}])_0 \oplus (Q'[z_{j-2048}^{(0)}])_0. \qquad (27)$$

Since $Q'[z_{j-2038}^{(0)}]$ and $Q'[z_{j-2048}^{(0)}]$ are two 32-bit elements from different positions in the same $Q'$ array, they are equal with uniform probability. That is, $(Q'[z_{j-2038}^{(0)}])_0$ and $(Q'[z_{j-2048}^{(0)}])_0$ are equal with probability 1/2. This implies that (27) and hence (24) holds with probability 1/2. This, in turn, implies that (8) and hence (7) holds with uniform probability 1/2. Now, let us suppose only two of the above cases occurs; for example, cases 1 and 2. Then, we will have four terms - $(Q'[z_{j-2038}^{(0)}])_0$, $(Q'[z_{j-2048}^{(0)}])_0$, $(Q'[z_{j-2038}^{(1)}])_0$ and $(Q'[z_{j-2048}^{(1)}])_0$ - with four different array indices, and hence their XOR-sum is zero with uniform probability 1/2. Hence, it follows that (7) holds with probability 1/2.

Extending the above argument to other events that result in the outcome $z_{j-2038} \neq z_{j-2048}$ (for example, the occurrence of cases 1, 2 and 3 but not case 4), one can similarly verify that (7) holds with probability 1/2. For the other events comprising $S_2^c$, we arrive at the same result; however, a complete treatment is beyond the scope of this paper.

# A Generic Construction of Timed-Release Encryption with Pre-open Capability

Yasumasa Nakai, Takahiro Matsuda, Wataru Kitada, and Kanta Matsuura

The University of Tokyo, Tokyo, Japan
{tig,tmatsuda,kitada,kanta}@iis.u-tokyo.ac.jp

**Abstract.** In 2005, Hwang et al. proposed a concept of timed-release encryption with pre-open capability (TRE-PC), where a receiver can decrypt a ciphertext not only by using a time-release key which is provided after its release-time, but also using a secret information called a pre-open key provided from a sender even before the release-time. Though there are several concrete constructions of TRE-PC proposed so far, no generic construction has been known. In this paper, we show a generic construciton of TRE-PC. Specifically, we construct a TRE-PC scheme from a chosen-ciphertext secure public key encryption scheme (PKE), a chosen plaintext secure identity-based encryption (IBE) scheme with specific property that we call *target collision resistance for randomness*, and a one-time signature scheme.

Interestingly, our proposed construction of TRE-PC is essentially the same as the generic construciton of (normal) TRE based on multiple encryption of IBE and PKE. As one of the consequences of our result, we can build a TRE-PC scheme secure in the standard model based on weaker assumptions than the ones used by the existing standard model TRE-PC scheme.

**Keywords:** timed-release encryption, pre-open capability, generic construction, public key encryption, identity-based encryption.

## 1 Introduction

*Background.* Timed-release encryption (TRE) is a kind encryption proposed by May [17] in 1993. Roughly, the functionality that TRE provides is that even a legitimated receiver cannot decrypt a ciphertext until the release-time decided by a sender. Several constructions and its applications have been considered and proposed so far. In this paper, we only consider *public key* TRE which is realized by utilizing the trusted *time server* (TS) that sends (or broadcasts) a time-release key at the time decided by a sender. The receiver can decrypt a ciphertext with the time-release key.

In 2005, Hwang *et al.* [15] proposed the concept of *Timed-Release Encryption with Pre-Open Capability* (TRE-PC). In TRE-PC, a receiver can decrypt a ciphertext by using not only a time-release key which is sent (or broadcast) by the TS at the release-time decided by a sender, but also a secret information

T. Takagi and M. Mambo (Eds.): IWSEC 2009, LNCS 5824, pp. 53–70, 2009.

called a *pre-open key* which is sent by the sender before the release-time. This pre-open capability will provide more flexibility with the use of TRE, and some application is introduced in the same paper. It is naturally required that even if the curious TS gets a pre-open key, it should not get any information on a plaintext, and even a legitimated receiver cannot decrypt a ciphertext until the release-time or without a pre-open key.

Hwang *et al.* [15] also gave a first concrete construciton of a TRE-PC scheme secure in the random oracle model based on the bilinear Diffie-Hellman (BDH) assumption. Dent *et al.* [11] revisited and formalized the security definition of TRE-PC, established a hybrid encryption composition framework, and proposed, via their composition framework, a concrete TRE-PC scheme which is secure in the random oracle model based on the BDH assumption. Chow *et al.* [10] showed a TRE-PC scheme which is secure in the standard model based on the modified decisional 3-party Diffie-Hellman (3-MDDH) and the decisional 3-party Diffie-Hellman (3-DDH) assumptions.

We note that these schemes are based on the hardness of number theoretic problems, and especially, no generic construction of TRE-PC has been known so far.

*Our Contribution.* In this paper, we propose a generic construction of TRE-PC, and give formal security proofs for our scheme. Specifically, we construct a TRE-PC scheme, which is secure in the model of [11], from a chosen-ciphertext secure (IND-CCA secure) public key encryption (PKE) scheme, a chosen-plaintext secure (IND-ID-CPA secure) identity-based encryption (IBE) scheme which satisfies a certain mild assumption, and a one-time signature scheme. Interestingly, the construction of our scheme is essentially the same as a (normal) TRE scheme based on multiple encryption [12] of a PKE and an IBE schemes introduced in [7,8], so we do not need any other cryptographic primitives or techniques other than our mild assumption on IBE, such as the non-interactive zero-knowledge proofs, to achieve pre-open capability. Therefore, if there is a normal TRE scheme constructed by the generic construction from PKE and IBE with our assumption, we can construct TRE-PC without the cost.

We believe that our generic construction will give important insights and be useful for a first step towards more practical constructions of TRE-PC secure in the standard model. As evidence of it, due to our results, we can build a TRE-PC scheme secure in the standard model based on weaker assumptions than the ones used in [10], by using the existing IBE and PKE schemes.

Though the underlying building blocks from which we construct TRE-PC are the same as the ones used for the generic construction of (normal) TRE addressed in [7,8], the security proofs are not a trivial extension from it, since we have to consider security properties specific to TRE-PC and also we have to deal with a pre-open key.

Though we introduce the assumption on IBE which is not so standard (we call it *target collision resistance for randomness*), many existing IBE schemes satisfy this assumption, and so we think the generality of our construction is not lost by this assumption. See Section 2.2 for details.

*Related Works.* There are two major approaches for realizing TRE. One approach is to use the time-lock puzzles [19,16]. In this approach a sender makes a ciphertext which cannot be finished decrypting until the release-time by a receiver's environment, even if the receiver keeps computing to decrypt after he receives the ciphertext. This imposes heavy computational cost on the receiver, and moreover, it is difficult to estimate the required time that the receiver finishes decrypting. Hence, it is difficult to ensure that the receiver can decrypt the ciphertext at the release-time certainly.

The other approach is, as we already mentioned, to use the TS, which is adopted by many previous works regarding TRE.

There are several TRE schemes that have special functionalities. Blake *et al.* [6] proposed the TRE scheme which needs no interaction with the TS, which is anonymous based on bilinear pairng. Based on this scheme, Hristu-Varsakelis *et al.* [14,5] constructed a more efficient anonymous TRE scheme. Hwang *et al.* [15] proposed TRE-PC, which we have already mentioned. Cheon *et al.* [7,8] proposed TRE with authentication, and introduced a way to construct it generically from PKE, IBE, and one time signature as well as concrete constructions.

*Paper Organization.* In Section 2, we briefly review the definitions necessary for describing our result. We also introduce the target collision resistance for randomness of IBE schemes. In Section 3, we review the definition of algorithms and security of TRE-PC schemes, adopted from [11]. In Section 4, we present our proposed generic construction of a TRE-PC scheme from PKE and IBE and signature, and show its security proofs. In Section 5, we discuss the consequences of our result.

## 2   Preliminaries

In this section, we review the definitions of the terms and security used in this paper.

*Notations.* In this paper, "$x \leftarrow y$" denotes that $x$ is chosen uniformly at random from $y$ if $y$ is a finite set, $x$ is output from $y$ if $y$ is a function or an algorithm, or $y$ is assigned to $x$ otherwise. "$x||y$" denotes a concatenation of $x$ and $y$. If $\mathcal{A}$ is probabilistic algorithm then $y \leftarrow \mathcal{A}(x; r)$ denotes that $\mathcal{A}$ computes $y$ as output, taking $x$ as input and using $r$ as randomness. "PPT" denotes probabilistic polynomial time. We say that a function $f(\kappa)$ is negligible in $\kappa$ if $f(\kappa) \leq 1/p(\kappa)$ for any positive polynomial $p(\kappa)$ and all sufficiently large $\kappa$. In this paper, when we say a function is negligible then we always mean that it is negligible in the security parameter $\kappa$.

### 2.1   Public Key Encryption

A public key encryption (PKE) scheme $\Pi$ consists of the following three (probabilistic) algorithms. A key generation algorithm PKE.KG takes $1^\kappa$ (security parameter $\kappa$) as input, and outputs a pair of a secret key $sk$ and a public key $pk$. An encryption algorithm PKE.Enc takes a public key $pk$ and a plaintext $m \in \mathcal{M}$ as input, and outputs a ciphertext $c \in \mathcal{C}$ (where $\mathcal{M}$ and $\mathcal{C}$ are a plaintext space and a ciphertext space of $\Pi$, respectively). A decryption algorithm PKE.Dec takes a secret key $sk$ and a ciphertext $c$ as input, and outputs a plaintext $m \in \mathcal{M} \cup \{\bot\}$. We require PKE.Dec$(sk, \text{PKE.Enc}(pk, m)) = m$ for all $(sk, pk)$ output from PKE.KG and all $m \in \mathcal{M}$.

*IND-CCA Security.* Indistinguishability against adaptive chosen ciphertext attacks (IND-CCA) of a PKE scheme $\Pi$ is defined using the following IND-CCA game between an adversary $\mathcal{A}$ and the challenger $\mathcal{CH}$:

**Setup.** $\mathcal{CH}$ runs PKE.KG$(1^\kappa)$ and obtains a pair of $sk$ and $pk$. $\mathcal{CH}$ gives $pk$ to $\mathcal{A}$ and keeps $sk$ to itself.

**Phase 1.** $\mathcal{A}$ can adaptively issue decryption queries $c$ to $\mathcal{CH}$. $\mathcal{CH}$ responds to each query $c$ by returning $m \leftarrow \text{PKE.Dec}(sk, c)$.

**Challenge.** $\mathcal{A}$ chooses two distinct plaintexts $(m_0, m_1)$ of equal length and sends them to $\mathcal{CH}$. $\mathcal{CH}$ flips a coin $b_C \in \{0, 1\}$ uniformly at random, then returns the challenge ciphertext $c^* \leftarrow \text{PKE.Enc}(pk, m_{b_C})$ to $\mathcal{A}$.

**Phase 2.** $\mathcal{A}$ can issue decryption queries in the same way as Phase 1, except that $\mathcal{A}$ is not allowed to issue $c^*$ as a decryption query.

**Guess.** $\mathcal{A}$ outputs a bit $b_A$ as its guess for $b_C$.

We define the IND-CCA advantage of $\mathcal{A}$ attacking $\Pi$ as follows:

$$\text{Adv}_{\Pi, \mathcal{A}}^{\text{IND-CCA}} = |\Pr[b_A = b_C] - \frac{1}{2}|.$$

**Definition 1.** *We say that a PKE scheme $\Pi$ is IND-CCA secure if* $\text{Adv}_{\Pi, \mathcal{A}}^{\text{IND-CCA}}$ *is negligible for any PPT algorithm $\mathcal{A}$.*

## 2.2   Identity-Based Encryption

An identity-based encryption (IBE) scheme $\Pi$ consists of the following four (probabilistic) algorithms. A setup algorithm IBE.Setup takes $1^\kappa$ (security parameter $\kappa$) as input, and outputs a pair of a master secret key msk and global parameters prm. A key extraction algorithm IBE.Ext takes global parameters prm, a master secret key msk, and an identity ID $\in \mathcal{I}$ as input, and outputs a decryption key $d_{\text{ID}}$ corresponding to ID (where $\mathcal{I}$ is an identity space of $\Pi$). An encryption algorithm IBE.Enc takes global parameters prm, an identity ID $\in \mathcal{I}$, and a plaintext $m \in \mathcal{M}$ as input, and outputs a ciphertext $c \in \mathcal{C}$ (where $\mathcal{M}$ and $\mathcal{C}$ are a plaintext space and a ciphertext space of $\Pi$, respectively). A decryption algorithm IBE.Dec takes a decryption key $d_{\text{ID}}$ and a ciphertext $c$ as input, and outputs a plaintext $m \in \mathcal{M} \cup \{\bot\}$. We require IBE.Dec(IBE.Ext(prm, msk, ID), IBE.Enc(prm, ID, $m$)) $= m$ for all (msk, prm) output from IBE.Setup, all ID $\in \mathcal{I}$, and all $m \in \mathcal{M}$.

*IND-ID-CPA Security.* Indistinguishability against adaptive identity, chosen plaintext attacks (IND-ID-CPA) of an IBE scheme $\Pi$ is defined using the following IND-ID-CPA game between an adversary $\mathcal{A}$ and the challenger $\mathcal{CH}$:

**Setup.** $\mathcal{CH}$ runs IBE.Setup($1^\kappa$) and obtains a pair of msk and prm. $\mathcal{CH}$ gives prm to $\mathcal{A}$ and keeps msk to itself.

**Phase 1.** $\mathcal{A}$ can adaptively issue extraction queries ID to $\mathcal{CH}$. $\mathcal{CH}$ responds to each query ID by returning $d_{\mathsf{ID}} \leftarrow$ IBE.Ext(prm, msk, ID).

**Challenge.** $\mathcal{A}$ chooses two distinct plaintexts $(m_0, m_1)$ of equal length and a challenge identity $\mathsf{ID}^*$ that has not been issued as an extraction query in Phase 1, and sends them to $\mathcal{CH}$. $\mathcal{CH}$ flips a coin $b_C \in \{0, 1\}$ uniformly at random, then returns the challenge ciphertext $c^* \leftarrow$ IBE.Enc(prm, $\mathsf{ID}^*, m_{b_C}$) to $\mathcal{A}$.

**Phase 2.** $\mathcal{A}$ can issue extraction queries in the same way as Phase 1, except that $\mathcal{A}$ is not allowed to issue $\mathsf{ID}^*$ as an extraction query.

**Guess.** $\mathcal{A}$ outputs a bit $b_A$ as its guess for $b_C$.

We define the IND-ID-CPA advantage of $\mathcal{A}$ attacking $\Pi$ as follows:

$$\mathsf{Adv}_{\Pi,\mathcal{A}}^{\mathrm{IND\text{-}ID\text{-}CPA}} = |\Pr[b_A = b_C] - \frac{1}{2}|.$$

**Definition 2.** *We say that an IBE scheme $\Pi$ is IND-ID-CPA secure if* $\mathsf{Adv}_{\Pi,\mathcal{A}}^{\mathrm{IND\text{-}ID\text{-}CPA}}$ *is negligible for any PPT algorithm $\mathcal{A}$.*

*Target Collision Resistance for Randomness.* We introduce target collision resistance for randomness required for security proof of the proposal scheme. Roughly speaking, this security ensures that any adversary who is given a randomness, that is used in an encryption algorithm, and even a master secret key, cannot come up with a message, an identity, and another randomness such that the encryption using each randomness collides. The reason why we use the term *target collision restance* is because an adversary has no control over one of randomness, as is the same with the target collision resistance for a hash function [18,1].

Formally, we define the advantage of an adversary $\mathcal{A}$ against target collision resistance for randomness of IBE scheme $\Pi$ (with randomness space $\mathcal{R}_{IBE}$) as follows.

$\mathsf{Adv}_{\Pi,\mathcal{A}}^{\mathrm{Rand}} =$
$\Pr[(\mathsf{msk}, \mathsf{prm}) \leftarrow$ IBE.Setup($1^\kappa$); $R_{IBE} \leftarrow \mathcal{R}_{IBE}$; $(m', \mathsf{ID}', R'_{IBE}) \leftarrow \mathcal{A}(\mathsf{msk}, \mathsf{prm}, R_{IBE})$
$\quad:$ IBE.Enc(prm, $\mathsf{ID}', m'; R'_{IBE}$) = IBE.Enc(prm, $\mathsf{ID}', m'; R_{IBE}$) $\wedge R'_{IBE} \neq R_{IBE}$].

**Definition 3.** *We say that an IBE scheme $\Pi$ has target collision resistance for randomness if* $\mathsf{Adv}_{\Pi,\mathcal{A}}^{\mathrm{Rand}}$ *is negligible for any PPT algorithm $\mathcal{A}$.*

Note that most practical IBE schemes, such as [2,21,13], satisfy this security without any assumption. Actually, target collision resistance for randomness is satisfied unconditionally by many pairing-based IBE schemes with a pairing $e$ :

$\mathbb{G}_1 \times \mathbb{G}_2 \to \mathbb{G}_T$ where orders of $\mathbb{G}_1$, $\mathbb{G}_2$ and $\mathbb{G}_T$ are a prime $p$ and a generator $g_1 \in$ $\mathbb{G}_1$ and $g_2 \in \mathbb{G}_2$, whose randomness space is $\mathbb{Z}_p$ and whose ciphertext contains a random group element $g_1^r$, $g_2^r$, or $e(g_1, g_2)^r$ with $r \in \mathbb{Z}_p$ as a randomness. In these schemes, any ciphertext using different randomness will be different from one another. It is easy to see the schemes [2,21,13] are included in this type of construction.

## 2.3   Signature

A signature scheme $\Sigma$ consists of the following three (probabilistic) algorithms. A key generation algorithm SigKG takes $1^\kappa$ (security parameter $\kappa$) as input, and outputs a pair of a signing key $SK$ and a verification key $VK$. A signing algorithm Sign takes a signing key $SK$ and a message $m \in \mathcal{M}$ as input, and outputs a valid signature $\sigma$ on $m$ under $VK$ (where $\mathcal{M}$ is a message space of $\Sigma$). A verification algorithm Verify takes a verification key $VK$, a message $m$, and a signature $\sigma$ as input, and outputs *accept* if $\sigma$ is a valid signature on $m$ or *reject* otherwise. We require $\mathsf{Verify}(VK, m, \mathsf{Sign}(SK, m)) = accept$ for all $(SK, VK)$ output from SigKG and all $m \in \mathcal{M}$.

*Strong One-Time Security.* Strong one-time (SOT) security of a signature scheme $\Sigma$ is defined using the following SOT game between an adversary $\mathcal{A}$ and the challenger $\mathcal{CH}$:

**Setup.** $\mathcal{CH}$ runs $\mathsf{SigKG}(1^\kappa)$ and obtains a pair of $SK$ and $VK$. $\mathcal{CH}$ gives $VK$ to $\mathcal{A}$ and keeps $SK$ to itself.

**Query.** $\mathcal{A}$ can issue a signing query $m$ to $\mathcal{CH}$ at most once. $\mathcal{CH}$ responds to the query by running $\sigma \leftarrow \mathsf{Sign}(SK, m)$ and returning $\sigma$.

**Output.** $\mathcal{A}$ outputs a message-signature pair $(m', \sigma')$ as a forgery under the verification key $VK$.

We define the SOT advantage of $\mathcal{A}$ attacking $\Sigma$ as follows:

$$\mathsf{Adv}_{\Sigma, \mathcal{A}}^{\mathrm{SOT}} = \Pr[\mathsf{Verify}(VK, m', \sigma') = accept \wedge (m, \sigma) \neq (m', \sigma')].$$

**Definition 4.** *We say that a signature scheme $\Sigma$ is strongly one-time (SOT) secure if $\mathsf{Adv}_{\Sigma, \mathcal{A}}^{\mathrm{SOT}}$ is negligible for any PPT algorithm $\mathcal{A}$. We also say that $\Sigma$ is a one-time signature scheme.*

# 3   TRE-PC

In this section, we briefly review the definition of algorithms and security of TRE-PC schemes. We adopt the model from [11].

*Algorithms.* A TRE-PC scheme $\Pi$ consists of the following six (probabilistic) algorithms.

TRE.Setup: A setup algorithm that takes $1^\kappa$ (security parameter $\kappa$) as input, and outputs a pair of a master secret key msk and global parameters prm.

TRE.Ext: A time-release key extraction algorithm that takes global parameters prm, a master secret key msk, and a release-time $T \in \mathcal{T}$ as input, and outputs a time-release key $s_T$ corresponding to release-time $T$.

TRE.UKG: A user key generation algorithm that takes $1^{\kappa}$ (security parameter $\kappa$) as input, and outputs a pair of a secret key $sk_u$ and a public key $pk_u$.

TRE.Enc: An encryption algorithm that takes global parameters prm, a receiver's public key $pk_u$, a release-time $T \in \mathcal{T}$, and a plaintext $m \in \mathcal{M}$ as input, and outputs a ciphertext $c \in \mathcal{C}$ and a pre-open key $V$.

TRE.Dec$_{\mathsf{RK}}$: A pre-open decryption algorithm that takes global parameters prm, a receiver's secret key $sk_u$, a pre-open key $V$, and a ciphertext $c$ as input, and outputs a plaintext $m \in \mathcal{M} \cup \{\bot\}$.

TRE.Dec$_{\mathsf{PK}}$: A release-time decryption algorithm that takes global parameters prm, a receiver's secret key $sk_u$, a time-release key $s_T$, and a ciphertext $c$ as input, and outputs a plaintext $m \in \mathcal{M} \cup \{\bot\}$.

where $\mathcal{T}$, $\mathcal{M}$, and $\mathcal{C}$ are a release-time space, a plaintext space, and a ciphertext space of $\Pi$, respectively. For all (msk, prm) output from TRE.Setup, all $(sk_u, pk_u)$ output from TRE.UKG, all $m \in \mathcal{M}$, and all $T \in \mathcal{T}$, we require that if $(c, V) \leftarrow$ TRE.Enc(prm, $pk_u, T, m$) then TRE.Dec$_{\mathsf{PK}}$(prm, $sk_u$, TRE.Ext(prm, msk, $T$), $c$) $= m$ and TRE.Dec$_{\mathsf{RK}}$(prm, $sk_u, V, c$) $= m$ hold.

## 3.1   Security

For TRE-PC schemes, Dent *et al.* [11] introduced the following four kinds of security and gave a formal definition for each of them. Specifically, they considered outsider security, time server security, insider security, and binding. In [11], it is proved that the outsider security is implied by the time server security, so we show the three kinds of security except the outsider security.

*Time Server Security.* This security ensures that a curious TS who has a master key cannot get any information of a plaintext from a ciphertext without a receiver's secret key. It is defined by the following game between an adversary $\mathcal{A}$ and the challenger $\mathcal{CH}$.

**Setup.** $\mathcal{CH}$ runs TRE.Setup($1^{\kappa}$) and TRE.UKG($1^{\kappa}$), and obtains (msk, prm) and $(sk_u, pk_u)$, respectively. $\mathcal{CH}$ gives (msk, prm, $pk_u$) to $\mathcal{A}$ and keeps $sk_u$ to itself.

**Phase 1.** $\mathcal{A}$ can adaptively issue pre-open decryption queries $(c, V)$ and release-time decryption queries $(c, T)$ to $\mathcal{CH}$. $\mathcal{CH}$ responds to each pre-open decryption query $(c, V)$ by returning $m \leftarrow$ TRE.Dec$_{\mathsf{RK}}$(prm, $sk_u, V, c$) to $\mathcal{A}$. $\mathcal{CH}$ responds to each release-time query $(c, T)$ by first computing $s_T \leftarrow$ TRE.Ext(prm, msk, $T$) then returning $m \leftarrow$ TRE.Dec$_{\mathsf{PK}}$(prm, $sk_u, s_T, c$) to $\mathcal{A}$.

**Challenge.** $\mathcal{A}$ chooses two distinct plaintexts $(m_0, m_1)$ of equal length and a challenge release-time $T^*$, and sends them to $\mathcal{CH}$. $\mathcal{CH}$ flips a coin $b_C \in \{0, 1\}$ uniformly at random, and then returns the challenge ciphertext and its corresponding pre-open key $(c^*, V^*) \leftarrow$ TRE.Enc(prm, $pk_u, T^*, m_{b_C}$) to $\mathcal{A}$.

**Phase 2.** $\mathcal{A}$ can issue pre-open decryption queries and release-time decryption queries in the same way as Phase 1, except that $\mathcal{A}$ is not allowed to issue $(c^*, V^*)$ as a pre-open decryption query, and $(c^*, T^*)$ as a release-time decryption query.

**Guess.** $\mathcal{A}$ outputs a bit $b_A$ as its guess for $b_C$.

Note that in Challenge phase, $\mathcal{CH}$ gives not only a challenge ciphertext but also its corresponding pre-open key to $\mathcal{A}$.

We define the IND-TR-CCA$_{TS}$ advantage of $\mathcal{A}$ attacking $\Pi$ as:

$$\mathsf{Adv}_{\Pi,\mathcal{A}}^{\text{IND-TR-CCA}_{\text{TS}}} = |\Pr[b_A = b_C] - \frac{1}{2}|.$$

**Definition 5.** *We say that a TRE-PC scheme $\Pi$ is IND-TR-CCA$_{TS}$ secure if* $\mathsf{Adv}_{\Pi,\mathcal{A}}^{\text{IND-TR-CCA}_{\text{TS}}}$ *is negligible for any PPT algorithm $\mathcal{A}$.*

*Insider Security.* This security ensures that the receiver who has his secret key cannot get any information of a plaintext from a ciphertext without a time-release key or a pre-open key. It is defined by the following game between an adversary $\mathcal{A}$ and the challenger $\mathcal{CH}$.

**Setup.** $\mathcal{CH}$ runs TRE.Setup($1^\kappa$) and TRE.UKG($1^\kappa$), and obtains (msk, prm) and $(sk_u, pk_u)$, respectively. $\mathcal{CH}$ gives (prm, $sk_u, pk_u$) to $\mathcal{A}$ and keeps msk to itself.

**Phase 1.** $\mathcal{A}$ can adaptively issue extraction queries $T$ to $\mathcal{CH}$. $\mathcal{CH}$ responds to each extraction query $T$ by returning $s_T \leftarrow$ TRE.Ext(prm, msk, $T$) to $\mathcal{A}$.

**Challenge.** $\mathcal{A}$ chooses two distinct plaintexts $(m_0, m_1)$ of equal length and a challenge release-time $T^*$, and sends them to $\mathcal{CH}$. $\mathcal{CH}$ flips a coin $b_C \in \{0, 1\}$ uniformly at random, then computes $(c^*, V^*) \leftarrow$ TRE.Enc(prm, $pk_u, T^*, m_{b_C}$), and sends $c^*$ to $\mathcal{A}$ (but keeps $V^*$ to itself). $T^*$ chosen here should be larger than any $T$ issued in Phase 1.

**Phase 2.** $\mathcal{A}$ can issue extraction queries in the same way as Phase 1, except that $\mathcal{A}$ is not allowed to issue $T \geq T^*$ as an extraction query.

**Guess.** $\mathcal{A}$ outputs a bit $b_A$ as its guess for $b_C$.

We define the IND-TR-CPA$_{IS}$ [1] advantage of $\mathcal{A}$ attacking $\Pi$ as:

$$\mathsf{Adv}_{\Pi,\mathcal{A}}^{\text{IND-TR-CPA}_{\text{IS}}} = |\Pr[b_A = b_C] - \frac{1}{2}|.$$

**Definition 6.** *We say that a TRE-PC scheme $\Pi$ is IND-TR-CPA$_{IS}$ secure if* $\mathsf{Adv}_{\Pi,\mathcal{A}}^{\text{IND-TR-CPA}_{\text{IS}}}$ *is negligible for any PPT algorithm $\mathcal{A}$.*

---

[1] The reason why we only consider the "CPA" adversary in this security can be found in the original paper [11]. Refer to it for details.

*Binding.* This is the security that the sender cannot make the ciphertext corresponding to a release-time $T$ that the decryption by running TRE.Dec$_{RK}$ with a pre-open key $V$ is different from the decryption by running TRE.Dec$_{PK}$ with a time-release key $s_T$. It is defined by the following game between $\mathcal{A}$ and $\mathcal{CH}$.

**Setup.** $\mathcal{CH}$ runs TRE.Setup($1^{\kappa}$) and TRE.UKG($1^{\kappa}$), and obtains (msk, prm) and $(sk_u, pk_u)$, respectively. $\mathcal{CH}$ gives (prm, $pk_u$) to $\mathcal{A}$ and keeps msk, $sk_u$ to itself.

**Query.** $\mathcal{A}$ can adaptively issue three kinds of queries. $\mathcal{CH}$ responds to pre-open decryption queries $(c, V)$ by returning $m \leftarrow$ TRE.Dec$_{RK}$(prm, $sk_u, V, c$) to $\mathcal{A}$, release-time decryption queries $(c, T)$ by first computing $s_T \leftarrow$ TRE.Ext(prm, msk, $T$) and then returning $m \leftarrow$ TRE.Dec$_{PK}$(prm, $sk_u, s_T, c$) to $\mathcal{A}$, and extraction queries $T$ by returning $s_T \leftarrow$ TRE.Ext(prm, msk, $T$) to $\mathcal{A}$.

**Output.** $\mathcal{A}$ outputs a pair of $(c^*, T^*, V^*)$.

We define the binding advantage of $\mathcal{A}$ attacking $\Pi$ as follows:

$$\mathsf{Adv}_{\Pi, \mathcal{A}}^{\mathrm{BINDING}} = \Pr[\bot \neq \mathsf{Dec}_{RK}(\mathrm{prm}, sk_u, V^*, c^*) \neq \mathsf{Dec}_{PK}(\mathrm{prm}, sk_u, s_T^*, c^*) \neq \bot],$$

where $s_T^* \leftarrow$ TRE.Ext(prm, msk, $T^*$).

**Definition 7.** *We say that a TRE-PC scheme $\Pi$ is binding if* $\mathsf{Adv}_{\Pi, \mathcal{A}}^{\mathrm{BINDING}}$ *is negligible for any PPT algorithm $\mathcal{A}$.*

# 4   A Proposed Generic Construction

In this section, we show a generic construction of TRE-PC, and prove that the proposed scheme achieves the security we reviewed in Section 3.1. In particular, we construct our TRE-PC scheme from an IND-CCA secure PKE scheme, an IND-ID-CPA secure IBE scheme which has the target collision resistance for randomness, and a one-time signature scheme.

Our construction is as follows. Let $\Pi = $ (PKE.KG, PKE.Enc, PKE.Dec) be a PKE scheme, $\Pi' = $ (IBE.Setup, IBE.Ext, IBE.Enc, IBE.Dec) be an IBE scheme, and $\Sigma = $ (SigKG, Sign, Verify) be a signature scheme. Then, we construct the TRE-PC scheme $\Gamma$ as in Fig. 1. In Fig. 1, $\mathcal{M}$ is the message space of $\Gamma$, and $\mathcal{R}_{IBE}$ is the randomness space of (an encryption algorithm of) $\Pi'$.

As noted before, this scheme is essentially the same construction as a (normal) TRE scheme based on multiple encryption with a PKE scheme and an IBE scheme (which is introduced in [7,8]). In particular, we do not use any other primitives or techniques such as the non-interactive zero-knowledge proofs.

## 4.1   Security

*Idea.* Before we show the formal security proofs, we give an intuitive explanation why this scheme can achieve the security of TRE-PC. The feature of this scheme is to use $(r_2, \mathcal{R}_{IBE})$ as a pre-open key where $r_2$ is one of the shares of

| TRE.Setup($1^\kappa$): | TRE.Dec$_{\mathsf{RK}}$(prm, $sk_u, V, CT$): |
|---|---|
| Output (msk, prm) $\leftarrow$ IBE.Setup($1^\kappa$). | $(VK, T, c_1, c_2, \sigma) \leftarrow CT$ |
| TRE.Ext(prm, msk, $T$): | $(r_2, R_{IBE}) \leftarrow V$ |
| $d_T \leftarrow$ IBE.Ext(prm, msk, $T$) | If Verify($VK, (T\|c_1\|c_2), \sigma$) = $reject$ |
| Output $s_T \leftarrow (d_T, T)$. | then output $\perp$ and stop. |
| TRE.UKG($1^\kappa$): | $(VK'\|r_1) \leftarrow$ PKE.Dec($sk_u, c_1$) |
| Output $(sk_u, pk_u) \leftarrow$ PKE.KG($1^\kappa$). | $c_2' \leftarrow$ IBE.Enc(prm, $T, (VK\|r_2); R_{IBE}$) |
| TRE.Enc(prm, $T, pk_u, m$): | If $c_2 = c_2'$ and $VK = VK'$ |
| $r_1 \leftarrow \mathcal{M}$ | then output $m = r_1 \oplus r_2$ else output $\perp$. |
| $r_2 \leftarrow m \oplus r_1$ | TRE.Dec$_{\mathsf{PK}}$(prm, $sk_u, s_T, CT$): |
| $R_{IBE} \leftarrow \mathcal{R}_{IBE}$ | $(VK, T, c_1, c_2, \sigma) \leftarrow CT$ |
| $(SK, VK) \leftarrow$ SigKG($1^\kappa$) | $(d_T, T') \leftarrow s_T$ |
| $c_1 \leftarrow$ PKE.Enc($pk_u, (VK\|r_1)$) | If Verify($VK, (T\|c_1\|c_2), \sigma$) = $reject$ or $T \neq T'$ |
| $c_2 \leftarrow$ IBE.Enc(prm, $T, (VK\|r_2); R_{IBE}$) | then output $\perp$ and stop. |
| $\sigma \leftarrow$ Sign($SK, (T\|c_1\|c_2)$) | $(VK'\|r_1) \leftarrow$ PKE.Dec($sk_u, c_1$) |
| $CT \leftarrow (VK, T, c_1, c_2, \sigma)$ | $(VK''\|r_2) \leftarrow$ IBE.Dec($d_T, c_2$) |
| $V \leftarrow (r_2, R_{IBE})$ | If $VK = VK' = VK''$ |
| Output $(CT, V)$. | then output $m = r_1 \oplus r_2$ else output $\perp$. |

**Fig. 1.** Proposed TRE-PC Scheme

the plaintext, and $R_{IBE}$ is the randomness used to encrypt $r_2$. That is, a pre-open key contains all the information about the IBE part $c_2$ of the ciphertext $CT$. The reason why this is possible is that the information of the plaintext of $CT$ cannot be obtained only from the share $r_2$. Moreover, $R_{IBE}$ does not leak the information of the plaintext more than $r_2$. Therefore, as long as the adversary (who has even a master key of TRE-PC) does not have the receiver's secret key, he cannot obtain the information of the plaintext from $(r_2, R_{IBE})$ without breaking the IND-CCA security of the underlying PKE scheme, which leads to the time server security. However, we found that there is a certain type of the decryption queries we cannot handle only with the power of IND-CCA security of the underlying PKE scheme. Hence in order to overcome it we had to require another assumption about the randomness for the underlying IBE scheme, which we feel is a quite mild assumption (see Section 2.2 for discussion on it).

The security against a curious receiver, who has the receiver's secret key and tries to obtain the information before the release-time, is achieved by the security of the underlying IBE as is the same with the generic construction of a (normal) TRE scheme from a PKE scheme and an IBE scheme [8].

When the receiver decrypts the ciphertext by a pre-open key, he cannot decrypt $c_2$ because he does not have the time-release key. But he can compute $c_2$ deterministically for checking the validity of the ciphertext by using the pre-open key $(r_2, R_{IBE})$, and reject if it is different from that in the received ciphertext. This process leads to the binding property.

$VK$ in a plaintext of $c_1$ and $c_2$ works like a session-identity of a ciphertext $CT$, meaning that it strongly binds the ciphertexts of the underlying IBE scheme and the PKE scheme as a single ciphertext of TRE-PC, and makes it possible to reject the ill-formed ciphertext.

In the following, we show the formal proofs of the three kinds of security.

**Theorem 1.** *Our scheme $\Gamma$ is IND-TR-CCA$_{TS}$ secure if the underlying PKE scheme $\Pi$ is IND-CCA secure, the underlying IBE scheme $\Pi'$ has target collision resistance for randomness, and the underlying signature scheme $\Sigma$ is SOT secure.*

*Proof.* Suppose $\mathcal{A}$ is an adversary that breaks IND-TR-CCA$_{TS}$ security of $\Gamma$, which means that $\mathcal{A}$ wins the IND-TR-CCA$_{TS}$ game with probability $\frac{1}{2} +$ $\mathsf{Adv}_{\Gamma,\mathcal{A}}^{\mathrm{IND\text{-}TR\text{-}CCA_{TS}}}$. Then we construct a simulator $\mathcal{S}$ who can break IND-CCA security of the underlying PKE scheme $\Pi$ using $\mathcal{A}$. Suppose $\mathsf{Adv}_{\Gamma,\mathcal{A}}^{\mathrm{IND\text{-}TR\text{-}CCA_{TS}}}$ is not negligible in order to show the contradiction. Our simulator $\mathcal{S}$, simulating the IND-TR-CCA$_{TS}$ game for $\mathcal{A}$, plays the IND-CCA game with the IND-CCA challenger $\mathcal{CH}$ as follows.

**Setup.** $\mathcal{S}$ is given $pk_u$ from $\mathcal{CH}$, and generates $(\mathsf{msk}, \mathsf{prm})$ by running IBE.Setup($1^\kappa$). $\mathcal{S}$ gives $(\mathsf{msk}, \mathsf{prm}, pk_u)$ to $\mathcal{A}$.

**Phase 1.** $\mathcal{S}$ responds to $\mathcal{A}$'s pre-open decryption queries $(CT, V)$ and release-time decryption queries $(CT, T)$ as follow. In the former case, $\mathcal{S}$ decrypts $CT$ by following the procedure of TRE.Dec$_{\mathsf{RK}}$ and gives $m$ to $\mathcal{A}$. In the latter case, $\mathcal{S}$ computes $s_T$ by running IBE.Ext($\mathsf{prm}, \mathsf{msk}, T$), and then gives $m$ to $\mathcal{A}$ by following the procedure of TRE.Dec$_{\mathsf{PK}}$ with using $s_T$. In both decryption procedure, $\mathcal{S}$ issues $c_1$ to $\mathcal{CH}$ as his decryption query and uses the returned value from $\mathcal{CH}$, instead of running PKE.Dec by himself.

**Challenge.** When $\mathcal{A}$ submits $(m_0, m_1, T^*)$ to $\mathcal{S}$, $\mathcal{S}$ returns the challenge ciphertext $CT^*$ to $\mathcal{A}$ generated as follows. Run SigKG and get $(SK^*, VK^*)$. Choose randomness $r_2^* \leftarrow \mathcal{M}$ (equal length to $m_0$) and $R_{IBE}^* \leftarrow \mathcal{R}_{IBE}$ uniformly at random, and computes $c_2^* \leftarrow$ IBE.Enc($\mathsf{prm}, T^*, (VK^*\|r_2^*); R_{IBE}^*$). Set $M_0 = (VK^*\|m_0\oplus r_2^*)$ and $M_1 = (VK^*\|m_1\oplus r_2^*)$. Submit $(M_0, M_1)$ to $\mathcal{CH}$ as $\mathcal{S}$'s challenge and obtain $c_1^*$ from $\mathcal{CH}$. Compute $\sigma^* \leftarrow$ Sign($SK^*, (T^*\|c_1^*\|c_2^*)$). Give $CT^* = (VK^*, T^*, c_1^*, c_2^*, \sigma^*)$ to $\mathcal{A}$.

**Phase 2.** $\mathcal{S}$ responds to $\mathcal{A}$'s pre-open decryption queries $(CT = (VK, T, c_1, c_2, \sigma), V = (r_2', R_{IBE}'))$ as follows. The followings are done in a sequential way.

**(1)** If Verify($VK, (T\|c_1\|c_2), \sigma) = reject$: Return $m \leftarrow \perp$.
**(2)** If $c_1 \neq c_1^*$: Return $m$ in the same way as the pre-open decryption queries in Phase 1.
**(3)** If $c_1 = c_1^* \wedge VK = VK^* \wedge c_2 =$ IBE.Enc($\mathsf{prm}, T, (VK\|r_2'); R_{IBE}'$): Give up the simulation and abort.
**(4) Otherwise:** Return $m \leftarrow \perp$.

Likewise, $\mathcal{S}$ responds to $\mathcal{A}$'s release-time decryption queries $(CT = (VK, T, c_1, c_2, \sigma), T')$ as follows. The following are done in a sequential way.

**(1)** If Verify($VK, (T\|c_1\|c_2), \sigma) = reject$ or $T \neq T'$ : Return $m \leftarrow \perp$.
**(2)** If $VK = VK^*$: Give up the simulation and abort.
**(3)** If $c_1 = c_1^*$: Return $m \leftarrow \perp$.

**(4) Otherwise:** Return $m$ in the same way as the release-time decryption queries in Phase 1.

**Guess.** $\mathcal{A}$ outputs a bit $b_A$. $\mathcal{S}$ outputs $b_A$ as its guess.

We define the three events as follows.

Succ: Finally, $\mathcal{S}$ wins the IND-CCA game.

Abort$_{RK}$: In Phase 2, $\mathcal{A}$ issues at least one pre-open decryption query that makes $\mathcal{S}$ abort, that is, $\mathcal{A}$ issues at least one query satisfying $\mathsf{Verify}(VK, (T\|c_1\|c_2), \sigma) = accept \wedge c_1 = c_1^* \wedge VK = VK^* \wedge c_2 = \mathsf{IBE.Enc}(\mathrm{prm}, T, (VK\|r_2'); R_{IBE}')$.

Abort$_{PK}$: In Phase 2, $\mathcal{A}$ issues at least one release-time decryption query that makes $\mathcal{S}$ abort, that is, $\mathcal{A}$ issues at least one query satisfying $\mathsf{Verify}(VK, (T\|c_1\|c_2), \sigma) = accept \wedge VK = VK^* \wedge T' = T^*$.

The probability $\mathcal{S}$ wins its own IND-CCA game is estimated as follows.

$$\Pr[\mathsf{Succ}] \geq \Pr[\mathsf{Succ} \wedge \overline{\mathsf{Abort_{RK}}} \wedge \overline{\mathsf{Abort_{PK}}}]$$
$$= \Pr[\mathsf{Succ}|\overline{\mathsf{Abort_{RK}}} \wedge \overline{\mathsf{Abort_{PK}}}] \cdot \Pr[\overline{\mathsf{Abort_{RK}} \vee \mathsf{Abort_{PK}}}]$$
$$\geq \Pr[\mathsf{Succ}|\overline{\mathsf{Abort_{RK}}} \wedge \overline{\mathsf{Abort_{PK}}}] - \Pr[\mathsf{Abort_{RK}}] - \Pr[\mathsf{Abort_{PK}}]$$

We show the three lemmas to complete the proof as follows.

**Lemma 1.** $\Pr[\mathsf{Succ}|\overline{\mathsf{Abort_{RK}}} \wedge \overline{\mathsf{Abort_{PK}}}] = \frac{1}{2} + \mathsf{Adv}_{\Gamma,\mathcal{A}}^{\mathrm{IND\text{-}TR\text{-}CCA}_{TS}}$.

*Proof.* (of Lemma 1) In this game, it is clear that the keys that $\mathcal{S}$ gives to $\mathcal{A}$ are distributed identically to those in the IND-TR-CCA$_{TS}$ game. $\mathcal{S}$ makes the challenge ciphertext of $\mathcal{A}$ in a different way from our scheme. In particular, though $r_2$ is made from the XOR of $m$ and uniformly chosen $r_1$ in our scheme, $\mathcal{S}$ makes $r_1$ from the XOR of $m$ and uniformly chosen $r_2$ in the above game. But, for any $m$ in both cases the distribution of $r_1$ and $r_2$ is perfectly indistinguishable. Therefore, the challenge phase is perfectly simulated for $\mathcal{A}$.

Here, we consider the $\mathcal{S}$'s simulation of the response to decryption queries when Abort$_{RK}$ and Abort$_{PK}$ do not occur.

**(1) The response to the pre-open decryption queries**

- If $\mathsf{Verify}(VK, (T\|c_1\|c_2), \sigma) = reject$, $\mathcal{S}$ returns $\bot$ and clealy this is a perfect simulation.
- If $c_1 \neq c_1^*$, $\mathcal{S}$ can issue $c_1$ as a decryption query to $\mathcal{CH}$, and use the returned value from $\mathcal{CH}$ for computing the plaintext of $CT$. In this case $\mathcal{S}$ can perfectly simulate for $\mathcal{A}$.
- If $c_1 = c_1^* \wedge c_2 \neq \mathsf{IBE.Enc}(\mathrm{prm}, T, (VK\|r_2'); R_{IBE}')$, $\mathcal{S}$ returns $\bot$ to $\mathcal{A}$ and this is a perfect simulation, because $\bot$ is returned if $c_2 \neq \mathsf{IBE.Enc}(\mathrm{prm}, T, (VK\|r_2'); R_{IBE}')$ in our scheme.
- If $c_1 = c_1^* \wedge VK \neq VK^*$, because $c_1$ equals to $c_1^*$, the decryption result of $c_1$ is $(VK^*\|r_1^*)$ with $r_1^*$ unknown to $\mathcal{S}$. However, since $VK \neq VK^*$, the decryption of $CT$ is $\bot$, and in this case $\mathcal{S}$ also returns $\bot$ to $\mathcal{A}$. Therefore, $\mathcal{S}$ can perfectly simulate for $\mathcal{A}$.

**(2) The response to the release-time decryption queries**

- If $\mathsf{Verify}(VK, (T||c_1||c_2), \sigma) = reject$ or $T \neq T'$, $\mathcal{S}$ returns $\perp$ and clearly this is a perfect simulation. $T \neq T'$ implies that the time-release key corresponding to $T'$ includes $T'$ itself and this does not satisfy the first check of our release-time decryption algorithm. (Rejection of the signature of course means that $CT$ decrypts to $\perp$.)
- If $c_1 = c_1^*$, though $\mathcal{S}$ cannot issue $c_1$ as a decryption query to $\mathcal{CH}$, it can find that the decryption result is $(VK^*||r_1^*)$ with $r_1^*$ unknown to $\mathcal{S}$. However, since $VK \neq VK^*$, the decryption of $CT$ is $\perp$, and in this case $\mathcal{S}$ also returns $\perp$ to $\mathcal{A}$. Therefore, $\mathcal{S}$ can perfectly simulate for $\mathcal{A}$.
- If $c_1 \neq c_1^*$, $\mathcal{S}$ can issue $c_1$ as a decryption query to $\mathcal{CH}$, and use the returned value from $\mathcal{CH}$ for computing the plaintext of $CT$. In this case $\mathcal{S}$ can perfectly simulate for $\mathcal{A}$.

Since $\mathcal{S}$ perfectly simulates the IND-TR-CCA$_{TS}$ game for $\mathcal{A}$ if both Abort$_\mathsf{RK}$ and Abort$_\mathsf{PK}$ do not occur, $\mathcal{S}$ wins the IND-CCA game with the same probability that $\mathcal{A}$ wins the IND-TR-CCA$_{TS}$ game, that is, $\frac{1}{2} + \mathsf{Adv}_{\Gamma, \mathcal{A}}^{\text{IND-TR-CCA}_{TS}}$. This completes the proof of Lemma 1. □

**Lemma 2.** $\Pr[\mathsf{Abort}_\mathsf{PK}]$ *is negligible.*

*Proof.* (of Lemma 2) First of all, note that if Abort$_\mathsf{PK}$ occurs, then $\mathcal{A}$ issues at least one release-time decryption query $(CT, T)$ satisfying $CT = (VK^*, T, c_1, c_2, \sigma) \wedge \mathsf{Verify}(VK^*, (T||c_1||c_2), \sigma) = accept$ (especially note that $T$'s in the ciphertext $CT$ and in the query are identical). Since $\mathcal{A}$ is the adversary of IND-TR-CCA$_{TS}$, $(CT, T) \neq (CT^*, T^*)$ is satisfied, and any query satisfying this condition always satisfies $(T, c_1, c_2, \sigma) \neq (T^*, c_1^*, c_2^*, \sigma^*)$.

We construct an adversary $\mathcal{F}$ who can break SOT security of the underlying signature scheme $\Sigma$ using $\mathcal{A}$ who causes the event of Abort$_\mathsf{PK}$ with $\Pr[\mathsf{Abort}_\mathsf{PK}] = p_A$. Suppose $p_A$ is not negligible. The description of $\mathcal{F}$ is as follows.

$\mathcal{F}$ receives $VK^*$ from $\mathcal{CH}$. Then, $\mathcal{F}$ runs IBE.Setup and PKE.KG, and gets (msk, prm) and $(sk_u, pk_u)$, respectively. $\mathcal{F}$ gives (msk, prm, $pk_u$) to $\mathcal{A}$. $\mathcal{F}$ can perfectly respond to two kinds of the decryption queries of $\mathcal{A}$ since he has msk and $sk_u$. If $\mathcal{A}$ outputs $(m_0, m_1, T^*)$ as the challenge, $\mathcal{F}$ chooses $R_{IBE}^* \leftarrow \mathcal{R}, r_2^* \leftarrow \mathcal{M}$, and $b_S \leftarrow \{0, 1\}$ uniformly at random, and computes $r_1^* = m_{b_S} \oplus r_2$. Then $\mathcal{F}$ computes $c_1^* \leftarrow \mathsf{PKE.Enc}(pk_u, (VK^*||r_1^*))$ and $c_2^* \leftarrow \mathsf{IBE.Enc}(\mathsf{prm}, T^*, (VK^*||r_2^*);$ $R_{IBE}^*)$, then issues $(T^*||c_1^*||c_2^*)$ as a signature query and gets $\sigma^*$. $\mathcal{F}$ gives the challenge ciphertext $CT^* = (VK^*, T^*, c_1^*, c_2^*, \sigma^*)$ and its corresponding pre-open key $V^* = (r_2^*, R_{IBE}^*)$ to $\mathcal{A}$. After $\mathcal{A}$ outputs $b_A$, $\mathcal{F}$ finds out the query satisfying $VK = VK^* \wedge \mathsf{Verify}(VK^*, (T||c_1||c_2), \sigma) = accept \wedge (T, c_1, c_2, \sigma) \neq (T^*, c_1^*, c_2^*, \sigma^*)$ in the release-time decryption queries issued by $\mathcal{A}$ in this game, and outputs $((T||c_1||c_2), \sigma)$. If $\mathcal{F}$ cannot find such query, it aborts.

It is easy to see that $\mathcal{F}$ can certainly forge the signature if $\mathcal{A}$ issues a release-time decryption query that causes the event Abort$_\mathsf{PK}$. Therefore, we have $\mathsf{Adv}_{\Sigma, \mathcal{F}}^{\text{SUF-OT}_{\text{sig}}} = p_A$, and it contradicts that $\Sigma$ is SOT secure. Hence $\Pr[\mathsf{Abort}_\mathsf{PK}]$ is negligible, which completes the proof of Lemma 2. □

**Lemma 3.** $\Pr[\mathsf{Abort_{RK}}]$ *is negligible.*

*Proof.* (of Lemma 3) First of all, note that if $\mathsf{Abort_{RK}}$ occurs, then $\mathcal{A}$ issues at least one pre-open decryption query satisfying $CT = (VK^*, T, c_1^*, c_2, \sigma) \wedge c_2 = \mathsf{IBE.Enc}(\mathsf{prm}, T, (VK^*\|r_2'); R_{IBE}') \wedge \mathsf{Verify}(VK^*, (T^*\|c_1^*\|c_2), \sigma) = accept$. Since $\mathcal{A}$ is the adversary of IND-TR-CCA$_{TS}$, $(CT, V) \neq (CT^*, V^*)$ is satisfied, and any query satisfying this condition always satisfies either (i) $(T, c_2, \sigma) \neq (T^*, c_2^*, \sigma^*)$, or (ii) $(T, c_2, \sigma) = (T^*, c_2^*, \sigma^*) \wedge V = (r_2', R_{IBE}') \neq (r_2^*, R_{IBE}^*)$, and these queries cover all possibilities. We divide the event $\mathsf{Abort_{RK}}$ into two sub-events $\mathsf{Forge}$ and $\mathsf{Rand}$, where the former is that $\mathcal{A}$ issues the query that causes (i), and the latter (ii). Then $\Pr[\mathsf{Abort_{RK}}]$ is estimated as $\Pr[\mathsf{Abort_{RK}}] = \Pr[\mathsf{Forge}] + \Pr[\mathsf{Rand}]$.

Here, we consider the probability that each sub-event occurs.

(1) $\Pr[\mathsf{Forge}]$: This is negligible due to the SOT security of $\Sigma$. We omit the proof because this proof is almost the same as that of Lemma 2.

(2) $\Pr[\mathsf{Rand}]$: If $\mathsf{Rand}$ occurs, $r_2' = r_2^*$ is satisfied by the correctness of the decryption of the underlying IBE scheme, because $c_2^* = \mathsf{IBE.Enc}(\mathsf{prm}, T^*, (VK^*\|r_2');$ $R_{IBE}')$.

We construct an adversary $\mathcal{H}$ who can break target collision resistance for randomness of the underlying IBE scheme $\Pi'$ using $\mathcal{A}$ who causes the event $\mathsf{Rand}$ with $\Pr[\mathsf{Rand}] = p_B$. Suppose $p_B$ is not negligible.

$\mathcal{H}$ receives $(\mathsf{msk}, \mathsf{prm}, R_{IBE}^*)$ from $\mathcal{CH}$. Then, $\mathcal{H}$ runs $\mathsf{PKE.KG}$, and gets $(sk_u, pk_u)$. $\mathcal{H}$ gives $(\mathsf{msk}, \mathsf{prm}, pk_u)$ to $\mathcal{A}$. $\mathcal{H}$ can perfectly respond to two kinds of the decryption queries of $\mathcal{A}$ since he has $\mathsf{msk}$ and $sk_u$. If $\mathcal{A}$ outputs $(m_0, m_1, T^*)$ as the challenge, $\mathcal{H}$ chooses $r_2^* \leftarrow \mathcal{M}, b_S \leftarrow \{0,1\}$ uniformly at random, and computes $r_1^* = m_{b_S} \oplus r_2$. Then $\mathcal{H}$ runs $\mathsf{SigKG}$ and gets $(SK^*, VK^*)$. $\mathcal{H}$ computes $c_1^* \leftarrow \mathsf{PKE.Enc}(pk_u, (VK^*\|r_1^*)), c_2^* \leftarrow \mathsf{IBE.Enc}(\mathsf{prm}, T^*, (VK^*\|r_2^*); R_{IBE}^*)$, and $\sigma^* \leftarrow \mathsf{Sign}(SK^*, (T^*\|c_1^*\|c_2^*))$. $\mathcal{H}$ gives the challenge ciphertext $CT^* = (VK^*, T^*, c_1^*, c_2^*, \sigma^*)$ and its corresponding pre-open key $V^* = (r_2^*, R_{IBE}^*)$ to $\mathcal{A}$. After $\mathcal{A}$ outputs $b_A$, $\mathcal{H}$ finds out the query that causes $\mathsf{Rand}$ in the pre-open decryption queries issued by $\mathcal{A}$ in this game, and outputs $((VK^*\|r_2^*), T^*, R_{IBE}')$. If $\mathcal{H}$ cannot find such query, it aborts.

It is easy to see that $\mathcal{H}$ can certainly break the target collision resistance for randomness if $\mathcal{A}$ issues a pre-open decryption query that causes $\mathsf{Rand}$. Therefore, we have $\mathsf{Adv}_{\Pi', \mathcal{H}}^{\mathsf{Rand}} = p_B$. But it contradicts that $\Pi'$ has the target collision resistance for randomness, so $\Pr[\mathsf{Rand}]$ is negligible.

From (1) and (2), $\Pr[\mathsf{Abort_{RK}}] = \Pr[\mathsf{Forge}] + \Pr[\mathsf{Rand}]$ is negligible. This completes the proof of Lemma 3. $\square$

From the Lemmas 1 ,2 and 3, we can estimate $\Pr[\mathsf{Succ}]$ as follows:

$$\Pr[\mathsf{Succ}] \geq \frac{1}{2} + \mathsf{Adv}_{\Gamma, \mathcal{A}}^{\mathsf{IND\text{-}TR\text{-}CCA}_{TS}} - \Pr[\mathsf{Abort_{RK}}] - \Pr[\mathsf{Abort_{PK}}].$$

Therefore, since we assumed that $\mathsf{Adv}_{\Gamma, \mathcal{A}}^{\mathsf{IND\text{-}TR\text{-}CCA}_{TS}}$ is not negligible, $\mathsf{Adv}_{\Pi, \mathcal{S}}^{\mathsf{IND\text{-}CCA}} = |\Pr[\mathsf{Succ}] - \frac{1}{2}|$ is not negligible. However, this contradicts that $\Pi$ is an IND-CCA secure PKE scheme. This completes the proof of Theorem 1. $\square$

**Theorem 2.** *Our scheme $\Gamma$ is IND-TR-CPA$_{IS}$ secure if the underlying IBE scheme $\Pi'$ is IND-ID-CPA secure.*

*Proof.* Suppose $\mathcal{A}$ is an adversary that breaks IND-TR-CPA$_{IS}$ security of $\Gamma$, which means that $\mathcal{A}$ wins the IND-TR-CPA$_{IS}$ game with probability $\frac{1}{2}$ + Adv$_{\Gamma,\mathcal{A}}^{\text{IND-TR-CPA}_{IS}}$. Then we construct a simulator $\mathcal{S}$ who can break IND-ID-CPA security of the underlying IBE scheme $\Pi'$ using $\mathcal{A}$. Suppose Adv$_{\Gamma,\mathcal{A}}^{\text{IND-TR-CPA}_{IS}}$ is not negligible in order to show the contradiction. Our simulator $\mathcal{S}$, simulating the IND-TR-CPA$_{IS}$ game for $\mathcal{A}$, plays the IND-ID-CPA game with the IND-ID-CPA challenger $\mathcal{CH}$ as follows.

**Setup.** $\mathcal{S}$ is given prm from $\mathcal{CH}$, and generates $(sk_u, pk_u)$ by running PKE.KG$(1^\kappa)$. $\mathcal{S}$ gives (prm, $sk_u, pk_u$) to $\mathcal{A}$.

**Phase 1.** $\mathcal{S}$ responds to $\mathcal{A}$'s extraction queries $T$ as follows. $\mathcal{S}$ regards $T$ as an identity of IBE, and issues $T$ as an extraction query to $\mathcal{CH}$ then receives $d_T$. $\mathcal{S}$ sets $s_T \leftarrow (d_T, T)$ and then returns $s_T$ as a time-release key to $\mathcal{A}$.

**Challenge.** When $\mathcal{A}$ submits $(m_0, m_1, T^*)$ to $\mathcal{S}$, $\mathcal{S}$ returns the challenge ciphertext $CT^*$ to $\mathcal{A}$ as follows. Run SigKG and gets $(SK^*, VK^*)$. Choose a randomness $r_1 \leftarrow \mathcal{M}$ (equal length to $m_0$) uniformly at random, and compute $c_1^* \leftarrow$ PKE.Enc$(pk_u, (VK^*||r_1^*))$. Set $M_0 = (VK^*||m_0 \oplus r_1^*)$ and $M_1 = (VK^*||m_1 \oplus r_1^*)$. Submit $(M_0, M_1)$ and $T^*$ to $\mathcal{CH}$ as $\mathcal{S}$'s challenge and obtain $c_2^*$ from $\mathcal{CH}$. Compute $\sigma^* \leftarrow$ Sign$(SK^*, (T^*||c_1^*||c_2^*))$. Give $CT^* = (VK^*, T^*, c_1^*, c_2^*, \sigma^*)$ to $\mathcal{A}$.

**Phase 2.** $\mathcal{S}$ responds to $\mathcal{A}$'s extraction queries in the same way as Phase 1.

**Guess.** $\mathcal{A}$ outputs a bit $b_A$. $\mathcal{S}$ outputs $b_A$ as its guess.

Note that $\mathcal{S}$ simulates perfectly to $\mathcal{A}$, because $\mathcal{S}$ gives correct key pairs, gives correct time-release key $s_T$ for $\mathcal{A}$'s extraction queries $T$ in both Phase 1 and Phase 2 by using extraction queries to $\mathcal{CH}$, and gives the correct challenge ciphertext to $\mathcal{A}$ by receiving $c_2^*$ from $\mathcal{CH}$ and giving $CT^*$ using $c_2^*$. Consequently, $\mathcal{S}$'s advantage can be estimated as Adv$_{\Pi',\mathcal{S}}^{\text{IND-ID-CPA}} =$ Adv$_{\Gamma,\mathcal{A}}^{\text{IND-TR-CPA}_{IS}}$. Since we assumed that Adv$_{\Gamma,\mathcal{A}}^{\text{IND-TR-CPA}_{IS}}$ is not negligible, this contradicts that $\Pi'$ is an IND-ID-CPA secure IBE scheme. This completes the proof of Theorem 2. $\square$

**Theorem 3.** *Our scheme $\Gamma$ is binding against any (even computationally unbounded) adversary.*

*Proof.* Suppose that an adversary $\mathcal{A}$ in the binding game outputs $CT = (VK, T, c_1, c_2, \sigma)$ and $V = (r_2, R_{IBE})$, and suppose $d_T \leftarrow$ IBE.Ext(prm, msk, $T$) and $s_T = (d_T, T)$. We can estimate Adv$_{\Gamma,\mathcal{A}}^{\text{BINDING}}$ as follows.

$$\text{Adv}_{\Gamma,\mathcal{A}}^{\text{BINDING}}$$

$$= \Pr[\text{TRE.Dec}_{\text{RK}}(\text{prm}, sk_u, V, CT) \neq \bot \wedge \text{TRE.Dec}_{\text{PK}}(\text{prm}, sk_u, s_T, CT) \neq \bot$$
$$\wedge \text{TRE.Dec}_{\text{RK}}(\text{prm}, sk_u, V, CT) \neq \text{TRE.Dec}_{\text{PK}}(\text{prm}, sk_u, s_T, CT)]$$

$$= \Pr[\text{Verify}(VK, (T||c_1||c_2), \sigma) = accept \wedge \text{PKE.Dec}(sk_u, c_1) = (VK||r_1)$$
$$\wedge c_2 = \text{IBE.Enc}(\text{prm}, T, (VK||r_2); R_{IBE}) \wedge \text{IBE.Dec}(d_T, c_2) = (VK||r_2')$$
$$\wedge r_1 \oplus r_2 \neq r_1 \oplus r_2']$$

$$\leq \Pr[c_2 = \text{IBE.Enc}(\text{prm}, T, (VK||r_2); R_{IBE}) \wedge \text{IBE.Dec}(d_T, c_2) = (VK||r_2') \wedge r_2 \neq r_2']$$

$$= \Pr[r_2 = r_2' \wedge r_2 \neq r_2'],$$

where the last equation is due to the correctness of the underlying IBE scheme $\Pi'$. Clearly $r_2 = r_2' \wedge r_2 \neq r_2'$ never occurs, and so $\mathsf{Adv}_{\Gamma,\mathcal{A}}^{\mathrm{BINDING}}$ is zero for any adversary of any running time. This completes the proof of Theorem 3.      □

## 5   Discussions

Here, we discuss the consequences of our result.

*Existence of TRE-PC.* As was discussed by Cheon et al. [8], the exsitence of TRE (without pre-open capability) is implied by the exsitence of IBE.

On the other hand, we can say that the existence of TRE-PC secure in the sense of [11] is, due to our result, implied by the exsitence of IBE which has target collision resistance for randomness. This is because the existence of IBE trivially implies the existence of one-way functions, which in turn implies the existence of the one-time signatures [18,20]. Moreover, the existence of IBE implies the existence of IND-CCA secure PKE [4].

Thus, it may be challenging to consider whether we can avoid the assumption about the randomness of the underlying IBE scheme so that we can show the existence of TRE-PC in the sense of [11] only from the existence of IBE schemes.

*Standard Model Constructions from Weaker Assumptions.* Chow et al. [10] showed a TRE-PC scheme secure in the standard model whose time server security and insider security are proved based on the 3-MDDH assumption and the 3-DDH assumption, respectively, and which has binding without any assumption. [2] We note that if we consider the 3-MDDH and the 3-DDH assumptions in the bilinear groups, then these assumptions are strictly stronger than the decisional bilinear Diffie-Hellman (DBDH) assumption.

On the other hand, due to our result, we can construct a TRE-PC scheme secure in the standard model whose time server security and insider security can be proven both based on the DBDH assumption and which has binding property without any assumption. Specifically, we can use the Waters IBE scheme [21] for the underlying IND-ID-CPA secure IBE scheme, and the Boyen et al. PKE scheme [3] for the underlying IND-CCA secure PKE scheme. The security of both schemes are proven based on the DBDH assumption. In addition, as mentioned in Section 2.2, the Waters IBE scheme satisfies target collision resistance for randomness without any computational assumption. We note that the efficiency (the computation costs for encryption and decryption and the ciphertext overhead) of the TRE-PC scheme obtained via our generic construction will be worse than that of the Chow et al. scheme [10]. However, we believe that our generic construction will give important insights and be useful for a first step towards more practical constructions of TRE-PC secure in the standard model.

---

[2] Their security model is somewhat different from the one in [11] and actually slightly stronger in the sense that their model considers the multi-receiver setting. In this paper we only consider the model of [11].

# Acknowledgement

The authors also would like to thank anonymous reviewers of IWSEC'09 for their invaluable comments. The second anthor Takahiro Matsuda is supported by the Japan Society for Promotion of Science (JSPS) as a research fellow.

# References

1. Bellare, M., Rogaway, P.: Collision-resistant hashing: Towards making uOWHFs practical. In: Kaliski Jr., B.S. (ed.) CRYPTO 1997. LNCS, vol. 1294, pp. 470–484. Springer, Heidelberg (1997)
2. Boneh, D., Franklin, M.: Identity-based encryption from the weil pairing. In: Kilian, J. (ed.) CRYPTO 2001. LNCS, vol. 2139, pp. 213–229. Springer, Heidelberg (2001)
3. Boyen, X., Mci, Q., Waters, B.: Direct chosen ciphertext security from identity-based techniques. In: ACM CCS, pp. 320–329 (2005)
4. Canetti, R., Halevi, S., Katz, J.: Chosen-ciphertext security from identity-based encryption. In: Cachin, C., Camenisch, J.L. (eds.) EUROCRYPT 2004. LNCS, vol. 3027, pp. 207–222. Springer, Heidelberg (2004)
5. Chalkias, K., Hristu-Varsakelis, D., Stephanides, G.: Improved anonymous timed-release encryption. In: Biskup, J., López, J. (eds.) ESORICS 2007. LNCS, vol. 4734, pp. 311–326. Springer, Heidelberg (2007)
6. Chan, A.C.-F., Blake, I.F.: Scalable, server-passive, user-anonymous timed release cryptography. In: ICDCS, pp. 504–513 (2005)
7. Cheon, J.H., Hopper, N., Kim, Y., Osipkov, I.: Timed-release and key-insulated public key encryption. In: Di Crescenzo, G., Rubin, A. (eds.) FC 2006. LNCS, vol. 4107, pp. 191–205. Springer, Heidelberg (2006)
8. Cheon, J.H., Hopper, N., Kim, Y., Osipkov, I.: Provably secure timed-release public key encryption. ACM Trans. Inf. Syst. Secur. 11(2) (2008)
9. Chow, S.S.M., Roth, V., Rieffel, E.G.: General certificateless encryption and timed-release encryption. In: Ostrovsky, R., De Prisco, R., Visconti, I. (eds.) SCN 2008. LNCS, vol. 5229, pp. 126–143. Springer, Heidelberg (2008)
10. Chow, S.S.M., Yiu, S.M.: Timed-release encryption revisited. In: Baek, J., Bao, F., Chen, K., Lai, X. (eds.) ProvSec 2008. LNCS, vol. 5324, pp. 38–51. Springer, Heidelberg (2008)
11. Dent, A.W., Tang, Q.: Revisiting the security model for timed-release encryption with pre-open capability. In: Garay, J.A., Lenstra, A.K., Mambo, M., Peralta, R. (eds.) ISC 2007. LNCS, vol. 4779, pp. 158–174. Springer, Heidelberg (2007)
12. Dodis, Y., Katz, J.: Chosen-ciphertext security of multiple encryption. In: Kilian, J. (ed.) TCC 2005. LNCS, vol. 3378, pp. 188–209. Springer, Heidelberg (2005)
13. Gentry, C.: Practical identity-based encryption without random oracles. In: Vaudenay, S. (ed.) EUROCRYPT 2006. LNCS, vol. 4004, pp. 445–464. Springer, Heidelberg (2006)
14. Hristu-Varsakelis, D., Chalkias, K., Stephanides, G.: Low-cost anonymous timed-release encryption. In: IAS, pp. 77–82 (2007)
15. Hwang, Y.-H., Yum, D.H., Lee, P.J.: Timed-release encryption with pre-open capability and its application to certified e-mail system. In: Zhou, J., López, J., Deng, R.H., Bao, F. (eds.) ISC 2005. LNCS, vol. 3650, pp. 344–358. Springer, Heidelberg (2005)

16. Mao, W.: Timed-release cryptography. In: Vaudenay, S., Youssef, A.M. (eds.) SAC 2001. LNCS, vol. 2259, pp. 342–358. Springer, Heidelberg (2001)
17. May, T.: Timed-release crypto. (Unpublished manuscript) (1993)
18. Naor, M., Yung, M.: Universal One-Way Hash Functions and their Cryptographic Applications.In STOC, pp. 33–43 (1989)
19. Rivest, R.L., Shamir, A., Wagner, D.A.: Time-lock Puzzles and Timed-release Crypto. MIT LCS Tech. Report MIT/LCS/TR-684 (1996)
20. Rompel, J.: One-way functions are necessary and sufficient for secure signatures. In: STOC, pp. 387–394 (1990)
21. Waters, B.: Efficient identity-based encryption without random oracles. In: Cramer, R. (ed.) EUROCRYPT 2005. LNCS, vol. 3494, pp. 114–127. Springer, Heidelberg (2005)

# An Efficient Identity-Based Signcryption Scheme for Multiple Receivers

S. Sharmila Deva Selvi[1], S. Sree Vivek[1,*], Rahul Srinivasan[2], and Chandrasekaran Pandu Rangan[1,*]

[1] Theoretical Computer Science Laboratory
Department of Computer Science and Engineering
Indian Institute of Technology Madras
Chennai, India
{sharmila,svivek,prangan}@cse.iitm.ac.in
[2] Department of Computer Science and Engineering
Indian Institute of Technology Bombay
Mumbai, India
rahul.srinivasan@iitb.ac.in

**Abstract.** This paper puts forward a new efficient construction for Multi-Receiver Signcryption in the Identity-based setting. We consider a scenario where a user wants to securely send a message to a dynamically changing subset of the receivers in such a way that non-members of this subset cannot learn the message. One obvious solution is to signcrypt the message to each member of the subset and transmit it to each of them individually. This requires a very long transmission (the number of receivers times the length of the message) and high computation cost. Another simple solution is to provide a key for every possible subset of receivers. This requires every user to store a huge number of keys. In this case, the storage efficiency is compromised. The goal of this paper is to provide a solution which is efficient in all three measures i.e. transmission length, storage of keys and computation at both ends. We propose a new scheme that achieves both confidentiality and authenticity simultaneously in this setting and is the most efficient scheme to date, in the parameters described above. It breaks the barrier of ciphertext length of linear order in the number of receivers, and achieves constant sized ciphertext, independent of the size of the receiver set. This is the first Multi-receiver Signcryption scheme to do so. We support the scheme with security proofs in the random oracle model under precisely defined security model.

**Keywords:** Multiple Receivers, Signcryption, Identity-Based Cryptography, Provable Security.

## 1 Introduction

Two fundamental tools of Public Key Cryptography are privacy and authenticity, achieved through encryption and signature respectively. Signcryption, introduced

* Work supported by Project No. CSE/05-06/076/DITX/CPAN on Protocols for Secure Communication and Computation sponsored by Department of Information Technology, Government of India.

T. Takagi and M. Mambo (Eds.): IWSEC 2009, LNCS 5824, pp. 71–88, 2009.

by Zheng [16], is a cryptographic primitive that offers confidentiality and unforgeability simultaneously similar to the sign-then-encrypt technique, but with lesser
computational complexity and lower communication cost. The security notion for
signcryption was first formally defined in 2002 by Baek et al. in [1].

The concept of an Identity based (ID-based) cryptosystem was introduced by
Shamir [13] in 1984. The idea is that users within a system could use their online
identifiers (combined with certain system-wide information) as their public keys.
This greatly reduces the problems with key management and provides a more
convenient alternative to conventional public key infrastructure. In 2001, the first
fully practical identity-based encryption (IBE) scheme, using bilinear mappings
over elliptic curves was proposed by Boneh et al. [4].

ID-based signcryption schemes achieve the functionality of signcryption with
the added advantage that ID-based cryptography provides. To date, some of the
most efficient ID-based signcryption schemes are that of Chen et al. [5], and
Barreto et al. [2]

## 1.1 Motivation

Assume that there are $n$ receivers, numbered 1 to $n$, and that each of them keeps
a private and public key pair denoted by $(sk_i, pk_i)$. A sender then encrypts a
message $M$ directed to receiver $i$ using $pk_i$ for $i = 1$ to $n$ and sends $(C_1, \ldots C_n)$ as
the ciphertext. Upon receiving the ciphertext, receiver $i$ extracts $C_i$ and decrypts
it using its private key $sk_i$. This setting of public key encryption is generally
referred to as *Multi-receiver Public Key Encryption* in literature.

The objective of a multi-receiver ID-based signcryption scheme is to efficiently
broadcast a single ciphertext to different receivers while achieving the security
properties of authenticity and unforgeability. In practice, broadcasting a message
to multiple users in a secure and authenticated manner is an important facility for
a group of people who are jointly working on the same project to communicate
with one another. When we consider the case of an organization with several
managers, each of whom wants to securely send messages to employees of the
company, independently, the issue of message authentication will arise, apart
from confidentiality.

## 1.2 Related Work

In the multi-receiver identity-based setting, we are interested in the situation
where there is not only a single sender to multiple receivers, but also multiple
senders. In such cases, it is desirable to achieve confidentiality and authenticity simultaneously. To our knowledge, identity-based signcryption in the multi-
receiver setting has not been much treated in the literature. One might argue
that by adding sender authentication by using a secure digital signature scheme
to a multi-receiver encryption scheme will achieve this purpose. However, such
combinations may suffer from hidden security weakness as observed by Duan
and Cao in [7]. Also, they proposed the first mIBSC scheme and specified the
formal security notions for the same. The multi-receiver scheme proposed by

Duan and Cao was shown to be insecure by Tan[14], by demonstrating an attack on the confidentiality of the scheme. Yu et al.[15] also proposed an mIBSC scheme in 2008. Sharmila et al. in [12] showed that this scheme is not secure in the sense that it is forgeable and is not confidential. They also provide a fix for the scheme. To the best of our knowledge the scheme with the fix is the only secure identity-based scheme available in Multi receiver Signcryption literature till date.

### 1.3   Our Contribution

Following the above discussion, a natural question one can ask is how to design a multi-receiver identity-based signcryption scheme that achieves both confidentiality and authenticity, and broadcasts a message with a high-level of computational and storage efficiency and optimal transmission length while retaining security. In this paper, we introduce an efficient scheme to answer this question, which is inspired by the signcryption scheme proposed by Barreto et. al. [2]. The major advantage of our scheme is, it sends only three components to all the receivers. That is the size of the ciphertext is a constant and is independent of the number of receivers. However, all the other systems existing in the literature have ciphertext size proportional to the number of receivers. But this is achieved at the cost of storage efficiency. The size of the public key grows as the maximal size of the subset of receivers in the group (which can be significantly less than the total number of people in the group). This is the most efficient Identity based Multi Receiver Scheme to date. This construction, when converted to a Broadcast Encryption scheme [8], is comparable to the Identity-Based Broadcast Encryption (IBBE) schemes proposed by Furukawa [11] and Delerablée [6]. We also provide formal security notions for Multi-receiver Identity-Based Signcryption (mIBSC) schemes and formally prove the construction secure in the random oracle model by reducing its security to standard assumptions related to the Bilinear Diffie Hellman Problems.

| Scheme | Storage Cost | | Computational Cost - No. of pairings for (Signcrypt, Designcrypt) | Header Size[2] | Status |
|---|---|---|---|---|---|
| | Public Key Size[1] | Private Key Size | | | |
| Duan and Cao [7] | $O(1)$ | $O(1)$ | $(1,4)$ | $O(t)$ | *Broken* |
| Yu et al.[15] | $O(1)$ | $O(1)$ | $(1,3)$ | $O(t)$ | *Broken* |
| Sharmila et al.[12] | $O(1)$ | $O(1)$ | $(1,3)$ | $O(t)$ | *Secure* |
| Our Construction | $O(N)$ | $O(1)$ | $(0,3)$ | $O(1)$ | *Secure* |

*Remark.* It is a common practice in group oriented protocols to ignore the part of the broadcast ciphertext that identifies the target subset of receivers. We distinguish between the set identification transmission and the message signcryption transmission. Our goal is the study of latter and their requirements. What is

---

[1] $N$ is the maximal size of the receiver set.
[2] $t$ is the size of the receiver set.

called ciphertext size usually refers to the size of the header that corresponds to the message signcryption alone.

## 2    Preliminaries

Let $\mathbb{G}_1$ be an additive cyclic group of prime order $p$, with generators $P$ and $Q$, and $\mathbb{G}_2$ be a multiplicative cyclic group of the same order $p$.

### 2.1    Bilinear Pairing

A bilinear pairing is a map $e : \mathbb{G}_1 \times \mathbb{G}_1 \to \mathbb{G}_2$ with the following properties.

- **Bilinearity.** For all $P, Q, R \in \mathbb{G}_1$,
  - $e(P + Q, R) = e(P, R)e(Q, R)$
  - $e(P, Q + R) = e(P, Q)e(P, R)$
  - $e(aP, bQ) = e(P, Q)^{ab}$
- **Non-Degeneracy.** There exist $P, Q \in \mathbb{G}_1$ such that $e(P, Q) \neq I_{\mathbb{G}_2}$, where $I_{\mathbb{G}_2}$ is the identity element of $\mathbb{G}_2$.
- **Computability.** There exists an efficient algorithm to compute $e(P, Q)$ for all $P, Q \in \mathbb{G}_1$.

### 2.2    Computational Assumptions

In this section, we review the computational assumptions related to bilinear maps that are relevant to the protocol we discuss.

Let $\mathcal{B} = (p, \mathbb{G}_1, \mathbb{G}_2, \mathbb{G}_T, e(\cdot, \cdot))$ be a bilinear map group system such that $\mathbb{G}_1 = \mathbb{G}_2 = \mathbb{G}$. Let $G_0 \in \mathbb{G}$ be a generator of $\mathbb{G}$, and set $g = e(G_0, G_0) \in \mathbb{G}_T$ .

#### 2.2.1    $l$-Strong Diffie Hellman Problem ($l - SDHP$)
The $l$-Strong Diffie-Hellman problem ($l - SDHP$) in the group $\mathbb{G}$ consists of, given $G_0, sG_0, s^2G_0,$
$\ldots, s^lG_0$, finding a pair $(c, \frac{1}{c+s}G_0)$ with $c \in \mathbb{Z}_p^*$.

**Definition 1.** *The advantage of any probabilistic polynomial time algorithm $\mathcal{A}$ in solving the $l - SDHP$ in $\mathbb{G}$ is defined as $Adv_{\mathcal{A}}^{l-SDHP} = Pr\left[\mathcal{A}(G_0, sG_0, s^2G_0, \ldots, s^lG_0) = (c, \frac{1}{c+s}G_0) \mid c \in \mathbb{Z}_p^*\right]$ The $l$-SDHP Assumption is that, for any probabilistic polynomial time algorithm $\mathcal{A}$, the advantage $Adv_{\mathcal{A}}^{l-SDHP}$ is negligibly small.*

#### 2.2.2    The General Diffie-Hellman Exponent Assumption
We make use of the generalization of the Diffie-Hellman exponent assumption due to Boneh, Boyen and Goh [3]. Let m, n be positive integers and $U, V \in \mathbb{F}_p[X_1, ..., X_n]^m$ be two m-tuples of n-variate polynomials over $\mathbb{F}_p$. Thus, $U$ and $V$ are just two sets containing m multivariate polynomials each. We write $U = (u_1, u_2, ..., u_m)$ and $V = (v_1, v_2, ..., v_m)$ as tuples of polynomials and impose

that $u_1 = v_1 = 1$; that is, the constant polynomials 1. For a set $\Omega$, a function $h : \mathbb{F}_p \rightarrow \Omega$ and vector $(x_1, ..., x_n) \in \mathbb{F}_p^n$, we write

$$h(U(x_1, ..., x_n)) = (h(u_1(x_1, ..., x_n)), ..., h(u_m(x_1, ..., x_n))) \in \Omega^m$$

We use a similar notation for the m-tuple $V$. Let $F \in \mathbb{F}_p[X_1, ..., X_n]$. It is said that $F$ depends on $(U, V)$, which we denote by $F \in \langle U, V \rangle$, when there exists a linear decomposition

$$F = \sum_{1 \leq i, j \leq m} a_{i,j} \cdot u_i \cdot u_j + \sum_{1 \leq i \leq m} b_i \cdot v_i, \quad a_{i,j}, b_i \in \mathbb{Z}_p$$

Let $U, V$ be as above and $F \in \mathbb{F}_p[X_1, ..., X_n]$. The $(U, V, F)$-General Diffie-Hellman Exponent problems are defined as follows.

**Definition 2 ($(U, V, F)$-GDHE).** *Given the tuple*

$$H(x_1, ..., x_n) = \left( [U(x_1, ..., x_n)]G_0, \; g^{V(x_1, ..., x_n)} \right) \in \mathbb{G}^m \times \mathbb{G}_T^m,$$

*$(U, V, F)$-GDHE asks to compute $g^{F(x_1, ..., x_n)}$.*

**Definition 3 ((U, V, F)-GDDHE).** *Given $H(x_1, ..., x_n) \in \mathbb{G}^m \times \mathbb{G}_T^m$ as above and $T \in \mathbb{G}_T$, $(U, V, F)$-GDDHE problem is to decide whether $T = g^{F(x_1, ..., x_n)}$.*

**Definition 4.** *The advantage of any probabilistic polynomial time algorithm $\mathcal{A}$ in solving the $(U, V, F) - GDDHE$ problem in $\mathbb{G}$ is defined as*

$$Adv_{\mathcal{A}}^{(U,V,F)-GDDHE} = |Pr[\mathcal{A}(U, V, F, g^{F(x_1, ..., x_n)}) = 1] - Pr[\mathcal{A}(U, V, F, T) = 1]|$$

*The $(U, V, F)$-GDDHE Assumption is that, for any probabilistic polynomial time algorithm $\mathcal{A}$, the advantage $Adv_{\mathcal{A}}^{(U,V,F)-GDDHE}$ is negligibly small.*

**Complexity Bound in Generic Bilinear Groups.** We state the following upper bound in the framework of the generic group model. We are given oracles to compute the induced group action on $\mathbb{G}, \mathbb{G}_T$, and an oracle to compute a non-degenerate bilinear map $e : \mathbb{G} \times \mathbb{G} \rightarrow \mathbb{G}_T$. We refer to $\mathbb{G}$ as a generic bilinear group. The following theorem gives an upper bound on the advantage of a generic algorithm in solving the decision $(U, V, F) - GDDHE$ problem.

**Theorem 1.** *Let $U, V \in \mathbb{F}_p[X_1, ..., X_n]$ be two m-tuples of n-variate polynomials over $\mathbb{F}_p$ and let $F \in \mathbb{F}_p[X_1, ..., X_n]$. Let $d_U$ (respectively. $d_V, d_F$) denote the maximal degree of elements of $U$ (respectively. of $V$, $F$) and pose $d = max(2d_U, d_V, d_F)$. If $F \notin \langle U, V \rangle$ then for any generic-model adversary $\mathcal{A}$ totaling at most $q$ queries to the oracles (group operations in $\mathbb{G}, \mathbb{G}_T$ and evaluations of $e$) which is given $H(x_1, ..., x_n)$ as input and tries to distinguish $g^{F(x_1, ..., x_n)}$ from a random value in $\mathbb{G}_T$, one has*

$$Adv(\mathcal{A}) \leq \frac{(q + 2m + 2)^2 \cdot d}{2p}$$

We refer to [3] for a proof that $(U, V, F) - GDHE$ and $(U, V, F) - GDDHE$ have generic security when $F \notin \langle U, V \rangle$. In our constructions, the order of the groups $(p)$ that we consider is exponential in the security parameter $\lambda$.

## 2.3   Multi-receiver Identity-Based Signcryption($mIBSC$)

A generic $mIBSC$ for sending a single message to $t$ users consists of the following probabilistic polynomial time algorithms,

- **Setup**$(k, N)$. Given a security parameter $k$ and the size of the maximal set of receivers[3] $N$, the Private Key Generator (PKG) generates the public parameters *params* and master private key $MSK$ of the system.
- **Extract**$(ID, MSK)$. Given an identity $ID$, the PKG computes the corresponding private key $S_{ID}$
- **Signcrypt**$(m, ID_A, ID_1, ID_2, ....ID_t, S_A)$. To send a message $m$ to $(ID_1, ID_2, ....ID_t)$, a user with identity $ID_A$ runs this algorithm to obtain the signcryption $\sigma$ of $m$ from $ID_A$ to $(ID_1, ID_2, ...., ID_t)$.
- **Designcrypt**$(\sigma, ID_A, ID_i, S_i)$. When a user with identity $ID_i$ and private key $S_i$ receives a signcryption $\sigma$, runs this algorithm to obtain either the plain text $m$ or $\perp$ according as whether $\sigma$ is a valid signcryption from identity $ID_A$ to $(ID_1, ID_2, ...., ID_t)$ or not.

## 2.4   Security Model

The notion of semantic security of public key encryption was extended to identity-based signcryption scheme by Malone-Lee in [9]. We describe the security models for *confidentiality* and *unforgeability* below.

### 2.4.1   Confidentiality

The standard notion for confidentiality of $mIBSC$ schemes is *Chosen Ciphertext Security (CCA)* and *Chosen Plaintext Security (CPA)* against Static Adversaries.

A multi-receiver ID-based signcryption scheme is semantically secure against chosen ciphertext attacks (IND-mIBSC-CCA) if no probabilistic polynomial time adversary $\mathcal{A}$ has a non-negligible advantage in the following game.

1. Setup : The adversary $\mathcal{A}$ first outputs the set of target receiver identities $\mathcal{S}^* = \{ID_1^*, ID_2^*, \ldots, ID_t^*\}$ to $\mathcal{R}$. The challenger $\mathcal{R}$ runs the *Setup* algorithm to generate the master public parameters *params* and the master private key $MSK$. $\mathcal{R}$ gives *params* to the adversary $\mathcal{A}$.
2. In the first phase, $\mathcal{A}$ makes polynomially bounded number of queries to the following oracles.
   (a) **Extract Oracle** $(\mathcal{O}_{Extract})$ — $\mathcal{A}$ produces an identity $ID$ and queries for the private key of $ID$. The *Extract Oracle* returns $S_{ID}$ to $\mathcal{A}$ provided $ID \notin \mathcal{S}^*$.

---

[3] This input is optional. Certain specific schemes may not need this input.

(b) **Signcrypt Oracle** ($\mathcal{O}_{Signcrypt}$) — $\mathcal{A}$ produces a message $m$, sender identity $ID_A$ and a list of receiver identities $ID_1, ID_2, \ldots, ID_t$. $\mathcal{R}$ computes the private key $S_A$ by using $Extract(ID_A, MSK)$ and returns to the adversary $\mathcal{A}$, the signcryption $\sigma$ by using $Signcrypt$ $(m, ID_A, ID_1, ID_2, \ldots, ID_t, S_A)$.

(c) **Designcrypt Oracle** ($\mathcal{O}_{Designcrypt}$) — $\mathcal{A}$ produces a sender identity $ID_A$, receiver identity $ID_B$ and a signcryption $\sigma$. The challenger $\mathcal{R}$ computes the private key $S_B$ from $Extract(ID_B, MSK)$, returning the result of $Designcrypt(\sigma, ID_A, ID_B, S_B)$ to $\mathcal{A}$. The result returned is $\perp$ if $\sigma$ is an invalid signcryption from $ID_A$ to $ID_B$.

3. $\mathcal{A}$ produces two messages $m_0$ and $m_1$ of equal length from the message space $\mathcal{M}$ and an arbitrary sender identity $ID_A^*$. The challenger $\mathcal{R}$ flips a coin, sampling a bit $b \leftarrow \{0,1\}$ and computes the challenge signcryption as $\sigma^* = Signcrypt(m_b, ID_A^*, ID_1^*, ID_2^*, \ldots, ID_t^*, S_A^*)$. $\sigma^*$ and returns to $\mathcal{A}$.

4. $\mathcal{A}$ is allowed to make polynomially bounded number of new queries as in Step 2 with the restrictions that it should not query the *Designcryption Oracle* for the designcryption of $\sigma^*$ and the *Extract Oracle* for the private keys corresponding to $\{ID_1^*, ID_2^*, \ldots, ID_t^*\}$, but he is allowed to query the private key of the sender $ID_A^*$.

5. At the end of this game, $\mathcal{A}$ outputs a bit $b'$. $\mathcal{A}$ wins the game if $b' = b$.

We define the advantage of the adversary $\mathcal{A}$ as

$$Adv_{\mathcal{A}}^{mIBSC-CCA} = |Pr[b = b'] - \frac{1}{2}|$$

Note. We analogously define security against chosen plaintext attacks (IND-mIBSC-CPA) by preventing the adversary from issuing Designcryption Queries in the above game.

### 2.4.2 Unforgeability

A signcryption scheme is existentially unforgeable under chosen message attack (EUF-mIBSC-CMA) if no probabilistic polynomial time adversary $\mathcal{A}$ has a non-negligible advantage in the following game.

1. $\mathcal{A}$ first outputs the target sender's identity $ID^*$ on which he would like to generate the forgery. The challenger $\mathcal{R}$ runs the *Setup* algorithm to generate the master public parameters *params* and master private key $MSK$ respectively. $\mathcal{R}$ gives system public parameters *params* to $\mathcal{A}$.

2. The adversary $\mathcal{A}$ makes polynomially bounded number of queries to the oracles as described in Step 2 of the confidentiality game with the constraint that no *Extract* query is made on $ID^*$.

3. Finally $\mathcal{A}$ produces a signcryption $\sigma^*$ from $ID^*$ to $\{ID_i^*\}_{(i=1\,to\,t)}$. $\mathcal{A}$ wins the game if
   - The result of $Designcrypt(\sigma^*, ID_A^*, ID_i^*)$ for some $1 \le i \le t$ results in a valid message $m^*$.
   - No query to $\mathcal{O}_{Signcrypt}$ involved $m^*, ID_A^*$ and any set of receivers.

**Note.** The above definitions for security in the sense of *Confidentiality* and *Unforgeability* only model the case where the adversary is static. We can analogously define security against adaptive adversaries by not posing the restriction of specifying the set that the adversary is going to attack beforehand. Modeling a scheme that is secure against adaptive adversaries is an open problem.

# 3      Multi-receiver Identity-Based Signcryption($mIBSC$) ($m\mathcal{IBSC}$)

In this section, we present a scheme that achieves constant-sized ciphertexts and private keys and prove that it is secure in the random oracle model. The size of the public keys is that of the maximal subset of receivers.

## 3.1      The Scheme

$m\mathcal{IBSC}$ has the following algorithms.

- **Setup**($\lambda, N$) The security parameter of the scheme is $\lambda$ and $N$ is the maximal size of the set of receivers. $\mathbb{G}_1$, $\mathbb{G}_2$ are two groups of prime order $p$, where $|p| = \lambda$. $P$ and $Q$ are generators of $\mathbb{G}_1$ and $e$ is a bilinear map defined as $e : \mathbb{G}_1 \times \mathbb{G}_1 \to \mathbb{G}_2$. Let $n_0$ and $n_1$ denote the number of bits required to represent an identity and a message respectively. Three hash functions $H_1 : \{0,1\}^{n_0} \to \mathbb{Z}_p^*$, $H_2 : \{0,1\}^{n_1} \times \mathbb{G}_2 \to \mathbb{Z}_p^*$, $H_3 : \mathbb{G}_2 \to \{0,1\}^{(n_1)+|\mathbb{G}_1|}$ are used. The PKG chooses $s \in_R \mathbb{Z}_p^*$ and computes $R = sP$ and $g = e(P, Q)$. The public parameters are

$$params = \langle \mathbb{G}_1, \mathbb{G}_2, R, Q, sQ, s^2Q, \ldots, s^NQ, g, e(\cdot, \cdot), H_1, H_2, H_3 \rangle.$$

  The Master Secret Key is

$$MSK = \langle s, P \rangle.$$

- **Extract**($ID, MSK$) The public key and private key of identity $ID$ are $H_1(ID)$ and $S_{ID} = \frac{1}{H_1(ID)+s}P$ respectively.
- **Signcrypt**($m, ID_A, ID_1, ID_2, \ldots, ID_t, S_A$) Suppose $A$ wants to signcrypt a message $m$ to $t$ receivers with identities $ID_1, ID_2, \ldots, ID_t$. User $A$ does the following.
  1. Choose $r$ uniformly and random from $\mathbb{Z}_p^*$
  2. Compute the following.
     (a) $\alpha = g^r$
     (b) $X = -rR$
     (c) $h = H_2(m, \alpha)$
     (d) $Z_A = (r + h) S_A$
     (e) $c = m\|Z_A \oplus H_3(\alpha)$
     (f) $y = \left[\prod_{i=1}^t (s + H_1(ID_i))\right] rQ$

3. The signcryption is $\sigma = \langle c, X, y, \mathcal{L} \rangle$, where $\mathcal{L}$ is the list of receivers who can designcrypt $\sigma$.

- **Designcrypt**$(\sigma, ID_A, ID_i, S_i)$ A receiver with identity $ID_i$ uses his private key $S_i$ to designcrypt $\sigma = \langle c, X, y, \mathcal{L} \rangle$ from $ID_A$ as follows.

  1. Compute the following.

     (a) $\alpha' = \left[ e\left(S_i, y\right) . e\left(X, \frac{1}{s} \left[ \prod_{j=1, j\neq i}^{t} (s + H_1(ID_j)) - \prod_{j=1, j\neq i}^{t} H_1(ID_j) \right] Q \right) \right]^{\frac{1}{\prod_{j=1, j\neq i}^{t} H_1(ID_j)}}$

     (b) $m \| Z'_A = c \oplus H_3(\alpha')$

     (c) $h = H_2(m, \alpha')$

  2. If $\alpha' = e\left(Z'_A, (H_1(ID_A)Q + sQ)\right) g^{-h}$, return $m$. Otherwise, return $\perp$.

**Note :** To compute the expression

$$\frac{1}{s} \left[ \prod_{j=1, j\neq i}^{t} (s + H_1(ID_j)) - \prod_{j=1, j\neq i}^{t} H_1(ID_j) \right] Q$$

the explicit knowledge about the component of the master private key, $s$, is not necessary. The expression $\left[ \prod_{j=1, j\neq i}^{t} (s + H_1(ID_j)) - \prod_{j=1, j\neq i}^{t} H_1(ID_j) \right]$ is a polynomial of degree $(t-1)$ in $s$, without the presence of a constant term, and hence is divisible by $s$. Thus the coefficient expression $\frac{1}{s} \left[ \prod_{j=1, j\neq i}^{t} (s + H_1(ID_j)) - \prod_{j=1, j\neq i}^{t} H_1(ID_j) \right]$ is a polynomial, say $f(s)$, of degree $(t-2)$ in $s$. Since $sQ, s^2 Q, \ldots, s^{(t-2)}Q$ where $t \leq N$, are all available in master public parameters $params$, the required expression $f(s)Q$, can be computed without the explicit knowledge of $s$.

*Correctness.* It is easy to see that the above decryption algorithm is consistent. Indeed, if $\sigma$ is a valid ciphertext to $ID_i$,

$$\beta = e\left(S_i, y\right) . e\left(X, \frac{1}{s}\left[ \prod_{j=1, j\neq i}^{t} (s + H_1(ID_j)) - \prod_{j=1, j\neq i}^{t} H_1(ID_j) \right]Q\right)$$

$$= e\left(P, Q\right)^{r \cdot \left\{ \prod_{j=1, j\neq i}^{t} [s + H_1(ID_j)] - \left[ \prod_{j=1, j\neq i}^{t} (s + H_1(ID_j)) - \prod_{j=1, j\neq i}^{t} H_1(ID_j) \right] \right\}}$$

$$= g^{r \cdot \prod_{j=1, j\neq i}^{t} H_1(ID_j)}$$

*Hence,* $\alpha = \beta^{\frac{1}{\prod_{j=1, j\neq i}^{t} H_1(ID_j)}}$.

### 3.2 Security Properties

**Definition 5** $((U, V, F)-GDDHE)$. *Let* $\mathcal{B} = (p, \mathbb{G}_1, \mathbb{G}_2, e(,))$ *be a bilinear map group system and let* $f$ *and* $g$ *be two coprime polynomials with pairwise distinct roots, of respective orders* $l$ *and* $t$. *Let* $P_0$ *and* $Q_0$ *be generators of* $\mathbb{G}_1$. *Given*

$$\begin{pmatrix} P_0, sP_0, \ldots, s^{l-1}P_0 & s.f(s)P_0, s^2.f(s)P_0, s^3.f(s)P_0 & \gamma.s.f(s)P_0 \\ Q_0, sQ_0, \ldots, s^{N+3}Q_0 & & \gamma.s.g(s)Q_0 \end{pmatrix}$$

*and* $T \in \mathbb{G}_2$, *solving the* $(U, V, F) - GDDHE$ *problem consists of deciding whether* $T$ *is equal to* $e(P_0, Q_0)^{\gamma \cdot f(s)}$ *or is some random element of* $\mathbb{G}_2$.

**Corollary 1 (Generic security of $(U,V,F)$–$GDDHE$).** *For any probabilistic algorithm $\mathcal{A}$ that totalizes of at most $q$ queries to the oracles performing the group operations in $\mathbb{G}_1, \mathbb{G}_2$ and the bilinear map $e(\cdot, \cdot)$,*

$$Adv^{GDDHE}(U,V,F,\mathcal{A}) \leq \frac{(q + 2(l + N + 9) + 2)^2 \cdot d}{2p}$$

*with $d = 2 \cdot max(N + 3, l + 1)$.*

*Proof.* Refer Appendix A.

### 3.2.1  Confidentiality

**Theorem 2.** *Assume that an IND-mIBSC-CCA adversary $\mathcal{A}$ has an advantage $\epsilon$ against mIBSC, asking at most $l$ extraction queries. Then there is an algorithm $\mathcal{R}$ to solve the $(U,V,F) - GDDHE$ problem with advantage*

$$\epsilon' \geq \epsilon/2$$

*Proof.* Both the adversary and the challenger are given as input N, the maximal size of a set of included users $\mathcal{S}$, and $l$ the total number of extraction queries and $q$ the total number of random oracle queries that can be issued by the adversary. Algorithm $\mathcal{R}$ is given as input a group system $\mathcal{B} = (p, \mathbb{G}_1, \mathbb{G}_2, e(,))$, and a $(U,V,F) - GDDHE$ instance in $\mathcal{B}$. We thus have $f$ and $g$, two coprime polynomials with pairwise distinct roots, of respective orders $l$ and $t$ respectively, and

$$\begin{pmatrix} P_0, sP_0, \ldots, s^{l-1}P_0 & s.f(s)P_0, s^2.f(s)P_0, s^3.f(s)P_0 & \gamma.s.f(s)P_0 \\ Q_0, sQ_0, \ldots, s^{N+2}Q_0 & & \gamma.s.g(s)Q_0 \end{pmatrix}$$

and $T \in \mathbb{G}_2$, which is either equal to $e(P_0, Q_0)^{\gamma.f(s)}$ or to some random element of $\mathbb{G}_2$

Notations.

- $f(X) = \prod_{i=1}^{l}(X + x_i)$
- $g(X) = \prod_{i=l+1}^{l+t}(X + x_i)$
- $f_i(x) = \frac{f(x)}{x+x_i}$ for $i \in [1, l]$, which is a polynomial of degree $l - 1$.

**Init Phase:** The adversary A outputs a $t$-set $\mathcal{S}^* = \{ID_1^*, ..., ID_t^*\}$ of identities that he wants to attack.

**Setup Phase:** To generate the system parameters, $\mathcal{R}$ formally sets $P = f(s)P_0$ (i.e. without computing it) and sets

- $Q = Q_0$
- $R = s.f(s)P_0 = sP$
- $g = e(P_0, Q_0)^{f(s)} = e(P, Q)$

$\mathcal{R}$ then defines the Public Key PK as $Q, sQ, s^2Q, \ldots, s^NQ, R, g$. Note $\mathcal{R}$ cannot compute the value of $P$.

**Query phase 1:** At any time the adversary $\mathcal{A}$ can query the following random oracles. To respond to these queries, $\mathcal{R}$ maintains three lists $\mathcal{L}_{H_1}, \mathcal{L}_{H_2}, \mathcal{L}_{H_3}$.

1. $H_1$ Queries: The list $\mathcal{L}_{H_1}$ contains at the beginning: $(*, x_i)_{i=1}^{l}$ $(ID_i, x_i)_{i=l+1}^{l+t}$ (we choose to note $*$ an empty entry in $\mathcal{L}_{H_1}$). When the adversary issues a hash query on identity $ID_i$,
   - If $ID_i$ already appears in the list $\mathcal{L}_{H_1}$, R responds with the corresponding $x_i$.
   - Otherwise, $\mathcal{R}$ picks an $x_i$ for some $(*, x_i)$ in $\mathcal{L}_{H_1}$, returns $H(ID_i) = x_i$, and completes the list with $(ID_i, x_i)$.
2. Extraction query $(ID_i)$: The challenger runs Extract on $ID_i \notin S^*$ and forwards the resulting private key to $\mathcal{A}$. To generate the keys,
   - If $\mathcal{A}$ has already issued a hash query on $ID_i$, then $\mathcal{R}$ uses the corresponding $x_i$ to compute
     $$S_{ID_i} = f_i(s)P_0 = \frac{1}{s+x_i}P$$
   - Otherwise, $\mathcal{R}$ sets $H(ID_i) = x_i$, computes the corresponding $S_{ID_i}$ exactly as above, and completes the list $\mathcal{L}_{H_1}$ for $ID_i$.
3. $H_2$ queries: To respond to these queries $\mathcal{R}$ maintains a list of tuples called the $\mathcal{L}_{H_2}$ list. Each entry in the list is a tuple of the form $(m_i, \alpha_i, h_i)$. Initially the list is empty. To respond to query $(m_i, \alpha_i)$ algorithm $\mathcal{R}$ does the following:
   - If the query $(m_i, \alpha_i)$ already appears in the list in a tuple $(m_i, \alpha_i, h_i)$ then respond with $H_2(m_i, \alpha_i) = h_i$.
   - Otherwise, $\mathcal{R}$ just picks a random $h_i \leftarrow \mathbb{Z}_p^*$ and adds the tuple $(m_i, \alpha_i, h_i)$ to the list
   - It responds to $\mathcal{A}$ with $H_2(m_i, \alpha_i) = h_i$.
4. $H_3$ queries: To respond to these queries $\mathcal{R}$ maintains a list of tuples called the $\mathcal{L}_{H_3}$ list. Each entry in the list is a tuple of the form $(\alpha_i, h_i)$. Initially the list is empty. To respond to query $\alpha_i$ algorithm $\mathcal{R}$ does the following:
   - If the query $\alpha_i$ already appears in the list in a tuple $(\alpha_i, h_i)$ then respond with $H_3(\alpha_i) = h_i$.
   - Otherwise, $\mathcal{R}$ just picks a random $h_i \leftarrow \{0, 1\}^n$ where $n$ is the number of bits in a message and adds the tuple $(\alpha_i, h_i)$ to the list
   - It responds to $\mathcal{A}$ with $H_3(\alpha_i) = h_i$.
5. Signcryption Queries : Of the form $(m, ID_A, ID_1, ID_2, \ldots, ID_n)$ If $ID_A \notin S^*$, $\mathcal{R}$ proceeds as in normal *Signcrypt* algorithm. Otherwise, $\mathcal{R}$ does the following:
   - Picks $r \in_R \mathbb{Z}_p^*$ and sets $Z_A = r.sP$
   - Picks $h \in_R \mathbb{Z}_p^*$
   - Computes $y = r\left(s(x_A + s) - h\right)\prod_{i=1}^{n}(s + x_i)Q$ and $X = r.\left(s(s + x_A) - h\right)sP$
   - Computes $\alpha = e(Z_A, (s + x_A)Q).g^{-h \cdot r}$ and picks a random string $V$ of length same as the message
   - Returns $\langle m \| Z_A \oplus V, X, y \rangle$ and enters the tuples $(m, \alpha, h \cdot r)$ and $(\alpha, V)$ in $\mathcal{L}_2$ and $\mathcal{L}_3$ respectively.

As one can see, the returned ciphertext will pass off as a valid one,

$$e(Z_A, (s + x_A)Q).g^{-h \cdot r} = g^{r \cdot (s(s + x_A) - h)}$$

$$= \beta^{\frac{1}{\prod_{j=1, j \neq i}^{t} H_1(ID_j)}}$$

where $\beta = e(S_i, y).e\left(X, \frac{1}{s}\left[\prod_{j=1, j \neq i}^{n} (s + H_1(ID_j)) - \prod_{j=1, j \neq i}^{n} H_1(ID_j)\right] Q\right)$
and $ID_i = ID_A$.

6. Designcryption Queries : Of the form $(\sigma, ID_A, ID_i)$ $\mathcal{R}$ retrieves $Z_A$ from $\sigma$ and searches $\mathcal{L}_2$ for an entry of the form $(m_j, \alpha_j, h_j)$ and corresponding entry $(\alpha_j, V_j)$ from list $L_3$ that satisfies the following condition,

$$m \| Z_A = c \oplus V_j$$
$$\alpha_j = e(Z_A, H_1(ID_A)Q + sQ) \cdot g^{-h_j}$$

If such an entry is present, $\mathcal{R}$ returns $m_j$. Otherwise, returns $\perp$.

We note that if $\sigma$ is a valid ciphertext, then $h_j$ is the correct value of $H_2(m_j, \alpha_j)$. If $\mathcal{A}$ has queried the $H_2$ oracle for these values, then an entry of the form $(m_j, \alpha_j, h_j)$ will be present in $\mathcal{L}_2$, which $\mathcal{R}$ retrieves. The only other case in which $\mathcal{A}$ produces a valid ciphertext is by correctly guessing the hash value. In a perfect simulation, this ciphertext using the correct guessed value should pass of as a valid one. But in our simulation, this does not happen. However we note that this event occurs only with a probability of $1/p$ which is of the order of $1/2^k$, which is negligible in the security parameter $k$.

**Challenge Phase:** When $\mathcal{A}$ decides that phase 1 is over, he gives two messages $m_0$ and $m_1$ and a sender's identity $ID_A$, algorithm $\mathcal{R}$ sets $\alpha = T$, picks random $c$ and responds with the challenge ciphertext $\sigma^* = \langle c, X, y, \mathcal{L} \rangle$ where $X = r.s.f(s)P_0$, $y = \gamma.s.g(s)Q_0$. Note that if $T = g^\gamma$, then $(X, y)$ is a valid encryption of $\alpha = g^\gamma$, although $\sigma^*$ may not be a valid ciphertext.

**Query phase 2:** The adversary continues to issue queries with the constraint that no extraction query is made on $ID_i$ for $ID_i \in \mathcal{S}^*$

**Guess Phase:** Finally, the adversary A outputs a guess $b$

$\mathcal{R}$ ignores the answer and searches $\mathcal{L}_{H_3}$ for an entry of the form $(T, *)$. If present, $\mathcal{R}$ outputs 1 (indicating that $T = g^\gamma$). Otherwise, $\mathcal{R}$ outputs 0.

We note that if $(X, y)$ is a valid encryption of $T$, then an adversary with a non-negligible advantage in the above game must have issued a $H_3$ query on $T$, in which case an entry of the form $(T, *)$ will be present in $\mathcal{L}_{H_3}$.

$$Adv_{\mathcal{R}}^{GDDHE}(U_3, V_3, F_3) = Pr[b = b' | real] - Pr[b = b' | random]$$
$$= \frac{1}{2} \cdot Adv_{\mathcal{A}}^{mIBSC-CCA}$$

### 3.2.2 Unforgeability

**Theorem 3.** *Assume that an EUF-mIBSC-CMA adversary $\mathcal{A}$ making $l$ extraction queries, $q_{H_i}$ queries to random oracles $H_i$ (i= 1,2,3) and $q_{sc}$ signcryption queries, has an advantage $\epsilon \geq 10(q_{sc} + 1)(q_{sc} + q_{H_2})/2^k$ has an advantage $\epsilon$ against mIBSC. Then there is an algorithm $\mathcal{R}$ to solve the $(l + N) - SDHP$ with advantage*

$$\epsilon' \geq 1/9$$

*Proof.* Let $l$ be the maximum number of extraction queries that can be queried by the adversary $\mathcal{A}$ and $N$ be the maximal size of the receiver set. Algorithm $\mathcal{R}$ takes as input $(Q, sQ, s^2Q, \ldots, s^{l+N}Q)$ and aims to find a pair $(c, \frac{1}{c+s}Q)$. In a setup phase, it builds a generator $G \in \mathbb{G}_1$, such that it knows $l - 1$ pairs $(x_i, \frac{1}{x_i+s}G)$ for $x_1, \ldots, x_{l-1} \in_R \mathbb{Z}_p^*$. To do so,

- It picks $\beta \in_R \mathbb{Z}_p^*$ and sets $P = \beta Q$
- It picks $x_1, x_2, \ldots, x_{l-1} \in_R \mathbb{Z}_p^*$ and expands $f(z) = \prod_{i=1}^{l-1}(z + x_i)$ to obtain $c_0, c_1, \ldots, c_{l-1} \in \mathbb{Z}_p^*$ so that $f(z) = \sum_{i=0}^{l-1} c_i z^i$.
- It sets generators $H = \sum_{i=0}^{l-1} c^i(s^iQ) = f(s)Q$ and $G = \beta H = f(s)P$. It then computes $\sum_{i=1}^{l} c_{i-1}(s^iQ) = sH, s^2H, \ldots, s^NH$ and $g = e(G, H)$ and makes $\langle sG, H, sH, s^2H, s^3H, \ldots, s^NH, g = e(G, H)\rangle$ public.
- For $1 \leq i \leq l - 1$, $\mathcal{R}$ expands $f_i(z) = \frac{f(z)}{(z+x_i)} = \sum_{i=0}^{l-2} d_i z^i$ and $\beta \cdot f_i(s)P = \frac{1}{x_i+s}G$

$\mathcal{A}$ provides $\mathcal{R}$ the target user identity $ID^*$ on which $\mathcal{A}$ would like to generate the forgery. $\mathcal{R}$ is then ready to answer $\mathcal{A}$'s queries along the course of the game. It first initializes a counter $i$ to 1. For simplicity, we assume that queries to $H_1$ are distinct, and that any query involving an identifier $ID$ is preceded by the random oracle query $H_1(ID)$.

1. $H_1$ queries: On input of an identity $ID$ by $\mathcal{A}$, $\mathcal{R}$ returns a random $x^* \in_R \mathbb{Z}_p^*$ if $ID = ID^*$. Otherwise, $\mathcal{R}$ answers $x = x_i$ and increments $i$. $\mathcal{R}$ stores $(ID, x)$ in a list $\mathcal{L}_{H_1}$.
2. $H_2$ queries: To respond to these queries $\mathcal{R}$ maintains a list of tuples called the $\mathcal{L}_{H_2}$ list. Each entry in the list is a tuple of the form $(m_i, \alpha_i, h_i)$. Initially the list is empty. To respond to query $(m_i, \alpha_i)$ algorithm $\mathcal{R}$ does the following:
   - If the query $(m_i, \alpha_i)$ already appears in the list in a tuple $(m_i, \alpha_i, h_i)$ then respond with $H_2(m_i, \alpha_i) = h_i$.
   - Otherwise, $\mathcal{R}$ just picks a random $h_i \leftarrow \mathbb{Z}_p^*$ and adds the tuple $(m_i, \alpha_i, h_i)$ to the list. Also, $\mathcal{R}$ responds to $\mathcal{A}$ with $H_2(m_i, \alpha_i) = h_i$.
3. $H_3$ queries: To respond to these queries $\mathcal{R}$ maintains a list of tuples called the $\mathcal{L}_{H_3}$ list. Each entry in the list is a tuple of the form $(\alpha_i, h_i)$. Initially the list is empty. To respond to query $\alpha_i$ algorithm $\mathcal{R}$ does the following:
   - If the query $\alpha_i$ already appears in the list in a tuple $(\alpha_i, h_i)$ then respond with $H_3(\alpha_i) = h_i$.

- Otherwise, $\mathcal{R}$ just picks a random $h_i \leftarrow \{0,1\}^n$ where $n$ is the number of bits in a message and adds the tuple $(\alpha_i, h_i)$ to the list, $\mathcal{R}$ responds to $\mathcal{A}$ with $H_3(\alpha_i) = h_i$.

4. Key extraction queries on $ID \neq ID^*$: $\mathcal{R}$ recovers the matching pair $(ID, x)$ from $\mathcal{L}_1$ and returns the previously computed $\frac{1}{s+x}G$. Note : No extraction query on $ID^*$ can be made.

5. Signcryption query on $(m, ID_A, ID_1, ID_2, \ldots, ID_n)$: If $ID_A \neq ID^*$, proceed normally as in the *Signcrypt* algorithm. Else, $\mathcal{R}$ does the following
   - Picks $r, h \leftarrow \mathbb{Z}_p^*$ and a random string $V$ of length equal to that of the message.
   - Computes $Z_A = r.G$
   - Computes $y = r(x^* + s - h)\prod_{i=1}^{n}(x_i + s)H$
   - Computes $X = rs(x^* + s - h)G$
   - Computes $\alpha = e(Z_A, (x^* + s)H)g^{-h \cdot r}$
   - Adds the tuple $(h \cdot r, m, \alpha)$ in $\mathcal{L}_2$ and $(V, \alpha)$ in $\mathcal{L}_3$
   - Returns the ciphertext $\langle c = m \| Z_A \oplus V, X, y \rangle$.

   As one can see, the returned ciphertext will pass off as a valid one,

$$e(Z_A, (s + x_A)H).g^{-h \cdot r} = g^{r \cdot (s + x^* - h)}$$
$$= \beta^{\frac{1}{\prod_{j=1, j \neq i}^{t} H_1(ID_j)}}$$

   where $\beta = e(S_i, y).e\left(X, \frac{1}{s}\left[\prod_{j=1, j \neq i}^{n}(s + H_1(ID_j)) - \prod_{j=1, j \neq i}^{n} H_1(ID_j)\right]H\right)$

6. Designcryption Queries : Queries of the form $(\sigma, ID_A, ID_i)$. $\mathcal{R}$ searches $\mathcal{L}_2$ for an entry of the form $(m_j, \alpha_j, h_j)$ and retrieves $Z_A$ from $c = m \| Z_A \oplus \alpha$ and checks whether it satisfies the following condition

$$\alpha_j = e(Z_A, H_1(ID_A)Q + sQ) \cdot g^{-h_j}$$

If such an entry is present, $\mathcal{R}$ returns $m_j$. Otherwise, $\mathcal{R}$ returns $\perp$.

We note that if $\sigma$ is a valid ciphertext, then $h_j$ is the correct value of $H_2(m_j, \alpha_j)$, for some $(m_j, \alpha_j)$. If $\mathcal{A}$ has queried the $H_2$ oracle with these values, then an entry of the form $(m_j, \alpha_j, h_j)$ will be present in $\mathcal{L}_2$, which $\mathcal{R}$ retrieves. The only other case in which $\mathcal{A}$ can produce a valid ciphertext is by correctly guessing the hash value of $(m_j, \alpha_j)$ without querying it. In a perfect simulation, this ciphertext using the correct guessed value should pass of as a valid one. But in our simulation, this does not happen, and we return $\perp$. However we note that this event occurs only with a probability of $1/p$ which is of the order of $1/2^k$, which is negligible in the security parameter $k$.

We are ready to apply the forking lemma that essentially says the following: consider a scheme producing signatures of the form $(M, \alpha, h, Z_A)$, where each of $\alpha, h, Z_A$ corresponds to one of the three moves of a honest-verifier zero-knowledge protocol. In our setting, from a forger $\mathcal{A}$, we build an algorithm $\mathcal{A}'$ that replays $\mathcal{A}$ sufficient number of times to obtain two suitable forgeries $(M^*, \alpha, h_1, Z_1), (M^*, \alpha, h_2, Z_2)$ on $ID^*$. The reduction then works as follows. The simulator $\mathcal{R}$ on obtaining two forgeries $(M^*, \alpha, h_1, Z_1), (M^*, \alpha, h_2, Z_2)$ for the same message $M^*$ and commitment $\alpha$ recovers the pair $(ID^*, x^*)$ from list $\mathcal{L}_1$. If both forgeries satisfy the verification equation, we obtain the relations

$$e(Z_1, Q_{ID^*})e(G, H)^{-h_1} = e(Z_2, Q_{ID^*})e(G, H)^{-h_2}$$

with $Q_{ID^*} = H_1(ID^*)H + sH = (x^* + s)H$. Then, it comes that $e((h_1 - h_2)^{-1}(Z_1 - Z_2), Q_{ID^*}) = e(G, H)$ and hence $T^* = (h_1 - h_2)^{-1}(Z_1 - Z_2) = \frac{1}{w^*+s}G$ From $T^*$, $\mathcal{R}$ first obtains $a_{-1}, a_0, \ldots, a_{l-2}$ for which $\frac{f(z)}{(z+x^*)} = \frac{a_{-1}}{(z+x^*)} + \sum_{i=0}^{l-2} a_i z^i$ and eventually computes

$$\sigma^* = \frac{1}{a_{-1}}\left[T^* - \sum_{i=0}^{l-2} a_i s^i P\right] = \frac{1}{x^* + s}P$$

and $\beta^{-1} \cdot \sigma^* = \frac{1}{x^*+s}Q$ (Since $P = \beta Q$) before returning the pair $(x^*, \frac{1}{x^*+s}Q)$ as the solution to $(l+N) - SDHP$.

We note as in [10], if $Adv_A^{mIBSC} \geq 10(q_{sc}+1)(q_{sc}+q_{H_2})/2^k$, where $l$ extraction queries, $q_{H_i}$ queries to random oracles $H_i$ (i= 1,2,3) and $q_{sc}$ signcryption queries are made, then

$$Adv_{\mathcal{R}}^{(l+N)-SDHP} \geq 1/9$$

## 4    Conclusion

To the best of our knowledge, the only identity-based multi-receiver signcryption schemes reported in literature are [7] and [15]. However, [14] proved [7] insecure and [12] showed security flaws in [15] and provided a fix for the same. Hence the only existing correct scheme in the literature is the scheme reported in [12]. This paper makes a significant improvement over the scheme [12] and hence is by far the best available till date. We also formally prove the security of the new scheme in the sense of confidentiality and unforgeability, based on the $l - SDHP$ and the $GDDHE$ assumptions. The major flaws in all the broken systems are related to the insider security of the schemes. In the scheme proposed we have specifically addressed this issue and designed the scheme with proven insider security.

To our knowledge, no public key multi-receiver encryption scheme is known to resist fully adaptive adversaries. We leave this as an open problem. Another interesting problem would be to design a scheme that is secure under weaker assumptions and achieves efficiency comparable to ours.

## References

1. Baek, J., Steinfeld, R., Zheng, Y.: Formal proofs for the security of signcryption. In: Naccache, D., Paillier, P. (eds.) PKC 2002. LNCS, vol. 2274, pp. 80–98. Springer, Heidelberg (2002)
2. Barreto, P.S.L.M., Libert, B., McCullagh, N., Quisquater, J.-J.: Efficient and provably-secure identity-based signatures and signcryption from bilinear maps. In: Roy, B. (ed.) ASIACRYPT 2005. LNCS, vol. 3788, pp. 515–532. Springer, Heidelberg (2005)

3. Boneh, D., Boyen, X., Goh, E.-J.: Hierarchical identity based encryption with constant size ciphertext. In: Cramer, R. (ed.) EUROCRYPT 2005. LNCS, vol. 3494, pp. 440–456. Springer, Heidelberg (2005)
4. Boneh, D., Franklin, M.k.: Identity-based encryption from the weil pairing. In: Kilian, J. (ed.) CRYPTO 2001. LNCS, vol. 2139, pp. 213–229. Springer, Heidelberg (2001)
5. Chen, L., Malone-Lee, J.: Improved identity-based signcryption. In: Vaudenay, S. (ed.) PKC 2005. LNCS, vol. 3386, pp. 362–379. Springer, Heidelberg (2005)
6. Delerablée, C.: Identity-based broadcast encryption with constant size ciphertexts and private keys. In: Kurosawa, K. (ed.) ASIACRYPT 2007. LNCS, vol. 4833, pp. 200–215. Springer, Heidelberg (2007)
7. Duan, S., Cao, Z.-F.: Efficient and provably secure multi-receiver identity-based signcryption. In: Batten, L.M., Safavi-Naini, R. (eds.) ACISP 2006. LNCS, vol. 4058, pp. 195–206. Springer, Heidelberg (2006)
8. Fiat, A., Naor, M.: Broadcast encryption. In: Stinson, D.R. (ed.) CRYPTO 1993. LNCS, vol. 773, pp. 480–491. Springer, Heidelberg (1994)
9. Malone-Lee, J.: Identity-based signcryption. Cryptology ePrint Archive, Report 2002/098 (2002)
10. Pointcheval, D., Stern, J.: Security arguments for digital signatures and blind signatures. J. Cryptology 13(3), 361–396 (2000)
11. Sakai, R., Furukawa, J.: Identity-based broadcast encryption. Cryptology ePrint Archive, Report 2007/217 (2007), http://eprint.iacr.org/
12. Selvi, S.S.D., Vivek, S.S., Gopalakrishnan, R., Karuturi, N.N., Rangan, C.P.: Cryptanalysis of id-based signcryption scheme for multiple receivers. Cryptology ePrint Archive, Report 2008/238 (2008)
13. Shamir, A.: Identity-based cryptosystems and signature schemes. In: Blakely, G.R., Chaum, D. (eds.) CRYPTO 1984. LNCS, vol. 196, pp. 47–53. Springer, Heidelberg (1985)
14. Tan, C.-H.: On the Security of Provably Secure Multi-Receiver ID-Based Signcryption Scheme. IEICE Transactions on Fundamentals of Electronics, Communications and Computer Sciences E91-A(7), 1836–1838 (2008)
15. Yu, Y., Yang, B., Huang, X., Zhang, M.: Efficient identity-based signcryption scheme for multiple receivers. In: Xiao, B., Yang, L.T., Ma, J., Muller-Schloer, C., Hua, Y. (eds.) ATC 2007. LNCS, vol. 4610, pp. 13–21. Springer, Heidelberg (2007)
16. Zheng, Y.: Digital signcryption or how to achieve cost (Signature & encryption) << cost(Signature) + cost(Encryption). In: Kaliski Jr., B.S. (ed.) CRYPTO 1997. LNCS, vol. 1294, pp. 165–179. Springer, Heidelberg (1997)

# A   Intractability of $(U_i, V_i, F_i) - GDDHE$

In this section, we prove the intractability of distinguishing the two distributions involved in the $(U_i, V_i, F_i) - GDDHE$ problems in the proofs of Theorems 2, 4 and 6.

In order to prove Corollaries 1, 2 and 3, we need to prove the intractability of $(U_i, V_i, F_i) - GDDHE$ problem for $i = 1, 2, 3$ and then subsequently use the result of Theorem 1. We consider the case when $\mathbb{G}_1 = \mathbb{G}_2 = \mathbb{G}$ and thus pose $Q_0 = \beta P_0$ Our problem can be reformulated as $(P, Q, F) - GDHE$ where

$$P = \begin{pmatrix} 1, s, s^2, \ldots, s^{l-1}, & s.f(s), s^2.f(s), s^3.f(s), \gamma.s.f(s) \\ \beta, s.\beta, s^2.\beta. \ldots, s^{N+2}.\beta, \gamma.\beta.g_1(s), \gamma.\beta.g_2(s), \gamma.\beta.g_3(s), \ldots, \gamma.\beta.g_k(s) \end{pmatrix}$$

$$Q = 1$$

$$F = \gamma.\beta.f(s)$$

We have $k = 1, 2$ or $3$ and $deg(g_i) = 1, 3$ or $t$ for Corollaries 1,2 and 3 respectively. Degree of $f$ is $l$. We have to show that $F$ is independent of $(P, Q)$, i.e. that no coefficients $\{a_{i,j}\}_{i,j=1}^n$ and $b_1$ exist such that $F = \sum_{i,j=1}^n a_{i,j} p_i p_j + b_1 q_1$ where the polynomials $p_i$ and $q_1$ are the one listed in $P$ and $Q$ above. By making all possible products of two polynomials from $P$ which are multiples of $\gamma.\beta$, we want to prove that no linear combination among the polynomials from the list $R$ below leads to $F$:

$$R = \begin{pmatrix} \gamma.\beta.s.f(s), \gamma.\beta.s^2.f(s), \gamma.\beta.s^3.f(s), \ldots, \gamma.\beta.s^{N+3}.f(s), \\ \gamma.\beta.g_1(s), \gamma.\beta.s.g_1(s), \ldots, \gamma.\beta.s^{l-1}.g_1(s) \\ \gamma.\beta.g_2(s), \gamma.\beta.s.g_2(s), \ldots, \gamma.\beta.s^{l-1}.g_2(s) \\ \cdots \\ \cdots \\ \cdots \\ \gamma.\beta.g_k(s), \gamma.\beta.s.g_k(s), \ldots, \gamma.\beta.s^{l-1}.g_k(s) \\ \gamma.\beta.s.f(s).g_1(s), \gamma.\beta.s.f(s).g_2(s), \ldots, \gamma.\beta.s.f(s).g_k(s) \\ \gamma.\beta.s^2.f(s).g_1(s), \gamma.\beta.s^2.f(s).g_2(s), \ldots, \gamma.\beta.s^2.f(s).g_k(s) \\ \gamma.\beta.s^3.f(s).g_1(s), \gamma.\beta.s^3.f(s).g_2(s), \ldots, \gamma.\beta.s^3.f(s).g_k(s) \end{pmatrix}$$

Note that the every polynomial on the last three lines can be written as

$$\gamma.\beta.s^j.f(s).g_i(s) = \sum_{i=0}^{i=deg(g_i)} c_i.\gamma.\beta.s^{i+j}f(s)$$

for $j = 1, 2, 3$ and thus as a linear combination of the polynomials from the first line. We therefore simplify the task, by finding a linear combination of the elements of the list $R'$ below, which leads to $f(s)$

$$R' = \begin{pmatrix} s.f(s), s^2.f(s), \ldots, s^{N+3}.f(s), \\ g_1(s), s.g_1(s), \ldots, s^{l-1}g_1(s) \\ g_2(s), s.g_2(s), \ldots, s^{l-1}g_2(s) \\ \cdots \\ \cdots \\ \cdots \\ g_k(s), s.g_k(s), \ldots, s^{l-1}g_k(s) \end{pmatrix}$$

Any linear combination can be written as

$$f(s) = A(s).f(s) + B_1(s)g_1(s) + B_2(s)g_2(s) + \ldots + B_k(s)g_k(s)$$

where $A$ and $B$ are polynomials such that $A(0) = 0$, $deg(A) \leq N + 3$ and $deg(B) \leq l - 1$. Since $f$ and $g_i$ are coprime by assumption, we must have $f/B_i$. Since $deg(f) = l$ and $deg(B_i) \leq l - 1$ this implies $B_i = 0$ for $1 \leq i \leq k$. Hence $A = 1$ which contradicts $A(0) = 0$. Therefore

$$F_i \notin \langle P_i, Q_i \rangle \text{ for i} = 1,2,3.$$

# Universal Designated Verifier Signatures with Threshold-Signers*

Pairat Thorncharoensri, Willy Susilo, and Yi Mu

Centre for Computer and Information Security
School of Computer Science & Software Engineering
University of Wollongong, Australia
{pt78,wsusilo,ymu}@uow.edu.au

**Abstract.** The privacy and anonymity of a signer and the integrity and authenticity of a message are important. Generally, whenever the signer states the authenticity of a message (by producing a signature on that message), the privacy and anonymity of that signer on the respective message will immediately be exposed. Universal Designated Verifier Signature is a cryptographic primitive that is designed to preserve the signer's authenticity together with limiting the signer's privacy. This is obtained by allowing any signature holder to convince a third party that the signature produced by the signer is authentic. In this work, we extend this notion by *controlling* the ability of the signature holder to convince any verifier if and only if the signature holder holds *sufficient* signatures from $n$ signers on the same message. This kind of primitives is very useful in many scenarios. We formalize this notion as a *universal designated verifier signature with threshold-signers* and provide a concrete scheme to realize it.

## 1 Introduction

Consider the following scenario. Alice is a member of the online organization ABC. In order to elevate her status as a premium member, Alice has to show the organization that she has contributed to at least $t$ out of the possible $n$ activities provided by the organization. However, Alice does not want to reveal which $t$ activities that she has chosen due to her privacy. In order to satisfy this scenario, Alice will obtain $t$ different signatures from the activities providers and using these signatures, Alice should be able to convince the organization to get her status elevated.

In this scenario, we require a cryptographic primitive to allow Alice to "accumulate" the signatures from different vendors, and once the threshold $t$ is achieved, then she should be able to convince any third party about this fact without revealing which vendors that have been involved. At the first glance, the primitive seems to be straightforward, but none of the existing primitives in the literature can be used to satisfy this requirement.

---

* This work is partially supported by ARC Linkage Project Grant LP0667899.

T. Takagi and M. Mambo (Eds.): IWSEC 2009, LNCS 5824, pp. 89–109, 2009.

A different related scenario is the multi-level marketing (MLM). A MLM company is willing to reward a distributor based on the point of sale in the organization. When the distributor wants to convince the company in regards to his bonus, the distributor will need to convince the company that he has obtained sufficient points without revealing with identity of the sub-distributors under his domain. Therefore, this statement is required to be deniable.

Another motivating scenario is from the law-suit. When a group of witnesses wants to confirm an information or statement to a judge, their identities must be protected. A lawyer or district attorney will needs to gather the signatures of this convincing statement and then, after receiving sufficient statements, will need to convince the jury.

*Previous Works*

In 1996, Jakobsson, Sako and Impagliazzo introduced the notion of designated verifier signatures, which provides the integrity of a message, and the authenticity, non-repudiation and privacy of signers [12]. In this notion, a signature is equipped with a deniability property that allows the signer to deny the signature. Since a designated verifier signature can always be generated, the designated verifier is the only party that can be convinced of the authenticity of the signature on the message. Many researchers have undertaken further studies on designated verifier signatures areas and the outcomes on various topics include [16,15,18,19,8,28].

A feature that is very close to the requirements in the scenario mentioned earlier is a signature scheme proposed in Asiacrypt 2003 by Steinfeld, Bull, Wang and Pieprzyk [27] called the "Universal Designated-Verifier Signature (UDVS) Scheme". With additional functionality compared to those in an ordinary designated verifier signature scheme, a UDVS scheme introduced a *signature holder*, who is given the privilege of designating the signature to any verifier that is chosen by him/her. Similar to an ordinary designated verifier signature scheme, the UDVS scheme protects the privacy of the original signer, where a designated verifier signature generated by the signature holder is designed to convince only the designated verifier. Then, the first UDVS scheme without random oracle model was proposed by Zhang et al. in [31]. In SCN 2006, Laguillaumie et al. proposed two efficient UDVS schemes in the standard model [14]. A new formal definition for universal designated verifier that avoid delegatability attack was introduced by Huang et al. [9]. The notion of delegatability attack is originally inspired by Lipmaa et al. in ICALP 2005 [19]. The delegatability attack refers to the case where the signer or verifier releases some information without revealing his/her secret key such that a signature holder can generate a designated verifier signature on any message of his choice. They argued that this notion is necessary in many applications such as hypothetical e-voting protocol provided in [19]. For the delegatability of UDVS schemes in [27], they also mentioned in [19].

The notion of ring signatures, which provide the integrity of the message, and the authenticity, non-repudiation and anonymity of the signer, was introduced and formalized by Rivest, Shamir and Tauman in [23]. In this notion, *signer-ambiguity* is a key to achieve the anonymity of the signer. Intuitively, a signer alone (who does not need to cooperate with other signers) can generate a signature that looks as though it has been signed by one of the signers in a ring (a set of signers). Hence, from the verifier's point of view, a ring signature provides authentication of a message by one signer in the ring. Topics concerning ring signatures have been widely studied by many researchers, including [4,29,7,30,2,25,6,21,20]. A feature that is close to the requirements in the above-mentioned application for the terms of multi signers and anonymity is introduced in [4]. Bresson, Stern and Szydlo first formalized the notion of threshold ring signatures in [4]. Similar to ring signature schemes, threshold ring signature schemes support multi-signers, whereas ring signature schemes do not. Many researchers have extended these studies to various areas, including [29,21,20,11,5].

A related notion has been addressed in the primitive called universal designated verifier ring signature by Li and Wang [17]. Their goal is to designate a ring signature to a specific verifier. In general, it seems that this scheme has met the requirement where $t = 1$, however, we stress that the subtleties of the concepts are different. In a universal designated verifier ring signature, a signer generates a ring signature on a message and provides it to a signature holder. A signature holder cannot create the ring signature by himself and also he does not know who actually signed this message (among the signers in the ring). In our scenario, a signature holder knows who signs the message and the signature holder is the one who does not want to reveal the signer identity.

Although the existing primitives in the literature resemble several requirements that we need as stated in the above motivating scenarios, there is *no* single primitive that can be used to capture our requirements entirely. Furthermore, trivial combination among the existing primitives will not provide us with our requirements either. Therefore, we will need to create a new notion to capture these requirements, as we will formalize it as the *universal designated verifier signatures with threshold-signers*.

*Our Contributions*
In this paper, we introduce the notion of universal designated verifier signature with threshold-signers (TS-UDVS) schemes to capture the above requirements. We provide a model of the TS-UDVS scheme and its security notions to capture the integrity of a message, and the authenticity, non-repudiation, privacy and anonymity of the signers. A concrete scheme is also presented, together with proof of its security to show that our scheme is secure in our model. This is the first time this kind of primitive has been introduced into the literature.

*Paper Organization*
The paper is organized as follows. In the next Section, we will review some preliminaries that will be used throughout this paper. The definition of TS-UDVS and its security notations will be described in Sections 3 and 4. We will provide an overview of the building blocks required for constructing our concrete TS-UDVS scheme in Section 5. Next, our TS-UDVS scheme will be given in Section 6. Then, proof of the security of our concrete scheme is described in Section 7. Finally, we conclude the paper.

# 2   Preliminaries

## 2.1   Notation

For the sake of consistency, the following notations will be used throughout the paper. Let PPT denote a probabilistic polynomial-time algorithm. When a PPT algorithm $F$ privately accesses and executes another PPT algorithm $E$, we denote it by $F^{E(\cdot)}(.)$. We denote by $poly(.)$ a deterministic polynomial function. For all polynomials $poly(k)$ and for all sufficiently large $k$, if $q \leq poly(1^k)$ then we say that $q$ is polynomial-time in $k$. We say that a function $f : \mathbb{N} \to \mathbb{R}$ is *negligible* if, for all constant $c > 0$ and for all sufficiently large $n$, $f(n) < \frac{1}{n^c}$. Denote by $l \stackrel{\$}{\leftarrow} L$ the operation of picking $l$ at random from a (finite) set $L$. A collision of a function $h(.)$ refers to the case when there is a message pair $m, n$ of distinct points in its message space such that $h(m) = h(n)$. We denote by $\|$ the concatenation of two strings (or integers).

## 2.2   Bilinear Pairing

Let $\mathbb{G}_1$ and $\mathbb{G}_2$ be cyclic multiplicative groups generated by $g_1$ and $g_2$, respectively. The order of both generators is a prime $p$. Let $\mathbb{G}_T$ be a cyclic multiplicative group with the same order $p$. Let $\hat{e} : \mathbb{G}_1 \times \mathbb{G}_2 \to \mathbb{G}_T$ be a bilinear mapping with the following properties:

1. *Bilinearity:* $\hat{e}(g_1^a, g_2^b) = \hat{e}(g_1, g_2)^{ab}$ for all $g_1 \in \mathbb{G}_1, g_2 \in \mathbb{G}_2$ , $a, b \in \mathbb{Z}_p$.
2. *Non-degeneracy:* There exists $g_1 \in \mathbb{G}_1$ *and* $g_2 \in \mathbb{G}_2$ such that $\hat{e}(g_1, g_2) \neq 1$.
3. *Computability:* There exists an efficient algorithm to compute $\hat{e}(g_1, g_2)$ for all $g_1 \in \mathbb{G}_1$, $g_2 \in \mathbb{G}_2$.

Note that there exists a $\varphi(.)$ function which maps $\mathbb{G}_1$ to $\mathbb{G}_2$ or vice versa in one time unit.

## 2.3   Complexity Assumptions

**Definition 1 (Computation Diffie-Hellman (CDH) Problem).** *Given a 3-tuple $(g, g^x, g^y)$ as input, output $g^{x \cdot y}$. An algorithm $\mathcal{A}$ has the advantage $\epsilon$ in solving the CDH problem if*

$$\Pr\left[\mathcal{A}(g, g^x, g^y) = g^{x \cdot y}\right] \geq \epsilon$$

*where the probability is over the random choice of $x, y \in \mathbb{Z}_q^*$ and the random bits consumed by $\mathcal{A}$.*

**Assumption 1. $(t, \epsilon)$-Computation Diffie-Hellman Assumption**     We say that the $(t, \epsilon)$-CDH assumption holds if no PPT algorithm with time complexity $t(.)$ has the advantage of at least $\epsilon$ in solving the CDH problem.

# 3   Notion of Universal Designated Verifier Signature with Threshold-Signers Schemes (TS-UDVS)

All parties are assumed to comply with a registration protocol with a certificate of authority $CA$ to obtain certificates on their public parameters prior to communications with others. Let $\mathcal{L}$ be a list of all of the signers such that $\mathcal{L} = \{pk_{S_i}\}$ where $i$ is an index of the signer. We give a definition of a universal designated verifier signature with threshold-signers scheme as outlined below.

**Definition 2.** *A universal designated verifier signature with threshold-signers scheme $\Sigma$ is an 7-tuple.*

$$\Sigma = (SKeyGen, Sign, Verify, VKeyGen, TDesignate, DVerify, DSimulate)$$

*such that*

**Signature Scheme Setup :** *A signature scheme comprises three PPT algorithms*
*$(SKeyGen, Sign, Verify)$.*
  - *Signer's Public Parameters and Secret Key Generator ($\Sigma.SKeyGen$):*
    *On input a security parameter $\mathcal{K}$, $\Sigma.SKeyGen$ outputs the secret key $(sk_S)$ and the public parameter ($pk_S$) of the signer. That is $\{pk_S, sk_S\} \leftarrow \Sigma.SKeyGen(1^{\mathcal{K}})$.*
  - *Signature Signing ($\Sigma.Sign$):*
    *On input a signer's secret key $sk_S$, public parameters $pk_S$, and a message $M$, $\Sigma.Sign$ outputs the signer's signature $\sigma$. That is $\sigma \leftarrow \Sigma.Sign(M, sk_S, pk_S)$.*
  - *Signature Verification ($\Sigma.Verify$):*
    *On input the signer's public parameters $pk_S$, a message $M$ and a signature $\sigma$, $\Sigma.Sign$ outputs a verification decision $d \in \{Accept, Reject\}$. That is $d \leftarrow \Sigma.Verify(M, \sigma, pk_S)$.*

**Verifier's Public Parameters and Key Generator ($\Sigma.VKeyGen$):** *On input a security parameter $\mathcal{K}$, $\Sigma.VKeyGen$ outputs the secret key $sk_V$ and the public parameter $pk_V$ of the verifier. That is $\{pk_V, sk_V\} \leftarrow \Sigma.VKeyGen(1^{\mathcal{K}})$.*

**Signature Threshold-Signers Designation ($\Sigma.TDesignate$) :** *Let $t$ denote a number of signers who a signature holder possessed their signatures and $n$ is the total number of signers. On input the verifier's public parameters $pk_V$, the signers' public parameters $pk_{S_1}, ..., pk_{S_n}$, the signers' signatures $\sigma_1, ..., \sigma_t$, and a message $M$, $\Sigma.TDesignate$ outputs a designated verifier signature $\hat{\sigma}$. That is $\hat{\sigma} \leftarrow \Sigma.TDesignate(M, \sigma_1, ..., \sigma_t, pk_V, pk_{S_1}, ..., pk_{S_n})$.*

**Designated Verifier Signature Verification ($\Sigma.DVerify$):** *On input the verifier's public parameters $pk_V$, the signers' public parameters $pk_{S_1}, ..., pk_{S_n}$, a message $M$ and a designated verifier signature $\hat{\sigma}$, $\Sigma.DVerify$ outputs a verification decision $d \in \{Accept, Reject\}$. That is $d \leftarrow \Sigma.DVerify(M, \hat{\sigma}, pk_V, pk_{S_1}, ..., pk_{S_n})$.*

**Simulation of a Designated Verifier Signature ($\Sigma.DSimulate$):** *On input the verifier's public parameters $pk_V$, the verifier's secret key $sk_V$, the signers'* *public parameters $pk_{S_1}, ..., pk_{S_n}$, and a message $M$, $\Sigma.DSimulate$ outputs a designated verifier signature $\bar{\sigma}$ such that $Valid \leftarrow \Sigma.DVerify(M, \bar{\sigma}, pk_V, sk_V, pk_{S_1}, ..., pk_{S_n})$. That is $\bar{\sigma} \leftarrow \Sigma.DSimulate(M, pk_V, sk_V, pk_{S_1}, ..., pk_{S_n})$.*

*For all $\mathcal{K} \in \mathbb{N}$, all $(pk_S, sk_S) \in \Sigma.SKeyGen(1^{\mathcal{K}})$, all $(pk_V, sk_V) \in S.VKeyGen(1^{\mathcal{K}})$ and all messages $M$, $\Sigma$ must satisfy the following properties:*

**Completeness of a Signature:**

$$\forall \sigma \in \Sigma.Sign(M, sk_S, pk_S), \Pr[\Sigma.Verify(M, \sigma, pk_S) = Valid] = 1. \quad (1)$$

**Completeness of a TS-UDVS:**

$$\forall \hat{\sigma} \in \Sigma.TDesignate(M, \sigma_1, ..., \sigma_t, pk_V, pk_{S_1}, ..., pk_{S_n}),$$

$$\Pr[\Sigma.DVerify(M, \hat{\sigma}, pk_V, pk_{S_1}, ..., pk_{S_n}) = Valid] = 1. \quad (2)$$

**Completeness of a Simulated TS-UDVS:**

$$\forall \bar{\sigma} \in \Sigma.DSimulate(M, pk_V, sk_V, pk_{S_1}, ..., pk_{S_n}),$$

$$\Pr[\Sigma.DVerify(M, \bar{\sigma}, pk_V, pk_{S_1}, ..., pk_{S_n}) = Valid] = 1. \quad (3)$$

## 4   Notion of Security

Security notions for universal designated verifier signature with threshold-signers (TS-UDVS) schemes are described in the following subsections. They include unforgeability, non-transferable privacy and anonymity. To model the ability of adversaries in breaking the security of TS-UDVS schemes, the following oracles are required.

$\mathcal{SPO}$ **oracle :** At most $q_{SP}$, $\mathcal{A}$ can make a query for a public key of a signer. In response, $\mathcal{SPO}$ runs the $\Sigma.SKeyGen$ algorithm to generate a secret key $sk_S$ and public parameters $pk_S$ of the signer. $\mathcal{SPO}$ replies to $\mathcal{A}$ with $pk_S$.

$\mathcal{SSO}$ **oracle :** At most $q_{SS}$, $\mathcal{A}$ can make a query for a signature $\sigma$ on its choice of message $M$ under its choice of signer public parameters $pk_S$. In response, $\mathcal{SSO}$ runs the $\Sigma.Sign$ algorithm to generate a signature $\sigma$ on a message $M$ corresponding with $pk_S$. $\mathcal{SSO}$ then returns $\sigma, M$ to $\mathcal{A}$.

$\mathcal{VPO}$ **oracle :** At most $q_{VP}$, $\mathcal{A}$ can make a query for public parameters $pk_V$ of a verifier. In response, $\mathcal{VPO}$ runs the $\Sigma.VKeyGen$ algorithm to generate a secret key $sk_V$ and public parameters $pk_V$ of the verifier. $\mathcal{VPO}$ replies to $\mathcal{A}$ with $pk_V$.

$\mathcal{TPO}$ **oracle :** Let $\mathcal{L} = \{pk_{S_1}, ..., pk_{S_n}\}$ and $\mathcal{T} = \{pk_{S_j}\}$, where $j$ is an index of each signer in a threshold $t$ and $\mathcal{T} \subset \mathcal{L}$. At most $q_{TD}$, $\mathcal{A}$ can make a query for a designated verifier signature $\hat{\sigma}$ on its choice of message $M$ under its choice of a group of signer public parameters $\mathcal{L}$, a group of threshold signer public parameters $\mathcal{T}$ and verifier public parameters $pk_V$. In response, $\mathcal{TPO}$ runs the $\Sigma.TDesignate$ algorithm to generate a designated verifier signature $\hat{\sigma}$ on a message $m$ corresponding with $\mathcal{L}, \mathcal{T}, pk_V$. $\mathcal{TPO}$ then returns $\hat{\sigma}, M$ to $\mathcal{A}$.

$\mathcal{SDO}$ **oracle :** At most $q_{SD}$, under its choice of signer public parameters $pk_{S_1}$, ..., $pk_{S_n}$ and verifier public parameters $pk_V$, $\mathcal{A}$ can make a query for a (simulated) designated verifier signature $\bar{\sigma}$ on its choice of message $M$, where $\bar{\sigma}$ must indeed be generated by the verifier. In response, $\mathcal{SDO}$ runs the $\Sigma.DSimulate$ algorithm to generate a (simulated) designated verifier signature $\bar{\sigma}$ on a message $M$ corresponding with $pk_{S_1}, ..., pk_{S_n}, pk_V$. $\mathcal{SDO}$ then returns $\bar{\sigma}, M$ to $\mathcal{A}$.

$\mathcal{SKO}$ **oracle :** At most $q_{SK}$, $\mathcal{A}$ can make a query for a secret key $sk_S$ (or $sk_V$) corresponding to the public parameters $pk_S$ (or $pk_V$) of the signer (or verifier). $\mathcal{SKO}$ responds to $\mathcal{A}$ with a corresponding secret key $sk_S$ (or $sk_V$).

### 4.1   Unforgeability

In this paper, when we discuss the unforgeability property, we are referring to the "designated verifier unforgeability" in [27,9]. The unforgeability property in [9] provides security against existential unforgeability under an adaptive chosen message and chosen public key attack. It intentionally prevents an attacker corrupted with a signature holder from generating a designated verifier signature $\hat{\sigma}_*$ on a new message $M^*$. Formally, this unforgeability provides an assurance that one with access to a signing oracle, designation oracle, simulated signature oracle, and verification oracles, and with the signer public parameters $pk_S$, should be unable to produce a designated verifier signature on a new message even with arbitrarily choosing the verifier's public parameters $pk_V$ and message $M$ as inputs.

However, for TS-UDVS schemes, unforgeability has a slightly different notion from that in [27,9]. To provide security of unforgeability against insider corruption (up to $t-1$ signers) for TS-UDVS schemes, our unforgeability notion has adapted the notion of unforgeability in the ring signature schemes in [23,2,21,25,29,20,4]. Intuitively, the unforgeability property of TS-UDVS schemes provides security against existential unforgeability under an adaptive chosen message, chosen public key attack and insider corruption. It intentionally prevents an attacker corrupted with $(t-1)$ signers and a signature holder from generating a threshold-signers designated verifier signature $\hat{\sigma}_*$ on a new message $M^*$.

Here, our unforgeability provides assurance that, with access to a signing oracle, threshold-signers designation oracle, and simulated designated verifier signature oracle, and with signer public parameters $pk_{S_1}, ... pk_{S_n}$, arbitrarily chosen verifier's public parameters $pk_V^*$ and the knowledge of $t'$-signer secret keys $sk_{S_1^*}, ..., sk_{S_{t'}^*}$, one should not able to produce a designated verifier signature on a new arbitrarily chosen message $M^*$. Note that $t$ is a threshold, $t'$ is a number of colluded signers and $t' < t$.

We denote by $CM$-$CPK$-$A$ the adaptively chosen message, chosen public key attack and insider corruption. We also denote by $EUF$-$TS$-$UDVS$ the existential unforgeability of the TS-UDVS scheme. Let $\mathcal{A}_{EUF-TS-UDVS}^{CM-CPK-A}$ be the adaptively chosen message and chosen public key adversary and let $\mathcal{F}$ be a simulator. The following game between $\mathcal{F}$ and $\mathcal{A}$ is defined to describe the existential unforgeability of the TS-UDVS scheme: given a choice of messages $M$ and access to oracles $\mathcal{SPO}$, $\mathcal{SSO}$, $\mathcal{VPO}$, $\mathcal{TPO}$, $\mathcal{SDO}$ and $\mathcal{SKO}$, $\mathcal{A}$ arbitrarily make queries to the oracles. At the end of these queries, we assume that $\mathcal{A}$ outputs a forged signature $\hat{\sigma}_*$ on a new message $M^*$ with respect to the public parameters $pk^*_{S_1}, ..., pk^*_{S_n}, pk^*_V$. We say that $\mathcal{A}$ wins the game if:

1. $Accept \leftarrow \Sigma.DVerify(M^*, \hat{\sigma}_*, pk^*_V, pk^*_{S_1}, ..., pk^*_{S_n})$.
2. $pk^*_V$ has never been submitted as the input of a query for a secret key to the $\mathcal{SKO}$ oracle.
3. At least $n - t'$ of the challenge signer public keys have never been submitted as the input of a query for a secret key to the $\mathcal{SKO}$ oracle.
4. For each signer public key, $\mathcal{A}$ never makes a request for a signature on input $M^*, pk^*_{S_i}$ to the $\mathcal{SSO}$ oracle, where $i$ is an index of submitted signer public parameters.
5. $\mathcal{A}$ never makes a request for a designated verifier signature on input $M^*$, $pk^*_{S_1}, ..., pk^*_{S_n}$ to the $\mathcal{TPO}$ oracle.
6. $\mathcal{A}$ never makes a request for a simulated designated verifier signature on input $M^*, pk^*_V$ to the $\mathcal{SDO}$ oracle.

Let $Succ^{CM-CPK-A}_{EUF-TS-UDVS}(.)$ be a success probability function such that $\mathcal{A}^{CM-CPK-A}_{EUF-TS-UDVS}$ wins the above game.

**Definition 3.** *We say that the TS-UDVS scheme is $(t, q_H, q_{SP}, q_{SS}, q_{VP}, q_{TD}, q_{SD}, q_{SK}, \epsilon)$-secure existentially unforgeable under an adaptive chosen message, chosen public key attack and insider corruption if there is no PPT CM-CPK-A adversary $\mathcal{A}^{CM-CPK-A}_{EUF-TS-UDVS}$ such that the success probability $Succ^{CM-CPK-A}_{EUF-TS-UDVS}(k) = \epsilon$ is negligible in $k$, where $\mathcal{A}^{CM-CPK-A}_{EUF-TS-UDVS}$ runs in time at most $t$, makes at most $q_H$, $q_{SP}$, $q_{SS}$, $q_{VP}$, $q_{TD}$, $q_{SD}$, and $q_{SK}$ queries to the random oracles, $\mathcal{SPO}$ oracle, $\mathcal{SSO}$ oracle, $\mathcal{VPO}$ oracle, $\mathcal{TPO}$ oracle, $\mathcal{SDO}$ oracle, and $\mathcal{SKO}$ oracle, respectively.*

### 4.2   Non-transferable Privacy

Building on the non-transferable privacy property in [27,10,9], the non-transferable privacy property for TS-UDVS schemes is required that even one obtains many threshold-signers designated verifier signatures $\hat{\sigma}_1, ..., \hat{\sigma}_q$ on its choice of messages $M \in \{M_1, ..., M_q\}$ designated to the same or different verifiers, where $\hat{\sigma}_1, ..., \hat{\sigma}_q$ are generated by the same signature holder using the same set of signatures $\sigma_1, ..., \sigma_t$, it is hard to convince other party that a signer indeed generated a signature $\hat{\sigma} \in \{\hat{\sigma}_1, ..., \hat{\sigma}_q\}$ on a message $M \in \{M_1, ..., M_q\}$. This intentionally prevents a distinguisher from distinguishing a signer from a (simulated) threshold-signers designated verifier signature $\hat{\sigma}_*$ on any new message $M^*$.

Let $ENT$-$TS$-$UDVS$ denote the existential non-transferable privacy of TS-UDVS scheme. Let $\mathcal{A}^{CM-CPK-A}_{ENT-TS-UDVS}$ be the adaptively chosen message and chosen public key distinguisher and let $\mathcal{F}$ be a simulator. The following experiment between $\mathcal{F}$ and $\mathcal{A}$ is prescribed to demonstrate the existential non-transferable privacy of the TS-UDVS scheme. The experiment is divided into two phases, as described as follows.

1. **Phase** 1 : With any adaptive strategies, $\mathcal{A}$ arbitrarily sends queries to the $\mathcal{SPO}$, $\mathcal{SSO}$, $\mathcal{VPO}$, $\mathcal{TPO}$, $\mathcal{SDO}$ and $\mathcal{SKO}$ oracles. The oracles respond as their design in the prior section.
2. **Challenge** : At the end of the first phase, $\mathcal{A}$ decides to challenge and then outputs $M^*, pk_{S_1}^*, ..., pk_{S_n}^*, pk_V^*$ such that:
   a.  On input $pk_{S_1}^*, ..., pk_{S_n}^*$ and $M^*$, $\mathcal{A}$ never issues a request for a signature to the $\mathcal{SSO}$ oracle.
   b.  On input $pk_{S_1}^*, ..., pk_{S_n}^*$ and $M^*$, $\mathcal{A}$ never issues a request for a designated verifier signature to the $\mathcal{TPO}$ oracle.
   c.  On input $pk_V^*$ and $M^*$, $\mathcal{A}$ never issues a request for a designated verifier signature to the $\mathcal{SDO}$ oracle.
   d.  On input $pk_{S_1}^*, ..., pk_{S_n}^*$, $\mathcal{A}$ never issues a request for a secret key to the $\mathcal{SKO}$ oracle.

   After this, $\mathcal{F}$ chooses a random bit $b \xleftarrow{\$} \{0,1\}$. If $b = 1$ then, on input $pk_{S_1}^*, ..., pk_{S_n}^*$, $pk_V^*$ and $M^*$, $\mathcal{F}$ makes a request for a designated verifier signature to the $\mathcal{TPO}$ oracle and responds to $\mathcal{A}$ with $\hat{\sigma}$ as an output from the $\mathcal{TPO}$ oracle. Otherwise, on input $pk_{S_1}^*, ..., pk_{S_n}^*$, $pk_V^*$ and $M^*$, $\mathcal{F}$ makes a request for a simulated designated verifier signature to the $\mathcal{SDO}$ oracle and responds to $\mathcal{A}$ with $\hat{\sigma}$ as an output from the $\mathcal{SDO}$ oracle.
3. **Phase** 2 : In this phase, $\mathcal{A}$ can return to *Phase* 1 or *Challenge* as many times as it wants. One condition must be met that $\mathcal{A}$ must have at least one set of the challenge $M^*, pk_{S_1}^*, ..., pk_{S_n}^*, pk_V^*$ such that
   a.  $\mathcal{A}$ never submits a request for a signature on input $M^*, pk_{S_1}^*, ..., pk_{S_n}^*$ to the $\mathcal{SSO}$ oracle.
   b.  $\mathcal{A}$ never submits a request for a designated verifier signature on input $M^*, pk_{S_1}^*, ..., pk_{S_n}^*, pk_V^*$ to the $\mathcal{TPO}$ oracle.
   c.  $\mathcal{A}$ never submits a request for a designated verifier signature on input $M^*, pk_V^*$ to the $\mathcal{SDO}$ oracle.
   d.  $\mathcal{A}$ never submits any request for a secret key $sk_{S_i}^*$ corresponding with $pk_{S_i}^*$ to the $\mathcal{SKO}$ oracle, where $i$ is the index and $i \in \{1, ..., n\}$.
4. **Guessing** : On the challenge $M^*, pk_{S_1}^*, ..., pk_{S_n}^*, pk_V^*$, $\mathcal{A}$ finally outputs a guess $b'$. The distinguisher wins the game if $b = b'$.

Let $Succ_{ENT-TS-UDVS}^{CM-CPK-A}(.)$ be the success probability function such that $\mathcal{A}_{ENT-TS-UDVS}^{CM-CPK-A}$ wins the above game.

**Definition 4.** *We say that the TS-UDVS scheme is $(t, q_H, q_{SP}, q_{SS}, q_{VP}, q_{TD}, q_{SD}, q_{SK}, \epsilon)$-secure existentially non-transferable privacy under a chosen message and chosen public key attack if there is no PPT CM-CPK-A distinguisher $\mathcal{A}_{ENT-TS-UDVS}^{CM-CPK-A}$ such that the success probability $Succ_{ENT-TS-UDVS}^{CM-CPK-A}(k) = |\Pr[b = b'] - \Pr[b \neq b']| = \epsilon$ is negligible in $k$, where $\mathcal{A}_{ENT-TS-UDVS}^{CM-CPK-A}$ runs in time at most $t$, makes at most $q_H, q_{SP}, q_{SS}, q_{VP}, q_{TD}, q_{SD}, and q_{SK}$ queries to the random oracles, $\mathcal{SPO}$ oracle, $\mathcal{SSO}$ oracle, $\mathcal{VPO}$ oracle, $\mathcal{TPO}$ oracle, $\mathcal{SDO}$ oracle, and $\mathcal{SKO}$ oracle, respectively.*

### 4.3 Anonymity

We adopt the motivation of the anonymity property from ring signature schemes [23,2,21,25] and threshold ring signature schemes [29,20,4], and adapt their notations to realize the security of anonymity against full key exposure for TS-UDVS schemes. The anonymity property for TS-UDVS schemes requires that even one obtains all secret keys of both signers and verifiers, and reviews many designated verifier signatures $\hat{\sigma}_1, ..., \hat{\sigma}_q$ on its choice of a message $m$ designated to the same or different verifiers, where $\hat{\sigma}_1, ..., \hat{\sigma}_q$ are generated by the same signature holder using the same set of signatures $\sigma_1, ..., \sigma_t$, it is hard to persuade the other party which signer is indeed one of the threshold signers who generated a designated signature $\hat{\sigma} \in \{\hat{\sigma}_1, ..., \hat{\sigma}_q\}$ on a message $M \in \{M_1, ..., M_q\}$.

Let $EA\text{-}TS\text{-}UDVS$ denote the existential anonymity against a full key exposure of a TS-UDVS scheme. Let $\mathcal{A}_{EA-TS-UDVS}^{CM-CPK-A}$ be the adaptively chosen message and chosen public key distinguisher and let $\mathcal{F}$ be a simulator. The following experiment between $\mathcal{F}$ and $\mathcal{A}$ is prescribed to show the existential anonymity against a full key exposure of a TS-UDVS scheme.

1. **Learning** : With any adaptive strategies, $\mathcal{A}$ arbitrarily sends queries to the $\mathcal{SPO}$, $\mathcal{SSO}$, $\mathcal{VPO}$, $\mathcal{TPO}$ and $\mathcal{SDO}$ oracles. The oracles respond according to their design.
2. **Challenge** : Let $\mathcal{L}^* = \{pk_{S_1}^*, ..., pk_{S_n}^*\}$ and $\mathcal{T}^* = \{pk_{S_{j_1}}^*, ..., pk_{S_{j_t}}^*\}$, where $j_1, ..., j_t$ are indexes of signers in a threshold $t$ and $\mathcal{T} \subset \mathcal{L}$. When $\mathcal{A}$ decides to challenge $\mathcal{F}$, it outputs $i_0, i_1, M^*, \mathcal{L}^*, pk_V^*$. In return, $\mathcal{F}$ chooses a random bit $b \xleftarrow{\$} \{0,1\}$. On input $\mathcal{T}^* : pk_{S_{i_b}}^* \in \mathcal{T}^*; pk_{S_{i_{\sim b}}}^* \notin \mathcal{T}^*, \mathcal{L}^*,$ $pk_V^*$ and $M^*$, $\mathcal{F}$ makes a request for a designated verifier signature to the $\mathcal{TPO}$ oracle and responds to $\mathcal{A}$ with $\hat{\sigma}$ as an output from the $\mathcal{TPO}$ oracle.
3. **Guessing** : Now, $\mathcal{A}$ is given access to the $\mathcal{SKO}$ oracles. After this, $\mathcal{A}$ finally outputs a guess $b'$. The distinguisher wins the game if $b = b'$.

Let $Succ_{EA-TS-UDVS}^{CM-CPK-A}(.)$ be the success probability function such that $\mathcal{A}_{EA-TS-UDVS}^{CM-CPK-A}$ wins the above game.

**Definition 5.** *We say that the TS-UDVS scheme is* $(t, q_H, q_{SP}, q_{SS}, q_{VP}, q_{TD},$ $q_{SD}, q_{SK}, \epsilon)$-*secure existentially against a full key exposure attack if there is no PPT CM-CPK-A distinguisher* $\mathcal{A}_{EA-TS-UDVS}^{CM-CPK-A}$ *such that the success probability* $Succ_{EA-TS-UDVS}^{CM-CPK-A}(k) = |\Pr[b = b'] - \Pr[b \neq b']| = \epsilon - t/n$ *is negligible in k, where t is a threshold of n signers,* $\mathcal{A}_{EA-TS-UDVS}^{CM-CPK-A}$ *runs in time at most* **t**, *makes at most* $q_H, q_{SP}, q_{SS}, q_{VP}, q_{TD}, q_{SD}, and q_{SK}$ *queries to the random oracles,* $\mathcal{SPO}$ *oracle,* $\mathcal{SSO}$ *oracle,* $\mathcal{VPO}$ *oracle,* $\mathcal{TPO}$ *oracle,* $\mathcal{SDO}$ *oracle, and* $\mathcal{SKO}$ *oracle, respectively.*

# 5 Cryptographic Tools

## 5.1 Short Signature Scheme

Introduced by Boneh, Lynn and Shacham [3], a (BLS) short signature scheme $\Sigma$ is a triple ($KeyGen$, $Sign$, $Verify$). The definition of this signature scheme can be found in [3]. We elaborate the BLS signature scheme as follows:

$KeyGen$ : Let param $= (p, \hat{e}, g \in \mathbb{G}_1, H, \hat{e} : \mathbb{G}_1 \times \mathbb{G}_1 \rightarrow \mathbb{G}_T)$ be a system parameter. Choose a random secret key $x \in \mathbb{Z}_p$. Let us denote by $X = g^x$ a public key of the signer. Hence, $KeyGen$ returns $pk_S = X$ and $sk_S = x$ as the public key and a private key of the signer, respectively.

$Sign$ : Given a message $M$, $pk_S$ and $sk_S$, $S$ computes $\sigma = H(M)^x$ as a signature on message $M$.

$\Sigma.Verify$ : Given $pk_S$, $\sigma$ and a message $M$, a verifier $V$ checks whether $\hat{e}(\sigma, g) \stackrel{?}{=} \hat{e}(H(M), X)$ holds or not. If not, then it outputs reject. Otherwise, it outputs accept.

## 5.2 Trapdoor Commitment Scheme

A trapdoor commitment scheme $TC$ is a triple ($Setup$, $Tcom$, $Topen$) such that

$Setup(1^{\mathcal{K}})$ is an algorithm that, on input a security parameter $\mathcal{K}$, generates public parameters $pk$ and a trapdoor key $sk$.

$Tcom(pk, M, r)$ is an algorithm that, on input $pk, M, r$, outputs a commitment value $T$.

$Topen(sk, pk, M, M', r)$ is an algorithm that, on input $sk, pk, M, M', r$, outputs $r'$ such that
$$T = Tcom(pk, M, r) = Tcom(pk, M', r').$$

## 5.3 A Concrete Scheme of a Trapdoor Commitment Scheme

The idea of transforming an identification scheme into a trapdoor commitment scheme was presented by Kurosawa and Heng in PKC 2006 [13]. We elaborate the Schnorr trapdoor commitment scheme transformed from the Schnorr identification scheme [24] as follows:

$Setup$ : On input a security parameter $\mathcal{K}$, $Setup$ randomly selects a prime $\alpha$ such that $\alpha \approx poly(1^{\mathcal{K}})$. Next, let $\mathbb{G}_\alpha$ be a multiplicative group order $\alpha$ and then choose a random generator $g_\alpha \in \mathbb{G}_\alpha$ and a random number $y \in \mathbb{Z}_\alpha^*$. Let us denote by param $= (\alpha, g_\alpha)$ the system parameters and by $Y = g_\alpha^y$ a public key. Finally, $Setup$ outputs public parameters $pk = (\text{param}, Y)$ and a secret trapdoor key $sk = y$.

$Tcom$ : On input public parameters $pk$ and two integers $M, r \in \mathbb{Z}_\alpha^*$, $Tcom$ computes an output $T = g_\alpha^r Y^M$. Then, $Tcom$ responds with $T$.

$Topen$ : On input public parameters $pk$, a secret key $sk$ and three integers $M', M, r \in \mathbb{Z}_\alpha^*$, $Topen$ computes $r'$ such that $T = g_\alpha^r Y^M = g_\alpha^{r'} Y^{M'}$. Then, $Topen$ returns $r'$.

We supply the security of the above trapdoor commitment scheme as follows:

**Definition 6.** *We say that a trapdoor commitment scheme $TC$ is secure if, on input pk, it is computationally infeasible to compute $(M, r)$ and $(M', r')$ such that $Tcom(pk, M, r) = Tcom(pk, M', r')$ where $M \neq M'$. [13]*

**Theorem 1.** *The above trapdoor commitment scheme is secure if the discrete logarithm assumption holds.*

*Proof.* The proof can be found in [13].

# 6  Universal Designated Verifier Signature with Threshold-Signers Scheme

## 6.1  Concrete Scheme

In this section, we present our scheme based on the concept outlined above. First, we define some notations. Let $G_1, G_T$ be multiplicative groups of prime order $p$. We denote by $\hat{e} : G_1 \times G_1 \rightarrow G_T$ an efficient computationally bilinear mapping function $\hat{e}$ which maps $G_1$ to $G_T$. Let us denote by $H : \{0,1\}^* \rightarrow G_1$ a random one-way function that maps any string to group $G_1$ and by $h : \{0,1\}^* \rightarrow \mathbb{Z}_p^*$ a collision-resistant hash function. Then, the scheme works as follows:

$\Sigma.SKeyGen$ : On input a security parameter $\mathcal{K}$, a signer $S$ randomly chooses a prime $p \approx poly(1^{\mathcal{K}})$ and a random generator $g \in G_1$. Let param $= (p, \hat{e}, g, H, h)$ denote the system parameters. A private key and the public parameters of the signer are generated as follows. Choose a random integer $x \in \mathbb{Z}_p$. Let us denote by $X = g^x$ a public key of the signer. Hence, $SKeyGen$ returns $pk_S = (\text{param}, X)$ and $sk_S = x$ as the public parameters and a private key of the signer, respectively.

$\Sigma.VKeyGen$ : On input a security parameter $\mathcal{K}$, a verifier $V$ complies with a trapdoor commitment scheme's setup function $Setup(1^{\mathcal{K}})$ to generate $\alpha, g_\alpha$, $Y = g_\alpha^y, sk_V = y$. Let $\bar{h} : \{0,1\}^* \rightarrow \mathbb{Z}_\alpha^*$ denote a collision-resistant hash function selected by $V$. $V$ keeps $sk_V$ as a secret key and then publishes $pk_V = (\text{param} = (\alpha, g_\alpha, \bar{h}), Y)$ as its public parameters. Note that a reader should be reminded that both signer and verifier key generation uses the same security parameter $\mathcal{K}$ and, hence, $|\alpha| = |p|$ and $\alpha \approx p$.

$\Sigma.Sign$ : Given a message $M$, $pk_S$ and $sk_S$, $S$ computes $\sigma = H(M)^x$ as a BLS short signature on message $M$.

$\Sigma.Verify$ : Given $pk_S$, $\sigma$ and a message $M$, a signature holder $SH$ checks whether $\hat{e}(\sigma, g) \overset{?}{=} \hat{e}(H(M), X)$ holds or not. If not, then it outputs reject. Otherwise, it outputs accept.

$TDesignate$ : Let $\mathcal{T}$ be a set of signers where the signature holder holds their signatures and $t$ be a threshold where $t = |\mathcal{T}|$. Let $i$ represent an index of the signer in $\mathcal{L}$ where $\mathcal{T} \subset \mathcal{L}$. Given $pk_V, \sigma_1, ..., \sigma_t, pk_{S_1}, ..., pk_{S_n}$ and a message $M$, $SH$ computes a designated verifier signature $\hat{\sigma}$ on message $M$ as follows:

- First, provide the simulated signature of the signers $pk_{S_i} \in \mathcal{L} \setminus \mathcal{T}$ as follows. Select random integers $z_i, c_i \in \mathbb{Z}_p^*$ and compute

$$Z_i = H(M)^{z_i}, \quad R_i = \hat{e}(Z_i, g)\hat{e}(H(M), X_i)^{c_i}.$$

- Secondly, for the signers $pk_{S_i} \in \mathcal{T}$, compute as follows. Select a random integer $r_i \in \mathbb{Z}_p^*$ and compute $R_i = \hat{e}(H(M), g)^{r_i}$.
- Next, let $\mathcal{R} \overset{def}{=} R_1 || ... || R_n$. Then compute the first part of the designated verifier signature with a verifier public key as follows. Select a random integer $r_V \in \mathbb{Z}_\alpha$ and compute

$$M' \overset{def}{=} M || \mathcal{R} || pk_{S_1} || ... || pk_{S_n}, \quad c_0 = T_V = h(g_\alpha^{r_V} Y^{\bar{h}(M')}).$$

- Finally, from the Shamir's secret sharing techinque [26], let $f$ be a polynomial such that it satisfies the following conditions:

$$deg(f) = n - t \bigwedge f(0) = c_0 \bigwedge \forall i \in \mathcal{L} \setminus \mathcal{T} : f(i) = c_i.$$

Then, for every signer $i \in \mathcal{T}$, compute the rest of the designated verifier signature as follows:

$$c_i = f(i), \quad Z_i = H(M)^{r_i} \cdot \sigma_i^{-c_i}.$$

Therefore, a designated verifier signature $\hat{\sigma}$ is $(\mathcal{L}, f, Z_1, ..., Z_n, r_V)$. Output $\hat{\sigma}$ as a designated verifier signature on message $M$.

DVerify : Given $pk_{S_1}, ..., pk_{S_n}, pk_V, \hat{\sigma}$ and a message $M$, the designated verifier $V$ first computes as follows:

$$\forall i \in \mathcal{L} \bigcup \{0\}, c_i = f(i).$$
$$\mathcal{R} = \hat{e}(Z_1, g)\hat{e}(H(M), X_1)^{c_1} || ... || \hat{e}(Z_n, g)\hat{e}(H(M), X_n)^{c_n}.$$
$$M' = M || \mathcal{R} || pk_{S_1} || ... || pk_{S_n}.$$

Then $V$ checks whether $c_0 \overset{?}{=} h(g_\alpha^{r_V} Y^{\bar{h}(M')})$ holds or not. If not, then it outputs reject. Otherwise, it outputs accept.

DSimulate : On input $sk_V, pk_V, pk_{S_1}, ..., pk_{S_n}$ and a message $M$, $V$ computes as follows:

- First, randomly generate $c_0$ as follows: select a random integer $k', r'_V \in \mathbb{Z}_\alpha$ and compute $c_0 = h(g_\alpha^{r'_V} Y^{k'})$.
- Second, randomly select a polynomial $f$ such that

$$deg(f) = n - t \bigwedge f(0) = c_0.$$

Then, for every signer $i \in \mathcal{L}$, compute $c_i = f(i)$.
- Next, for each signer $pk_{S_i} \in \mathcal{L}$, compute the first part of the designated verifier signature as follows:

$$Z_i \overset{\$}{\leftarrow} \mathbb{G}_1, \quad R_i = \hat{e}(Z_i, g)\hat{e}(H(M), X_i)^{c_i}.$$

– Finally, recompute $r_V$ with the verifier secret key as follows:

$$M' = M||\mathcal{R}||pk_{S_1}||...||pk_{S_n}, \quad r_V = r'_V + y \cdot k' - y \cdot \bar{h}(M').$$

Therefore, a simulated designated verifier signature by the verifier is
$\hat{\sigma} = (\mathcal{L}, f, Z_1, ..., Z_n, r_V)$.

# 7   Security Analysis

## 7.1   Completeness

**Completeness of a Signature and a TS-UDVS:** These are straightforward,
and hence, they are omitted.

**Completeness of a Simulated TS-UDVS:** Given the public parameters of
the signers $\mathcal{L}$, public parameters of the designated verifier $pk_V$, a secret key of
the designated verifier $sk_V$, a message $M$ and a designated verifier signature
$\hat{\sigma}$, one first computes as follows:

$$\forall i \in \mathcal{L}\bigcup\{0\}, c_i = f(i).$$
$$\mathcal{R} = \hat{e}(Z_1, g)\hat{e}(H(M), X_1)^{c_1}||...||\hat{e}(Z_n, g)\hat{e}(H(M), X_n)^{c_n}.$$
$$M' = M||\mathcal{R}||pk_{S_1}||...||pk_{S_n}.$$

Then check $c_0 = h(g_\alpha^{r'_V} Y^{k'}) \overset{?}{=} h(g_\alpha^{r_V} Y^{\bar{h}(M')})$
$$h(g_\alpha^{r'_V} g_\alpha^{y \cdot k'}) \overset{?}{=} h(g_\alpha^{r'_V + y \cdot k' - y \cdot \bar{h}(M')} g_\alpha^{y \cdot \bar{h}(M')})$$
$$h(g_\alpha^{r'_V + y \cdot k'}) \overset{?}{=} h(g_\alpha^{r'_V + y \cdot k'}).$$

Hence, the above statements show that the simulated threshold-signers designated verifier signature does indeed hold.

## 7.2   Unforgeability

**Theorem 2.** *Our universal designated verifier signature with threshold-signers
scheme is existentially unforgeable under an adaptive chosen message, chosen
public key attack and insider corruption if the CDH assumption holds in the
random oracle model.*

*Proof.* Suppose that there exists a forger algorithm $\mathcal{A}$, which runs the existentially unforgeability game defined in Section 4.1, then we will show that there
exists an adversary $\mathcal{F}$ that solves the CDH problem by using $\mathcal{A}$. Start with the
construction oracles as they are designed in Section 4. Then construct $\mathcal{F}$ and run
it over $\mathcal{A}$ with the existentially unforgeability game defined in Section 4.1. Next,
summarize the success probability of the existentially unforgeability game under
an adaptive chosen message, chosen public key attack and insider corruption. Finally, from the existentially unforgeability game and its success probability, we
can draw a conclusion that the success probability of solving the CDH problem
is non-negligible if the success probability of the above game is non-negligible.

We construct the oracles and run the existentially unforgeability game as follows: on input $g$, $g^a$ and $g^b$ as an instance of the CDH problem, $\mathcal{F}$ sets $g^b$ as one of the answers for the hash query to the random oracle. Next, $\mathcal{F}$ sets $X^* = g^{x^*} = g^a$ in one of the signer public parameters defined as $pk_{S^*}$. Our aim is to obtain $g^{ab}$ from running the existentially unforgeability experiment. Assume that there exists an algorithm managing the list of each queries and such algorithm will be omitted. Let $M' = M||\sigma_1||pk_S$ and $\check{M} = M^*||\sigma_1^*||pk_S$. From the above setting, it is easy for $\mathcal{F}$ to construct the $\mathcal{SPO}$, $\mathcal{SSO}$, $\mathcal{VPO}$, $\mathcal{TPO}$, $\mathcal{SDO}$, $\mathcal{SKO}$ and the random oracles $\mathcal{HO}$ as follows:

$\mathcal{HO}$ **oracle :** Select $d \xleftarrow{\$} \{0,1\}$ such that the probability of $d = 1$ is $\frac{1}{q_H}$. If $d = 1$ then set $M = \check{M}$ and $H(M) = g^b$ and return $H(M)$. Otherwise, $k \xleftarrow{\$} \mathbb{Z}_p$; $H(M) = g^k$ and return $H(M)$. Then $\mathcal{HO}$ keeps a pair of $H(M)$ and $k$ in the list, which it is accessible only by $\mathcal{F}$. For a query for $h(M')$, $\mathcal{HO}$ randomly selects $k_1 \xleftarrow{\$} \mathbb{Z}_p$; $h(M') = k_1$ and return $h(M')$.

$\mathcal{SPO}$ **oracle :** Let param $= (p, \hat{e}, h, H, g)$ be the system parameters for each signer. $\mathcal{SPO}$ chooses $\dot{d} \xleftarrow{\$} \{0,1\}$ such that the probability of $\dot{d} = 1$ is $\frac{1}{q_{SP}}$. If $\dot{d} = 1$ then set $X^* = g^a$ and return $pk_S^* = (\text{param}^*, X^*)$. Otherwise, $t \xleftarrow{\$} \mathbb{Z}_p$; $X = g^t$ and then return $pk_S = (\text{param}, X)$ and keep $t$ as a secret key.

$\mathcal{SKO}$ **oracle :** $\mathcal{SKO}$ oracle responds to every query on input $pk_S$ and $pk_V$ with its corresponding secret key. Expect for $pk_S^*$, $\mathcal{SKO}$ outputs $\bot$.

$\mathcal{SSO}$ **oracle :** Let $r_1 \xleftarrow{\$} \mathbb{Z}_p$. On input $pk_S$ and $M$, $\mathcal{SSO}$ outputs $\sigma = H(M)^t$ for every query except when $pk_S = pk_S^*$ and $M = M^*$. In the case of $(pk_S^*, M^*)$, it outputs $\bot$.

$\mathcal{TPO}$ **oracle :** Let $t_i$ be a secret of $i$-th signer in $\mathcal{L}$. On input $\mathcal{L}$, $\mathcal{T}$, $pk_V$ and $M$, where $pk_S^* \notin \mathcal{T}$ and $M \neq \check{M}$, $\mathcal{TPO}$ obtains each signer's secret key $t_i$ of the public parameters in $\mathcal{T}$ from $\mathcal{SPO}$. Then $\mathcal{TPO}$ computes a threshold-signers designated verifier signature as described in $Sign$ and $TDesignate$ in Section 6.1. In the case of $pk_S^* \in \mathcal{T}$ and $M \neq \check{M}$, $\mathcal{F}$ obtains a random integer $k$ associated with $H(M)$ from a list of $H(M)$ and $k$ maintained by $\mathcal{HO}$. $\mathcal{F}$ then gives it to $\mathcal{TPO}$. $\mathcal{TPO}$ computes $\sigma_i = X_i^k$, where $i$ is an index of each signer in $\mathcal{T}$. Then $\mathcal{TPO}$ computes a threshold-signers designated verifier signature as described in $TDesignate$ in Section 6.1. In the case of $pk_S^* \in \mathcal{T}$ and $M = \check{M}$, $\mathcal{TPO}$ outputs $\bot$.

$\mathcal{VPO}$ **and** $\mathcal{SDO}$ **oracles :** These oracles are straightforward as described in Section 4.

Access to the above oracles is provided to $\mathcal{A}$. Assume that a hash of message $M$ from the random oracle $\mathcal{HO}$ is always queried before $\mathcal{A}$ makes a query to the $\mathcal{SSO}$, $\mathcal{TPO}$ and $\mathcal{SDO}$ oracles, or before it outputs a potential forgery, denoted by $(M^*, \hat{\sigma_*}, \mathcal{L}^*, pk_V^*)$.

In the end, after processing an adaptive strategy with the above oracles, $\mathcal{A}$ outputs a forged threshold-signers designated verifier signature $\hat{\sigma_*}$ on a message

$M^*$ with respect to $\mathcal{L}^*, pk_V^*$. $\mathcal{A}$ wins the game if a message $M^*$ is never submitted to the $\mathcal{SSO}$, $\mathcal{TPO}$ and $\mathcal{SDO}$ oracles and at least $n + 1 - t$ signers' secret keys in $\mathcal{L}$ have never been queried to the $\mathcal{SKO}$ oracle. After condutcting the above experiment, we obtain a valid threshold-signers designated verifier signature $\hat{\sigma}_*$ on a message $M^*$ with respect to $\mathcal{L}^*, pk_V^*$. From the above signature, we will first show the probability of success in the next paragraph and then, after running the second experiment, we will demonstrate how to obtain the original signature $\sigma^* = H(\check{M})^{x^*} = (g^b)^a = g^{ab}$, which is also an answer for the CDH problem. Let $e$ denote the base of the natural logarithm and $q$ be a polynomial upper bound on the number of queries that $\mathcal{A}$ makes to the $\mathcal{HO}$ and $\mathcal{SKO}$ oracles. Now the probability of events such that $\mathcal{F}$ does not abort during the simulation is analyzed as follows:

- $E_1$: $\mathcal{F}$ does not abort during the issuing of queries to the $\mathcal{SKO}$.
  The probability of this event is greater than $(1 - \frac{1}{q_{SP}})^{q_{SP}-1} \approx \frac{q_{SP}}{e \cdot (q_{SP}-1)}$.
- $E_2$: $\mathcal{F}$ does not abort when issuing queries to the $\mathcal{SSO}$.
  The fact is that $\mathcal{A}$ needs at least one hash value and one signer secret to output a forgery, and hence, $q_{SS} \leq (q_H - 1) \cdot (q_{SP} - 1)$. Therefore, the probability of this event is greater than $(1 - \frac{1}{q_H \cdot q_{SP}})^{q_{SS}} = (1 - \frac{1}{q_H \cdot q_{SP}})^{(q_H-1) \cdot (q_{SP}-1)} \approx \frac{1}{e} \cdot (\frac{q_H \cdot q_{SP}}{q_H \cdot q_{SP}-1})^{(q_H+q_{SP}-1)}$.
- $E_3$: $\mathcal{F}$ does not abort during the issuing of queries to the $\mathcal{TPO}$.
  Similar to the $E_2$ event, where $q_{TD} \leq (q_H - 1) \cdot (q_{SP} - 1)$, the probability of this event is greater than $(1 - \frac{1}{q_H \cdot q_{SP}})^{q_{TD}} = (1 - \frac{1}{q_H \cdot q_{SP}})^{(q_H-1) \cdot (q_{SP}-1)} \approx \frac{1}{e} \cdot (\frac{q_H \cdot q_{SP}}{q_H \cdot q_{SP}-1})^{(q_H+q_{SP}-1)}$.

Let $Succ_{EUF-TS-UDVS}^{CM-CPK-A} = \epsilon$ be the probability that $\mathcal{A}$ wins the game.

The probability that $\mathcal{A}$ wins the above game and outputs a message $M^*$ and signer public parameters $pk_S^*$ is $\frac{\epsilon}{q_H \cdot q_{SP} - max(q_{TD}, q_{SS})} \leq \frac{\epsilon}{q_H + q_{SP} - 1}$ where $q_{SS} \leq (q_H - 1) \cdot (q_{SP} - 1)$, $q_{TD} \leq (q_H - 1) \cdot (q_{SP} - 1)$, and $q_H$ and $q_{SP}$ are the maximum number of queries that $\mathcal{A}$ made to the random oracle and the $\mathcal{SPO}$ oracle, respectively. Putting the above probabilities together, we resolve the probability such that $\mathcal{F}$ does not abort during the simulation and $\mathcal{A}$ wins the game with $M^*, pk_S^*$ is about $\frac{\epsilon}{q_H + q_{SP} - 1} \cdot \frac{q_{SP}}{e \cdot (q_{SP} - 1)} \cdot (\frac{1}{e} \cdot (\frac{q_H \cdot q_{SP}}{q_H \cdot q_{SP}-1})^{q_H+q_{SP}-1})^2 = \frac{\epsilon}{q_H + q_{SP} - 1} \cdot \frac{q_{SP}}{e^3 \cdot (q_{SP} - 1)} \cdot (\frac{q_H \cdot q_{SP}}{q_H \cdot q_{SP}-1})^{2(q_H+q_{SP}-1)} > \frac{\epsilon}{e^3(q_H+q_{SP}-1)}$.

From the above probability, it is obvious that the probability, where $\mathcal{F}$ successfully runs the above simulation and $\mathcal{A}$ wins the game with $M^* = \check{M}$ and $pk_S^* \in \mathcal{L}^*$, is non-negligible compared with the probability that $\mathcal{A}$ wins the game where $q > (q_H + q_{Sp} - 1)$.

Hence, with a non-negligible running time due to the forking lemma [22,1], $\mathcal{F}$ also obtains another set of forgeries by rerunning the experiment with $\mathcal{A}$ as follows:

- First, reset $\mathcal{A}$ to the initial state.
- Second, provide the same setting as in the previous experiment but with a new set of verifier public parameters.

– Finally, rerun the experiment with the same random tape as the first experiment.

At the end of the second experiment, $\mathcal{F}$, with non-negligible probability, outputs a forgery $(M^*, \hat{\sigma}_{**}, \mathcal{L}^*, pk_V^{**})$. Since the setting is the same as the first experiment, $\mathcal{A}$ outputs $M^*, \mathcal{L}^*$ such that $pk_S^* \in \mathcal{L}^*$ with the same probability as in the first experiment. However, in the second experiment, $\mathcal{A}$ is given with a new set of verifier public parameters, hence, $\mathcal{A}$ outputs $\hat{\sigma}_{**}, pk_V^{**}$ which are different outputs from those in the first experiment.

From the above outputs by $\mathcal{A}$, $\mathcal{F}$ obtains $Z^* = H(\check{M})^{r^*} \cdot \sigma_*^{-c^*}$ and $Z^{**} = H(\check{M})^{r^{**}} \cdot \sigma_{**}^{-c^{**}}$ from $\hat{\sigma}_*, \hat{\sigma}_{**}$, where both $Z^*$ and $Z^{**}$ are associated with $pk_S^*$ and $H(\check{M})$. Since $r^* = r^{**}$, $\mathcal{F}$ computes $\sigma^* = (Z^*/Z^{**})^{1/(c^{**}-c^*)}$. In fact, $\sigma^* = H(\check{M})^{x^*} = (g^b)^a = g^{ab}$. Therefore, $\mathcal{F}$ outputs $\sigma^*$ as an output for the CDH problem with non-negligible probability as mentioned above. The above simulation shows that the probability of success in attacking our TS-UDVS scheme by existentially unforgeability under an adaptive chosen message, chosen public key attack and insider corruption is negligible since the probability of solving the CDH problem is negligible.

### 7.3  Non-transferable Privacy

**Theorem 3.** *In the random oracle model, the proposed universal designated verifier signature with threshold-signers scheme offers existentially non-transferable privacy an against adaptively chosen message and chosen public key distinguisher* $\mathcal{A}_{ENT-TS-UDVS}^{CM-CPK-A}$.

*Proof.* We prove Theorem 3 by running the existentially non-transferable privacy game defined in Section 4.2 and showing that the success probability of distinguisher $\mathcal{A}$ in that game attacking our TS-UDVS scheme is negligible. Start with a construction of oracles and the existentially non-transferable privacy game defined in Section 4.2. Then show that both probabilities of the distribution of the DVS signature generated by the signature holder and designated verifier are equal. We will finally conclude the indistinguishability of both valid or simulated designated verifier signatures in our TS-UDVS scheme.

The following simulation shows that, running on both the signer and the verifier, a simulator $\mathcal{F}$ generates a designated verifier signature which is indistinguishable whether a signer or a verifier indeed generated it. In the first step, since $\mathcal{F}$ can arbitrarily generate a public-secret key pair for $\mathcal{A}$, $\mathcal{F}$ constructs straightforward oracles as described in Section 4. $\mathcal{A}$ is given access to those oracles. Note that for every secret key corresponding to its queried public parameters, $\mathcal{F}$ keeps them secretly to itself.

Then, we analyze the distribution of the $\mathcal{TPO}$ oracle. There is one random integer involved in the production of the signature for each signer, $n - t$ random integers involved in the production of a polynomial function and one random integer involved in the production of the designated verifier signature related to the verifier. Therefore, there are in total $2n - t + 1$ uniformly random numbers used in the generation of the designated verifier signature besides the secret keys of the signers. Let $\hat{\sigma}_{DV}$ denote a designated verifier signature in the distribution of the $\mathcal{TPO}$ oracle. With the above random integers and secret keys of the signer $sk_{S_1}, \ldots, sk_{S_t}$, $\mathcal{F}$ randomly produces the designated verifier signature as described in the $TDesignate$ algorithm in Section 6.1. Hence, since each random integer is selected from $\mathbb{Z}_p^*$ or $\mathbb{G}_1$, if we randomly choose a designated verifier signature $\hat{\sigma}_*$ then the probability that $\hat{\sigma}_*$ is in the distribution of the $\mathcal{TPO}$ oracle is $\Pr[\hat{\sigma}_{DV} = \hat{\sigma}_*] = \frac{1}{p^{(2n-t+1)}}$.

Next, we analyze the distribution of the $\mathcal{SDO}$ oracle. There is one random integer involved in the production of the signature for each signer, $n - t$ random integers involved in the production of a polynomial function. There are also other two random integers ($k', r'_V$) involved in the production of the designated verifier signature signature related to the verifier; however, these two integers work to achieve one output, which is $r_V$. Hence, these are viewed together as one random variable. Therefore, there are in total $2n - t + 1$ uniformly random numbers used in the generation of the simulated designated verifier signature, besides the secret key of the verifier. Let $\hat{\sigma}_{DS}$ denote a designated verifier signature in the distribution of the $\mathcal{SDO}$ oracle. With the above random integers and secret keys of the signer $sk_{S_1}, \ldots, sk_{S_t}$, $\mathcal{F}$ randomly produces the designated verifier signature as described in the $DSimulate$ algorithm in Section 6.1. More precisely, since each random integer is selected from $\mathbb{Z}_p^*$ or $\mathbb{G}_1$, if we randomly choose a designated verifier signature $\hat{\sigma}_*$ then the probability that $\hat{\sigma}_*$ is in the distribution of the $\mathcal{SDO}$ oracle is $\Pr[\hat{\sigma}_{DS} = \hat{\sigma}_*] = \frac{1}{p^{(2n-t+1)}}$.

Finally, the above probabilities claim that one cannot distinguish whether a randomly given valid universal designated verifier signature is generated by the $\mathcal{TPO}$ or $\mathcal{SDO}$ oracles. Hence, our TS-UDVS scheme satisfies the non-transferable privacy property.    □

## 7.4    Anonymity

**Theorem 4.** *With probability at most $t/n + \epsilon$, where $\epsilon$ is negligible, our universal designated verifier signature with threshold-signers scheme offers anonymity against a full key exposer.*

*Proof.* We prove Theorem 4 by showing that the success probability of distinguisher $\mathcal{A}$ attacking our TS-UDVS scheme when running anonymity against the full key exposer game defined in Section 4.3 is negligible, when it excludes $t/n$. The following simulation shows that, running on signers, a simulator $\mathcal{F}$ generates a designated verifier signature that is indistinguishable in which signer is in a list of threshold signers. In the first step, since $\mathcal{F}$ can arbitrarily generate a public-secret key pair for $\mathcal{A}$, $\mathcal{F}$ constructs straightforward oracles as described in Section 4. Except for the $\mathcal{VPO}$ oracle, since $\mathcal{A}$ has taken over control of the verifier, $\mathcal{A}$ can arbitrarily run $VKeyGen$ to generate a public-private key pair for the verifier by itself. Then, $\mathcal{A}$ is given access to those oracles and is run with anonymity against the full key exposer game defined in Section 4.3. Note that for every secret key corresponding to its queried public parameters, $\mathcal{A}$ can arbitrarily issue a request for the signer's secret key to the $\mathcal{SKO}$ oracle.

*Discussion*

First, the polynomial $f$ in the $T Designate$ algorithm in Section 6.1 uniquely outputs $c_0$ and $c_i$, where $i \in \mathcal{T}$. $c_0$ and $c_i$ are uniquely generated by the random oracle and random tapes consumed by $\mathcal{F}$. Therefore, the polynomial $f$ can be considered as a random function selected from the entire polynomials over $GF(p)$ with degree $n - t$. Hence, the distribution of $c_i$, where $i \in \mathcal{T}$, is also uniform over $GF(p)$. Second, for each $Z_j$, where $j \in \mathcal{L}$, a random variable (either $z_j$ or $r_j$) is independently chosen and uniformly distributed over $GF(p)$. Therefore, $Z_j$ is uniformly distributed over $GF(p)$. Finally, we can see that, for a fixed message $M$ and a fixed set of signers' public keys $\mathcal{L}$, there are $p^n$ possible solutions for $\mathcal{F}$ to output $(Z_1, ..., Z_n)$. The possible solutions above are uniformly and independently distributed, hence, it does not matter whether $\mathcal{A}$ possesses unbound computing resources and all the secret keys, and how many participant signers ($t$) there are to generate signatures. To identify any one of the participant signers, advantage over random guessing is negligible.                                    □

## 8    Conclusion

In this paper, we introduced the notion of universal designated verifier signature with threshold-signers schemes to capture the need for the privacy and anonymity of signers and the authenticity of the message produced by signers. A model of a TS-UDVS scheme and its security notions that capture the integrity of the message, and the authenticity, non-repudiation, privacy and anonymity of the signers was also presented. We provided a concrete scheme and its proof of security. We showed that our scheme is secure in our model and in its security notions.

## References

1. Bellare, M., Neven, G.: Multi-signatures in the plain public-key model and a general forking lemma. In: ACM Conference on Computer and Communications Security, pp. 390–399 (2006)
2. Bender, A., Katz, J., Morselli, R.: Ring signatures: Stronger definitions, and constructions without random oracles. In: Halevi, S., Rabin, T. (eds.) TCC 2006. LNCS, vol. 3876, pp. 60–79. Springer, Heidelberg (2006)
3. Boneh, D., Lynn, B., Shacham, H.: Short signatures from the weil pairing. In: Boyd, C. (ed.) ASIACRYPT 2001. LNCS, vol. 2248, pp. 514–532. Springer, Heidelberg (2001)
4. Bresson, E., Stern, J., Szydlo, M.: Threshold ring signatures and applications to ad-hoc groups. In: Yung, M. (ed.) CRYPTO 2002. LNCS, vol. 2442, pp. 465–480. Springer, Heidelberg (2002)
5. Chow, S.S.M., Hui, L.C.K., Yiu, S.M.: Identity based threshold ring signature. In: Park, C.-s., Chee, S. (eds.) ICISC 2004. LNCS, vol. 3506, pp. 218–232. Springer, Heidelberg (2005)

6. Fujisaki, E., Suzuki, K.: Traceable ring signature. In: Okamoto, T., Wang, X. (eds.) PKC 2007. LNCS, vol. 4450, pp. 181–200. Springer, Heidelberg (2007)
7. Herranz, J., Sáez, G.: Forking lemmas for ring signature schemes. In: Johansson, T., Maitra, S. (eds.) INDOCRYPT 2003. LNCS, vol. 2904, pp. 266–279. Springer, Heidelberg (2003)
8. Huang, X., Mu, Y., Susilo, W., Zhang, F.T.: Short designated verifier proxy signature from pairings. In: Enokido, T., Yan, L., Xiao, B., Kim, D.Y., Dai, Y.-S., Yang, L.T. (eds.) EUC-WS 2005. LNCS, vol. 3823, pp. 835–844. Springer, Heidelberg (2005)
9. Huang, X., Susilo, W., Mu, Y., Wu, W.: Universal designated verifier signature without delegatability. In: Ning, P., Qing, S., Li, N. (eds.) ICICS 2006. LNCS, vol. 4307, pp. 479–498. Springer, Heidelberg (2006)
10. Huang, X., Susilo, W., Mu, Y., Wu, W.: Secure universal designated verifier signature without random oracles. Int. J. Inf. Sec. 7(3), 171–183 (2008)
11. Isshiki, T., Tanaka, K.: An $(n-t)$-out-of-$n$ threshold ring signature scheme. In: Boyd, C., González Nieto, J.M. (eds.) ACISP 2005. LNCS, vol. 3574, pp. 406–416. Springer, Heidelberg (2005)
12. Jakobsson, M., Sako, K., Impagliazzo, R.: Designated Verifier Proofs and Their Applications. In: Maurer, U.M. (ed.) EUROCRYPT 1996. LNCS, vol. 1070, pp. 143–154. Springer, Heidelberg (1996)
13. Kurosawa, K., Heng, S.-H.: The power of identification schemes. In: Yung, M., Dodis, Y., Kiayias, A., Malkin, T.G. (eds.) PKC 2006. LNCS, vol. 3958, pp. 364–377. Springer, Heidelberg (2006)
14. Laguillaumie, F., Libert, B., Quisquater, J.-J.: Universal designated verifier signatures without random oracles or non-black box assumptions. In: De Prisco, R., Yung, M. (eds.) SCN 2006. LNCS, vol. 4116, pp. 63–77. Springer, Heidelberg (2006)
15. Laguillaumie, F., Vergnaud, D.: Designated verifier signatures: Anonymity and efficient construction from any bilinear map. In: Blundo, C., Cimato, S. (eds.) SCN 2004. LNCS, vol. 3352, pp. 105–119. Springer, Heidelberg (2005)
16. Laguillaumie, F., Vergnaud, D.: Multi-designated verifiers signatures: anonymity without encryption. Inf. Process. Lett. 102(2-3), 127–132 (2007)
17. Li, J., Wang, Y.: Universal designated verifier ring signature (Proof) without random oracles. In: Zhou, X., Sokolsky, O., Yan, L., Jung, E.-S., Shao, Z., Mu, Y., Lee, D.C., Kim, D.Y., Jeong, Y.-S., Xu, C.-Z. (eds.) EUC Workshops 2006. LNCS, vol. 4097, pp. 332–341. Springer, Heidelberg (2006)
18. Li, Y., Lipmaa, H., Pei, D.: On delegatability of four designated verifier signatures. In: Qing, S., Mao, W., López, J., Wang, G. (eds.) ICICS 2005. LNCS, vol. 3783, pp. 61–71. Springer, Heidelberg (2005)
19. Lipmaa, H., Wang, G., Bao, F.: Designated verifier signature schemes: Attacks, new security notions and a new construction. In: Caires, L., Italiano, G.F., Monteiro, L., Palamidessi, C., Yung, M. (eds.) ICALP 2005. LNCS, vol. 3580, pp. 459–471. Springer, Heidelberg (2005)
20. Liu, J.K., Wei, V.K., Wong, D.S.: A separable threshold ring signature scheme. In: Lim, J.-I., Lee, D.-H. (eds.) ICISC 2003. LNCS, vol. 2971, pp. 12–26. Springer, Heidelberg (2004)
21. Liu, J.K., Wong, D.S.: On the security models of (Threshold) ring signature schemes. In: Park, C.-s., Chee, S. (eds.) ICISC 2004. LNCS, vol. 3506, pp. 204–217. Springer, Heidelberg (2005)
22. Pointcheval, D., Stern, J.: Security arguments for digital signatures and blind signatures. J. Cryptology 13(3), 361–396 (2000)

23. Rivest, R.L., Shamir, A., Tauman, Y.: How to leak a secret. In: Boyd, C. (ed.) ASIACRYPT 2001. LNCS, vol. 2248, pp. 552–565. Springer, Heidelberg (2001)
24. Schnorr, C.-P.: Efficient signature generation by smart cards. J. Cryptology 4(3), 161–174 (1991)
25. Shacham, H., Waters, B.: Efficient ring signatures without random oracles. In: Okamoto, T., Wang, X. (eds.) PKC 2007. LNCS, vol. 4450, pp. 166–180. Springer, Heidelberg (2007)
26. Shamir, A.: How to share a secret. Commun. ACM 22(11), 612–613 (1979)
27. Steinfeld, R., Bull, L., Wang, H., Pieprzyk, J.: Universal designated-verifier signatures. In: Laih, C.-S. (ed.) ASIACRYPT 2003. LNCS, vol. 2894, pp. 523–542. Springer, Heidelberg (2003)
28. Susilo, W., Zhang, F., Mu, Y.: Identity-based strong designated verifier signature schemes. In: Wang, H., Pieprzyk, J., Varadharajan, V. (eds.) ACISP 2004. LNCS, vol. 3108, pp. 313–324. Springer, Heidelberg (2004)
29. Tsang, P.P., Wei, V.K., Chan, T.K., Au, M.H., Liu, J.K., Wong, D.S.: Separable linkable threshold ring signatures. In: Canteaut, A., Viswanathan, K. (eds.) INDOCRYPT 2004. LNCS, vol. 3348, pp. 384–398. Springer, Heidelberg (2004)
30. Zhang, F., Kim, K.: ID-based blind signature and ring signature from pairings. In: Zheng, Y. (ed.) ASIACRYPT 2002. LNCS, vol. 2501, pp. 533–547. Springer, Heidelberg (2002)
31. Zhang, R., Furukawa, J., Imai, H.: Short signature and universal designated verifier signature without random oracles. In: Ioannidis, J., Keromytis, A.D., Yung, M. (eds.) ACNS 2005. LNCS, vol. 3531, pp. 483–498. Springer, Heidelberg (2005)

# Reducing Complexity Assumptions for Oblivious Transfer

K.Y. Cheong and Takeshi Koshiba

Division of Mathematics, Electronics and Informatics,
Graduate School of Science and Engineering, Saitama University
255 Shimo-Okubo, Sakura, Saitama 338-8570, Japan
{kaiyuen,koshiba}@tcs.ics.saitama-u.ac.jp

**Abstract.** Reducing the minimum assumptions needed to construct various cryptographic primitives is an important and interesting task in theoretical cryptography. *Oblivious transfer*, one of the most basic cryptographic building blocks, could be also studied under this scenario. Reducing the minimum assumptions for oblivious transfer seems not an easy task, as there are a few impossibility results under black-box reductions.

Until recently, it is widely believed that oblivious transfer can be constructed with trapdoor permutations. Goldreich pointed out some flaw in the folklore and introduced some enhancement to cope with the flaw. Haitner then revised the enhancement more properly. As a consequence they showed that some additional properties for trapdoor permutations are necessary to construct oblivious transfers. In this paper, we discuss possibilities of basing not on trapdoor permutations but on trapdoor functions in general. We generalize previous results and give an oblivious transfer protocol based on a collection of trapdoor functions with some extra properties with respect to the length-expansion and the pre-image size. We discuss that our reduced assumption is almost minimal and show the necessity for the extra properties.

**Keywords:** oblivious transfer, trapdoor one-way functions.

## 1 Introduction

### 1.1 Oblivious Transfer

*Oblivious Transfer* (OT) is an important two-party cryptographic protocol. The first known OT system was introduced by Rabin [27] in 1981 where a message is received with probability 1/2 and the sender cannot know whether his message reaches the receiver. Prior to this, Wiesner [31] introduced a primitive called multiplexing, which is equivalent to the 1-out-of-2 OT [10] known today, but it was then not seen as a tool in cryptography. In 1985, Even et al. defined the 1-out-of-2 OT [10], where the sender has two secrets $\sigma_0$ and $\sigma_1$ and the receiver can choose one of them in an oblivious manner. That is, the sender cannot know the receiver's choice $i \in \{0, 1\}$ and the receiver cannot know any information

T. Takagi and M. Mambo (Eds.): IWSEC 2009, LNCS 5824, pp. 110–124, 2009.

on $\sigma_{1-i}$. The former property is called *receiver's privacy* and the latter *sender's privacy*. Later, Crépeau [7] showed that Rabin's OT and the 1-out-of-2 OT are equivalent. Furthermore, the more general 1-out-of-$N$ OT (where the sender has $N$ secrets), the more specific 1-out-of-2 *bit* OT (where the secrets are one bit long), are similarly defined and the reductions among the variants of OT have been discussed in the literature, e.g. [2,3,8].

OT protocols are fundamental building blocks of modern cryptography. Most notably, it is known that any multi-party secure computation can be based on OT [22,14]. Various implementations of OT protocols have been proposed, and they are all based on some computational assumptions. As an efficient implementation, Naor and Pinkas has proposed a protocol [24] based on Diffie and Hellman [9] type of problems. More recently, a universally composable [4] OT protocol has been constructed based on a variety of assumptions [25].

## 1.2   Complexity Assumptions of OT

With limited exceptions such as one-time-pad encryption [30] and secret sharing scheme [29], most cryptographic primitives rely on certain computational assumptions. In 1-out-of-2 OT, by simple arguments it can be seen that either sender's privacy or receiver's privacy must be protected by some computational assumptions, where the other party may be protected in the information theoretic sense. The symmetry of 1-out-of-2 bit OT [32] implies that we have the freedom to choose which side to protect in which way when we are given a protocol.

We are interested to know the minimum computational assumptions necessary for building OT. Unavoidably, for each OT protocol proposed, we may have to rely on some unproven computational assumptions for its security. To some extent, this is acceptable, since most cryptographic protocols require the existence of one-way functions [20]. This in particular implies $P \neq NP$, which is unproven.

On the other hand, since it is impossible to avoid all the computational assumptions, we would like to construct protocols based upon as little assumptions as possible. In any cryptographic protocol, less underlying assumptions means more confidence on the security. Therefore, the study of minimum computational assumptions of various cryptographic primitives is an important part in cryptographic research. For example, while one-way permutation is known to imply statistically-hiding commitment [23], this assumption has been reduced in [17]. And finally, Haitner and Reingold [18] recently proved that statistically-hiding commitment can be constructed from any one-way function. That enables us to rely on one-way functions to use zero-knowledge arguments.

The situation for OT is more complicated. From the discussion in [19], it is known that OT can be based on one-way functions if there exists a *witness retrievable compression algorithm* for some type of SAT formulas. But on the other hand, the oracle separation [21] between one-way permutations and OT rules out the possibility of blackbox reductions from OT to one-way functions. In general, it is believed that it will be very difficult, if not impossible, to build OT with one-way functions only.

In the original paper of [10], trapdoor permutations with some extra properties are used to construct OT. In [15], Haitner proposed a similar protocol which in theory reduced the computational assumptions required by [10]. The protocol uses a collection of *dense* trapdoor permutations. In [26], another construction of [10] is made from a new type of trapdoor functions (called *lossy trapdoor functions*) with some specific properties. However, the definition comes rather from concrete problems such as the Diffie-Hellman problem and lattice problems than from the theoretical origin.

In this paper, we focus on two issues. We explore the possibility to further reduce the computational assumptions of OT as stated in [15]. We like to know if trapdoor functions, rather than trapdoor permutations, can be used to construct OT. Also, we investigate the essential properties of trapdoor functions necessary for OT. For example, Bellare et al. showed that many-to-one trapdoor functions with exponential pre-image size can be constructed from one-way functions [1]. This fact says that many-to-one trapdoor functions with polynomial pre-image size may have very different properties from those of super-polynomial pre-image size. It also suggests that OT may not be constructible from many-to-one trapdoor functions with super-polynomial pre-image size.

While public key encryptions can be constructed from many-to-one trapdoor functions with polynomial pre-image size as stated in [1], there exists an oracle separation in [11] between public key encryptions and OT. Thus, it is natural to ask whether OT can be constructed from many-to-one trapdoor functions with polynomial pre-image size.

As the main result of this paper, we show that the protocol of [15] can be improved to make it applicable to *general* trapdoor functions. The permutation property is thus not essential. This possibility is actually discussed in the concluding remarks of [15]. But the trapdoor functions used in our protocol have some extra properties (and restrictions) with respect to pre-image size and length expansion. Consequently, we have an OT construction based on a weaker assumption than the previous results, because a trapdoor permutation is a trapdoor function with strictly single pre-image and zero length expansion. Also, we provide arguments that these extra properties are necessary, and are close to the minimum in blackbox reductions.

## 1.3   Relation to Previous Results

The original paper of [10] for 1-out-of-2 OT opens the discussion for the minimum computational assumptions of OT. In [10], a public key encryption scheme with an extra property is used to construct OT. Stated explicitly, the property is that a valid ciphertext can be uniformly sampled from the plaintext domain. This condition is explained in [15] such that, in general, a trapdoor permutation suffices for OT if it is possible to sample an image of it without knowing the pre-image. The term Enhanced Trapdoor Permutation is used in [12] to represent such a trapdoor permutation.

Following the construction of [10] and discussion of [12], Haitner reduced the assumption further by using a set of dense trapdoor permutations [15]. This essentially establishes the sampling property without requiring it explicitly. This seems to be close to minimal, as [21] shows the impossibility for blackbox reduction from OT to one-way permutations. In this paper, we follow the insights and techniques of [15] to further reduce the computational assumptions such that trapdoor functions, rather than trapdoor permutations, may be used to construct OT. Near the end of [15], the possibility of using trapdoor functions for OT has been considered, but the further assumptions required for such a trapdoor function are not clearly discussed.

Taking the impossibility results implied by [1] and [11], we see that the preimage size and length-expansion of the trapdoor function are vital for OT possibility. Therefore, we consider these issues and try to build OT with what may be regarded as minimum assumptions in this framework.

## 2 Preliminaries

### 2.1 Blackbox Reduction

Our work is about basing OT on a primitive with as few assumptions as possible. We focus on blackbox reductions only, where the primitive used as the building block is treated as a blackbox. This means the protocol only deals with the input and output of the underlying primitive, but not its internal calculations. Most known reductions and impossibility results are based on blackbox reductions. The impossibility results initiated by [21] shows that OT cannot be based on one-way functions in blackbox reductions. In [1] and [11], other impossibility results concerning OT are also shown based on [21]. These results are related to our protocol.

As discussed in [21], blackbox reductions may be divided into fully-blackbox reductions and semi-blackbox reductions. In a fully-blackbox reduction, any adversary who breaks the constructed primitive can be used as a blackbox for another algorithm which breaks the building-block primitive. The semi-blackbox reduction basically does not have this requirement. Therefore, a fully-blackbox reduction seems to imply a closer relation between the constructing and constructed primitives. On the other hand, [28] shows that the difference between fully-blackbox and semi-blackbox reductions is not as great as what may be perceived in [21].

In this paper, we focus on fully-blackbox reductions. Any adversary who breaks our protocol can be used as a blackbox to break the trapdoor function used. In fact, in our OT protocol, only the sender's privacy is protected computationally. The receiver's privacy is protected in information theoretic sense. Therefore it is the sender's privacy that is equivalent to the security of the trapdoor function.

### 2.2 Semi-honest Model

We limit ourselves to the semi-honest model in our OT protocol. In a semi-honest protocol, all parties are assumed to follow the protocol properly, except that they may try to extract extra information from the communications, possibly by performing some computations afterwards. In [12] it is shown that a protocol for semi-honest model can be used to construct an equivalent protocol in the general malicious model, where nothing is assumed about the parties. Moreover, in [16] and [6] it is further shown that such a construction can be done in the blackbox way, where the semi-honest protocol is used as a blackbox.

These known constructions of protocols for the malicious model from the semi-honest model are based on commitment schemes or zero-knowledge proofs. Regarding to complexity assumptions, they also require the existence of one-way functions, which is a rather basic assumption for most cryptographic primitives including OT. Using the combination of these results, we can obtain OT in the general model simply by constructing a semi-honest OT protocol. The use of semi-honest model can simplify both the definition and the construction of OT.

## 2.3   1-out-of-2 Bit OT

In this paper, we consider only the 1-out-of-2 bit OT. It is known that other versions of OT can be constructed using 1-out-of-2 bit OT as building blocks. The sender has two secret bits $(\sigma_0, \sigma_1)$ and the receiver has a choice bit $i$. In the correct output, the receiver will get $\sigma_i$ and not $\sigma_{1-i}$, whereas the sender will get no information about $i$. More formally, let $V_S(\sigma_0, \sigma_1, i)$ and $V_R(\sigma_i, \sigma_{1-i}, i)$ be the random variables for the sender's and receiver's view of the protocol respectively, given the receiver's choice $i$ and the sender's secrets $\sigma_0$ and $\sigma_1$. Note that the notation of $V_R(\sigma_i, \sigma_{1-i}, i)$ is informal because the order of parameters is not fixed. This is not a problem because the receiver always knows $i$ and the order of the other two parameters are decided accordingly. Also, these variables have to exist because we assume the OT protocol is run in a semi-honest way. The privacy properties of OT can then be defined as, for all possible $i$, $\sigma_0$ and $\sigma_1$:

1. *Sender's privacy*: Receiver gains no computational knowledge about $\sigma_{1-i}$. That is, for any probabilistic polynomial time algorithm $M$,

$$|\Pr[M(V_R(\sigma_i, 1, i)) = 1] - \Pr[M(V_R(\sigma_i, 0, i)) = 1]| < neg(n) \qquad (1)$$

where $neg(n)$ stands for a negligible function of $n$.[1]

2. *Receiver's privacy*: Sender gains no computational knowledge about $i$.

$$|\Pr[M(V_S(\sigma_0, \sigma_1, 0)) = 1] - \Pr[M(V_S(\sigma_0, \sigma_1, 1)) = 1]| < neg(n) \qquad (2)$$

for any probabilistic polynomial time algorithm $M$.

The standard definition of OT above requires that both parties are at least protected computationally. Nonetheless, in an OT system, it is known that at most one party's privacy can be perfectly protected in information theoretic sense. In that case, even if the other party is computationally unbounded, the first party's privacy is still maintained.

---

[1]   A negligible function of $n$, denoted by $neg(n)$, is defined as a function of $n$ where $|neg(n)| < |\frac{1}{g(n)}|$ for any polynomial $g(n)$, for large enough $n$.

## 2.4  Weak OT

A Weak OT protocol (WOT) is a relaxed version of OT. The weakness is described by three parameters. In a $(\epsilon_1, \epsilon_2, \epsilon_3)$-WOT, the secret required by the receiver is only guaranteed to pass correctly with a probability no less than $1 - \epsilon_1$. This is called the *correctness* of the protocol. On the other hand, the receiver does not gain more computational advantage about $\sigma_{1-i}$ than $\epsilon_2$, and the sender does not gain more computational advantage about $i$ than $\epsilon_3$. Similar to the normal OT, we have:

1. *Sender's privacy:* For any probabilistic polynomial time algorithm $M$,

$$|\Pr[M(V_R(\sigma_i, 1, i)) = 1] - \Pr[M(V_R(\sigma_i, 0, i)) = 1]| \leq \epsilon_2. \qquad (3)$$

2. *Receiver's privacy:* For any probabilistic polynomial time algorithm $M$,

$$|\Pr[M(V_S(\sigma_0, \sigma_1, 0)) = 1] - \Pr[M(V_S(\sigma_0, \sigma_1, 1)) = 1]| \leq \epsilon_3. \qquad (4)$$

Note that, under our definition, a $(neg(n), neg(n), neg(n))$-WOT is equal to OT.

## 2.5  Pairwise Independent Universal Hash Functions

In this paper we also need a construction called the pairwise independent universal hash function. For a parameter $n$, let there be two sets $L_1 = \{1, 2, \ldots, 2^n\}$ and $L_2 = \{1, 2, \ldots, l\}$ such that $l \leq 2^n$. From [5] it is known that, for any choice of $l$, there exists an efficient family of hash functions $H_n$ with the following properties:

1. Any function $h \in H_n$ has domain $L_1$ and range $L_2$.
2. There exists a polynomial-time algorithm to sample $h \in H_n$ uniformly.
3. There exists a polynomial-time algorithm to evaluate $h(x)$ given $h$ and $x \in L_1$.
4. When $h$ is uniformly sampled, for every distinct $x_1, x_2 \in L_1$ and every $y_1, y_2 \in L_2$,

$$\Pr[h(x_1) = y_1 \wedge h(x_2) = y_2] = \frac{1}{l^2}. \qquad (5)$$

## 3  Trapdoor Functions for OT

In this paper we are constructing OT based on a special type of trapdoor function. We first define the normal trapdoor function, and add some extra restrictions suitable for our purpose. At the same time, we try to minimize the assumptions we make. In general, a collection of (non-injective) trapdoor functions $F$ have the following properties:

1. There exists an efficient algorithm which uniformly selects a function $f_\alpha$ in $F$, represented by $\alpha$, and generates the trapdoor $t$ at the same time.

2. Denote the domain of the function by $D_\alpha$. If $x \in D_\alpha$ then $f_\alpha(x)$ can be computed efficiently.
3. Without the trapdoor $t$, for a uniformly chosen $x \in D_\alpha$, when given $f_\alpha(x)$ it is computationally infeasible to obtain any $x' \in D_\alpha$ such that $f_\alpha(x') = f_\alpha(x)$.
4. For any $x \in D_\alpha$, given $f_\alpha(x)$ and $t$, there exist an efficient algorithm to find one $x' \in D_\alpha$ such that $f_\alpha(x') = f_\alpha(x)$. That is, we can calculate $x' = f_\alpha^{-1}(t, y)$ where $y = f_\alpha(x')$, if in the first place $y = f_\alpha(x)$ for some $x$ in the domain.

In any practical use of such a trapdoor function, we can assume either $D_\alpha = \{0, 1\}^n$ or $D_\alpha \subset \{0, 1\}^n$ for some parameter $n$. The former is called full domain while the latter normally further requires a sampling algorithm for finding elements in $D_\alpha$. For our trapdoor function, the full domain is preferred, but we can relax the assumption a bit, due to the results of [15]. Without loss of generality, $D_\alpha \subset \{0, 1\}^n$. But we also assume that $D_\alpha$ is dense in $\{0, 1\}^n$. This *dense domain assumption* is the first assumption we add to our otherwise general trapdoor function. It means there exist a polynomial $p(n)$ such that, for all $\alpha$, we have

$$\frac{|D_\alpha|}{2^n} > \frac{1}{p(n)}. \tag{6}$$

Next, for all $x \in \{0, 1\}^n$ we assume $f_\alpha(x)$ can be evaluated in general using the same algorithm evaluating the function, and the algorithm will halt in polynomial time, producing some output. In practice, this has to be justified by adding a measure which terminates the algorithm when the running time exceeds some fixed value, and gives a default output. That is, even if $x \notin D_\alpha$ the algorithm will still run and produce a string as output. The definition of $f_\alpha(x)$ is extended to handle any $x \in \{0, 1\}^n$. As we do not assume we can detect $x \notin D_\alpha$, nothing is assumed about the output string in this case.

In the same way, for all $x \in D_\alpha$ we assume $f_\alpha(x) \in \{0, 1\}^m$ for some fixed $m$. And for all $y \in \{0, 1\}^m$, we assume the function $f_\alpha^{-1}(t, y)$ can be evaluated using the same algorithm evaluating the inverse function, and the algorithm will halt in polynomial time, producing some output. In other words, the definition of $f_\alpha^{-1}(t, y)$ is extended for all $y \in \{0, 1\}^m$.

## 3.1   Extra Assumptions

In order to construct our OT protocol, we require the trapdoor functions to have a few more properties. We call them the Extra Assumptions, in order to distinguish our trapdoor functions from the general ones.

1. *Pre-image assumption*: For any $\alpha$, when $x \in D_\alpha$ and $y = f_\alpha(x)$, the number of pre-images of $y$ is bounded by a polynomial. That is, there exists a polynomial $q_1(n)$ such that, for all $\alpha$ and $y$,

$$I_{\alpha,y} = \{x \in D_\alpha : f_\alpha(x) = y\} \tag{7}$$
$$|I_{\alpha,y}| \leq q_1(n). \tag{8}$$

2. *Expansion assumption*: For $x \in D_\alpha$ we have $f_\alpha(x) \in \{0,1\}^m$ with $m = n + \log q_2(n)$ where $q_2(n)$ is a polynomial in $n$. That is equal to saying that the expansion (in terms of the length of strings) of the function is in $O(\log n)$.

## 3.2   Necessity of the Extra Assumptions

We clarify that our aim is to define a general set of trapdoor functions with specific restrictions, such that any trapdoor functions meeting these restrictions can be used to construct OT. Therefore, when we investigate a particular set of such restrictions, one single counterexample of OT impossibility under a trapdoor function meeting these restrictions suffices to indicate that the set of restrictions in question is not tight enough. The counterexamples can be specially designed for this purpose, and may only exist theoretically.

To see the necessity of the Extra Assumptions, first look at the pre-image assumption due to [1], where non-injective trapdoor functions are studied. The following trapdoor function with exponential pre-image size can be blackbox constructed from a one-way permutation.

1. A one-way permutation $f_1(x)$ is given for $x \in \{0,1\}^n$.
2. Choose a trapdoor value $t \in \{0,1\}^n$. Let $\alpha = f_1(t)$. For $v, u, x \in \{0,1\}^n$ we define

$$f_2(v, u, x) = \begin{cases} v & \text{if } f_1(u) = \alpha \\ f_1(x) & \text{otherwise.} \end{cases} \tag{9}$$

3. This is a trapdoor function in the sense that, if $t$ is known, we can calculate from an image $y$ a value $(y, t, x)$ as a pre-image, using any $x$. The function $f_2$ is also one-way because when $t$ is unknown, its inversion requires the inversion of $f_1$ on either $y$ or $\alpha$.

On the other hand, it is known that no OT (including semi-honest model) can be blackbox reduced to one-way permutation [21]. This implies that semi-honest OT cannot be blackbox constructed from a trapdoor function with exponential pre-image size.

The expansion assumption is related to [11], which shows an example of a trapdoor function with linear length expansion. Arguments are presented relative to a world with a PSPACE-complete oracle. The following random (oracle) functions are constructed as the only source of computational hardness, but OT does not exist in this world. This implies that OT cannot be blackbox constructed from any such functions in the real world.

1. $\alpha = f_3(t)$ is a uniformly distributed, length-tripling function. It generates an identifier $\alpha$ by inputting trapdoor $t$, an arbitrary string, to the function.
2. $y = f_4(x, r, \alpha)$ is an injective, uniformly distributed, length-tripling function on the set of valid inputs. Input $\alpha$ is valid if there exists $t$ such that $\alpha = f_3(t)$. Also, $x$ and $r$ are valid if $|x| = |r| = |t|$. On any invalid input the function outputs $\perp$.
3. $f_5$ is a function basically for inverting $f_4$, such that $x = f_5(y, t)$ whenever $y = f_4(x, r, f_3(t))$ for some $(x, r)$. There is at most one such $x$, as $f_4$ is injective. When there is no such $x$, $f_5(y, t) = \perp$.

An injective trapdoor function can be based on $f_4$ simply by fixing $r = 0$ all the time. It is length-expanding in $O(n)$. The length-expanding property of this trapdoor function makes it difficult to sample valid images of the function without knowing the pre-image. This is one main reason why OT cannot be based on it.

Note that in these two examples of OT impossibility, the trapdoor function with exponential pre-image size is not length-expanding, and the length-expanding trapdoor function is injective, as shown above. That means in our trapdoor function for OT possibility, both the pre-image assumption and the expansion assumption are required at the same time.

Moreover, our trapdoor function $f_2$ with exponential pre-image size is a full domain trapdoor function, as it takes any string (in the right format) as input. The length-expanding trapdoor function $f_4$ also has a full domain as we only consider $x$ as the input. This further shows the necessity of the pre-image assumption and the expansion assumption, regardless of the dense domain assumption.

On the other hand, we do not rule out OT possibilities based on other assumptions. For instance, in [11] it is implied that if $\alpha$ can be sampled independent of $t$, then OT may be based on such a trapdoor function, regardless of length expansion. Although we do not see it as a minimal assumption in general, this assumption is indeed rather independent of ours.

We also note that there is still space between our construction and the known impossibility results, for both the pre-image assumption and the expansion assumption. A possible gap between super-polynomial and exponential functions is neglected up to this point. For pre-image size, while impossibility results are known for the exponential, our construction is for the polynomial. Similarly, for length expansion, while impossibility results are for the linear, our construction is for the logarithm of polynomial. In this sense, we say that our Extra Assumptions are close, but may not be equal to the real minimum.

## 4    The Protocol

We point out that the construction of our OT protocol is mostly same as [15]. Every step is basically the same, while there are some modifications only due to the differences of the trapdoor functions involved. A semi-honest WOT protocol is first constructed. After that, the process to enhance it to a semi-honest OT is exactly the same as [15].

First of all, we select a collection of pairwise independent universal hash functions $H_n$ with domain $\{0,1\}^n$ and range $\{1, 2, \ldots, g(n)p(n)q_1(n)\}$ where $g(n) > 1$ is a relatively large polynomial of our choice. The actual choice of $g(n)$ is related to the WOT parameters and will be discussed later. The sender has secret bits $(\sigma_0, \sigma_1)$ and the receiver has the choice bit $i$. The protocol is:

1. The sender uniformly selects a trapdoor function $(\alpha, t)$ and a hash function $h \in H_n$.
2. The sender sends $(h, \alpha)$ to the receiver.

3. The receiver selects uniformly $s \in \{0,1\}^n$ and calculates $f_\alpha(s)$. If $f_\alpha(s) \notin \{0,1\}^m$ another $s$ is selected iteratively until $f_\alpha(s) \in \{0,1\}^m$. After that the receiver sets $r_i = f_\alpha(s)$ and selects uniformly $r_{1-i} \in \{0,1\}^m$ where $r_i \neq r_{1-i}$.
4. The receiver sends $\{r_0, r_1\}$ in random order to the sender.
5. Not knowing the order of $\{r_0, r_1\}$, for both $j = 0,1$ the sender checks that the following conditions are satisfied.

$$f_\alpha^{-1}(t, r_j) \in \{0,1\}^n \tag{10}$$
$$f_\alpha(f_\alpha^{-1}(t, r_j)) = r_j. \tag{11}$$

If the answer is negative, the sender aborts the current iteration and restarts the protocol. Otherwise the protocol continues with the sender setting for $j = 0,1$

$$v_j = h(f_\alpha^{-1}(t, r_j)). \tag{12}$$

6. The sender sends $\{v_0, v_1\}$ in the same order as he received $\{r_0, r_1\}$ from the receiver before.
7. Receiver checks that $v_i = h(s)$. If the result is negative, the current iteration aborts and the protocol is restarted. Otherwise, the receiver reveals the true order of $(r_0, r_1)$ to the sender. From here, both $r_0$ and $r_1$ are thought to be good candidates as the keys in the OT protocol. The receiver is thought to know the pre-image of exactly one of them, whereas the sender does not know which one.
8. For both $j = 0,1$ the sender chooses $z_j \in \{0,1\}^n$ uniformly and sets

$$c_j = \sigma_j \oplus b(f_\alpha^{-1}(t, r_j), z_j) \tag{13}$$

where $b(x, y)$ is the inner product of $x, y$ modulus 2, a hardcore predicate.
9. The sender sends $(c_0, c_1, z_0, z_1)$ to the receiver.
10. The receiver outputs $\sigma_i' = b(s, z_i) \oplus c_i$. This is the secret required.

## 5    Analysis of Protocol

To make the analysis easier, we define the following sets before we proceed.

$$D_\alpha' = \{x \in D_\alpha : x = f_\alpha^{-1}(t, f_\alpha(x))\} \tag{14}$$
$$R_\alpha = f_\alpha(D_\alpha) = f_\alpha(D_\alpha') \tag{15}$$

where $R_\alpha$ is the range of the trapdoor function. Also, there is a one-to-one relationship between $D_\alpha'$ and $R_\alpha$. Next, we define the following sets, acting as an extension of the domain of the trapdoor function.

$$D_\alpha'' = \{x \in \{0,1\}^n : x = f_\alpha^{-1}(t, f_\alpha(x)) \wedge f_\alpha(x) \in \{0,1\}^m\} \tag{16}$$
$$R_\alpha'' = f_\alpha(D_\alpha''). \tag{17}$$

Naturally, there is also a one-to-one relationship between elements in $D_\alpha''$ and $R_\alpha''$. Also we see that $D_\alpha' = D_\alpha \cap D_\alpha''$.

## 5.1   Running Time

Observe that, due to the dense property of $D_\alpha$ in $\{0,1\}^n$ and $D'_\alpha$ in $D_\alpha$, $D'_\alpha$ is also dense in $\{0,1\}^n$. As $|D'_\alpha| = |R_\alpha|$ and $m = n + \log q_2(n)$, $R_\alpha$ is dense in $\{0,1\}^m$. To be more precise, in our protocol we have, in each iteration,

$$\Pr(s \in D'_\alpha) > \frac{1}{p(n)q_1(n)} \tag{18}$$

$$\Pr(r_{1-i} \in R_\alpha) > \frac{1}{p(n)q_1(n)q_2(n)}. \tag{19}$$

In one iteration, if $s \in D'_\alpha$ and $r_{1-i} \in R_\alpha$ then the protocol will reach the end successfully. It is easy to see that the total expected number of iterations is polynomial in $n$. Thus, we say the protocol runs in expected polynomial time. To be precise, in order to guarantee that the protocol will come to a halt, we need to set a counter for the number of iterations. The protocol is terminated when the counter exceeds some predetermined number. In this case, the running time will be polynomial, while the weakness parameter for correctness in WOT will be increased by a negligible amount.

Also, we see how the properties of the trapdoor function affect the running of the protocol. Both the expansion and pre-image size affect the density of usable elements in the domain and range of the trapdoor function. Here they are required for the running time to be polynomial.

## 5.2   Correctness

With the discussion above, the protocol will be prematurely terminated with a negligible probability. If this does not happen, the protocol is executed to the last step. In the last iteration of the protocol, the receiver can get the required secret correctly if $s = f_\alpha^{-1}(t, r_i)$.

For any initial choice of $s$ and $r_{1-i}$, failure occurs if $s \neq f_\alpha^{-1}(t, r_i)$ and at the same time $h(s) = v_i$. This is independent of the choice of $r_{1-i}$, even though $r_{1-i}$ may lead to an aborted round in the protocol. For probability we write:

$$\Pr(s = f_\alpha^{-1}(t, r_i)) > \frac{1}{p(n)q_1(n)} \tag{20}$$

$$\Pr(s \neq f_\alpha^{-1}(t, r_i) \wedge h(s) = v_i) < (1 - \frac{1}{p(n)q_1(n)})(\frac{1}{g(n)p(n)q_1(n)}) \tag{21}$$

and the remaining probability is that the iteration does not reach the end of the protocol. Thus, the probability of correctness, given that the protocol is completely finished, would be

$$1 - \epsilon_1 > \frac{\frac{1}{p(n)q_1(n)}}{\frac{1}{p(n)q_1(n)} + (1 - \frac{1}{p(n)q_1(n)})(\frac{1}{g(n)p(n)q_1(n)})}$$

$$= \frac{g(n)}{g(n) + (1 - \frac{1}{p(n)q_1(n)})}$$

$$> 1 - \frac{1}{g(n)} \tag{22}$$

as $p(n) \geq 1$ and $q_1(n) \geq 1$. This gives the required result that $\epsilon_1 < 1/g(n)$. If we also consider the minor case that the protocol may not run through the end, we have $\epsilon_1 < 1/g(n) + neg(n)$.

### 5.3  Privacy of Receiver

First of all we argue that, when $s = f_\alpha^{-1}(t, r_i)$, we have $s \in D_\alpha''$. On the other hand, if the protocol is run through the end in an iteration, then it must be that $r_{1-i} \in R_\alpha''$. Due to the one-to-one relation between elements of $D_\alpha''$ and $R_\alpha''$, we conclude in this case that both $r_0$ and $r_1$ will appear uniformly distributed in $R_\alpha''$, protecting the privacy of the receiver. This is guaranteed at the time the order of $(r_0, r_1)$ is revealed to the sender. As a result, the only problem occurs when $s \neq f_\alpha^{-1}(t, r_i)$. Thus the weakness parameter for receiver's privacy is bounded by the same events that determine correctness, giving $\epsilon_3 < 1/g(n)$.

At this point, it is important to see that when $s = f_\alpha^{-1}(t, r_i)$ the receiver's privacy is protected in information theoretic sense, without requiring permutation properties in the trapdoor functions. In previous works, the permutation property in trapdoor permutations is usually needed to protect the receiver's privacy in information theoretic sense, while the sender's privacy is protected by computational hardness of the inverse function.

### 5.4  Privacy of Sender

The main weakness of our WOT protocol is on the sender's privacy. After all, $r_{1-i}$ is finally not even guaranteed to be in $R_\alpha$ with high probability. We can assume nothing about the computational hardness of inverting $f_\alpha$ in that case.

But if $r_{1-i} \in R_\alpha$, the sender's privacy should be protected. In this case we can see that if the receiver has non-negligible advantage in guessing $\sigma_{1-i}$ then he also has non-negligible advantage guessing $b(f_\alpha^{-1}(t, r_{1-i}), z_{1-i})$. From the theory for this hardcore predicate [13], this means the receiver has a non-negligible advantage to compute $f_\alpha^{-1}(t, r_{1-i})$.

Note that the receiver is holding $r_{1-i}$ and $h(f_\alpha^{-1}(t, r_{1-i}))$ to help his computation. But if there is such an efficient algorithm $M$ to find $f_\alpha^{-1}(t, r_{1-i})$ in this case, then we also have a polynomial time algorithm solving $f_\alpha^{-1}(t, r_{1-i})$ from $r_{1-i}$ alone, by running $M$ with the setting of $h(f_\alpha^{-1}(t, r_{1-i})) = y$ for each $y \in \{1, 2, \ldots, g(n)p(n)q_1(n)\}$. Each iteration is terminated at a reasonable time limit if it does not give an output. Any potential solution $x$ for $f_\alpha^{-1}(t, r_{1-i})$ can be checked by $f_\alpha(x)$.

Finally, if $f_\alpha^{-1}(t, r_{1-i})$ can be calculated from $r_{1-i}$ in our protocol with non-negligible probability, the computational hardness of the trapdoor function must be violated because $r_{1-i}$ is generated by uniform sampling in the first place. This results in a contradiction. Therefore, we conclude that when $r_{1-i} \in R_\alpha$, the sender's privacy is maintained.

The event $r_{1-i} \in R_\alpha$ is only related to the density of $R_\alpha$ in $\{0,1\}^m$. Thus we have

$$\epsilon_2 < 1 - \frac{1}{p(n)q_1(n)q_2(n)} \tag{23}$$

where again we see that the privacy of sender depends on all properties of our trapdoor function: the dense property $p(n)$, the pre-image property $q_1(n)$ and expansion property $q_2(n)$.

## 6 Strengthening the Weak OT

As a result, we have a WOT with $\epsilon_1 < \frac{1}{g(n)} + neg(n)$, $\epsilon_2 < 1 - \frac{1}{G(n)}$ and $\epsilon_3 < \frac{1}{g(n)}$, where $G(n) = p(n)q_1(n)q_2(n)$. The value of $g(n)$ is of our choice. It is possible to strengthen WOT to standard OT [33] under some conditions in general. In our protocol, exactly the same method of [15] can be used to strengthen the WOT to OT in the semi-honest model. From [15], it works with $g(n) = 3n^2G(n)$. The WOT is used as a blackbox a number of times to suppress the weakness parameters until they become negligible. This completes the last step of the construction of standard OT with blackbox usage of our trapdoor functions.

## 7 Concluding Remarks

We believe the main contribution of this paper is two-fold. In the constructive sense, we follow [15] and continue the work to remove the strict permutation requirement in trapdoor functions for constructing OT. We show that trapdoor functions with three extra properties are sufficient. They are the dense assumption, pre-image assumption and expansion assumption.

On the other hand, through the known blackbox impossibility results, we argue that the pre-image assumption and expansion assumption are hard to remove. The one question remains is about OT possibility if the dense assumption is removed, keeping only the other two assumptions. This question can be divided into two cases. The first case is that the trapdoor function is not required to be a permutation. Then the answer is negative, as a counterexample can easily be constructed by setting $D_\alpha = \{0,1\}^{\frac{m}{15}}$ with $R_\alpha \subset \{0,1\}^m$ and following exactly the same arguments for linear expansion mentioned in this paper. If a trapdoor permutation is used, then we are back to an old question. We know that the Enhanced Trapdoor Permutation [12] suffices, but OT based on trapdoor permutation only is an interesting open question, and the answer is still being awaited.

## References

1. Bellare, M., Halevi, S., Sahai, A., Vadhan, S.P.: Many-to-one trapdoor functions and their relation to public-key cryptosystems. In: Krawczyk, H. (ed.) CRYPTO 1998. LNCS, vol. 1462, pp. 283–299. Springer, Heidelberg (1998)

2. Brassard, G., Crépeau, C., Santha, M.: Oblivious transfers and intersecting codes. IEEE Transactions on Information Theory 42(6), 1769–1780 (1996)
3. Brassard, G., Crépeau, C., Wolf, S.: Oblivious transfers and privacy amplification. Journal of Cryptology 16(4), 219–237 (2003)
4. Canetti, R.: Universally composable security: A new paradigm for cryptographic protocols. In: Proc. 42nd IEEE Symposium on Foundations of Computer Science, pp. 136–145 (2001)
5. Carter, J., Wegman, M.: Universal classes of hash functions. Journal of Computer and System Sciences 18(2), 143–154 (1979)
6. Choi, S.G., Dachman-Soled, D., Malkin, T., Wee, H.: Simple, black-box constructions of adaptively secure protocols. In: Theory of Cryptography Conference 2009. LNCS, vol. 5444, pp. 387–402 (2009)
7. Crépeau, C.: Equivalence between two flavours of oblivious transfers. In: Pomerance, C. (ed.) CRYPTO 1987. LNCS, vol. 293, pp. 350–354. Springer, Heidelberg (1988)
8. Crépeau, C., Savvides, G.: Optimal reductions between oblivious transfers using interactive hashing. In: Vaudenay, S. (ed.) EUROCRYPT 2006. LNCS, vol. 4004, pp. 201–221. Springer, Heidelberg (2006)
9. Diffie, W., Hellman, M.: New directions in cryptography. IEEE Transactions on Information Theory 22(6), 644–654 (1976)
10. Even, S., Goldreich, O.: A Lempel: A randomized protocol for signing contracts. Communications of the ACM 28(6), 637–647 (1985)
11. Gertner, Y., Kannan, S., Malkin, T., Reingold, O., Viswanathan, M.: The relationship between public key encryption and oblivious transfer. In: Proc. 41st IEEE Symposium on Foundations of Computer Science, pp. 325 335 (2000)
12. Goldreich, O.: Foundations of Cryptography, vol II. Cambridge University Press, Cambridge (2004)
13. Goldreich, O., Levin, L.: A hard-core predicate for all one-way functions. In: Proc. 21st ACM Symposium on Theory of Computing, pp. 25–32 (1989)
14. Goldreich, O., Micali, S., Wigderson, A.: How to play any mental game or A completeness theorem for protocols with honest majority. In: Proc. 19th ACM Symposium on Theory of Computing, pp. 218–229 (1987)
15. Haitner, I.: Implementing oblivious transfer using collection of dense trapdoor permutations. In: Naor, M. (ed.) TCC 2004. LNCS, vol. 2951, pp. 394–409. Springer, Heidelberg (2004)
16. Haitner, I.: Semi-honest to malicious oblivious transfer—the black-box way. In: Canetti, R. (ed.) TCC 2008. LNCS, vol. 4948, pp. 412–426. Springer, Heidelberg (2008)
17. Haitner, I., Horvitz, O., Katz, J., Koo, C.-Y., Morselli, R., Shaltiel, R.: Reducing complexity assumptions for statistically-hiding commitment. In: Cramer, R. (ed.) EUROCRYPT 2005. LNCS, vol. 3494, pp. 58–77. Springer, Heidelberg (2005)
18. Haitner, I., Reingold, O.: Statistically-hiding commitment from any one-way function. In: Proc. 39th ACM Symposium on Theory of Computing, pp. 1–10 (2007)
19. Harnik, D., Naor, M.: On the compressibility of NP instances and cryptographic applications. In: Proc. 47th IEEE Symposium on Foundations of Computer Science, pp. 719–728 (2006)
20. Impagliazzo, R., Luby, M.: One-way functions are essential for complexity based cryptography. In: Proc. 30th IEEE Symposium on Foundations of Computer Science, pp. 230–235 (1989)

21. Impagliazzo, R., Rudich, S.: Limits on the provable consequences of one-way permutations. In: Proc. 21st ACM Symposium on Theory of Computing, pp. 44–61 (1989)
22. Kilian, J.: Founding cryptography on oblivious tranfer. In: Proc. 20th ACM Symposium on Theory of Computing, pp. 20–31 (1988)
23. Naor, M., Ostrovsky, R., Venkatesan, R., Yung, M.: Perfect zero-knowledge arguments for NP using any one-way permutation. Journal of Cryptology 11(2), 87–108 (1998)
24. Naor, M., Pinkas, B.: Efficient oblivious transfer protocols. In: Proc. 12th ACM-SIAM Symposium on Discrete Algorithms, pp. 448–457 (2001)
25. Peikert, C., Vaikuntanathan, V., Waters, B.: A framework for efficient and composable oblivious transfer. In: Wagner, D. (ed.) CRYPTO 2008. LNCS, vol. 5157, pp. 554–571. Springer, Heidelberg (2008)
26. Peikert, C., Waters, B.: Lossy trapdoor functions and their applications. In: Proc. 40th ACM Symposium on Theory of Computing, pp. 187–196 (2008)
27. Rabin, M.: How to exchange secrets by oblivious transfer, Technical Report TR-81, Aiken Computation Laboratory, Harvard University (1981)
28. Reingold, O., Trevisan, L., Vadhan, S.P.: Notions of reducibility between cryptographic primitives. In: Naor, M. (ed.) TCC 2004. LNCS, vol. 2951, pp. 1–20. Springer, Heidelberg (2004)
29. Shamir, A.: How to share a secret. Communications of the ACM 22(11), 612–613 (1979)
30. Shannon, C.: Communication theory of secrecy systems. Bell System Technical Journal 28(4), 656–715 (1949)
31. Wiesner, S.: Conjugate coding. SIGACT News 15(1), 78–88 (1983)
32. Wolf, S., Wullschleger, J.: Oblivious transfer is symmetric. In: Vaudenay, S. (ed.) EUROCRYPT 2006. LNCS, vol. 4004, pp. 222–232. Springer, Heidelberg (2006)
33. Wullschleger, J.: Oblivious-transfer amplification. In: Naor, M. (ed.) EUROCRYPT 2007. LNCS, vol. 4515, pp. 555–572. Springer, Heidelberg (2007)

# Tamper-Tolerant Software: Modeling and Implementation

Mariusz H. Jakubowski[1], Chit Wei (Nick) Saw[1],
and Ramarathnam Venkatesan[1,2]

[1] Microsoft Research
One Microsoft Way, Redmond, WA 98052, USA
{mariuszj,chitsaw}@microsoft.com
[2] Microsoft Research India
196/36 2nd Main, Sadashivnagar, Bangalore 560 080, India
venkie@microsoft.com

**Abstract.** Common software-protection systems attempt to detect malicious observation and modification of protected applications. Upon tamper detection, anti-hacking code may produce a crash or gradual failure, rendering the application unusable or troublesome. Such a response is designed to complicate attacks, but has also caused problems for developers and end users, particularly when bugs or other problems invoke anti-tampering measures accidentally. To address these issues, an alternative approach is to detect and fix malicious changes. This paper presents a scheme to transform programs into tamper-tolerant versions that use self-correcting operation as a response against attacks. Combining techniques from the fields of fault tolerance and software security, the approach transforms programs via code individualization and redundancy. We also describe security enhancements through error correction, delayed responses and checkpointing. For security analysis, we adapt a graph-based model of attacks and defenses in the context of software tamper-resistance. This helps to estimate the difficulty of breaking our scheme in practical scenarios.

## 1 Introduction

On modern computing systems, certain software requires protection against malicious tampering and unauthorized usage. For example, DRM (Digital Rights Management) systems attempt to prevent software piracy, as well as illegal distribution of music, video and other content. Running on open PCs, however, such security-sensitive applications are subject to observation and modification by hackers. Consequently, developers have employed *tamper-resistant software (TRS)* [5,9,18,19], which involves a variety of program obfuscation and hardening tactics to complicate hacker eavesdropping and tampering [12,32,4,29]. While no provably secure and practical methods have been deployed, various TRS heuristics extend the time and effort required to break protection.

Among the most popular protection techniques is *integrity checking*, or verifying that a program and its execution are tamper-free. Specific methods

T. Takagi and M. Mambo (Eds.): IWSEC 2009, LNCS 5824, pp. 125–139, 2009.

include computation of hashes over program code and data, along with periodic checks for mismatches between pre-computed and runtime values [10,19]. Upon detection of incorrect program code or behavior, a protection system typically responds by crashing or degrading the application (e.g., via slowdown and erratic operation) [29]. Often obfuscated, this response mechanism serves both to delay hackers and deny illegitimate usage of the application.

This typical "pessimistic" response to tampering has caused issues with application development, including testing and debugging, as well as with end-user experience. For example, application bugs sometimes manifest themselves only in tamper-protected instances of applications, forcing developers to face their own (or third-party) protection measures. Bugs in the actual protection system can be especially troublesome, particularly when interacting with protected applications. Given random application failures and erratic behavior, legitimate end users may find it difficult or impractical to file bug reports and receive support. These and other problems have contributed to general unpopularity of software protection.

A more constructive response to attacks is not to render an application unusable, but to correct the effects of tampering and allow the program to continue. The basic notion of such *tamper-tolerant software (TTS)* is appealing from the perspectives of both developers and end users, since TTS works actively to keep a program running correctly despite attacks – much like fault-tolerant systems protect against system breakdown due to malfunctioning components. Along these lines, some earlier protection schemes have used multiple copies of code to guard against tampering [9,11].

Fault tolerance [16,21,27] is a rich area that has seen much theoretical and practical work, but aims mainly to defend against "random" or unintentional failures, not against intelligent malicious attackers. However, TTS can derive from the basic concepts of fault tolerance, including redundancy, failover, and checkpoints with rollback. Likewise, error-correction methods [24] are geared mainly towards addressing noisy data transmission, but are useful in TTS as well. TTS can be considered as an adaptation and extension of fault tolerance and error correction to the intelligent-attacker scenario in software protection.

Evaluating the real-life effectiveness of software protection has been a traditionally problematic task. Most implementations in practice tend to use "ad hoc" techniques that offer only heuristic security assessments, if any. Even schemes that reduce to solving "difficult" problems can often be broken when attacks violate their idealized models or assumptions. Nonetheless, a recent line of work on graph-based modeling of tamper-resistance [15] offers some promise. In this framework, execution is modeled as a walk on program graphs, while attacks are analyzed as a "graph game" between hackers and defenders. We provide a simple adaptation of this model to our tamper-tolerance framework. As a step towards security analysis, this approach estimates the number of runtime observations and modifications required by any successful tampering attack.

The rest of this paper is structured as follows. Section 2 describes our basic TTS approach, including background on fault tolerance and software protection.

In Section 3, we present a graph-based security model for evaluating the strength of TTS. Section 4 presents a test implementation and experimental results on SPEC benchmarks. We provide a final assessment in Section 5.

## 2  Tamper-Tolerant Software

The essential idea of tamper-tolerant software is to detect tampering and fix its effects at runtime. This is distinct from traditional anti-tampering responses, which use techniques such as delayed crashes and graceful degradation [29,15] to block illegitimate usage and hinder attackers. Much the same effects are achieved if the program silently corrects its operation instead of failing. However, clear practical advantages come into play when applications continue to function as intended despite attacks. As with delayed responses in TRS, TTS may actually allow some tampered execution, but only temporarily.

To construct TTS schemes, our approach relies on several well known techniques from the fields of fault tolerance and software protection. Below we briefly review these techniques in the context of software security.

### 2.1  Building Blocks

Fault-tolerant systems typically use redundant and diversified components to resist random or non-malicious failures. With some extensions, such methods also help against intelligent attackers. We leverage the following main elements of fault tolerance:

- **Redundancy**: Duplication of system components into distinct, independently functioning units. This is a means of implementing *failover*, or switching to a fresh component if one stops working correctly. In addition, *voting* schemes compute results from multiple redundant components and select the most frequently occurring values. For example, the well known TMR/V scheme (triple modular redundancy with voting) uses three duplicate components and picks the majority answer [28].
- **Individualization**: Alteration of software code without affecting its functionality (synonymous with *diversification* [4]). Such transformations can implement the same operations in different ways, leading to potentially more robust systems. This can also make the same code appear different to adversaries, ideally forcing them to duplicate analysis efforts. Both code and data may be individualized statically (i.e., prior to runtime [1]) or dynamically (i.e., periodically during runtime [3]).
- **Checkpointing**: Upon tamper detection, rollback of execution to an earlier point. Checkpoints (i.e., summaries of program state sufficient to restart execution) are saved periodically for this purpose. This is the essential idea behind *recovery-block schemes* [26,30]. One motivation for this is attacks that alter program state without patching code, so that canceling and redoing operations can effectively fix the tampering. Alternately, a different redundant

component can redo the computation. Such checkpointing is also used by so-called "time-travel" (or "omniscient") debuggers to execute code backwards or roll execution back to some arbitrary point [8]. We may take advantage of existing checkpoint technology from such debuggers and simulators.

TTS also uses a number of techniques from the field of software protection:

- **Integrity checks**: Runtime verification of correct program operation. A traditional method is to compute checksums or hashes of code bytes, comparing at runtime against precomputed correct values [18,9]. Without reading instruction bytes, the technique of *oblivious hashing* computes and verifies hashes based on runtime variable values and control-flow transfers (e.g., by updating a hash value upon every variable assignment and branch [10,19]). Similarly, *integrity-checking expressions (ICEs)* can be used to verify integrity of execution by computing predicates over runtime state [20].
- **Delayed responses**: Separation of tamper detection and correction in space and time. This is to prevent easy identification of the TTS mechanism, mainly by disguising and hiding corrective response mechanisms [29,15]. One example technique is corrupting pointers so that future dereferencing will result in an invalid access, crashing the program [29].
- **Result correction**: Combination of several (possibly encoded) outputs from individualized copies of a code block, and output of the block's correct result despite tampering with one or more of the copies. This is a generalization of the idea of majority decoding in error correction (e.g., TMR/V, as described earlier [24]).
- **Data encoding and shuffling**: Encryption or scrambling of a program's working data, including usage of standard authentication (e.g., hashes or MACs) and error-correction codes. Variables may be continually transformed and moved in memory to prevent easy dataflow analysis and tracking [31,2].

## 2.2   Tamper-Tolerance Schemes

Following the core principles and terminology of fault tolerance, our basic TTS approach uses the notion of *individualized modular redundancy (IMR)*. In essence, the methodology duplicates code blocks at various granularities (e.g., basic blocks or entire functions), transforming the copies into diversified but functionally equivalent versions. We treat these code blocks as deterministic functions that map inputs to outputs and have no side effects. At runtime, the different copies may execute at various times or in parallel, producing individual intermediate outputs (all of which should be the same if no tampering occurs). Fig. 1 shows the basic conception of tamper-tolerant software.

This general IMR framework may be specialized in various ways. For concreteness, we present three specific practical schemes. We use acronyms and terminology derived from literature on fault tolerance [28,27,16,21]:

- **IMR with voting (IMR/V)**: This is IMR combined with a baseline form of result correction (similar to N-version programming [6]). From among the

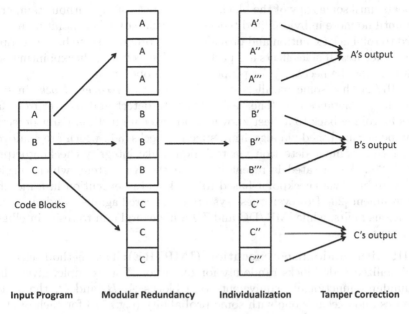

**Fig. 1.** High-level overview of tamper-tolerant software

results computed by individualized code blocks, a voting mechanism selects the final output. Given no tampering, the vote will be unanimous – i.e., all redundant copies generate the same output. This voting scheme can be considered as a simple means of implementing result correction.

For more secure result correction, we use the general concept of a *tamper-correcting transform* that accepts a number of encrypted (or scrambled) and potentially corrupted intermediate results. Individualized copies of a code block compute such results; the transform then decrypts (or unscrambles) these values and uses error correction on them to produce one final answer. As described above, the simplest form of this transform is equivalent to error correction via majority voting – i.e., the intermediate results are in plaintext, and the most commonly appearing value is selected as the final output. In general, however, the decryption (or unscrambling) and error correction (or voting) may be coalesced into a single transform that performs these distinct operations implicitly.

- **IMR with detection and correction (IMR/DC):** In this scheme, the protection system resorts to redundant execution only if tampering is detected. Using the integrity-verification techniques described earlier, the system checks the execution of each code block for correctness (e.g., via verifying code-byte checksums or oblivious hashes of execution). Upon tamper detection, the system selects and executes an individualized copy of the block, also verifying its runtime integrity. The system may simply call another individualized version of the block, or overwrite the tampered code with new code from a repository of possibly encrypted redundant blocks. This process repeats until some copy of the block executes successfully without tampering (or until no more individualized blocks are available). Checkpointing may be used to roll back execution and provide correct program state before a copied block executes. If side effects are part of block execution, checkpointing with rollback may be necessary for proper program operation.

IMR/DC has some parallels with the notion of *recovery blocks* in standard fault tolerance [26]. The basic idea is to detect and recover from failures by rolling back to a "last known good" execution state. Fault detection may be accomplished via algorithm-specific checks [30], which are analogous to runtime tamper detection via techniques like integrity-checking expressions [20]. Also related is recent work on the Rx system, which survives software bugs via checkpoint-based rollback and re-execution in a modified environment [25]. However, these systems are geared against random or non-malicious faults, while IMR/DC and TTS in general aim to resist intelligent attackers.

- **IMR with randomized execution (IMR/RE):** This method selects individualized code blocks randomly for execution. For example, given three redundant, functionally equivalent code blocks $A$, $B$, and $C$, the system chooses and executes one with some probability (e.g., $1/3$ for each of $A$, $B$, and $C$). If an attacker tampers with only $A$, execution will still be correct with probability $2/3$, since $B$ and $C$ may be picked. Controlled by opaque predicates or other possibly obfuscated means [14,13], block selection may vary during runtime and between runs of a program. Such an approach cannot be used standalone to ensure tamper tolerance, but may be combined with other methods to enhance security of tolerance. In particular, combining IMR/RE with checkpointing (or rollback to an earlier point upon tamper detection) can undo tampering.

In a typical implementation, various other software-protection techniques would be incorporated into a tamper-tolerance system. These include data transformations [31,2], delayed responses [29], as well as other applicable tamper-resistance and obfuscation techniques. The main goal is to strengthen the above basic schemes, as well as to satisfy "engineering assumptions" required by the security model we adapt [15], as described later.

## 2.3    Tamper-Tolerance Algorithms

Using the above concepts, we present a general algorithm outline to implement TTS in practice. Given a program $P$ to be protected, along with optional user-specified security and maintenance parameters, the algorithm transforms $P$ into a new tamper-tolerant version $P'$. $P$ is typically a single application, library module or driver running in either user or kernel mode. The following are general basic steps of the transformation process to protect $P$:

1. Break up $P$ into a number of blocks, which may range in granularity from individual instructions to the entire program $P$. In practice, subdivision

into standard basic blocks (i.e., code sections with no incoming or outgoing internal branches) or functions is likely to suffice.

2. Duplicate, individualize and rearrange the blocks within the program, relying on user-specified parameters to determine number(s) of copies and specifics of individualization (e.g., types and degrees of diversifying transformations).

3. Inject appropriate code to implement IMR/V, IMR/DC, IMR/RE, or a combination of two or three thereof, as specified by user parameters. Such code may include opaque predicates for block selection.

4. Optionally inject code to manage result correction, data transformations, delayed responses, checkpointing, or a combination of two or more thereof. Also optional is injection of any additional obfuscation measures.

5. For enhanced security, optionally iterate the above steps two or more times, so that the tamper-tolerance measures are themselves protected by one or more layers of tamper tolerance. This is important for leveraging the basic IMR approach.

## 3   Security Modeling

This section presents a security model to evaluate the effectiveness of TTS schemes. Our main goal is a method to estimate the complexity of breaking TTS in practice (e.g., in terms of the number of observations and modifications required by any successful attacker). Different applications require different levels of resistance; e.g., a few weeks without cracks might suffice for copy protection on some games, while even a few hours may be enough for quickly refreshed Web-based code. Although "unbreakable" software protection remains an open problem, this is not necessary in many, if not most, business contexts.

Theoretical treatment of obfuscation has yielded negative general results [7,17]. This indicates that no tool can protect all possible programs, but certain limited classes of functionality are amenable to obfuscation [22,33]. However, this is in a very strict "all or nothing" model, where any non-negligible information extracted efficiently from obfuscated code is considered a break. On the other hand, our modeling approach is geared mainly towards estimating the time and effort required to defeat protection.

To assess security of TTS, we adapt a *graph-game* tamper-resistance framework that treats a program as a graph and execution as a walk on the graph [15]. The program is protected by integrity checks contained in some nodes, and the attacker's goal is to isolate all such nodes. Although originally intended for modeling tamper-resistant software, this approach can be adapted naturally to TTS. We provide an informal but self-contained summary of this framework, along with a description of our changes to model TTS.

### 3.1   Graph-Game Model

The main elements of the graph-game model [15] are as follows:

- **Program**: The program $P$ to be protected is viewed as a graph $G$, such as a control-flow graph (CFG). This CFG should be "semi-random," which is achieved via transformations that add nodes and edges.
- **Execution**: This is modeled as a "semi-random" walk on the graph $G$. Most program CFGs result in walks that are not particularly random, given typical patterns of control flow. The model relies on various transformations to randomize the runtime walk.
- **Integrity checks**: Unknown to the attacker, some nodes in the CFG execute probabilistic checks to verify correct program operation at a particular time and place. In practice, this abstract notion of an integrity check may be implemented in various ways, such as code-byte checksums [18,9], oblivious hashing [10,19], and integrity-checking expressions [20]
- **Tamper responses**: When certain sets of checks fail, a tamper response is initiated. This is typically a delayed crash, or a program failure designed to deflect attention away from its causes (i.e., tampering with nodes).

With these elements, the graph game involves an attacker able to run the protected program, tamper with nodes, and observe program behavior. The program's response to tampering (i.e., time and place of failure) reveals information about the placement of integrity checks. Once the attacker identifies a node containing such a check, he may disable it. His goal is to identify all nodes responsible for integrity verification, which he can then eliminate to unprotect the program.

The analysis in [15] essentially shows that in order to achieve success, the attacker must perform a large number of program observations and node modifications. This number may be quadratic (or higher) in terms of the workload required to protect the program. In general, this is our main goal – i.e., the attacker should expend an order of magnitude more effort than the protector.

## 3.2    TTS Modeling

The graph-game framework is almost directly applicable to TTS. Our only main change is to replace the notion of delayed crashes with *delayed fixes*. More specifically, instead of responding to the attacker's tampering by eventually crashing, the program will correct its operation and continue running. When the attacker tampers with graph nodes, he may observe altered program behavior for some time, after which the program resumes its untampered operation. Like a delayed crash, this length of time gives the attacker information about whether any of the tampered nodes contained integrity checks. With this modification, the original analysis of the graph-game model [15] essentially applies as is.

For concreteness, we describe a simplified variant of this modeling approach. Assume the protected program contains $n$ integrity checks, each executed with probability $p$. Let $d$ denote the average time required by the attacker to determine that a node contains an integrity check. To identify all integrity checks, the attacker must run the program an average of $n/p$ times, each taking time $d$.

Thus, the time required by the attacker is $dn/p$. If we set $p$ to $1/n$, the time becomes $dn^2$, or quadratic in the number of checks.

Like the original graph-game model, this approach makes a number of "engineering assumptions" that must be approximated in practice. For example, all integrity checks must be distinct, so that an attacker cannot easily use knowledge of one check to identify others. In addition, converting a typical CFG to a "semi-random" graph, along with approximating execution as a "semi-random" walk, may incur significant performance and code-size penalties. Nonetheless, software-protection techniques like individualization and opaque predication can help satify these requirements. In fact, the previously described elements of TTS can be viewed as a set of engineering techniques to satisfy the model's practical assumptions about tamper-tolerance.

### 3.3 Impossibility Results

While general-purpose obfuscation has been proved impossible in the model of Barak et al. [7], we are not aware of analogous work for tamper-resistance. However, it is straightforward to show that general-purpose tamper-resistance (or tamper-tolerance) is impossible as well. Informally, if we assume the existence of a generic tool to tamper-protect any program, we can simply feed such a tool's output to itself. Since any tamper protection involves some form of program transformations, this would essentially force the tool to break its own tamper protection in order to modify the tamper-resistant program. Thus, such a tool cannot exist.

The graph-game model [15] actually does propose an approach for general-purpose tamper-protection. However, this model implicitly assumes that the input program is not already tamper-protected, thus rendering the above impossibility argument irrelevant. In addition, the argument assumes that the transformation tool uses no secret key or other non-public information, but the scenario is somewhat different if this is allowed. A more detailed analysis of related results for tamper-resistance and -tolerance may appear elsewhere.

## 4   Implementation and Experiments

We have implemented an initial version of a tool that applies some of the tamper-tolerance techniques described in this paper by transforming and compiling high-level source code. The tool is built on top of a code transformation framework based on Phoenix [23]. Phoenix is a Microsoft program analysis and compiler framework based on a common intermediate representation (IR) that provides the building blocks of the program to be transformed.

This current section describes the tool in more detail, and includes some experimental results obtained by applying the tool to several SPEC CPU2006 benchmarks.

## 4.1   Tool Implementation

In this initial version of the tool, we implemented the IMR/RE scheme, which incorporates many of the building blocks upon which the other schemes may be built. In addition, we also implemented a stack-based checkpointing and rollback mechanism in order to illustrate the performance under simulated tampering and detection conditions. Future work will enhance the tool to implement the IMR/V and IMR/DC schemes.

The tool processes each function in an input program and creates a configurable number of copies of the basic blocks in the function. The number of copies may be specified in a configuration file. Additionally, the functions to be processed may also be specified, and a parameter may be used to control the code coverage, or percentage of blocks processed within the functions. We could have instead opted to copy entire functions rather than basic blocks, but copying at the basic-block level provides a finer level of granularity that could allow for more targeted applications of the technique.

The multiple copies are each individualized, which in the case of our tool is achieved by applying a different combination of simple chaff-code injection and code-substitution transformations to each code block in a way that does not alter the functionality of the block. In practice, any individualization scheme that produces functionally equivalent individualized code may be used. Finally, the tool inserts code to select (randomly, as is the case for the IMR/RE scheme) one of the multiple copies to execute. In our prototype, a simple pseudo-random number generator is inlined in the code to select randomly one of the code blocks to which to transfer control.

## 4.2   Experimental Results

This section presents experimental results obtained by running the tool on selected SPEC CPU2006 benchmarks (data compression, transportation scheduling, database search, chess and video compression). The benchmarks were run and timed on a Pentium 3.0 GHz workstation with 3 GB of RAM. In the set of tables that follow, we measured for each benchmark the binary code size and runtime performance before and after applying the tamper-tolerance transformations. We express these measures in the tables as *ratios* relative to the baseline benchmark with no tamper-tolerance applied. The results show the impact of the addition of tamper-tolerance on the code size and runtime performance of the program.

Tables 1 and 2 show how applying IMR/RE by duplicating a random sampling of 25% of the code blocks affects the code-size and performance respectively relative to the baseline. Because not all blocks are the same size, and because we perform the duplication of blocks in high-level source code, it does not necessarily follow that the size of the resulting executable file will increase by exactly the same amount as statically-linked library code is not seen at compile-time and will not be subjected to the transformation. In addition, the random-block-selection code will add to both the code size and performance overhead. We repeated the

**Table 1.** Code-size impact of block redundancy, 25% code coverage

| Benchmark | Number of redundant copies ($n$) | | | |
| | $n = 2$ | $n = 4$ | $n = 8$ | $n = 16$ |
|---|---|---|---|---|
| 401.bzip2 | 1.650 | 2.319 | 3.525 | 5.875 |
| 429.mcf | 1.189 | 1.400 | 1.611 | 2.256 |
| 456.hmmer | 1.879 | 2.640 | 4.109 | 7.298 |
| 458.sjeng | 1.776 | 2.475 | 3.929 | 6.859 |
| 464.h264ref | 1.907 | 2.770 | 4.414 | 8.054 |

**Table 2.** Performance impact of block redundancy, 25% code coverage

| Benchmark | Number of redundant copies ($n$) | | | |
| | $n = 2$ | $n = 4$ | $n = 8$ | $n = 16$ |
|---|---|---|---|---|
| 401.bzip2 | 2.267 | 2.674 | 3.287 | 4.903 |
| 429.mcf | 2.010 | 2.352 | 2.762 | 2.238 |
| 456.hmmer | 2.275 | 2.389 | 2.310 | 4.629 |
| 458.sjeng | 2.840 | 3.797 | 4.858 | 6.274 |
| 464.h264ref | 2.222 | 3.655 | 3.909 | 5.274 |

**Table 3.** Code-size impact of block redundancy, 50% code coverage

| Benchmark | Number of redundant copies ($n$) | | | |
| | $n = 2$ | $n = 4$ | $n = 8$ | $n = 16$ |
|---|---|---|---|---|
| 401.bzip2 | 2.325 | 3.394 | 5.375 | 10.65 |
| 429.mcf | 1.333 | 1.667 | 2.222 | 3.644 |
| 456.hmmer | 2.599 | 4.119 | 7.023 | 13.07 |
| 458.sjeng | 2.475 | 3.886 | 6.529 | 11.79 |
| 464.h264ref | 2.701 | 4.394 | 7.699 | 14.32 |

measurements for number of copies $n = 4$, 8 and 16. This clearly shows the increase in code size due to the additional redundant code as more copies are introduced. The performance overhead may be attributed to the block-selection code as well as changes to the spatial and temporal ordering of code blocks which can affect the efficacy of CPU-based optimizations such as caching and branch prediction. These performance impacts can also vary depending on the profile of the code running the benchmark and the actual blocks selected for redundancy. For instance, duplicating a block within a performance-critical, tight inner loop would cause the block-selection code to be run on every iteration of the loop, thereby amplifying the performance overhead.

Tables 3 through 6 repeat the measurements for expanded code-coverage values of 50% and 100%. As the code coverage is increased, both code size and performance are impacted, the latter due to the increased frequency of block-selection code execution and the reduced efficacy of CPU-based optimizations. This can be seen most clearly at the 100% code-coverage level, where the

**Table 4.** Performance impact of block redundancy, 50% code coverage

| Benchmark | Number of redundant copies ($n$) | | | |
| | $n = 2$ | $n = 4$ | $n = 8$ | $n = 16$ |
| --- | --- | --- | --- | --- |
| 401.bzip2 | 3.840 | 5.580 | 7.099 | 9.530 |
| 429.mcf | 2.388 | 2.447 | 3.340 | 4.301 |
| 456.hmmer | 2.834 | 3.738 | 5.808 | 4.803 |
| 458.sjeng | 4.311 | 6.509 | 7.547 | 11.56 |
| 464.h264ref | 4.364 | 5.395 | 6.854 | 10.04 |

**Table 5.** Code-size impact of block redundancy, 100% code coverage

| Benchmark | Number of redundant copies ($n$) | | | |
| | $n = 2$ | $n = 4$ | $n = 8$ | $n = 16$ |
| --- | --- | --- | --- | --- |
| 401.bzip2 | 3.394 | 5.725 | 10.33 | 19.42 |
| 429.mcf | 1.722 | 2.356 | 3.700 | 6.533 |
| 456.hmmer | 4.149 | 7.235 | 13.26 | 25.50 |
| 458.sjeng | 3.890 | 6.765 | 12.00 | 22.53 |
| 464.h264ref | 4.307 | 7.802 | 14.31 | 27.45 |

**Table 6.** Performance impact of block redundancy, 100% code coverage

| Benchmark | Number of redundant copies ($n$) | | | |
| | $n = 2$ | $n = 4$ | $n = 8$ | $n = 16$ |
| --- | --- | --- | --- | --- |
| 401.bzip2 | 6.205 | 9.307 | 12.13 | 16.74 |
| 429.mcf | 3.990 | 5.324 | 6.618 | 10.10 |
| 456.hmmer | 4.934 | 7.293 | 9.651 | 13.49 |
| 458.sjeng | 8.255 | 12.31 | 16.70 | 25.71 |
| 464.h264ref | 6.801 | 9.880 | 12.76 | 18.07 |

redundancy is applied to every block in the source code. We should also point out that the block-selection code was not optimized by the compiler, which may account in part for the slower execution times as the degree of redundancy is increased. This could be addressed by encoding the block-selection code using low-level jump tables.

In order to illustrate in general how checkpointing and rollback could be used in conjunction with IMR/RE as an effective means of result correction in the presence of tampering, we implemented a simple stack-based scheme to checkpoint the execution environment of the program before a function call, and rollbacks to restore the execution to the most recent checkpoint. This scheme does not currently support saving and restoring global state, so we are limited to applying this only in the absence of global side-effects.

We assume different probabilities of tampering within the program, and simulate detection and correction by injecting code in each function to perform a rollback to the previous checkpoint with probability $p$. Upon a successful rollback,

**Table 7.** Performance impact of rollback

| Benchmark | Probability of tampering ($p$) | | | | |
| --- | --- | --- | --- | --- | --- |
| | $p = 0.9$ | $p = 0.8$ | $p = 0.7$ | $p = 0.6$ | $p = 0.5$ |
| 401.bzip2 | 2.720 | 1.875 | 1.571 | 1.432 | 1.324 |
| 429.mcf | 5.735 | 3.373 | 2.578 | 2.137 | 1.863 |
| 456.hmmer | 2.175 | 1.611 | 1.415 | 1.332 | 1.262 |
| 458.sjeng | 6.132 | 3.755 | 2.943 | 2.542 | 2.222 |
| 464.h264ref | 9.679 | 5.395 | 3.936 | 3.159 | 2.651 |

execution will resume from the previous checkpoint, and will have a probability of $(1 - p)$ of successfully proceeding beyond the tampered block. In the IMR/RE scheme, the probability that the same tampered block will be executed is $1/n$, where $n$ corresponds to the number of copies made of the code block.

The performance impact of checkpointing and rollback under different tampering probabilities is presented in Table 7. The values in the table are again expressed as a ratio relative to the baseline execution with no tampering or rollback. As the probability $p$ of encountering tampering decreases, the performance improves due to a greater likelihood that the tampered code is avoided upon restoration of execution following a rollback.

In all of the experiments, we applied the transformation over a set percentage of all code blocks in order to be able to perform relative measurements across the selected benchmarks. More realistic usage may involve targeted selection of sensitive code sections on which to apply tamper-tolerance, as well as protecting less critical parts of the program to avoid drawing attention to the former. As with other software-protection schemes, these need to be balanced with the code-size and performance impacts. While the current version of the tool applies the transformations to high-level source code for cross-platform compatibility, the methods described in this paper may equally be applied to low-level machine code. Finally, practical application of this and other tamper-tolerance schemes should always be done in conjunction with other protection methods as part of an overall software-protection solution.

# 5    Conclusion

This paper proposed the general concept of *tamper-tolerant software*, or the notion of an attacked program correcting its own operation upon tamper detection, as opposed to traditional responses that involve crashes or graceful degradation. Tamper-tolerance enables a program to continue executing rather than to fail upon attack detection. TTS is based on *individualized modular redundancy*, namely a combination of software protection and fault-tolerance techniques adapted to the malicious-attacker scenario. The approach detects tampering and fixes malicious changes via voting, result correction, randomized re-execution, or rollback. We model TTS by adapting a graph-based tamper-resistance framework [15], enabling security analysis and estimation of attack resistance in practice.

Future work will analyze possibility and impossibility results for TRS and TTS, extending the informal discussion from Section 3. In particular, we are investigating classes of programs in terms of how well TRS and TTS can protect them, both with and without secret keys and other auxiliary information. A main goal is to put TRS and TTS on a sound yet practically useful formal foundation, eliminating the need for "ad hoc" heuristics and unpredictable security in real-world contexts.

# References

1. Anckaert, B., Jakubowski, M.H., Venkatesan, R.: Proteus: Virtualization for diversified tamper-resistance. In: DRM 2006: Proceedings of the ACM Workshop on Digital Rights Management, pp. 47–58. ACM Press, New York (2006)
2. Anckaert, B., Jakubowski, M.H., Venkatesan, R.: Runtime protection via dataflow flattening. In: IARIA SECURWARE 2009 (to appear, 2009)
3. Anckaert, B., Jakubowski, M.H., Venkatesan, R., De Bosschere, K.: Run-time randomization to mitigate tampering. In: Miyaji, A., Kikuchi, H., Rannenberg, K. (eds.) IWSEC 2007. LNCS, vol. 4752, pp. 153–168. Springer, Heidelberg (2007)
4. Anckaert, B., De Sutter, B., De Bosschere, K.: Software piracy prevention through diversity. In: DRM 2004: Proceedings of the 4th ACM Workshop on Digital Rights Management, pp. 63–71. ACM Press, New York (2004)
5. Aucsmith, D.: Tamper resistant software: An implementation. In: Anderson, R. (ed.) IH 1996. LNCS, vol. 1174, pp. 317–333. Springer, Heidelberg (1996)
6. Avizienis, A.: The methodology of N-version programming. In: Lyu, M.R. (ed.) Software Fault Tolerance,ch. 2, pp. 23–46. Wiley, Chichester (1995)
7. Barak, B., Goldreich, O., Impagliazzo, R., Rudich, S., Sahai, A., Vadhan, S., Yang, K.: On the (im)possibility of obfuscating programs. In: Kilian, J. (ed.) CRYPTO 2001. LNCS, vol. 2139, pp. 1–18. Springer, Heidelberg (2001)
8. Bhansali, S., Chen, W.-K., de Jong, S., Edwards, A., Murray, R., Drinić, M., Mihočka, D., Chau, J.: Framework for instruction-level tracing and analysis of program executions. In: VEE 2006: Proceedings of the 2nd international conference on Virtual execution environments, pp. 154–163. ACM, New York (2006)
9. Chang, H., Atallah, M.J.: Protecting software code by guards. In: Digital Rights Management Workshop, pp. 160–175 (2001)
10. Chen, Y., Venkatesan, R., Cary, M., Pang, R., Sinha, S., Jakubowski, M.H.: Oblivious hashing: A stealthy software integrity verification primitive. In: Information Hiding 2002, Noordwijkerhout, The Netherlands (October 2002)
11. Cloakware Corporation. Software Security Suite (2009)
12. Collberg, C., Thomborson, C., Low, D.: A taxonomy of obfuscating transformations. Technical Report 148, Department of Computer Science, The University of Auckland, New Zealand (July 1997)
13. Collberg, C., Thomborson, C., Low, D.: Breaking abstractions and unstructuring data structures. In: International Conference on Computer Languages, pp. 28–38 (1998)
14. Collberg, C., Thomborson, C., Low, D.: Manufacturing cheap, resilient, and stealthy opaque constructs. In: Principles of Programming Languages, POPL 1998, pp. 184–196 (1998)

15. Dedić, N., Jakubowski, M.H., Venkatesan, R.: A graph game model for software tamper protection. In: Proceedings of the 2007 Information Hiding Workshop (June 2007)
16. Denning, P.J.: Fault tolerant operating systems. ACM Comput. Surv. 8(4), 359–389 (1976)
17. Goldwasser, S., Kalai, Y.T.: On the impossibility of obfuscation with auxiliary input. In: FOCS 2005: Proceedings of the 46th IEEE Symposium on Foundations of Computer Science (2005)
18. Horne, B., Matheson, L.R., Sheehan, C., Tarjan, R.E.: Dynamic self-checking techniques for improved tamper resistance. In: Digital Rights Management Workshop, pp. 141–159 (2001)
19. Jacob, M., Jakubowski, M.H., Venkatesan, R.: Towards integral binary execution: Implementing oblivious hashing using overlapped instruction encodings. In: 2007 ACM Multimedia and Security Workshop, Dallas, TX (September 2007)
20. Jakubowski, M.H., Naldurg, P., Patankar, V., Venkatesan, R.: Software integrity checking expressions (ICEs) for robust tamper detection. In: Furon, T., Cayre, F., Doërr, G., Bas, P. (eds.) IH 2007. LNCS, vol. 4567, pp. 96–111. Springer, Heidelberg (2008)
21. Linden, T.A.: Operating system structures to support security and reliable software. ACM Comput. Surv. 8(4), 409 445 (1976)
22. Lynn, B., Prabhakaran, M., Sahai, A.: Positive results and techniques for obfuscation. In: Cachin, C., Camenisch, J.L. (eds.) EUROCRYPT 2004. LNCS, vol. 3027, pp. 20–39. Springer, Heidelberg (2004)
23. Microsoft Corporation. Phoenix compiler framework (2008)
24. Moon, T.K.: Error Correction Coding: Mathematical Methods and Algorithms. Wiley-Interscience, Hoboken (2005)
25. Feng, Q., Joseph, T., Yuanyuan, Z., Jagadeesan, S.: Rx: Treating bugs as allergies—a safe method to survive software failures. ACM Trans. Comput. Syst. 25(3), 7 (2007)
26. Randell, B.: System structure for software fault tolerance. In: Proceedings of the International Conference on Reliable Software, Los Angeles, California, pp. 437–449. ACM, New York (1975)
27. Randell, B., Lee, P., Treleaven, P.C.: Reliability issues in computing system design. ACM Comput. Surv. 10(2), 123–165 (1978)
28. Siewiorek, D.P., Swarz, R.S.: Theory and Practice of Reliable System Design. Digital Press, Bedford (1982)
29. Tan, G., Chen, Y., Jakubowski, M.H.: Delayed and controlled failures in tamper-resistant software. In: Proceedings of the 2006 Information Hiding Workshop (july 2006)
30. Tyrrell, A.M.: Recovery blocks and algorithm-based fault tolerance. In: EUROMICRO Conference, vol. 0, p. 292 (1996)
31. Varadarajan, A.V., Venkatesan, R., Rangan, C.P.: Data structures for limited oblivious execution of programs while preserving locality of reference. In: DRM 2007: Proceedings of the 2007 ACM workshop on Digital Rights Management, pp. 63–69. ACM, New York (2007)
32. Wang, C., Hill, J., Knight, J., Davidson, J.: Software tamper resistance: Obstructing static analysis of programs. Technical Report CS-2000-12, University of Virginia (December 2000)
33. Wee, H.: On obfuscating point functions. In: STOC 2005: Proceedings of the Thirty-seventh Annual ACM Symposium on Theory of Computing, pp. 523–532. ACM Press, New York (2005)

# An Error-Tolerant Variant of a Short 2-Secure Fingerprint Code and Its Security Evaluation*

Koji Nuida

Research Center for Information Security (RCIS), National Institute of Advanced
Industrial Science and Technology (AIST)
Akihabara-Daibiru Room 1003, 1-18-13 Sotokanda, Chiyoda-ku, Tokyo 101-0021,
Japan
k.nuida@aist.go.jp

**Abstract.** In recent research on collusion-secure fingerprint codes, some relaxation of the conventional security assumption (Marking Assumption) have been introduced from a viewpoint of reality in practical situations, and several fingerprint codes have been proposed under those assumptions. In this article, we consider such a relaxed assumption and give an extension of short 2-secure codes (under Marking Assumption) recently proposed by Nuida et al. (IEICE Trans. A, 2009) to our assumption. We perform theoretical and numerical evaluation of security and required code lengths. For example, to bound the error probability by 0.01% for 10,000 users, 162-bit, 220-bit and 329-bit lengths are sufficient even if each bit of the fingerprint codeword is either flipped (in addition to other collusion attacks) with probabilities 1%, 2.5% and 5%, respectively, or erased with probabilities 2%, 5% and 10%, respectively.

**Keywords:** Digital fingerprint, collusion-attack, 2-secure code, error-tolerance, digital rights management.

## 1 Introduction

### 1.1 Backgrounds

Recently, digital content distribution services have been widespread with support of the progress of information processing/communication technology. Digitization of contents and content distribution has been promoted convenience for many people. However, it does also work better for malicious pirates, and the number of illegal content copying/redistribution has increased very rapidly. Thus technical countermeasures for such illegal activities are strongly desired.

Digital fingerprinting is a possible solution for the above problems. Here we focus on code-based schemes; a content server first encodes each user's ID and then embeds each codeword into a content that will be sent to the user. This intends to be able to determine the pirate from the codeword in a pirated content when a

---

* This work was supported by 2007 Research Grants of the Science and Technology
Foundation of Japan (JSTF).

T. Takagi and M. Mambo (Eds.): IWSEC 2009, LNCS 5824, pp. 140–157, 2009.

single pirate redistributes the received content. However, it has been pointed out that, if two or more pirates collude, then strong attacks (collusion attacks) to the embedded codeword are possible. Thus any fingerprint code should be equipped with an appropriate pirate tracing algorithm that determines a pirate correctly with an overwhelming probability even from an attacked codeword. Such a code is called $c$-secure [4] if it works properly against at most $c$ pirates. Under the conventional Marking Assumption [4] several $c$-secure codes (e.g., [4,8,9,12,14,15]), including 2-secure ones (e.g., [2,5,7,11,13,16]), have been proposed. In particular, to our best knowledge, the 2-secure codes recently proposed by Nuida et al. [11] have shortest code lengths under several practical parameters among those existing codes in the present time.

## 1.2  Motivation

The conventional Marking Assumption [4] mentioned in the previous subsection is, roughly speaking, the following: If existence of a bit in a pirate's codeword cannot be detected by mutual comparison of all pirates' codewords, then this bit will be left unchanged in the pirated codeword (the codeword embedded into the pirated content). See Sect. 2 for a precise description. The Marking Assumption has been standard in the research on fingerprint codes, and several fingerprint codes (including the above-mentioned ones [11]) have been proposed under the Marking Assumption as we have mentioned in the previous subsection.

However, it has also been pointed out that Marking Assumption somewhat lacks practicality, as it is difficult to realize a fingerprint embedding scheme that ensures Marking Assumption. Thus there have been proposed some relaxation of the Marking Assumption to consider more practical situations. Guth and Pfitzmann [8] considered the situation that each bit of a pirate's codeword is changed independently with a certain probability, even if this bit is undetectable in the above sense. The robustness of the fingerprint embedding scheme required by the relaxed Marking Assumption is weaker than that required by the original (strict) Marking Assumption, therefore the fingerprint codes become more practical by basing on the relaxed Marking Assumption instead of the original Marking Assumption. The aim of this article is to give a modification of the above-mentioned short 2-secure codes [11], together with its security evaluation, under a relaxed Marking Assumption that is closely related to the assumption in [8].

A part of significance of studying 2-secure codes can be explained as follows. First, in some situations where the users are less anonymous for the content server (e.g., a case to prevent information leakage in development of a new product, where the "content server" is a company and "users" are the development staffs), it would be difficult to make a large malicious coalition confidentially, hence the 2-secure property would make sense. On the other hand, the code lengths can be significantly reduced by restricting the construction to 2-secure case than applying $c$-secure codes (valid for any $c$) to the special case $c = 2$.

## 1.3    Our Contributions and Organization of the Article

In Sect. 2, we give a formulation of the notion of fingerprint codes, definitions of some notations and terminology, and formal descriptions of Marking Assumption and its relaxed variant considered in this article, called *Marking Assumption with $(\delta_f, \delta_e)$-Error*. The relaxed assumption states that, in addition to perform any attack allowed under Marking Assumption, the pirates flip and erase each bit of the codeword with probabilities $\delta_f$ and $\delta_e$, respectively. We call a fingerprint code $(\delta_f, \delta_e)$-*tolerant c-secure* if it is secure under this assumption against at most $c$ pirates. Then in Sect. 3, we summarize the construction and some properties of 2-secure codes in [11], in particular, a special subroutine of the pirate tracing algorithm called Partner Search that is a main ingredient of the 2-secure codes.

In Sect. 4, we give the construction of the fingerprint codes of our proposal. First, in Sect. 4.1 we introduce a variant of the above Partner Search, called *T-Tolerant Partner Search*, where $T$ is a parameter that will be related to the quantities $\delta_f$ and $\delta_e$. Its difference from the original Partner Search is motivated by that we are now concerning Marking Assumption with $(\delta_f, \delta_e)$-Error instead of the original Marking Assumption. The definition of our fingerprint codes is given in Sect. 4.2 by modifying the definition of the original 2-secure codes [11]. Their difference (except some technical points) is that our codes use $T$-Tolerant Partner Search instead of Partner Search used in the original codes.

In Sect. 5, we give a formula of error probabilities of our fingerprint codes under Marking Assumption with $(\delta_f, \delta_e)$-Error, for each of the cases with one pirate or two pirates, respectively (Sect. 5.1). We also give proofs of the formulae in Sect. 5.2 and Sect. 5.3. Note that, in our security evaluation, $\alpha\%$ bit flipping and $2\alpha\%$ bit erasure by the pirates are equivalent with each other.

Finally, Sect. 6 deals with a choice of the parameter $T$ and gives numerical examples for our fingerprint codes. First, in Sect. 6.1, we discuss how to choose an appropriate parameter $T$ for given values of the code length $m$, the bound $\varepsilon$ of error probability, and the parameter $\delta = \delta_f + \delta_e/2$ for our assumption. We propose a "formula" of the parameter $T$ from a viewpoint of a certain statistical property of the pirates' codewords and its approximation by Central Limit Theorem. By using the parameter $T$, in Sect. 6.2 we derive the required code lengths of our codes for some parameters $N$ (the number of users), $\varepsilon$, and $\delta = \delta_f + \delta_e/2$ by computer calculation. For example, when $N = 10^4$, and $\delta = 0.01, 0.025$ and $0.05$ (i.e., each bit of the codeword is either flipped by pirates with probabilities 1%, 2.5% and 5%, or erased with probabilities 2%, 5% and 10%, respectively), the bit lengths $m = 162, 220$ and $329$ are sufficient to bound the error probability by $\varepsilon = 10^{-4}$, respectively. On the other hand, the code length for the original 2-secure code [11] is $m = 88$ for the same parameters $N$ and $\varepsilon$ under Marking Assumption. Which of the two codes is more efficient depends on, for example, whether or not embedding 329-bit fingerprint into a content with tolerance of 5% bit flipping or 10% bit erasure is more practical than embedding 88-bit fingerprint without such tolerance. The author thinks that our result in this article would in fact increase practicality of the fingerprint codes significantly.

## 1.4  Related Works

As we have mentioned in Sect. 1.2, several relaxation of Marking Assumption have been already studied. First, Guth and Pfitzmann [8] proposed a modification of $c$-secure codes by Boneh and Shaw [4] under the relaxed assumption mentioned in Sect. 1.2. On the other hand, Nuida et al. [12] considered a similar but different situation that at most a limited number of undetectable bits in pirates' codewords may be changed, where whether each bit is changed or not may depend on the other bits. They also constructed $c$-secure codes under their relaxed assumption. Moreover, recently Sirvent [17] considered another relaxation of Marking Assumption (that is very similar to the one by Nuida et al.) in connection with traitor tracing schemes with short ciphertext. He also proposed a modification of the $c$-secure codes by Boneh and Shaw under his assumption (see also Boneh and Naor [3]). Note that the assumption by Guth and Pfitzmann (relevant to our proposal) and the remaining two assumptions may be closely related, but there seems not to exist a simple implication from one to the other. Despite of those works, to the author's best knowledge there have not been fingerprint codes that focus on the case of two pirates under such relaxed assumptions; when restricted to the case of two pirates, such preceding fingerprint codes have much longer code lengths than our proposal in this article.

# 2  Fingerprint Codes

## 2.1  Basic Formulation

In this article, we define a *fingerprint code* as a pair (Gen, Tr) of a *codeword generation algorithm* Gen and a *tracing algorithm* Tr. The algorithm Gen outputs an $N \times m$ binary matrix $W$, with each row corresponding to a *user* for the code, where $N$ denotes the number of users and $m$ denotes the code length. (In general Gen may also output some auxiliary parameter for performing the tracing algorithm later, but here we omit the issue since the fingerprint codes considered in this article do not use such an auxiliary parameter.) Let $w_i$ denote the codeword of $i$-th user $u_i$, i.e., the $i$-th row of $W$. On the other hand, the algorithm Tr takes the matrix $W$ and a codeword $y$ of length $m$ as input, and outputs a (possibly empty) set of users. This $y$ signifies the pirated codeword; and the codeword $y$ is supposed to have an expanded alphabet $\{0, 1, ?\}$ instead of the binary alphabet $\{0, 1\}$, since we also deal with the case that some bit in the pirated codeword is not only flipped but also made unreadable (erased). We write such a bit as '?', and call each '?' in $y$ an *unreadable bit*.

  Now we consider the situation that $\ell$ of the $N$ users $u_{i_1}, \ldots, u_{i_\ell}$ are adversaries, called *pirates*, who create a codeword $y \in \{0, 1, ?\}^m$ as above (called a *pirated codeword*) from their codewords $w_{i_1}, \ldots, w_{i_\ell}$ by using an attack algorithm. Let $U$ and $U^{\mathrm{P}}$ denote the sets of all users and of all pirates, respectively. Users in $U \setminus U^{\mathrm{P}}$ are called *innocent users*. In this article, superscripts 'P' and 'I' (such as $u^{\mathrm{P}}$ and $w^{\mathrm{I}}$) indicate "pirate" and "innocent user", respectively. We assume that $\ell \leq c$ for a fixed constant $c$. The events $\mathrm{Tr}(W, y) \cap U^{\mathrm{P}} = \emptyset$ and $\mathrm{Tr}(W, y) \not\subset U^{\mathrm{P}}$

are called *false-negative* and *false-positive*, respectively, and their union is called a *tracing error* (or an *error* in short). Assumptions on the choice of the pirates' attack algorithm are described in the next subsection.

## 2.2  Assumptions on Attack Algorithms

We say that $j$-th position in the codewords ($1 \leq j \leq m$) is *undetectable* if the $j$-th bits $w_{i_1,j}, \ldots, w_{i_\ell,j}$ of all pirates' codewords coincide with each other. Then the conventional *Marking Assumption* [4] is described as follows:

**Marking Assumption:** If $j$-th position is undetectable, then the $j$-th bit $y_j$ of the pirated codeword $y$ satisfies that $y_j = w_{i_1,j}$.

A fingerprint code is called *c-secure (with $\varepsilon$-error)* [4] if the tracing error probability is not higher than a sufficiently small value $\varepsilon$ under Marking Assumption (and the implicit assumption $\ell \leq c$). As we have mentioned in Sect. 1, most of the preceding fingerprint codes are based on the Marking Assumption.

On the other hand, Guth and Pfitzmann [8] considered a relaxed variant of the Marking Assumption. Following their idea, here we introduce the following assumption, where $\delta_f \geq 0$ and $\delta_e \geq 0$ are parameters:

**Marking Assumption with $(\delta_f, \delta_e)$-Error:** If $j$-th position is undetectable, then the $j$-th bit $y_j$ of the pirated codeword $y$ satisfies $Pr[y_j = 1 - w_{i_1,j}] = \delta_f$ and $Pr[y_j = ?] = \delta_e$. Moreover, the behavior of each undetectable bit in $y$ is independent of the remaining positions.

Note that the above assumption is not exactly the same as the one in [8]; here we adopt the assumption to simplify the argument. Note also that the case $\delta_f = \delta_e = 0$ coincides with the original Marking Assumption. We say that a fingerprint code is $(\delta_f, \delta_e)$-*tolerant c-secure (with $\varepsilon$-error)* if the tracing error probability is not higher than a sufficiently small value $\varepsilon$ under Marking Assumption with $(\delta_f, \delta_e)$-Error (whenever $\ell \leq c$). As we have mentioned in Sect. 1, the aim of this article is to modify 2-secure codes in [11] for making them $(\delta_f, \delta_e)$-tolerant. See Sect. 1.4 for other relaxed variants of Marking Assumption.

## 3  The Original Codes

This section summarizes the construction of 2-secure codes proposed by Nuida et al. in [11] that can be regarded as an improvement of Tardos's $c$-secure codes [15] (specialized to the case $c = 2$). Based on this, in later sections we will propose a $(\delta_f, \delta_e)$-tolerant variant of the codes. In fact, they proposed two variants of the 2-secure codes (called "basic codes" and "advanced codes" in [11]); here we focus on the latter "advanced" one since that was the main proposal of [11].

### 3.1  The Codeword Generation Algorithm

The codeword generation algorithm $\mathsf{Gen}_{org}$ of the original 2-secure code [11] outputs an $N \times m$ binary matrix $W$ uniformly at random. Thus each bit $w_{i,j}$ of each user's codeword $w_i$ is chosen from $\{0, 1\}$ independently and uniformly at random.

## 3.2   The Tracing Algorithm

The following subroutine PS, called *Partner Search*, is a main ingredient of the tracing algorithm $\mathsf{Tr}_{\mathrm{org}}$ of the original 2-secure code [11]:

**Definition 1.** *Given a pirated codeword $y$ and a user ID (say, of $i$-th user $u_i$), the subroutine $\mathsf{PS}(u_i)$ returns YES if there is another (say, $i'$-th) user $u_{i'}$ such that their codewords $w_i$ and $w_{i'}$ satisfy the following condition:*

$$\text{For each } 1 \leq j \leq m, \text{ we have } y_j = w_{i,j} \text{ if } w_{i,j} = w_{i',j}; \tag{1}$$

*and returns NO if there does not exist such a user.*

The key observation is that, under the Marking Assumption and the assumption $\ell \leq c = 2$, the condition (1) is a necessary condition for two users $u_i$ and $u_{i'}$ being the two pirates. By using this subroutine, the tracing algorithm $\mathsf{Tr}_{\mathrm{org}}$ is constructed as follows:

**Definition 2.** *Given a pirated codeword $y$ and the users' codewords as input, the tracing algorithm $\mathsf{Tr}_{\mathrm{org}}$ proceeds as follows:*

1. *Replace all the unreadable bits '?' in $y$ with '0'.*
2. *For each user $u_i$, calculate the score $S_i = S_{u_i}$ of $u_i$ by*

$$S_i = |\{j \in \{1, 2, \ldots, m\} \mid y_j = w_{i,j}\}| ,$$

   *i.e., $S_i = m - $ (Hamming distance of $y$ and $w_i$).*
3. *Sort all users in decreasing order of scores, as $u_{i_1}, u_{i_2}, \ldots, u_{i_N}$. (If two or more users have the same score, the order of them may be arbitrarily chosen.)*
4. *Set $h \leftarrow 1$.*
5. *If Partner Search $\mathsf{PS}(u_{i_h})$ for the user $u_{i_h}$ returns YES, then output the user $u_{i_h}$ and halt. If $\mathsf{PS}(u_{i_h})$ returns NO, then set $h \leftarrow h + 1$ and repeat this step unless $h = N$; otherwise (i.e., if $h = N$), output the empty set and halt.*

Table 1 shows code lengths of the 2-secure codes $(\mathsf{Gen}_{\mathrm{org}}, \mathsf{Tr}_{\mathrm{org}})$ (quoted from [11]) for achieving given bounds of error probabilities under the Marking Assumption.

**Table 1.** Required code lengths of 2-secure codes in [11]

| number $N$ of users | tracing error probability | | | | | |
|---|---|---|---|---|---|---|
| | $10^{-4}$ | $10^{-5}$ | $10^{-6}$ | $10^{-7}$ | $10^{-9}$ | $10^{-11}$ |
| $10^2$ | 61 | 71 | 81 | 91 | 112 | 133 |
| $10^3$ | 74 | 83 | 93 | 102 | 123 | 144 |
| $10^4$ | 88 | 97 | 105 | 114 | 134 | 155 |
| $10^5$ | 103 | 111 | 119 | 127 | 145 | 166 |
| $10^6$ | 118 | 126 | 134 | 141 | 158 | 177 |

# 4    Our Proposal

In this section, we present a modification of the 2-secure codes [11] summarized in Sect. 3. By the modification, the 2-secure codes will be $(\delta_f, \delta_e)$-tolerant for given parameters $\delta_f$ and $\delta_e$ (see Sect. 2.2 for the terminology). Analyses of security properties of the modified codes will be given in later sections.

## 4.1    $T$-Tolerant Partner Search

To make the codes $(\delta_f, \delta_e)$-tolerant, we modify the Partner Search algorithm (Definition 1) used in the original tracing algorithm $\mathsf{Tr}_{\mathrm{org}}$ in the following manner, where $T \geq 0$ is a parameter:

**Definition 3.** *Given a pirated codeword $y$ and a user ID (say, of $i$-th user $u_i$), the subroutine $\mathsf{PS}_T(u_i)$ returns YES if there is another (say, $i'$-th) user $u_{i'}$ such that their codewords $w_i$ and $w_{i'}$ satisfy the following condition:*

$$|\{j \in \{1, 2, \ldots, m\} \mid y_j \neq w_{i,j} = w_{i',j}\}| \leq T \ , \tag{2}$$

*and returns NO if there does not exist such a user.*

We call this subroutine $\mathsf{PS}_T$ *$T$-Tolerant Partner Search*. A key observation for the following construction is the following: Under Marking Assumption with $(\delta_f, \delta_e)$-Error, if $T$ is significantly larger than the average number of undetectable positions in which the pirated codeword differs from codewords of pirates, then the codewords of the two pirates will satisfy the condition (2) with high probability. Roughly speaking, the condition (2) is almost a necessary condition for two users being the pirates if $T$ is sufficiently large.

## 4.2    Construction of Our Codes

From now, we present our construction of $(\delta_f, \delta_e)$-tolerant 2-secure codes (Gen, Tr) based on the $T$-tolerant Partner Search introduced in the previous subsection. First, the codeword generation algorithm Gen is the same as the original one $\mathsf{Gen}_{\mathrm{org}}$: Each bit $w_{i,j}$ of each user's codeword $w_i$ is chosen from $\{0, 1\}$ independently and uniformly at random. We note that under some assumptions, the "worst-case attack" by two pirates is shown to be the uniform choice for each bit of a pirated codeword from the two codewords [1,6], and it can be shown that the evenness of occurrence probabilities of the bits 0 and 1 in codewords maximizes the mutual information between the pirate's codeword and the pirated codeword against this attack, suggesting the advantage of our codeword generation algorithm.

Secondly, the tracing algorithm Tr is obtained from the original one $\mathsf{Tr}_{\mathrm{org}}$ mainly by replacing the Partner Search with $T$-Tolerant Partner Search. Then the whole description of the algorithm Tr is the following:

**Definition 4.** *Given a parameter $T$, a pirated codeword $y$, and the users' codewords as input, the tracing algorithm Tr proceeds as follows:*

1. *Replace each unreadable bit '?' in* $y$ *with '0' or '1' independently and uniformly at random.*
2. *For each user* $u_i$, *calculate the score* $S_i = S_{u_i}$ *of* $u_i$ *by*

$$S_i = |\{j \in \{1, 2, \ldots, m\} \mid y_j = w_{i,j}\}|,$$

   *i.e.,* $S_i = m - $ *(Hamming distance of* $y$ *and* $w_i$).
3. *Sort all users in decreasing order of scores, as* $u_{i_1}, u_{i_2}, \ldots, u_{i_N}$. *(If two or more users have the same score, the order of them may be arbitrarily chosen.)*
4. *Set* $h \leftarrow 1$.
5. *If* $T$-*Tolerant Partner Search* $\mathsf{PS}_T(u_{i_h})$ *for the user* $u_{i_h}$ *returns YES, then output the user* $u_{i_h}$ *and halt. If* $\mathsf{PS}(u_{i_h})$ *returns NO, then set* $h \leftarrow h+1$ *and repeat this step unless* $h = N$; *otherwise (i.e., if* $h = N$), *output the empty set and halt.*

An appropriate choice of the parameter $T$ will be discussed in Sect. 6. Note that the scoring rule in the second step is essentially the same as Tardos's scoring rule [15] (specialized to the case that the occurrence probability of '1' is 1/2) up to affine transformation $S \leftrightarrow 2S - m$. Thus our tracing algorithm can be thought of as an improvement of that of Tardos's codes [15] implied by an idea of "joint decoding" (e.g., [1,10]). In contrast to some preceding works [2,13] that intend to almost perform an exhaustive decoding, which increases the running time significantly, a novel idea of the present work and the original one [11] is to reduce the running time of an exhaustive decoding by combining it with a "Tardos-like" scoring technique.

*Remark 1.* In the fifth step of the above tracing algorithm Tr, in the $T$-Tolerant Partner Search $\mathsf{PS}_T(u_{i_h})$ for the user $u_{i_h}$, it suffices to check whether there is another user $u_{i_{h'}}$ with $h' > h$ such that their codewords $w_i = w_{i_h}$ and $w_{i'} = w_{i_{h'}}$ satisfy the condition (2). Indeed, if there is another user $u_{i_{h'}}$ such that the condition (2) holds and $h' < h$, then the $T$-Tolerant Partner Search $\mathsf{PS}_T(u_{i_{h'}})$ that has been performed prior to $\mathsf{PS}_T(u_{i_h})$ should have returned YES, hence the tracing algorithm should have halted in that time. This fact is obvious but worthy to reduce the running time of the tracing algorithm Tr.

*Remark 2.* In contrast to the case of the original tracing algorithm $\mathsf{Tr}_{\mathrm{org}}$, in the algorithm Tr each '?' in $y$ is replaced with either '0' or '1' with the same probability by a technical reason. However, if no information on which of '0' and '1' is assigned to each undetectable position in the pirates' codewords is available by the pirates, then it can be seen that every '?' in $y$ may be safely replaced with '0', as it is done in the original algorithm $\mathsf{Tr}_{\mathrm{org}}$. This is also useful for simplifying the construction of the algorithm. (Note that another possible modification about the treatment of the symbols '?' is to *ignore* such symbols instead of replacing them with '0' or '1'. Evaluation of tracing performance based on this modification will be a future research topic.)

## 5    Error Probabilities of Our Codes

In this section, we evaluate theoretically the error probabilities of our fingerprint codes proposed in Sect. 4 under the Marking Assumption with $(\delta_f, \delta_e)$-Error. Some numerical examples based on the result of this section will be given in Sect. 6. In what follows, we put $\delta = \delta_f + \delta_e/2$ and assume that $N \geq 2$ for simplicity.

### 5.1    The Formulae

First, we summarize the result of this section as two formulae; proofs of them will be given in the following subsections. Before giving the formulae, we introduce some notations. For $0 \leq x \leq 1$ and $k > 0$, put $k * x = 1 - (1 - x)^k$. For any real number $x$, put $[x]_{\wedge 1} = \min\{x, 1\}$. For any integer $a$, put

$$\chi_o(a) = \begin{cases} 1 & \text{if } a \text{ is odd,} \\ 0 & \text{if } a \text{ is even,} \end{cases} \quad \chi_e(a) = \begin{cases} 0 & \text{if } a \text{ is odd,} \\ 1 & \text{if } a \text{ is even.} \end{cases}$$

Moreover, for any $0 \leq x \leq 1$ and integers $a, b$, put $P_x(a, b) = \binom{a}{b} x^b (1 - x)^{a-b}$. By using these notations, the formulae are described as follows:

**Theorem 1.** *Assume that there is precisely one pirate. Then, under the Marking Assumption with $(\delta_f, \delta_e)$-Error, the tracing error probability $p_{\mathrm{err}}$ is bounded by*

$$p_{\mathrm{err}} \leq \sum_{a=0}^{T} P_\delta(m, a) \left( (N - 1) * f_1(a) \right)$$

$$+ \sum_{a=T+1}^{m} P_\delta(m, a) \left[ (N - 1) * f_1(a) + (1 - f_2(a))^{N-1} \right]_{\wedge 1}, \tag{3}$$

*where $\delta = \delta_f + \delta_e/2$ and*

$$f_1(a) = \frac{1}{2^m} \sum_{b=0}^{a} \binom{m}{b}, \quad f_2(a) = \frac{1}{2^a} \sum_{a_0=0}^{T} \binom{a}{a_0} - \frac{1}{2^m} \sum_{a_0=0}^{T} \binom{a}{a_0} \sum_{b_0=0}^{a-a_0} \binom{m-a}{b_0}$$

*(see above for the other notations).*

**Theorem 2.** *Assume that there are precisely two pirates. Then, under the Marking Assumption with $(\delta_f, \delta_e)$-Error, the tracing error probability $p_{\mathrm{err}}$ is bounded by*

$$p_{\mathrm{err}} \leq \frac{1}{2^m} \sum_{a_0=0}^{m} \binom{m}{a_0} \left( \sum_{b_1=0}^{a_0-T-1} P_{1-\delta}(a_0, b_1) \left[ \max{}^* G_1(a_0, a_1, b_1) \right]_{\wedge 1} \right.$$

$$\left. + \sum_{b_1=a_0-T}^{a_0} P_{1-\delta}(a_0, b_1) \left[ \max{}^* G_2(a_0, a_1, b_1) \right]_{\wedge 1} \right), \tag{4}$$

*where*

$$G_1(a_0, a_1, b_1) = (N - 2 - \chi_e(N)) \left( \frac{N - 2 - \chi_0(N)}{2} * g_0 \right)$$
$$+ (N - 2) * g_2(a_1, b_1) + (N - 2) * g_3(a_0, a_1, b_1) + (1 - g_4(a_1, b_1))^{N-2},$$

$$G_2(a_0, a_1, b_1) = (N - 2 - \chi_e(N)) \left( \frac{N - 2 - \chi_0(N)}{2} * g_1(a_1, b_1) \right)$$
$$+ (N - 2) * g_2(a_1, b_1) + (N - 2) * g_3(a_0, a_1, b_1) ,$$

$$g_0 = \left( \frac{3}{4} \right)^m \sum_{k=0}^{T} \binom{m}{k} \frac{1}{3^k} ,$$

$$g_1(a_1, b_1) = g_0$$
$$- \frac{1}{4^m} \sum_{s=m+1-T-b_1-a_1}^{b_1+a_1-1} \binom{m}{s} \sum_{\ell=m+1-s-b_1-a_1}^{T} \binom{m-s}{\ell} \sum_{k=0}^{b_1+a_1+s+\ell-m-1} \binom{s}{k} ,$$

$$g_2(a_1, b_1) = \frac{1}{2^m} \sum_{\ell=0}^{T} \binom{m-b_1-a_1}{\ell} \sum_{k=2b_1+2a_1+\ell-m}^{b_1+a_1} \binom{b_1+a_1}{k} ,$$

$$g_3(a_0, a_1, b_1) = \frac{1}{2^m} \sum_{\ell=0}^{T} \binom{a_0+a_1-b_1}{\ell} \sum_{k=2b_1+\ell-a_0}^{m+b_1-a_0-a_1} \binom{m+b_1-a_0-a_1}{k} ,$$

$$g_4(a_1, b_1) = \frac{1}{2^{m-a_1-b_1}} \sum_{\ell=0}^{T} \binom{m-a_1-b_1}{\ell} ,$$

*and* max* *denotes the maximum over all integers* $a_1$ *such that* $(m-a_0)/2 \le a_1 \le m - a_0$ *(see above for the other notations).*

## 5.2   Proof of Theorem 1

The outline of the proof of Theorem 1 is as follows. Let $y$ denote the pirated codeword after the replacing process in the first step of Tr; thus $y \in \{0, 1\}^m$. Let $a$ be the number of positions in which $y$ differs from the codeword $w^P$ of the pirate $u^P$ (note that now there is just one pirate, thus every position is undetectable). By the definition of the first step of Tr and Marking Assumption with $(\delta_f, \delta_e)$-Error, in each position $y$ differs from $w^P$ with probability $\delta$ (since a '?' in $j$-th position is replaced with $w_j^P \in \{0, 1\}$ with probability $1/2$), therefore the probability that $y$ differs from $w^P$ in $a$ positions is $P_\delta(m, a)$.

In the case $a \le T$, $T$-Tolerant Partner Search $\mathsf{PS}_T(u^P)$ for the pirate $u^P$ always returns YES by the definition. Thus only the possibility of tracing error is that some innocent user $u^I$ comes prior to $u^P$ by the sorting in the third step of Tr and then $\mathsf{PS}_T(u^I)$ returns YES. Hence tracing error occurs only if the score $S_{u^I}$ of some $u^I$ is not less than $m-a$ ($= S_{u^P}$). We will prove the following lemma later, which shows that the tracing error probability conditioned on this case is not higher than $(N-1) * f_1(a)$:

**Lemma 1.** *In the above setting, the probability that $S_{u^{\mathrm{I}}} \geq m - a$ for some $u^{\mathrm{I}}$, conditioned on the choice of $w^{\mathrm{P}}$, is not higher than $(N - 1) * f_1(a)$.*

On the other hand, in the case $T + 1 \leq a \leq m$, only the possibility of tracing error is either (I) some $u^{\mathrm{I}}$ comes prior to $u^{\mathrm{P}}$ by the sorting and then $\mathsf{PS}_T(u^{\mathrm{I}})$ returns YES; or (II) $\mathsf{PS}_T(u^{\mathrm{P}})$ returns NO. A bound of the probability of (I) is given by Lemma 1. On the other hand, the case (II) occurs only if there does not exist a $u^{\mathrm{I}}$ such that $w^{\mathrm{P}}$ and $w^{\mathrm{I}}$ satisfy the condition (2). Since the case $S_{u^{\mathrm{I}}} \geq m - a$ is already included in Lemma 1, it suffices to consider the case (II') there does not exist a $u^{\mathrm{I}}$ such that $w^{\mathrm{P}}$ and $w^{\mathrm{I}}$ satisfy the condition (2) and $S_{u^{\mathrm{I}}} < m - a$. We will prove the following lemma later, which (together with Lemma 1) shows that the tracing error probability conditioned on this case is not higher than $\left[(N - 1) * f_1(a) + (1 - f_2(a))^{N-1}\right]_{\wedge 1}$ (note that the probability is not higher than 1):

**Lemma 2.** *In the above setting, the probability of the case (II'), conditioned on the choice of $w^{\mathrm{P}}$, is not higher than $(1 - f_2(a))^{N-1}$.*

Now Theorem 1 follows from the above argument. Finally, we give the proofs of the above two lemmas.

*Proof (Lemma 1).* By the definition of the operation $*$, since each user's codeword is generated independently, it suffices to show that $Pr[S_{u^{\mathrm{I}}} \geq m - a] = f_1(a)$ for each $u^{\mathrm{I}}$. This follows immediately from the definition of $f_1(a)$ (where the index $b$ signifies the number of positions in which $w^{\mathrm{I}}$ differs from $y$), since each bit of $w^{\mathrm{I}}$ is chosen from $\{0, 1\}$ independently and uniformly at random.     □

*Proof (Lemma 2).* It suffices to show that, for each $u^{\mathrm{I}}$, the probability that $w^{\mathrm{P}}$ and $w^{\mathrm{I}}$ satisfy the condition (2) and $S_{u^{\mathrm{I}}} < m - a$ is $f_2(a)$. Let

$$a_0 = |\{1 \leq j \leq m \mid w_j^{\mathrm{P}} \neq y_j \neq w_j^{\mathrm{I}}\}| \ , \quad b_0 = |\{1 \leq j \leq m \mid w_j^{\mathrm{P}} = y_j \neq w_j^{\mathrm{I}}\}| \ .$$

Then $w^{\mathrm{P}}$ and $w^{\mathrm{I}}$ satisfy the condition (2) if and only if $a_0 \leq T$; while $S_{u^{\mathrm{I}}} = m - a_0 - b_0$, therefore $S_{u^{\mathrm{I}}} < m - a$ if and only if $b_0 > a - a_0$. Thus the probability is

$$\sum_{a_0=0}^{T} \frac{1}{2^a} \binom{a}{a_0} \sum_{b_0=a-a_0+1}^{m-a} \frac{1}{2^{m-a}} \binom{m-a}{b_0}$$

$$= \sum_{a_0=0}^{T} \frac{1}{2^a} \binom{a}{a_0} \left(1 - \sum_{b_0=0}^{a-a_0} \frac{1}{2^{m-a}} \binom{m-a}{b_0}\right) = f_2(a) \ .$$

Hence Lemma 2 holds.     □

## 5.3   Proof of Theorem 2

The outline of the proof of Theorem 2 is as follows. Let $u_1^{\mathrm{P}}$ and $u_2^{\mathrm{P}}$ denote the two pirates. Let $y$ be as in Sect. 5.2. Put $[m] = \{1, 2, \ldots, m\}$, and define

$$A_{y,y} = \{j \in [m] \mid w_{1,j}^{\mathrm{P}} = y_j = w_{2,j}^{\mathrm{P}}\} \ , \quad A_{y,\times} = \{j \in [m] \mid w_{1,j}^{\mathrm{P}} = y_j \neq w_{2,j}^{\mathrm{P}}\} \ ,$$

$$A_{\times,y} = \{j \in [m] \mid w_{1,j}^{\mathrm{P}} \neq y_j = w_{2,j}^{\mathrm{P}}\} \ , \quad A_{\times,\times} = \{j \in [m] \mid w_{1,j}^{\mathrm{P}} \neq y_j \neq w_{2,j}^{\mathrm{P}}\} \ .$$

Then, since $w_1^P$ and $w_2^P$ coincide in a fixed position with probability $1/2$, the probability that $|A_{y,y}| + |A_{\times,\times}| = a_0$ (i.e., the number of undetectable positions is $a_0$) is $\binom{m}{a_0}/2^m$. On the other hand, by an argument similar to Sect. 5.2, the probability that $|A_{y,y}| = b_1$ conditioned on $|A_{y,y}| + |A_{\times,\times}| = a_0$ is $P_{1-\delta}(a_0, b_1)$. Thus it suffices to prove that, conditioned on the case that $|A_{y,y}| + |A_{\times,\times}| = a_0$ and $|A_{y,y}| = b_1$, the tracing error probability is not higher than $\max^* G_1(a_0, a_1, b_1)$ if $b_1 < a_0 - T$ and $\max^* G_2(a_0, a_1, b_1)$ if $b_1 \geq a_0 - T$, respectively (note that the probability is not higher than 1). In what follows, for any pair $(u_i, u_{i'})$ of two users we write $u_i \sim u_{i'}$ if and only if their codewords $w_i$ and $w_{i'}$ satisfy the condition (2).

First, we consider the case $b_1 < a_0 - T$. Suppose that $|A_{y,\times}| = a_1$. We may assume without loss of generality that $a_1 \geq (m - a_0)/2$ by symmetry on the two pirates. It suffices to show that the tracing error probability conditioned on this case is not higher than $G_1(a_0, a_1, b_1)$. Note that $S_{u_1^P} = |A_{y,y}| + |A_{y,\times}| = b_1 + a_1$ and $S_{u_2^P} = |A_{y,y}| + |A_{\times,y}| = b_1 + m - a_0 - a_1$, therefore $S_{u_1^P} \geq S_{u_2^P}$. Note also that $u_1^P \not\sim u_2^P$ since $|A_{\times,\times}| = a_0 - b_1 > T$. Now tracing error occurs only if one of the following four conditions is satisfied:

**(I)** There are two innocent users $u_1^I \neq u_2^I$ such that $u_1^I \sim u_2^I$.
**(II)** There is a $u^I$ such that $u^I \sim u_1^P$ and $S_{u^I} \geq b_1 + a_1$.
**(III)** There is a $u^I$ such that $u^I \sim u_2^P$ and $S_{u^I} \geq b_1 + a_1$.
**(IV)** There does not exist a $u^I$ such that $u^I \sim u_1^P$.

Indeed, if all of the four conditions fail, then $\mathsf{PS}_T(u^I)$ returns NO for any innocent user $u^I$ coming prior to $u_1^P$ by the sorting process (by the absence of (I)–(III)), while $\mathsf{PS}_T(u_1^P)$ returns YES (by the absence of (IV)); therefore this assertion follows. Thus the claim for the case $b_1 < a_0 - T$ is derived from the following four lemmas, which will be proven later:

**Lemma 3.** *In the above setting, the probability of the case (I), conditioned on the choice of $w_1^P$ and $w_2^P$, is not higher than*

$$(N - 2 - \chi_e(N))\left(\frac{N - 2 - \chi_0(N)}{2} * g_0\right).$$

**Lemma 4.** *In the above setting, the probability of the case (II), conditioned on the choice of $w_1^P$ and $w_2^P$, is not higher than $(N - 2) * g_2(a_1, b_1)$.*

**Lemma 5.** *In the above setting, the probability of the case (III), conditioned on the choice of $w_1^P$ and $w_2^P$, is not higher than $(N - 2) * g_3(a_0, a_1, b_1)$.*

**Lemma 6.** *In the above setting, the probability of the case (IV), conditioned on the choice of $w_1^P$ and $w_2^P$, is not higher than $(1 - g_4(a_1, b_1))^{N-2}$.*

Secondly, we consider the case $b_1 \geq a_0 - T$. Suppose that $|A_{y,\times}| = a_1$. We may assume without loss of generality that $a_1 \geq (m - a_0)/2$ by symmetry on the two pirates. It suffices to show that the tracing error probability conditioned on this case is not higher than $G_2(a_0, a_1, b_1)$. Note that $S_{u_1^P} = b_1 + a_1$ and

$S_{u_2^P} = b_1 + m - a_0 - a_1$, therefore $S_{u_1^P} \geq S_{u_2^P}$. Note also that $u_1^P \sim u_2^P$ since $|A_{\times,\times}| = a_0 - b_1 \leq T$. Now tracing error occurs only if one of the three conditions (II), (III) above and (I') below is satisfied:

**(I')** There are two innocent users $u_1^I \neq u_2^I$ such that $u_1^I \sim u_2^I$ and either $S_{u_1^I} \geq b_1 + a_1$ or $S_{u_2^I} \geq b_1 + a_1$.

Indeed, if all of the three conditions fail, then $\mathsf{PS}_T(u^I)$ returns NO for any innocent user $u^I$ coming prior to $u_1^P$ by the sorting process (by the absence of the three conditions), while $\mathsf{PS}_T(u_1^P)$ returns YES (since $u_1^P \sim u_2^P$); therefore this assertion follows. Thus the claim for the case $b_1 \geq a_0 - T$ is derived from Lemma 4, Lemma 5 and the following lemma, which will be proven later:

**Lemma 7.** *In the above setting, the probability of the case (I'), conditioned on the choice of $w_1^P$ and $w_2^P$, is not higher than*

$$(N - 2 - \chi_e(N)) \left( \frac{N - 2 - \chi_o(N)}{2} * g_1(a_1, b_1) \right).$$

Hence Theorem 2 follows from the above argument. From now, we give the proofs of the above lemmas. In the proof, we use the following auxiliary fact:

**Lemma 8.** *Let $x_1, \ldots, x_k$ be i.i.d. random variables, and let $\mathsf{P}$ be a property such that each unordered pair $x_i x_j$ ($i \neq j$) satisfies $\mathsf{P}$ with common probability $p$. Then $Pr[\text{at least one } x_i x_j \text{ satisfies } \mathsf{P}] \leq (k - \chi_e(k))(\frac{k - \chi_o(k)}{2} * p)$.*

*Proof.* First, the set of the $\binom{k}{2}$ unordered pairs $x_i x_j$ ($i \neq j$) has a partition into $k' = k - \chi_e(k)$ subsets $X_1, \ldots, X_{k'}$ of $(k - \chi_o(k))/2$ mutually disjoint pairs. This is an easy consequence of the well-known fact (see e.g., [18]) that the $k$-vertex complete graph $K_k$ has an edge $k'$-coloring. Now for each $h$, the events that $x_i x_j$ satisfies $\mathsf{P}$ are independent for all $x_i x_j \in X_h$, therefore at least one $x_i x_j \in X_h$ satisfies $\mathsf{P}$ with probability $\frac{k - \chi_o(k)}{2} * p$. This implies the desired bound. $\square$

This lemma is applied to prove Lemma 3 and Lemma 7, where the codewords of innocent users play the role of i.i.d. random variables $x_1, \ldots, x_k$ ($k = N - 2$). More precisely, by the lemma it suffices to show that, for each pair $(u_1^I, u_2^I)$ of two innocent users, we have $u_1^I \sim u_2^I$ with probability $g_0$, and we have $u_1^I \sim u_2^I$ and either $S_{u_1^I} \geq b_1 + a_1$ or $S_{u_2^I} \geq b_1 + a_1$ with probability $g_1(a_1, b_1)$ (note that $\chi_e(N - 2) = \chi_e(N)$ and $\chi_o(N - 2) = \chi_o(N)$). Since $j$-th bits of $w_1^I$ and $w_2^I$ satisfy $y_j \in \{w_{1,j}^I, w_{2,j}^I\}$ with probability $3/4$, we have $|\{j \in [m] \mid w_{1,j}^I \neq y_j \neq w_{2,j}^I\}| = k$ with probability $P_{1/4}(m, k) = (3/4)^m \binom{m}{k}/3^k$ for each $0 \leq k \leq T$. Thus the former assertion holds. For the latter assertion, it now suffices to show that we have $u_1^I \sim u_2^I$, $S_{u_1^I} < b_1 + a_1$ and $S_{u_2^I} < b_1 + a_1$ with probability equal to the second term of the definition of $g_1(a_1, b_1)$. Put

$$s = |\{j \in [m] \mid w_{1,j}^I = y_j\}| \ , \quad k = |\{j \in [m] \mid w_{1,j}^I = y_j = w_{2,j}^I\}| \ ,$$
$$\ell = |\{j \in [m] \mid w_{1,j}^I \neq y_j \neq w_{2,j}^I\}| \ .$$

Then the probability of $w_1^{\mathrm{I}}$ and $w_2^{\mathrm{I}}$ realizing these quantities is $\binom{m}{s}\binom{m-s}{\ell}\binom{s}{k}/4^m$. On the other hand, the conditions $u_1^{\mathrm{I}} \sim u_2^{\mathrm{I}}$, $S_{u_1^{\mathrm{I}}} < b_1 + a_1$ and $S_{u_2^{\mathrm{I}}} < b_1 + a_1$ are equivalent to $0 \leq \ell \leq T$, $0 \leq s < b_1 + a_1$ and $0 \leq k + m - s - \ell < b_1 + a_1$. Now by using the implicit conditions $k \geq 0$ and $s + \ell \leq m$, the above conditions for $s$, $\ell$ and $k$ are equivalent to

$$\max\{0, m + 1 - T - b_1 - a_1\} \leq s \leq b_1 + a_1 - 1 \ ,$$
$$\max\{0, m + 1 - s - b_1 - a_1\} \leq \ell \leq T \ , \quad 0 \leq k \leq b_1 + a_1 + s + \ell - m - 1 \ .$$

Since the sum of $\binom{m}{s}\binom{m-s}{\ell}\binom{s}{k}/4^m$ over the indices $s$, $\ell$ and $k$ in this range is equal to the second term of $g_1(a_1, b_1)$, the latter assertion holds. Hence Lemma 3 and Lemma 7 have been proven.

To prove Lemma 4 and Lemma 6, let $u^{\mathrm{I}}$ be a fixed innocent user, and put

$$\ell = |\{j \in A_{\times,y} \cup A_{\times,\times} \mid u_j^{\mathrm{I}} \neq y_j\}| \ , \quad k = |\{j \in A_{y,y} \cup A_{y,\times} \mid u_j^{\mathrm{I}} = y_j\}| \ .$$

Then we have $u^{\mathrm{I}} \sim u_1^{\mathrm{P}}$ if and only if $\ell \leq T$, while $w^{\mathrm{I}}$ realizes the quantity $\ell$ with probability $\binom{m-a_1-b_1}{\ell}/2^{m-a_1-b_1}$. Thus $u^{\mathrm{I}} \sim u_1^{\mathrm{P}}$ holds with probability $g_4(a_1, b_1)$, therefore Lemma 6 is proven. Moreover, we have $S_{u^{\mathrm{I}}} = k + m - a_1 - b_1 - \ell$, therefore $S_{u^{\mathrm{I}}} \geq b_1 + a_1$ if and only if $k \geq 2b_1 + 2a_1 + \ell - m$. Since $w^{\mathrm{I}}$ realizes the quantities $\ell$ and $k$ with probability $\binom{m-a_1-b_1}{\ell}\binom{b_1+a_1}{k}/2^m$, it follows that $u^{\mathrm{I}} \sim u_1^{\mathrm{P}}$ and $S_{u^{\mathrm{I}}} \geq b_1 + a_1$ hold with probability $g_2(a_1, b_1)$. Hence Lemma 4 is proven.

Finally, to prove Lemma 5, let $u^{\mathrm{I}}$ be a fixed innocent user, and put

$$\ell = |\{j \in A_{y,\times} \cup A_{\times,\times} \mid u_j^{\mathrm{I}} \neq y_j\}| \ , \quad k = |\{j \in A_{y,y} \cup A_{\times,y} \mid u_j^{\mathrm{I}} = y_j\}| \ .$$

Then we have $u^{\mathrm{I}} \sim u_2^{\mathrm{P}}$ if and only if $\ell \leq T$, while $w^{\mathrm{I}}$ realizes the quantities $\ell$ and $k$ with probability $\binom{a_0+a_1-b_1}{\ell}\binom{m+b_1-a_0-a_1}{k}/2^m$ (note that $|A_{\times,\times}| = a_0 - b_1$). Moreover, we have $S_{u^{\mathrm{I}}} = k + a_0 + a_1 - b_1 - \ell$, therefore $S_{u^{\mathrm{I}}} \geq b_1 + a_1$ if and only if $k \geq 2b_1 + \ell - a_0$. Thus $u^{\mathrm{I}} \sim u_2^{\mathrm{P}}$ and $S_{u^{\mathrm{I}}} \geq b_1 + a_1$ hold with probability $g_3(a_0, a_1, b_1)$, therefore Lemma 5 is proven.

Hence the proof of Theorem 2 is concluded.

# 6    Numerical Examples

## 6.1    On Choices of Parameter $T$

In this subsection, we discuss appropriate choices of the parameter $T$ for the tracing algorithm Tr of our $(\delta_{\mathrm{f}}, \delta_{\mathrm{e}})$-tolerant 2-secure codes. Note that the following argument is somewhat informal, however it still gives us a "yardstick" of how to decide the parameter $T$. In what follows, we focus on the case of two pirates.

First, recall from the argument in Sect. 5.3 that for each of $m$ positions in the codewords, the probability that it is undetectable and the pirated codeword $y$ (after the replacing process in the first step of Tr) differs from the pirates' codewords in this position is $\delta = \delta_{\mathrm{f}} + \delta_{\mathrm{e}}/2$. Let $a$ denote the number of such positions. A natural requirement for the parameter $T$ is that $Pr[a > T]$ does not exceed the parameter $\varepsilon$ for the bound of error probability (hence $T$ is not too small); if $a > T$, then the codewords of two pirates do not satisfy the condition (2), therefore it is not expected that Tr outputs a pirate correctly (except some accidental case that codewords of a pirate and an innocent user satisfy the condition (2)). On the other hand, it is also desirable that the parameter $T$ is not too large; if $T$ becomes too large, then the probability of codewords of two innocent users satisfying the condition (2) accidentally is also getting too high, which causes that false-positive probability increases as well.

Now we consider approximation of the distribution of $a$ by the normal distribution. Since $a$ follows the binomial distribution $B(m, \delta)$, the Central Limit Theorem implies that the distribution of $a$ is approximately the normal distribution $N(\mu, \sigma^2)$ (under a certain condition) with mean $\mu$ and variance $\sigma^2$ given by

$$\mu = m\delta \ , \ \ \sigma^2 = m\delta(1 - \delta) \ .$$

Under the approximation, we have

$$Pr[a > T] \approx Pr\big[N(\mu, \sigma^2) > T\big] = Pr[N(0, 1) > T'] \text{ where } T' = \frac{T - \mu}{\sigma} \ .$$

Note that $T = \sigma T' + \mu = \sqrt{m\delta(1 - \delta)}T' + m\delta$. By this observation, we determine the value of $T$ in the following manner: First calculate the value $x$ such that $Pr[N(0, 1) > x] = \varepsilon_0$ where $\varepsilon_0$ is a certain value with $0 \leq \varepsilon_0 < \varepsilon$ (by using the relation $Pr[N(0, 1) > x] = \mathrm{erfc}(x/\sqrt{2})/2$ where $\mathrm{erfc}(x)$ is the complementary error function) and then put

$$T = \left\lceil \sqrt{m\delta(1 - \delta)}x + m\delta \right\rceil \ . \tag{5}$$

We use this rule of determining $T$ in the following examples.

## 6.2  Code Lengths of Our Codes

Table 2 shows sufficient code lengths $m$ of our $(\delta_f, \delta_e)$-tolerant 2-secure codes for some parameters $N$, $\varepsilon$ and $\delta = \delta_f + \delta_e/2$, where the parameter $T$ is determined by the rule (5) with $Pr[N(0, 1) > x] = \varepsilon_0 = \varepsilon/2$. In the calculation of code lengths here, we mainly concern the tracing error probabilities in the case of two pirates (see Theorem 2); it is checked that the error probabilities in the case of one pirate (see Theorem 1) are much lower than $\varepsilon$ for the parameters in the table. Table 2 also includes the corresponding values of the parameter $T$. Due to the intricate shapes of the formulae of error probabilities, it is difficult to obtain a simple approximated formula of the code lengths of our codes in terms of the other parameters, which will be a future research topic.

Table 3 shows a comparison of code lengths for our $(\delta_f, \delta_e)$-tolerant codes and the original codes [11] for the same error probability $\varepsilon = 10^{-4}$ (cf. Table 1). Although the code lengths of our codes themselves are longer than those of the original codes [11], which of the two codes is more efficient actually depends on,

**Table 2.** Code lengths of the $(\delta_f, \delta_e)$-tolerant 2-secure codes (where $\delta = \delta_f + \delta_e/2$)

| | | $\delta = 0.005$ | | | $\delta = 0.01$ | | | $\delta = 0.025$ | | | $\delta = 0.05$ | | |
|---|---|---|---|---|---|---|---|---|---|---|---|---|---|
| | | tracing error probability $\varepsilon$ | | | | | | | | | | | |
| $N$ | | $10^{-2}$ | $10^{-3}$ | $10^{-4}$ | $10^{-2}$ | $10^{-3}$ | $10^{-4}$ | $10^{-2}$ | $10^{-3}$ | $10^{-4}$ | $10^{-2}$ | $10^{-3}$ | $10^{-4}$ |
| $10^2$ | $m$ | 66 | 84 | 101 | 81 | 99 | 116 | 102 | 133 | 157 | 152 | 195 | 237 |
| | $T$ | 2 | 3 | 4 | 4 | 5 | 6 | 7 | 10 | 12 | 15 | 20 | 25 |
| $10^3$ | $m$ | 92 | 102 | 119 | 100 | 118 | 135 | 130 | 161 | 192 | 195 | 238 | 286 |
| | $T$ | 3 | 3 | 4 | 4 | 5 | 6 | 8 | 11 | 14 | 18 | 23 | 29 |
| $10^4$ | $m$ | 110 | 127 | 145 | 127 | 144 | 162 | 164 | 189 | 220 | 237 | 286 | 329 |
| | $T$ | 3 | 4 | 5 | 5 | 6 | 7 | 10 | 12 | 15 | 21 | 27 | 32 |
| $10^5$ | $m$ | 127 | 145 | 163 | 145 | 163 | 180 | 192 | 224 | 248 | 279 | 329 | 378 |
| | $T$ | 3 | 4 | 5 | 5 | 6 | 7 | 11 | 14 | 16 | 24 | 30 | 36 |
| $10^6$ | $m$ | 145 | 163 | 181 | 163 | 189 | 207 | 219 | 251 | 283 | 321 | 371 | 414 |
| | $T$ | 3 | 4 | 5 | 5 | 7 | 8 | 12 | 15 | 18 | 27 | 33 | 38 |

**Table 3.** Comparison of code lengths for $\varepsilon = 10^{-4}$ (where $\delta = \delta_f + \delta_e/2$)

| $N$ | original [11] | $\delta = 0.005$ | $\delta = 0.01$ | $\delta = 0.025$ | $\delta = 0.05$ |
|---|---|---|---|---|---|
| $10^2$ | 61 | 101 | 116 | 157 | 237 |
| $10^3$ | 74 | 119 | 135 | 192 | 286 |
| $10^4$ | 88 | 145 | 162 | 220 | 329 |
| $10^5$ | 103 | 163 | 180 | 248 | 378 |
| $10^6$ | 118 | 181 | 207 | 283 | 414 |

for example, whether or not embedding 329-bit fingerprint into a content with tolerance of 5% bit flipping or 10% bit erasure is more practical than embedding 88-bit fingerprint without such tolerance. The author's naive opinion is that the former embedding with such tolerance would be much more practical than the latter embedding without such tolerance, hence our result in this article would in fact increase practicality of the fingerprint codes significantly. Theoretical or experimental consideration of such a comparison between the practicality of fingerprint embedding schemes with and without error tolerance, respectively, would be an interesting future research topic.

Finally, we give one more remark on the choice of the parameter $T$. Since this parameter $T$ is determined by using estimated values of the error rates $\delta_f$ and $\delta_e$, a problem in use of our codes is in fact *how to estimate the values of $\delta_f$ and $\delta_e$* in practical situations. A naive idea to resolve the problem is to append some common dummy bits to every user's codewords (that will always be undetectable bits). If the positions of dummy bits among the entire codeword can be hidden from the pirates (by, for instance, using secret random permutations), it would be possible to use the error rates restricted to the dummy bits (that can be explicitly determined) as a hint on what the actual error rates for non-dummy bits of the pirated codeword are. A rigorous evaluation of such an idea will be an interesting future research topic as well.

## 7    Conclusion

In this article, we studied 2-secure fingerprint codes in the situation that each bit is flipped or erased by the pirates with a certain probability in addition to other attacks, which is a more practical situation than that considered by the conventional Marking Assumption. We proposed a construction of such an error-tolerant 2-secure code based on the preceding scheme in [11], and evaluated its code length and security property. By comparing the code length of our code with the original scheme [11] that is not error-tolerant, the author conjectured that our code is more practical than the original scheme in a viewpoint of implementation. A theoretical or experimental evaluation of this conjecture will be a topic in future research.

## Acknowledgments

The author would like to thank Professor Keiichi Iwamura, Dr. Hyunho Kang, Dr. Takashi Kitagawa, Dr. Manabu Hagiwara, Dr. Hajime Watanabe, and Professor Hideki Imai, for their invaluable comments. Also, the author would like to thank the anonymous referees for their acute comments and suggestions.

## References

1. Amiri, E., Tardos, G.: High Rate Fingerprinting Codes and the Fingerprinting Capacity. In: Proc. SODA 2009, pp. 336–345. ACM, New York (2009)
2. Blakley, G.R., Kabatiansky, G.: Random Coding Technique for Digital Fingerprinting Codes. In: Proc. IEEE ISIT 2004, p. 202. IEEE, Los Alamitos (2004)
3. Boneh, D., Naor, M.: Traitor Tracing with Constant Size Ciphertext. In: Proc. ACM CCS 2008, pp. 501–510. ACM, New York (2008)
4. Boneh, D., Shaw, J.: Collusion-Secure Fingerprinting for Digital Data. IEEE Trans. Inform. Th. 44, 1897–1905 (1998)
5. Cotrina-Navau, J., Fernandez, M., Soriano, B.M.: A Family of Collusion 2-Secure Codes. In: Barni, M., Herrera-Joancomartí, J., Katzenbeisser, S., Pérez-González, F. (eds.) IH 2005. LNCS, vol. 3727, pp. 387–397. Springer, Heidelberg (2005)
6. Furon, T., Pérez-Freire, L.: Worst Case Attacks against Binary Probabilistic Traitor Tracing Codes. Preprint, arXiv:0903.3480v1 (2009)
7. Fernandez, M., Soriano, M.: Fingerprinting Concatenated Codes with Efficient Identification. In: Chan, A.H., Gligor, V. (Eds.), ISC 2002. LNCS, vol. 2433, pp. 459–470. Springer (2002)
8. Guth, H.-J., Pfitzmann, B.: Error- and Collusion-Secure Fingerprinting for Digital Data. In: Pfitzmann, A. (ed.) IH 1999. LNCS, vol. 1768, pp. 134–145. Springer, Heidelberg (2000)
9. Hagiwara, M., Hanaoka, G., Imai, H.: A short random fingerprinting code against a small number of pirates. In: Fossorier, M.P.C., Imai, H., Lin, S., Poli, A. (eds.) AAECC 2006. LNCS, vol. 3857, pp. 193–202. Springer, Heidelberg (2006)
10. Moulin, P.: Universal Fingerprinting: Capacity and Random-Coding Exponents. Preprint, arXiv:0801.3837v2 (2008)

11. Nuida, K., Fujitsu, S., Hagiwara, M., Imai, H., Kitagawa, T., Ogawa, K., Watanabe, H.: An Efficient 2-Secure and Short Random Fingerprint Code and Its Security Evaluation. IEICE Trans. Fundamentals E92-A(1), 197–206 (2009)
12. Nuida, K., Fujitsu, S., Hagiwara, M., Kitagawa, T., Watanabe, H., Ogawa, K., Imai, H.: An Improvement of Discrete Tardos Fingerprinting Codes. Des. Codes Cryptogr. 52, 339–362 (2009)
13. Nuida, K., Hagiwara, M., Kitagawa, T., Watanabe, H., Ogawa, K., Fujitsu, S., Imai, H.: A Tracing Algorithm for Short 2-Secure Probabilistic Fingerprinting Codes Strongly Protecting Innocent Users. In: Proc. IEEE CCNC 2007, pp. 1068–1072. IEEE, Los Alamitos (2007)
14. Nuida, K., Hagiwara, M., Watanabe, H., Imai, H.: Optimization of Tardos's Fingerprinting Codes in a Viewpoint of Memory Amount. In: Furon, T., Cayre, F., Doërr, G., Bas, P. (eds.) IH 2007. LNCS, vol. 4567, pp. 279–293. Springer, Heidelberg (2008)
15. Tardos, G.: Optimal Probabilistic Fingerprint Codes. J. ACM 55(2), 1–24 (2008)
16. Tô, V.D., Safavi-Naini, R., Wang, Y.: A 2-secure code with efficient tracing algorithm. In: Menezes, A., Sarkar, P. (eds.) INDOCRYPT 2002. LNCS, vol. 2551, pp. 149–162. Springer, Heidelberg (2002)
17. Sirvent, T.: Traitor Tracing Scheme with Constant Ciphertext Rate against Powerful Pirates. In: Proc. WCC 2007, pp. 379–388. INRIA (2007)
18. West, D.B.: Introduction to Graph Theory, 2nd edn. Prentice-Hall, Englewood Cliffs (2001)

# Efficient Intrusion Detection Based on Static Analysis and Stack Walks

Jingyu Hua[1], Mingchu Li[1], Kouichi Sakurai[2], and Yizhi Ren[1,2]

[1] School of Software, Dalian University of Technology,
Dalian 116620, China
huajingyu@gmail.com, li_mingchu@yahoo.com
[2] Dept.of Computer Science and Communication Engineering, kyushu University,
Fukuoka 812-0053, Japan
sakurai@csce.kyushu-u.ac.jp, renyizhi@gmail.com

**Abstract.** Some intrusion detection models such as the VPStatic first construct a behavior model for a program via static analysis, and then perform intrusion detection by monitoring whether its execution is consistent with this behavior model. These models usually share the highly desirable feature that they do not produce false alarms but they face the conflict between precision and efficiency. The high precision of the VPStatic is at the cost of high space complexity. In this paper, we propose a new context-sensitive intrusion detection model based on static analysis and stack walks, which is similar to VPStatic but much more efficient, especially in memory use. We replace the automaton in the VPStatic with a state transition table (STT) and all redundant states and transitions in VPStatic are eliminated. We prove that our STT model is a deterministic pushdown automaton (DPDA) and the precision is the same as the VPStatic. Experiments also demonstrate that our STT model reduces both time and memory costs comparing with the VPStatic, in particular, memory overheads are less than half of the VPStatic's. Thereby, we alleviate the conflict between precision and efficiency.

## 1 Introduction

When a program is attacked, such as injected malicious codes, it will behave in a manner inconsistent with its binary code, which can be made use of to perform intrusion detection. We can do a static analysis of the binary code to construct a behavior model, and then different kinds of attacks can be detected by monitoring whether the execution of this program deviates from this model. Actually, a lot of IDSs [2, 3, 4, 6, 9, 10, 11, 12] based on this idea has been proposed since 2000. Because of system calls are easy to be monitored at runtime, most of these systems use system calls to model the program behavior. These models usually do not produce any false alarms because they capture all correct execution behaviors via static analysis. This is the biggest reason why they are appreciated.

According to [3], the precision of intrusion detection models generated via static analysis can be divided into at least two levels. Models on the first level

T. Takagi and M. Mambo (Eds.): IWSEC 2009, LNCS 5824, pp. 158–173, 2009.
© Springer-Verlag Berlin Heidelberg 2009

are flow-sensitive and they just consider the order of execution of statements in the program, such as the system call sequences. Models on the second level are context-sensitive, which are more precise. They keep track of calling context of functions and are able to match the return of a function with the call site that invoked it. As a result, they are immune to the impossible path problem [4]. However, in most time, accurate is incompatible with efficient. Context-sensitive models are more accurate at the cost of higher program running time and space caused by the overheads of maintaining context information. Our purpose in this paper is right to decrease these overheads to construct an efficient context-sensitive intrusion detection model via static analysis.

## 1.1 Previous Work

In 2001, Wanger and Dean [4] proposed a precise abstract stack model generated via static analysis of C source code. This model uses stack states maintained in the abstract stack to model the call and return behaviors of function calls. Hence, this model is context-sensitive. Unfortunately, this model is a non-deterministic push down automaton (PDA). As a result, the time and space complexities are so high that it's not practical.

Feng and Giffin [2] pointed out severe non-determinism in the stack state is the major contributing factor to the high time and space complexities of PDA operations. They proposed two different models: Dyck and VPStatic to eliminate this non-determinism to improve the online detection efficiency.

The Dyck model [2, 12] is based on code instrumentation. It uses binary rewriting to insert code before and after each function call site to generate extra symbols needed for stack determinism. However, because the Dyck model is just a stack-deterministic PDA (sDPDA), not a complete deterministic PDA (DPDA), it still requires linear time when waking in the automaton. What's worse, its time efficiency is also affected by the overheads of new inserted codes. As a result, the time complexity for the Dyck model is still too high that slowdowns of 56% and 135% are reported for two linux self-contained programs: *cat* and *htzipd*.

The VPStatic [2] is a statically constructed variant of the dynamic context-sensitive VtPath model [7]. It also uses a statically constructed automaton to model the call and return behavior of function calls between two consecutive system calls, but stack walks are used to observe existing context-determining symbols to eliminate non-determinability. It is a provably DPDA and dose not do any instrumentation. Thereby, the time efficiency is much higher than the Dyck model. However, the VPStatic produces much lager automaton structures than the Dyck model which leads to a higher memory use. Increases of 183% and 194% are reported for *htzipd* and *cat* in memory uses.

## 1.2 Our Contribution

Our work is focused on constructing a model similar to VPStatic that is a DPDA and efficient in time but with a much lower memory use. Specifically, we make the following contributions:

- We propose a new context-sensitive intrusion detection model called STT based on static analysis and stack walks. We replace the automaton in the VPStatic with a state transition table, which records correct transitions among system call sites and corresponding execution contexts directly. The walk in the automaton is becoming a search in the table, which is more efficient. We use a delta optimization to solve the state explosion problem due to the use of the STT. There're no redundant states and transitions in our STT model. According to our analysis, the number of states in the STT is much less than half of that in the VPStatic for the same program. As a result, the memory overheads are greatly reduced.
- We formally define the STT model and prove it's a deterministic push down automaton (DPDA), which means its time efficiency is at least as high as the VPStatic.
- We prove our STT model has the same precision with the VPStatic. It accepts all VPStatic accepts and refuses all VPStatic refuses. So we improve the efficiency without reducing the precision.
- We implement dynamically-constructed VPStatic models and STT models for programs *gzip* and *cat*. Experiments results show the memory overheads of the STT models are less than half of the VPStatic models'.

```
1    char* filename; pid_t [2] pid;
2    int prepare(int index) {
3        char buf[20];
4        pid[index] = getpid();
5        strcpy(buf, filename);
6        return open(buf,O_RDWR);
7    }
8    void action(){
9        uid_t uid = getuid();
10       int handle;
11       if (uid!= 0)
12       {
13           handle = prepare(1);
14           read(handle, ...);
15       }
16       else
17       {
18           handle =prepare(0);
19           write(handle, ...);
20       }
21       close(handle);
22   }
```

**Fig. 1.** A sample program fragment. This fragment is composed by two functions: *prepare* and *action*. Functions *getpid*, *open*, *getuid*, *read*, *write* and *close* are system calls.

## 2  STT Model

Our model is a statically-constructed context-sensitive intrusion detection model. We will first use the sample program in Fig.1 to illustrate its basic idea.

### 2.1  Basic Idea

See Fig.1, assume we capture two consecutive system calls: *getuid* and *getpid* in an execution of the program and corresponding user stacks are presented in Fig.2. We can perform intrusion detection by checking whether such transitions for both system calls and stack states are possible according to the program's binary code. As we known, the stack state represents the real-time calling context of functions. According to the source code, the system call *getpid* is right following the system call *getuid*. Between them, only a function *prepare* is called (in line 13 or 18), so a new stack frame for *prepare* will be pushed into the call stack, which means the transition of the stack state is correct, too. Therefore, we say this program is still running normally by now. Our model is just based on this idea. We use a state transition table which is constructed via a static analysis of the binary of a program to record all these correct transitions. We perform online intrusion detection by verifying whether both the system call and stack state traces of the execution are consistent with the table. Because we make use of a state transition table, we name our model STT.

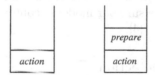

**Fig. 2.** Abstract stack states when *getuid* is called (left) and *getpid* is called (right)

### 2.2  Structure of the State Transition Table

In our model, we assume that when a system call is invoked, the monitored program will transfer to a new state. The STT is used to decide what new state the program should transfer to after a system call is invoked according to the binary.

Table 1 presents the STT for the sample program in Fig.1. The left header of the table are states of the program. We assign each an increasing unique id. Every state is corresponding to a system call site and composed by two parts: the address of the system call site and the stack state when the program executes to this site. In order to reduce the memory use of the STT, we use a fixed-length hash value of the return address list in the stack to represent the stack state. In this paper, we assume the hash function we use is so perfect that the probability of conflicts of hash values can be ignored. The first state $< h(a), s\_getuid >$ means the program invokes a system call *getuid* at address $s\_getuid$ and the

**Table 1.** State transition table for the sample program in Fig.1. $a$, $p1$ and $p0$ are return addresses of *action*, *prepare*(1) and *prepare*(0),respectively. String with the prefix $s_-$ represents the address of the corresponding system call.

| | getuid | getpid | open | read | close | write |
|---|---|---|---|---|---|---|
| 1:$< h(a), s\_getuid >$ | | 2,3 | | | | |
| 2:$< h(ap1), s\_getpid >$ | | | 4 | | | |
| 3:$< h(ap0), s\_getpid >$ | | | 5 | | | |
| 4:$< h(ap1), s\_open >$ | | | | 6 | | |
| 5:$< h(ap0), s\_open >$ | | | | | | 8 |
| 6:$< h(a), s\_read >$ | | | | | 7 | |
| 7:$< h(a), s\_close >$ | | | | | | |
| 8:$< h(a), s\_write >$ | | | | | 7 | |

stack state is $h(a)$ at this site, where h is the hash function. The top header of the table are system calls that trigger the program transferring from the current state to a new one. Assume we are at state 1, and then if the system call *getpid* is captured, according to the STT, the program should transfer to state 2 or state 3.

Because we take stack state into consideration, we define different states for the same system call site when it is executed in different contexts. For example, in the sample program, the system call *open* can be invoked either in *prepare*(0) or *prepare*(1). As a result, we define two sates: 4 and 5, for this single system call site. We do this to make sure our model is context sensitive and immune to the impossible path problem [4].

## 2.3   Online Intrusion Detection

If the STT for a program has been statically constructed, we can use it to monitor the execution of the program. Intrusion detection is performed every time when a new system call is captured. The whole process contains three steps:

1. Use the new captured system call $s$ and the last state to search for the expected state set $Q_e$ in the STT.
2. Walk the current user stack to extract the return address list $B$ and then compute the real state $q =< h(B), s\_s >$ the program is at.
3. Then, if $q \in Q_e$, nothing is wrong, but if $q \notin Q_e$, an attack is considered having occurred.

Let's use an overflow attack targeting to the sample program in Fig.1 to illustrate this process. Assume when the program is executing in the function call *prepare*(1), an attacker overflows $buf$ using *strcpy* (Line 5) and modifies the return address of this call to the address of *prepare*(0), then the system call sequence will become $getpid- > open- > getpid- > open- > write- > \cdots$.

The detection process for this attack is presented in Table 2. When the system call *open* is captured at the first time, the real state is $< h(ap0), s\_open >$.

**Table 2.** Online Detection Process for the overflow attack to the sample program in Fig.1

| Captured System Call | Last State | Expected States | Real State | Detect Result |
|---|---|---|---|---|
| *getpid* | 1 | 2,3 | $< h(ap1), s\_getpid >= 2$ | normal |
| *open* | 2 | 4 | $< h(ap0), s\_open > \neq 4$ | attack |

However, the current state is expected to be $< h(ap1), s\_open >$ according to the STT. Thereby, we detect the attack.

## 2.4 Delta Optimization

$$f_n \xrightarrow{a_{n-1}} f_{n-1} \xrightarrow{a_{n-2}} \cdots f_2 \xrightarrow{a_1} f_1 \xrightarrow{1} s$$

**Fig. 3.** A special situation where a system call $s$ is invoked by the first function $f_1$ at some site, $f_1$ itself is invoked at $a_1$ different sites by the second function $f_2$, $f_2$ is invoked at $a_2$ different sites by the third function and so on

### 2.4.1 State Explosion Problem

By now, our STT model suffers the state explosion problem. Because our model is context sensitive, we define different states for the same system call site in different execution contexts. Let's consider the special case presented in Fig.3. In this case, the system call $s$ can be invoked in $a_1 \times a_2 \times \cdots \times a_{n-1}$ different contexts, as a result, the total number of states defined for it is $a_1 \times a_2 \times \cdots \times a_{n-1}$. This is so called state explosion, which means our current model will scale poorly for large programs because of the soaring number of states. Fortunately, we can use a method named delta optimization by us to solve this problem.

### 2.4.2 Delta Optimization

We find that for two consecutive states, they must share a common prefix between their return address lists in the stack. For example, state 1 and state 2 in Table 1 are consecutive and their return address lists share $a$ as the common prefix. According to this, we redefine the state:

**Definition 1.** *Let $C$ be the common prefix between the current return address list $B$ and the last return address list $A$. Then, the state for the current system call site in the delta optimized STT is a triple $S =< l, d, s >$, where:*

*$l$ is the length of the postfix [1] of $B$ excluding $C$.*
*$d$ is the hash value of the postfix of $B$ excluding $C$.*
*$s$ is the address of the current system call site.*

This definition will reduce the number of states in the STT greatly. Let's consider the system call *open* in the sample program in Fig.1 again. Table 3 presents the

---

[1] This postfix is the delta part (different part) of $B$ compared with $A$. So we call this optimization method Delta Optimization.

**Table 3.** State definitions for the system call *open* of the sample program in Fig.1 in two different execution contexts

| Context | Last System Call Site | Last Return Address List | Current Return Address List | State Definition |
|---------|----------------------|--------------------------|-----------------------------|------------------|
| *prepare*(1) | *s_getpid* | *ap1* | *ap1* | $< 0, none, s\_open >$ |
| *prepare*(0) | *s_getpid* | *ap0* | *ap0* | $< 0, none, s\_open >$ |

**Table 4.** New state transition table for the sample program in Fig.1 after the delta optimization

| | *getuid* | *getpid* | *open* | *read* | *close* | *write* |
|---|----------|----------|--------|--------|---------|---------|
| 1:$< 1, h(a), s\_getuid >$ | | 1,2 | | | | |
| 2:$< 1, h(p1), s\_getpid >$ | | | 4 | | | |
| 3:$< 1, h(p0), s\_getpid >$ | | | 4 | | | |
| 4:$< 0, none, s\_open >$ | | | | $5 - (2, p1)$ | | $7 - (2, p0)$ |
| 5:$< 0, none, s\_read >$ | | | | | 6 | |
| 6:$< 0, none, s\_close >$ | | | | | | |
| 7:$< 0, none, s\_write >$ | | | | | 6 | |

state definition for this single site in two different execution contexts. We find that $l$, $d$, $s$ remain the same in the two different contexts. As a result, state 2 and state 3 in Table 1 are merged into one state $< 0, none, s\_open >$. In fact, if a function is called in $n$ different sites, after the delta optimization, we only define one state for each system call in the function except the first one [2], for which we still define $n$ states. Thereby, now the total number of states defined for $s$ in the case presented in Fig.3 is less than $a_1 + a_2 + \cdots + a_{n-1}$ , which is linear to the number of function calls. So, our new STT model can scale well for large programs.

Although we redefine the state, the online intrusion detection algorithm described in Sec.2.3 remains the same on the whole and the only difference is the way to compute the real state $q$. Before the delta optimization, $q$ is computed based on the current return address list $B$ got from the stack walks. However, now, we have to compute $q$ based on not only $B$ but also last state's return address list $A$. As a result, we need to keep track of the last state's return address list during the online monitoring.

Table 4 presents the new STT for the sample program in Fig.1 after the delta optimization. We will describe how to construct it via static analysis in Sec.2.5.

### 2.4.3  Side Effect of Delta Optimization

Unfortunately, the delta optimization has side effect that it will bring us impossible path problem again. See Table 4, after the optimization, state 4 can either

---

[2] Note that the first system call of a function refers to the first system call the program will invoke after entering the function, before leaving the function.

transfer to state 5 or state 7 with out any limit. Actually, state 4 can transfer to state 5 only when *open* is called in *prepare*(1) and to state 7 only when *open* is called in *prepare*(0). We find states suffering this problem are all last system calls [3] of functions. The reason behind this problem is we neglect the execution context of the function. When a function is called at different sites, we only define one state for its last system call (Assume the function will invoke more than one system call) after the delta optimization. Then, if the program transfers to different states when the same function returns from different sites, we have no ways to distinguish among them just based on the triple of the state. However, we should remember that the return address of the function exits in the return address list. We can turn to it to identify which call site we are returning from and then decide which state we should transfer to. So we add a transfer condition to each transition of these states. A condition specifies the position of the return address of the function in the return address list and what value it should be equal to if the program follows the corresponding transition. In Table 4, we add condition $(2, p1)$ to the transition from state 4 to state 5, which means if this transition takes place, the second address in the return address list of state 4 should be equal to $p1$. By this way, we can solve the impossible problem due to delta optimization completely.

## 2.5  Model Generation via Static Analysis

Before we can monitor the running of a program, we have to build a STT for it. The STT model for a program is built via a static analysis of its binary executable. We first disassemble the binary, and then we analyze the disassembled instructions recursively following the control flow of the program. We maintain a virtual stack to simulate the real stack: when the analyzer enters into a function, its return address is pushed into the virtual stack and when it leaves the function, the return address is popped out of the stack. In our algorithm, we don't care any other types of instructions except the following three ones:

**System Call Instructions:** When the analyzer comes to a system call instruction, we use the instruction address, current return address list in the virtual stack and the last state's return address list to create a new state according to Definition 1. If this state has been already in the STT, which means the current analysis path has been covered before, we stop going on analyzing along this path and return. Otherwise, we insert the new state into the STT and update the last state of the analyzer to be this new state. Then, we continue the analysis along this path. In addition, in both cases we need to add a new transition from the last state to the current state in the STT.

**Jump Instructions:** When the analyzer comes to a jump instruction, we first recursively invoke the analysis algorithm from the target address. Then, after that process returns, we continue at the address following the jump instruction.

---

[3] Note that the last system call of a function refers to the last system call the program will invoke after entering the function, before leaving the function.

**Function Call Instructions:** As we said before, except the first one, we only define one state for each system call site in the same function after the delta optimization. As a result, no need to analyze the same function repeatedly. When the analyzer comes to a function call, we first judge whether this function has been analyzed before. If not, we enter it and recursively invoke the analysis algorithm from the beginning of the function. When we create the first state of this function, we store the address $s$ of the system call and the postfix $R$ of its return address list, which starts after the return address of the function. After finishing the analysis, we store the last state of the function and the postfix $R'$ of its return address list, which also starts after the return address of the function. Then, when we revisit this function at other site $t$, no need to re-analyze this function but just do two things. Firstly, we create a new state $< length(R) + 1, h(tR), s >$, where $length(R)$ means the length of $R$, and then add a new transition from the last state before we come to the function to this new state in the STT. Secondly, we update the last state of the analyzer to be the last state of the function stored earlier and its return address list should be modified to $VtR'$, where $V$ is the address list in the virtual stack. Then, we go on analyzing at the address after the function call. When we come to a new state and add a new transition to the last state of the function, we have to add a transfer condition $(length(V) + 1, t)$ to this transition to avoid the side effect described in Sec.2.4.3.

# 3    Formal Proof That the STT Model Is a DPDA

Our STT model can be considered as a push down automaton (PDA). We use the formal language described in [2, 14] to define it formally and prove that it's deterministic.

**Definition 2.** *The STT model is a push down automaton* $P = (Q, \Sigma, \Gamma, \delta, q_0, z_0, F)$, *where:*

*$Q$ is the set of states. Every state is a triple defined as Definition 1.*

*$\Sigma$ is the input alphabet to the automaton. If $a \in \Sigma$, then $a = (s, z')$, where: $s$ is the address of the current system call site and $z'$ is the real return address list got from stack walks.*

*$\Gamma$ is the stack alphabet. $z \in \Gamma$ is the last state's return address list.*

*$\delta$ is the transition relation mapping $Q \times \Sigma \times \Gamma$ to $Q \times \Gamma$. Let $z' = b_1 b_2 \cdots b_n$, $z = a_1 a_2 \cdots a_m$ and $l$ be the length of the common prefix of $z'$ and $z$. Then, the real state the program located at is $q' =< n - l, hash(b_l b_{l+1} \cdots b_n), s >$. On the other hand, we can search the STT and find the expected state set $Q_e$. Then,*

$$\delta(q, a, z) = \begin{cases} none & q' \notin Q_e \\ (q', z') & q' \in Q_e \end{cases} \tag{1}$$

*$q_0 \in Q$ is the unique initial state and $z_0 \in \Gamma$ is the initial stack state. $F \subseteq Q$ is the set of accepting states.*

**Theorem 1.** *The STT Model is a deterministic PDA (DPDA).*

*Proof.* A PDA is called deterministic if the transition relation $\delta$ satisfies the following two conditions [2, 14]:

Condition 1: For all $q \in Q$ and $z \in \Gamma$, whenever $\delta(q, \varepsilon, z)$ is nonempty, then $\delta(q, a, z)$ is empty for all $a \in \Sigma$.

Condition 2: For all $q \in Q$, $a \in \Sigma \cup \{\varepsilon\}$ and $z \in \Gamma$, $\delta(q, a, z)$ contains at most one element.

First, $\varepsilon$-transition doesn't exist in our model. So Condition 1 is satisfied.

Second, according to (1), $\delta(q, a, z)$ contains none element or one element, so Condition 2 is also satisfied.

Therefore, we obtain the conclusion that the STT Model is a DPDA.

According to [2], the time complexity for processing an input symbol with a non deterministic PDA is $O(nm^2)$, where $n$ and $m$ denote the number of states and transitions, respectively. However, if the PDA is deterministic, the time complexity will be reduced to $O(1)$. So our STT model is efficient in PDA operation.

## 4 Comparison between STT and VPStatic

Both the STT and the VPStatic perform intrusion detection by monitoring the system call events of the program. The VPStatic uses a virtual path in a statically-constructed automaton to record the call and return behaviors of function calls between two consecutive system calls. In our STT model, we replace this automaton with a state transition table, which records context-sensitive transitions between two consecutive system calls directly. We do a comparison between the two models in precision, time complexity and space complexity.

### 4.1 Precision

STT performs intrusion detection each time a system call is made. Assume $s_B$ is the new captured system call and $b_{n+1}$ is its address. The return address list got from stack walks is $b_1 b_2 \cdots b_n$. Also assume $s_A$, $a_{m+1}$ are the last system call and its address, respectively. Its return address list is $a_1 a_2 \cdots b_m$. Suppose $l$ is the length of the common prefix of $A$ and $B$. We assume everything is ok when the program is at $a_{m+1}$.

Then, for the STT, if the following two conditions are both satisfied, it will accept the new system call $s_B$ and consider the program is running normally:

Condition 1: $S_B = < n - l, h(b_l b_{l+1} \cdots b_n) >$ is in the STT.

Condition 2: Let $S_A$ be the state corresponding to the last system call. Then, $S_A$ has a transition to $S_B$ in the STT and if this transition contains a condition-the return address list $A$ has to satisfy it.

For the VPStatic, it will generate a sequence of input symbols using $A$ and $B$, and then feed them to its automaton one by one. If every symbol in the sequence is accepted by this automaton, the new system call $s_B$ will be accepted, otherwise an alarm is raised. There are three kinds of input symbols: $e$, $g$ and $f$ in the VPStatic. The automaton for the sample program in Fig.1 is presented on the right side of Fig.4.

**Theorem 2.** *The STT Model has the same precision with the VPStatic Model, which means if $s_B$ is accepted by the VPStatic, it will also be accepted by the STT, and if it is refused by the VPStatic, it will be refused by the STT, too.*

*Proof.* First, assume the input sequence is accepted by VPStatic, which means $s_A$ and $s_B$ are really consecutive and the correct return address list at $b_{n+1}$ is truly $B$. So, according to the Definition 1 and the construction algorithm of the STT described in Sec.2.5, the state $S_B$ must be in STT and $S_A$ must have a transition to $S_B$. In addition, if this transition contains a condition, $A$ must also satisfy it. So we satisfy the two conditions above and $s_B$ is also accepted by the STT.

Secondly, assume the input sequence is not accepted by the VPStatic. Then, there're three cases:

Case 1: One $g$ symbol in the input sequence is not accepted. Let this incorrect symbol be $g(none, a_i, a_i)$, where $i > l$. This means $a_i$ dose not match the top symbol on the virtual stack of the VPStatic and the program returns to a wrong address. Thereby, this execution path does not exist in the real. In this situation, if $S_B$ is still in the STT, there is only one possibility: $s_A$ at $a_{m+1}$ can be invoked in another context [4], in which there is an execution path from $a_{m+1}$ to $b_{n+1}$, and we just define one state $S_A$ for them because of the delta optimization, which is similar to the state 4 in Table 4. However, we add transfer conditions to all the transitions of this kind of states, based on which we can distinguish between different contexts. So even if Condition 1 can be satisfied in this case, Condition 2 can't be satisfied because the corresponding transition condition can't be satisfied. So $s_B$ is not accepted by the STT, too.

Case 2: One $f$ symbol in the input sequence is not accepted. We can use the similar way in Case 1 to prove the transition either will not be accepted by our STT model. We omit it here.

Case 3: One $e$ symbol is not accepted. There're three sub-cases in this situation. If the incorrect symbol is $e(none, Exit(Func(a_i)))$, which means we can't return from the corresponding function at that time according to the binary. We may enter a new function or make a system call, which means the next symbol $g(none, a_{i-1}, a_{i-1})$ is either wrong. So we come to Case 1, which has been proved above. Else if the incorrect symbol is $e(none, b_i)$, which means we can't enter the function $Func(b_i)$ at present. Thereby, the last transition $f(none, Entry(Func(b_i)), b_{i-1})$ must be either wrong and we come to Case 2. At last if the incorrect symbol is $e(s_B, b_{n+1})$, which means we can't reach to $b_{n+1}$ at present following this execution path. Then, either $S_B$ is not in the STT or the corresponding transition condition is not satisfied, which can be proved similarly to Case 1. So an intrusion alarm will still be raised by the STT in this case.

Therefore, we obtain the result our STT model is as precious as the VPStatic. It accepts all VPStatic accepts and refuses all VPStatic refuses.

---

[4] To be more precise, the function corresponding to $a_i$ can be called at another site in the program.

## 4.2    Space Complexity

We can learn from Case 3 in the proof of Theorem 2 that all $e$ transitions except the last one are all redundant in the VPStatic Model. They are just equivalent to the next $g$ transitions or the last $f$ transitions. Therefore, all these transitions and corresponding states can be eliminated to compact the automaton. In STT, we replace the automaton in the VPStatic with a state transition table, which records the context-sensitive transitions among system calls directly. Every state in the STT is corresponding to a system call site and all those intermediate states and transitions between any two system call states, which are called virtual paths in the VPStatic, are all eliminated. As a result, the STT is much smaller than the VPStatic.

**Theorem 3.** *States in the STT are fewer than that in the VPStatic.*

*Proof.* The exact numbers of states in the two models for the same program are presented in Table 5, respectively. The VPStatic defines two states ('Entry' and 'Exit') for each function, two states ('f' and 'g') for each call site, and one state for each system call site. So there are totally $2m + 2n + p$ states in the VPStatic, where $m, n, p$ denote the number of function call sites, functions and system call sites in a program, respectively. The STT defines one state for each system call site if it is not the first one of a function. For those first system calls, the STT defines $t$ states for each one if the corresponding function is called in $t$ different sites. So there're totally $q + p - k$ states in the STT, where $k$ and $q$ denote the

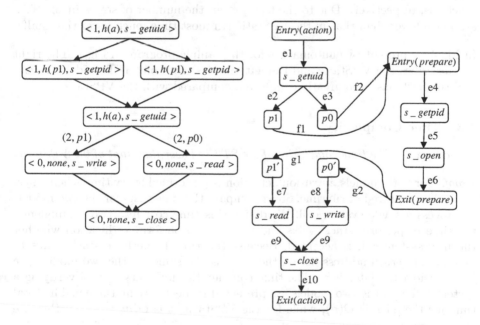

**Fig. 4.** STT and VPStatic automatons for the sample program in Fig.1. The left one is for the STT and the right one is for the VPStatic.

**Table 5.** Numbers of states in the STT and the VPStatic. Assume there are $n$ functions, $m$ call sites and $p$ system call sits in the monitored program. Among the $n$ functions, assume only $k$ ones invoke system calls and they are called at $q$ sites.

|  | VPStatic | STT |
|---|---|---|
| Number of States | $q + p - k$ | 2m+2n+p |

**Table 6.** Time complexities for every step of processing a system call with the STT and the VPStatic. The lengths of the return address lists of the last state and the current state are denoted by $m$ and $n$, respectively. The length of the common prefix of the two lists is denoted by $l$.

| Model | Intrusion Detection Step | Time Complexity |
|---|---|---|
| STT | Search expected states in the STT | $O(1)$ |
|  | Compute the real state | $O(n)$ |
|  | Compare between the real state and a expected state | $O(1)$ |
| VPStatic | Generate the input sequence | $O(l)$ |
|  | Walk the automaton | $O(m + n - 2 * l)$ |

number of functions which invoke system calls[5] and call sites of these special functions, respectively. Due to the fact $q < m$, the number of states in the STT are much fewer than that in the VPStatic (In most time much fewer than half).

In Fig.4 we present two automatons for the sample program in Fig.1. The right one describes the VPStatic and the left one describes our STT model. We can find the STT has been greatly compacted compared with the VPStatic.

## 4.3   Time Complexity

**Theorem 4.** *The time complexity of the STT is lower than that of the VPStatic.*

*Proof.* For both models, intrusion detection is performed every time when a system call is captured at runtime. So we compare the time costs for the two models to process a single system call. We divide this time cost into two components: the time to perform stack walks and the time to perform verification whether the new system call is accepted. Because the time to perform stack walks to extract the return address list on the stack is the same for the two models, we just consider the later here. The time complexities for every step of verifying a system call with the two models are presented respectively in Table 6. The total time for the STT is $O(n)$, while for the VPStatic it is $O(m + n - l)$. Because

---

[5] Note that we say a function invokes system calls so long as the program invokes any system calls after entering the function, before leaving the function.

$m > l$, we obtain the result that the time complexity of the STT is lower than that of the VPStatic.

Although we do improve the time efficiency, the improvement is not obvious: the time complexity to process a single system call is linear to the length of the return address list on the stack for both models. This is because the VPStatic is also a DPDA and its time efficiency is already very high. Actually, as we can see from the experiment results described in Sec.5, time overheads for both models are dominated by the time to perform stack walks and the time to perform verification is so small that can be ignored.

## 5  Experiments

Experiments are conducted to compare the time and memory overheads of the STT and VPStatic models. In this respect, we analyze two test programs: *gzip* and *cat*. Currently, we build the two models for these test programs via dynamic analysis but not static analysis. For every test program, we first execute it to finish a specific workload and capture all system calls and the corresponding stack states, based on which, we construct the STT and the VPStatic for this program. Then, for every model, we execute the program with the same workload for the second time. At this time, we use the model to monitor the execution of the program.

Due to the fact we can't cover all possible execution paths, these models built via dynamic analysis are far from complete and the true memory costs of models built via static analysis are much larger. However, comparisons between these dynamically constructed models still make sense. This is because they are constructed based on the same data. In addition, we can consider test programs we analyze are not *gzip* or *cat*, but just two new programs that formed by execution paths of *gzip* and *cat* we cover in the experiments. From this point, our models are truly complete.

Our experiments are carried on Fedora 7.0. We monitor the execution of a program in user space and process tracing is used to capture system call events. The workloads and corresponding execution statistics for each test program are presented in Table 7. Base time in the table refers to the time a program finishes its workload with process tracing enabled but doing nothing at each system call stop. We regard it as the execution time of a program without IDS.

Table 8 presents the accumulated time overheads for the dynamically constructed VPStatic and STT models to monitor the two test programs finishing their own workloads. We separate the models' runtime into two components: the time to perform stack walks and the time to perform verification. From this table, we find time overheads for both models are dominated by the time to perform stack walks. The STT does improve the time efficiency to perform verification but not obviously. Actually, compared with the overheads caused by stack walks, those caused by verification are so small that can be even ignored.

Numbers of states and memory overheads for the dynamically constructed VPStatic and STT models are presented in Table 9. From that we find our

**Table 7.** Workloads and corresponding execution statistics for test programs. Based times are measured in seconds.

| Program | Workloads | System Call Events | Base Time |
|---|---|---|---|
| gzip | Compress a 24.4 MB tar file | 2281 | 11.72 |
| cat | Concatenate 40 files totaling 500MB to a file | 520131 | 85.19 |

**Table 8.** Model execution times in seconds. Percentages compare against base execution.

| Program | Model | Stack Walks | % | Verification | % |
|---|---|---|---|---|---|
| gzip | STT | 9.25 | 79 | 0.03 | 0 |
| | VPStatic | 9.21 | 79 | 0.03 | 0 |
| cat | STT | 22.73 | 27 | 3.2 | 4 |
| | VPStatic | 22.75 | 27 | 5.12 | 6 |

**Table 9.** Numbers of states and memory uses in KB for models

| Program | Model | Number of States | Memory Use |
|---|---|---|---|
| gzip | STT | 41 | 0.750 |
| | VPStatic | 109 | 1.58 |
| cat | STT | 28 | 0.460 |
| | VPStatic | 87 | 0.94 |

STT models do reduce the numbers of states greatly. As a result, the memory overheads due to monitoring are also greatly reduced. In our experiments, all the memory uses of the STT models are less than half of the VPStatic models'.

## 6   Conclusion

We propose a novel efficient context-sensitive intrusion detection model via static analysis. It uses stack walks to eliminate non-determinability and is a provably DPDA, which is similar to the VPStatic. We replace the automaton in the VP-Static with a state transition table and the automaton walk in VPStatic is replaced by a search in the STT, which is more efficient. We perform a delta optimization to solve the state explosion problem of the STT and no redundant states and corresponding transitions, which exist in the automaton of the VP-Static, exist in our STT model. As a result, the memory use is greatly reduced. In our experiments, the memory overheads of the dynamically-constructed STT models for programs *gzip* and *cat* are both samller than half of the corresponding VPStatic models'. We prove that our STT model has the same precision with the VPStatic. Thereby, we improve the efficiency of the VPStatic greatly without reducing its precision, which alleviates the historical conflict between the efficiency and precision, which is suffered by similar intrusion detection models.

# References

[1] Forrest, S., Longstaff, T.: A sense of self for unix processes. In: 1996 IEEE Symposium on Security and Privacy, pp. 120–128. IEEE Press, Oakland (1996)

[2] Feng, H.H., Giffin, J.T., Huang, Y., Jha, S., Lee, W., Miller, B.P.: Formalizing sensitivity in static analysis for intrusion detection. In: 2004 IEEE Symposium on Security and Privacy, pp. 194–208. IEEE Press, California (2004)

[3] Gopalakrishna, R., Spafford, E.H., Vitek, J.: Efficient Intrusion Detection using Automaton Inlining. In: 2005 IEEE Symposium on Security and Privacy, pp. 18–21. IEEE Press, Washington (2005)

[4] Wagner, D., Dean, D.: Intrusion detection via static analysis. In: 2001 IEEE Symposium on Security and Privacy, p. 156. IEEE Press, Oakland (2001)

[5] Wagner, D., Soto, P.: Mimicry attacks on host-based intrusion detection systems. In: 9th ACM Conference on Computer and Communications Security, pp. 255–264. ACM Press, Washington (2002)

[6] Saidi, H.: Guarded Models for Intrusion Detection. In: 2007 Workshop on Programming languages and analysis for security, pp. 85–94. ACM Press, San Diego (2007)

[7] Feng, H., Kolesnikov, P.F., Lee, W.: Anomaly detection using call stack information. In: 2003 IEEE Symposium on Security and Privacy, p. 62. IEEE Press, Los Alamitos (2003)

[8] Gao, D., Reiter, M.K., Song, D.: Gray-box extraction of execution graphs for anomaly detection. In: 11th ACM Conference on Computer and Communications Security, pp. 318–329. ACM Press, Washington (2004)

[9] Giffin, J.T., Dagon, S., Jha, S., Lee, W., Miller, B.P.: Environment-sensitive intrusion detection. In: Valdes, A., Zamboni, D. (eds.) RAID 2005. LNCS, vol. 3858, pp. 185–206. Springer, Heidelberg (2006)

[10] Feng, H.: Dynamic monitoring and static analysis: new approaches for intrusion detection. PhD Dissertation, University of Massachusetts Amherst (2005)

[11] Castro, M., Costa, M., Harris, T.: Securing software by enforcing data-flow integrity. In: 6th Symposium on Operating Systems Design and Implementation, pp. 147–160. USENIX Association, Seattle (2006)

[12] Giffin, J.T., Jha, S., Lee, W., Miller, B.P.: Efficient context-sensitive intrusion detection. In: 11th Annual Network and Distributed Systems Security Symposium. Internet Society, San Diego (2004)

[13] Chen, S., Xu, J., Sezer, E.C., Gauriar, P., Iver, R.K.: Non-control- data attacks are realistic threats. In: 14th USENIX Security Symposium, pp. 1–12. USENIX Association, Baltimore (2005)

[14] Hopcroft, J., Motwani, R., Ullman, J.: Introduction to Automata Theory, Languages, and Computation. Addison Wesley, New Jersey (2001)

# Strongly Secure Authenticated Key Exchange without NAXOS' Approach

Minkyu Kim[1,*], Atsushi Fujioka[2], and Berkant Ustaoğlu[2]

[1] ISaC and Department of Mathematical Sciences
Seoul National University, Seoul 151-747, Korea
minkyu97@snu.ac.kr
[2] NTT Information Sharing Platform Laboratories
3-9-11 Midori-cho Musashino-shi Tokyo 180-8585, Japan
{fujioka.atsushi,ustaoglu.berkant}@lab.ntt.co.jp

**Abstract.** LaMacchia, Lauter and Mityagin [15] proposed the extended Canetti-Krawczyk (eCK) model and an AKE protocol, called NAXOS. Unlike previous security models, the adversary in the eCK model is allowed to obtain ephemeral secret information related to the test session, which makes the security proof difficult. To overcome this NAXOS combines an ephemeral private key $x$ with a static private key $a$ to generate an ephemeral public key $X$; more precisely $X = g^{H(x,a)}$. As a result, no one is able to query the discrete logarithm of $X$ without knowing both the ephemeral and static private keys. In other words, the discrete logarithm of an ephemeral public key, which is typically the ephemeral secret, is hidden via an additional random oracle.

In this paper, we show that it is possible to construct eCK-secure protocol without the NAXOS' approach by proposing two eCK-secure protocols. One is secure under the GDH assumption and the other under the CDH assumption; their efficiency and security assurances are comparable to the well-known HMQV [12] protocol. Furthermore, they are at least as secure as protocols that use the NAXOS' approach but unlike them and HMQV, the use of the random oracle is minimized and restricted to the key derivation function.

**Keywords:** AKE, eCK model, NAXOS' approach, trapdoor test.

## 1 Introduction

Using key exchange two parties can establish a common secret, called a session key, via a public communication channel. Diffie and Hellman [10] proposed the first key exchange protocol in which two parties exchange $X = g^x$, $Y = g^y$ and derive a session key from $g^{xy} = Y^x = X^y$. The original Diffie-Hellman (DH) protocol does not provide authentication and is vulnerable to active person-in-the-middle attacks. A key exchange protocol is authenticated key exchange

---

* This work was done while the first author was visiting NTT Information Sharing Platform Laboratories. He was partially supported by NAP of Korea Research Council of Fundamental Science and Technology.

T. Takagi and M. Mambo (Eds.): IWSEC 2009, LNCS 5824, pp. 174–191, 2009.

(AKE) if both parties are assured that only their intended peers can derive the session key.

Bellare and Rogaway [5] proposed the first security model and definition for authenticated key exchange that allows a rigorous analysis. Their model is indistinguishability based, where an adversary is required to differentiate between a random key and a session key. There have been several variations to the Bellare-Rogaway model and until recently, the Canetti-Krawczyk [8] (CK) model was regarded as one of the most significant BR modifications.

The CK model, however, fails to capture some desirable AKE properties. CK-secure protocols may still be vulnerable to key compromise impersonation (KCI) attack or may not be resilient to the leakage of ephemeral private keys (LEP). Resilience to LEP is motivated by scenarios where the session specific information is stored in an insecure place or the random number generator used by a party is corrupt.

To bring these attacks and properties within the scope of analysis, LaMacchia, Lauter and Mityagin changed the CK model, to the so called eCK model, and proposed NAXOS as an example of an eCK-secure protocol. Informally, the eCK aims to allow all adversary queries, except those that trivially break AKE protocols. In particular the eCK adversary is allowed to obtain ephemeral secret information related to the test session, which makes the security arguments in the eCK model difficult. To achieve eCK security, NAXOS requires that the ephemeral public key $X$ be computed from an exponent made up by hashing an ephemeral private key $x$ and the static private key $a$, more precisely, $X = g^{H(x,a)}$ instead of $X = g^x$. In this paper generating ephemeral public key as $X = g^{H(x,a)}$ is called *NAXOS' approach*. In NAXOS' approach no one is able to query the discrete logarithm of an ephemeral public key $X$ without the pair $(x,a)$; thus the discrete logarithm of $X$ is hidden via an extra random oracle. Using NAXOS' approach many protocols [25,11,16,17] were argued secure in the eCK model under the random oracle assumption. In the standard model, the only (to our knowledge) eCK-secure protocol is due to Okamoto [22]; it uses pseudo-random functions instead of hash functions.

In this paper, we show that it is possible to construct eCK-secure AKE protocols without NAXOS' approach by giving two example protocols. Protocol 1 relies on the Gap Diffie-Hellman and the random oracle assumptions. Protocol 2 is derived by applying the trapdoor technique introduced by Cash, Kiltz and Shoup [9] to Protocol 1, and thus uses Computational Diffie-Hellman assumption instead of the gap assumption.

Our protocols provide no less security assurances than protocols utilizing the NAXOS' approach in the sense that our analysis considers leakage of the discrete logarithm of ephemeral public keys. One advantage of this method (see [26]) is to reduce the risk of leaking the static private key, since the derivation of the ephemeral public key is independent from the static private key. This is in contrast to protocols that use the NAXOS' approach. In addition, unlike other eCK secure protocols and HMQV, which require at least two random oracles, we minimize the use of the random oracle, by applying it only to the session key derivation.

**Organization.** In section 2, we recall the security assumptions and the trapdoor test, which we use in this paper. In section 3, we briefly outline the eCK model and then propose our new protocols with security arguments in sections 4 and 5. In section 6 we compare our protocols with other relevant protocols and conclude in section 7.

## 2   Preliminaries

Let $G$ be a cyclic group of prime order $q$ and generator $g$. Let $\mathrm{dl}_g : G \to \mathbf{Z}_q$ be the discrete logarithm (DL) function which takes an input $X \in G$ and returns $x \in \mathbf{Z}_q$ such that $X = g^x$. Define the computational Diffie-Hellman (CDH) function $\mathrm{dh}_g : G^2 \to G$ as $\mathrm{dh}_g(X, Y) = g^{\mathrm{dl}_g(X)\mathrm{dl}_g(Y)}$, and the corresponding decisional predicate $\mathrm{ddh}_g : G^3 \to \{0, 1\}$ as a function which takes an input $(X, Y, Z) \in G^3$ and returns 1 if $Z = \mathrm{dh}_g(X, Y)$ and 0 otherwise.

The advantage of an algorithm $\mathcal{S}$ in solving the CDH problem, $\mathrm{Adv}^{\mathrm{CDH}}(\mathcal{S})$, is the probability that, given input $X, Y$ selected uniformly at random from $G$, $\mathcal{S}$ returns $\mathrm{dh}_g(X, Y)$. Similarly, the advantage of an algorithm $\mathcal{S}$ in solving the Gap Diffie-Hellman (GDH) problem, $\mathrm{Adv}^{\mathrm{GDH}}(\mathcal{S})$, is the probability that, given input $X, Y$ selected uniformly at random in $G$ and oracle access to $\mathrm{ddh}_g(\,\cdot\,,\,\cdot\,,\,\cdot\,)$, $\mathcal{S}$ returns $\mathrm{dh}_g(X, Y)$.

We say that $G$ satisfy the CDH (resp. GDH) assumption if no probabilistic polynomial-time bounded algorithm can solve the CDH (resp. GDH) problem on $G$ with non-negligible advantage.

In the security argument of Protocol 2 we will use the following theorem, called the trapdoor test, (see [9] for theorem details).

**Theorem 1 (Trapdoor Test in [9]).** *Let $G$ be a cyclic group of prime order $q$, generated by $g \in G$. Suppose $X_1, r, s$ are mutually independent random variables, where $X_1$ takes values in $G$, and each of $r, s$ is uniformly distributed over $\mathbf{Z}_q$, and define the random variable $X_2 := g^s / X_1^r$. Further, suppose that $\hat{Y}, \hat{Z}_1, \hat{Z}_2$ are random variables taking values in $G$, each of which is defined as some function of $X_1$ and $X_2$. Then we have:*

1. *$X_2$ is uniformly distributed over $G$;*
2. *$X_1$ and $X_2$ are independent;*
3. *if $X_1 = g^{x_1}$ and $X_2 = g^{x_2}$, then the probability that the truth value of*

$$\hat{Z}_1^r \hat{Z}_2 \overset{?}{=} \hat{Y}^s \tag{1}$$

*does not agree with the truth value of*

$$\hat{Z}_1 \overset{?}{=} \hat{Y}^{x_1} \wedge \hat{Z}_2 \overset{?}{=} \hat{Y}^{x_2} \tag{2}$$

*is at most $1/q$; moreover, if (2) holds, then (1) certainly holds.*

# 3  Security Model

For further eCK details and explanations see [15].

In the eCK model, each party is a probabilistic polynomial-time Turing machine and is assigned a static public and private key pair together with a certificate that binds party's identity to its public key. We denote a party's identity $\mathcal{A}, \mathcal{B}, \mathcal{C}, \ldots$ [1]. We assume that, the certificate authority (CA) does not require proof of possession of the corresponding private key included in a certificate. However, CA verifies that the public key is in $G^{\times} = G - \{\mathrm{id}_G\}$, where $\mathrm{id}_G$ is the identity element of $G$.

We outline the eCK model for two-pass Diffie-Hellman protocols, where two parties $\mathcal{A}$ and $\mathcal{B}$ exchange static and ephemeral public keys and thereafter compute a session key that depends on the exchanged public keys and identities of the parties.

**Session.** An invocation of a protocol is called a *session*. Session activation is made via an incoming message of the forms $(\mathcal{I}, \mathcal{A}, \mathcal{B})$ or $(\mathcal{R}, \mathcal{A}, \mathcal{B}, Y)$. If $\mathcal{A}$ was activated with $(\mathcal{I}, \mathcal{A}, \mathcal{B})$, then $\mathcal{A}$ is called the session *initiator*, otherwise it is called the session *responder*. After activation, session initiator $\mathcal{A}$ creates ephemeral public key $X$ and sends $(\mathcal{R}, \mathcal{B}, \mathcal{A}, X)$ to the session responder $\mathcal{B}$, who then prepares ephemeral public key $Y$, computes the session key and sends $(\mathcal{I}, \mathcal{A}, \mathcal{B}, X, Y)$ to $\mathcal{A}$. Upon receiving $(\mathcal{I}, \mathcal{A}, \mathcal{B}, X, Y)$, $\mathcal{A}$ also computes a session key for the session $\mathcal{A}$ owns. We say that a session is *completed* if its owner computes a session key.

If $\mathcal{A}$ is the initiator of a session, the session is identified via $(\mathcal{I}, \mathcal{A}, \mathcal{B}, X, \times)$ or $(\mathcal{I}, \mathcal{A}, \mathcal{B}, X, Y)$. For a responder $\mathcal{A}$ the session is identified via $(\mathcal{R}, \mathcal{A}, \mathcal{B}, Y, X)$. The *matching session* of $(\mathcal{I}, \mathcal{A}, \mathcal{B}, X, Y)$ is a session with identifier $(\mathcal{R}, \mathcal{B}, \mathcal{A}, X, Y)$ and vice versa. In the remainder of the paper we will omit $\mathcal{I}$ and $\mathcal{R}$ since these "role markers" are implicitly defined from the order of ephemeral public keys.

**Adversary.** The adversary $\mathcal{M}$ is modeled as a probabilistic Turing machine that controls all communications including session activation, performed via Send(message) query. The message has one of the following forms: $(\mathrm{pid}, \overline{\mathrm{pid}})$, $(\mathrm{pid}, \overline{\mathrm{pid}}, X)$, or $(\mathrm{pid}, \overline{\mathrm{pid}}, X, Y)$, where pid and $\overline{\mathrm{pid}}$ are identities. Each party submits its responses to the adversary, who decides the global delivery order.

The adversary does not have immediate access to a party's private information. However, leakage of private information is captured via the following adversary queries:

- EphemeralKeyReveal(sid) The adversary obtains the ephemeral secret key associated with the session sid.

- SessionKeyReveal(sid) The adversary obtains the session key for the session sid, provided that the session holds a session key.

---

[1] In the eCK model the adversary selects these identifier strings.

- StaticKeyReveal(pid) The adversary learns the static secret key of the party pid.

- EstablishParty(pid)[2] This query allows the adversary to register a static public key on behalf of a party pid; the adversary totally controls that party. If a party pid is established by EstablishParty(pid) query issued by adversary, then we call the party *dishonest*. If not, we call the party *honest*. This query models malicious insider.

To define eCK security we need the following definition.

**Definition 1 (Freshness).** *Let* sid* *be the session identifier of a completed session, owned by an honest party* $A$ *with peer* $B$*, who is also honest. If the matching session exists, then let* $\overline{\text{sid}^*}$ *be the session identifier of the matching session of* sid*. *Define* sid* *to be fresh if none of the following conditions hold:*

1. *Adversary issues a* SessionKeyReveal(sid*) *or* SessionKeyReveal($\overline{\text{sid}^*}$) *query (if* $\overline{\text{sid}^*}$ *exists)*
2. $\overline{\text{sid}^*}$ *exists and Adversary makes either of the following queries*
   - *both* StaticKeyReveal($A$) *and* EphemeralKeyReveal(sid*)*, or*
   - *both* StaticKeyReveal($B$) *and* EphemeralKeyReveal($\overline{\text{sid}^*}$)
3. $\overline{\text{sid}^*}$ *does not exist and Adversary makes either of the following queries*
   - *both* StaticKeyReveal($A$) *and* EphemeralKeyReveal(sid*)*, or*
   - StaticKeyReveal($B$)

**Security Experiment.** Initially, the adversary $M$ is given a set of honest parties, for whom $M$ selects identifiers. Then the adversary makes any sequence of the queries described above. During the experiment, $M$ makes a special query Test(sid*), where sid* is a fresh session, and is given with equal probability either the session key held by sid* or a random key; the query does not terminate the experiment. The experiment continues until $M$ makes a guess whether the key is random or not. The adversary *wins* the game if the test session sid* is still fresh and if $M$ guess was correct.

**Definition 2 (eCK security).** *The advantage of the adversary* $M$ *in the AKE experiment with AKE protocol* $\Pi$ *is defined as*

$$\text{Adv}_{\Pi}^{\text{AKE}}(M) = \Pr[M \ wins] - \frac{1}{2}.$$

*We say that an AKE protocol* $\Pi$ *is secure in the eCK model if the following conditions hold:*

---

[2] Formally, this query is not available in the eCK model [15], where the adversary is only allowed to selects identities of parties and establishes dishonest parties before starting the interaction with the parties. This does not present a deficiency in the model since the query gives the addition power to the adversary to decide (dishonest) party specific information after observing the behavior of honest parties.

1. *If two honest parties complete matching sessions, then, except with negligible probability, they both compute the same session key.*
2. *For any probabilistic polynomial-time bounded adversary $\mathcal{M}$, $\mathrm{Adv}_{\Pi}^{\mathrm{AKE}}(\mathcal{M})$ is negligible.*

# 4    Protocol 1

In sections 4 and 5, we offer two eCK-secure protocols without NAXOS' approach. The following are parameters used in the protocol descriptions.

**Parameters.** Let $k/2$ be the security parameter and $G$ be a cyclic group with generator $g$ and order a $k$-bit prime $q$. Let $H : \{0,1\}^* \to \{0,1\}^k$ be a cryptographic hash function modeled as a random oracle. Party $\mathcal{A}$'s static private key is a pair $a_1, a_2 \in \mathbf{Z}_q^\times$ and his public key is the pair $A_1 = g^{a_1}, A_2 = g^{a_2} \in G^\times$. Similarly, the party $\mathcal{B}$'s static keys are $b_1, b_2 \in \mathbf{Z}_q^\times, B_1 = g^{b_1}, B_2 = g^{b_2} \in G^\times$.

## 4.1    Protocol 1 Description

In the description, $\mathcal{A}$ is the session initiator and $\mathcal{B}$ is the session responder.

1. $\mathcal{A}$ chooses at random an ephemeral private key $x \in \mathbf{Z}_q^\times$, computes the ephemeral public key $X = g^x$ and sends $(\mathcal{B}, \mathcal{A}, X)$ to $\mathcal{B}$.

2. Upon receiving $(\mathcal{B}, \mathcal{A}, X)$, $\mathcal{B}$ verifies that $X \in G^\times$. If so, $\mathcal{B}$ chooses at random an ephemeral private key $y \in \mathbf{Z}_q^\times$ and computes the ephemeral public key $Y = g^y$. After computing the shared secrets $Z_1 = (XA_1)^{y+b_1}$, $Z_2 = (XA_2)^{y+b_2}$, the session key SK $= H(Z_1, Z_2, X, Y, \mathcal{A}, \mathcal{B})$ and sending $(\mathcal{A}, \mathcal{B}, X, Y)$ to $\mathcal{A}$, $\mathcal{B}$ completes the session with session key SK.

3. Upon receiving $(\mathcal{A}, \mathcal{B}, X, Y)$, $\mathcal{A}$ checks if he owns a session with session identifier $(\mathcal{A}, \mathcal{B}, X, \times)$. If so, $\mathcal{A}$ verifies that $Y \in G^\times$ and computes $Z_1 = (YB_1)^{x+a_1}$, $Z_2 = (YB_2)^{x+a_2}$ and completes the session $(\mathcal{A}, \mathcal{B}, X, Y)$ with session key SK $= H(Z_1, Z_2, X, Y, \mathcal{A}, \mathcal{B})$.

Both parties compute the shared secrets $Z_1 = g^{(x+a_1)(y+b_1)}, Z_2 = g^{(x+a_2)(y+b_2)}$ and therefore compute the same session key SK.

## 4.2    Protocol 1 Security Argument

**Theorem 2.** *If the GDH assumption holds in $G$ and $H$ is a random oracle, then the Protocol 1 is eCK-secure.*

*Proof.* Let $\mathcal{M}$ be a polynomially bounded adversary against Protocol 1, that runs in time $t(k)$, activates at most $n(k)$ honest parties, at most $s(k)$ sessions and makes at most $h(k)$ queries to the oracle $H$, where $t(k), n(k), s(k)$, and $h(k)$ are polynomially bounded in $k$. Assume also that $\mathrm{Adv}_{\mathrm{Protocol\ 1}}^{\mathrm{AKE}}(\mathcal{M})$ is non-negligible. Since $H$ is modeled as a random oracle, the adversary $\mathcal{M}$ has only three ways to distinguish a session key of the test session from a random string.

- A1. Guessing attack: $\mathcal{M}$ correctly guesses the session key.
- A2. Key replication attack: $\mathcal{M}$ creates a session that is not matching to the test session, but has the same session key as the test session.
- A3. Forging attack: $\mathcal{M}$ computes $Z_1$ and $Z_2$ used in the test session, and queries $H$ with $(Z_1, Z_2, X, Y, \mathcal{A}, \mathcal{B})$.

Since $H$ is a random oracle, the probability of guessing the output of $H$ is $\mathcal{O}(1/2^k)$, which is negligible. Since non-matching sessions have different communicating parties or ephemeral public keys, key replication is equivalent to finding an $H$-collision; therefore the probability, that event A2 occurs, is $\mathcal{O}(s(k)^2/2^k)$, which is also negligible. Thus events A1 and A2 can be ruled out.

Let M be the event that $\mathcal{M}$ wins the security game, H be the event that $\mathcal{M}$ queries $H$ with $(Z_1, Z_2, X, Y, \mathcal{A}, \mathcal{B})$, and $\overline{H}$ the complementary event of H. Since $H$ is a random oracle and events A1 and A2 were ruled out, we have $\Pr[M|\overline{H}] = \frac{1}{2}$ except with negligible difference. Then

$$\Pr[M] = \Pr[M \wedge H] + \Pr[M|\,\overline{H}]\Pr[\overline{H}] \leq \Pr[M \wedge H] + \frac{1}{2}$$

$$\mathrm{Adv}^{\mathrm{AKE}}_{\mathrm{Protocol}\ 1}(\mathcal{M}) \leq \Pr[M \wedge H] = \Pr[A3]$$

Since $\mathrm{Adv}^{\mathrm{AKE}}_{\mathrm{Protocol}\ 1}(\mathcal{M})$ is non-negligible, $\Pr[A3]$ is also non-negligible.

Now, consider the following complementary sub-events of A3.

- E1. A3 occurs and the test session has no matching session.
- E2. A3 occurs and the test session has a matching session.

Then

$$\Pr[A3] = \Pr[E1] + \Pr[E2]$$

Consider also the following sub-events of E1 so that $E1 = E1_a \vee E1_b$.

- $E1_a$. E1 occurs and $\mathcal{M}$ does not reveal the ephemeral private key of the owner of the test session, but may query for the static private key of the test session owner.
- $E1_b$. E1 occurs and the owner's static private key of the test session has never been revealed by $\mathcal{M}$, but may query for the ephemeral private key of the test session owner.

Consider also the following sub-events of E2 so that $E2 = E2_a \vee E2_b \vee E2_c \vee E2_d$.

- $E2_a$. E2 occurs and $\mathcal{M}$ does not reveal the ephemeral private keys of both the owner of the test session and its peer, but may query for the static private keys of the test session peers.
- $E2_b$. E2 occurs and $\mathcal{M}$ does not reveal the static private keys of both the test session and its matching session, but may query for the ephemeral private keys of the test session peers.
- $E2_c$. E2 occurs and the owner's ephemeral private key and the peer's static private key of the test session have never been revealed by $\mathcal{M}$, but $\mathcal{M}$ may query StaticKeyReveal with the identity of the test session owner and query EphemeralKeyReveal with the session matching to the test session.

- E2$_d$. E2 occurs and the owner's static private key and the peer's ephemeral private key of the test session have never been revealed by $\mathcal{M}$, but $\mathcal{M}$ may query StaticKeyReveal with the identity of the test session peer and EphemeralKeyReveal with the test session.

We then have

$$\Pr[\text{E1}] \leq \Pr[\text{E1}_a] + \Pr[\text{E1}_b] \tag{3}$$
$$\Pr[\text{E2}] \leq \Pr[\text{E2}_a] + \Pr[\text{E2}_b] + \Pr[\text{E2}_c] + \Pr[\text{E2}_d]. \tag{4}$$

We will show how to construct a GDH solver $\mathcal{S}$ that uses a Protocol 1 adversary $\mathcal{M}$. The solver $\mathcal{S}$ is given a CDH instance $(U, V)$, where $U$ and $V$ are selected uniform randomly in $G$, access to a $\text{ddh}_g(\cdot, \cdot, \cdot)$ oracle and has to compute $\text{dh}_g(U, V)$. Without loss of generality in the analysis, we denote the test session owner and peer by $\mathcal{A}$ and $\mathcal{B}$, respectively, and assume that $\mathcal{A}$ is the initiator.

**Analysis of E1$_a$.** We use $\mathcal{M}$ to construct a GDH solver $\mathcal{S}$ that succeeds with non-negligible probability provided that event E1$_a$ occurs. $\mathcal{S}$ prepares $n(k)$ honest parties, selects one party $\mathcal{B}$ to whom $\mathcal{S}$ assigns static public key $B_1 = V, B_2 = V^r$, where $\mathcal{S}$ randomly chooses $r \in \mathbf{Z}_q$. The remaining $n(k) - 1$ parties are assigned random static public and private key pairs. $\mathcal{S}$ also chooses a session sid*, owned by an honest party $\mathcal{A}$.

When $\mathcal{M}$ activates sessions between honest peers $\mathcal{S}$ follows the protocol description. Since $\mathcal{S}$ knows static private keys of at least one peer, it can respond all queries faithfully. The only exception is the session sid*, for which $\mathcal{S}$ sets the ephemeral public key of sid* to $U$, and chooses a random $\zeta \in \{0,1\}^k$ as the session key of sid*.

The simulator has difficulty in responding queries related to $\mathcal{B}$ because $\mathcal{S}$ does not know the static private key of $\mathcal{B}$. More precisely, for sessions owned by $\mathcal{B}$ with peer $\mathcal{C}$ controlled by $\mathcal{M}$, $\mathcal{S}$ cannot compute shared secrets $Z_1, Z_2$, but may have to answer SessionKeyReveal queries. Note that $\mathcal{M}$ can obtain session keys of these session by computing the shared secrets $Z_1, Z_2$ and query $H$. If two values do not coincide, then $\mathcal{S}$ fails its simulation. To handle this situations, $\mathcal{S}$ prepares $\text{R}^{\text{list}}$ with entries of the form $(\text{pid}, \overline{\text{pid}}, W, W', \text{SK}) \in \{0,1\}^* \times \{0,1\}^* \times G^2 \times \{0,1\}^k$, which is maintained for consistent responses to $H$ and SessionKeyReveal queries.

We next describe the action of $\mathcal{S}$ when $\mathcal{M}$ makes queries related to $\mathcal{B}$. In the following, $Y$ is generated by the party $\mathcal{B}$. Recall that if the session identifier is $(\mathcal{B}, \mathcal{C}, X, Y)$ (resp. $(\mathcal{B}, \mathcal{C}, Y, X)$), then $\mathcal{B}$ is the session responder (resp. initiator).

- Send($\mathcal{B}, \mathcal{C}$): $\mathcal{S}$ randomly selects $y \in \mathbf{Z}_q^\times$, computes $Y = g^y$, creates a new session with sid $(\mathcal{B}, \mathcal{C}, Y, \times)$ and returns $(\mathcal{C}, \mathcal{B}, Y)$ to $\mathcal{M}$.

- Send($\mathcal{B}, \mathcal{C}, X$): $\mathcal{S}$ randomly selects $y \in \mathbf{Z}_q^\times$, compute $Y = g^y$, creates a new session with sid $(\mathcal{B}, \mathcal{C}, X, Y)$ and returns $(\mathcal{C}, \mathcal{B}, X, Y)$ to $\mathcal{M}$.

- **Send**$(\mathcal{B}, \mathcal{C}, Y, X)$: $\mathcal{S}$ checks if $\mathcal{B}$ owns a session with sid $(\mathcal{B}, \mathcal{C}, Y, \times)$. If not, the session is aborted; otherwise, $\mathcal{S}$ updates sid to $(\mathcal{B}, \mathcal{C}, Y, X)$.

- $H(\cdot)$: $\mathcal{S}$ maintains an initially empty list $H^{\text{list}}$ with entries of the form $(\hat{Z}_1, \hat{Z}_2, W, W', \text{pid}, \overline{\text{pid}}, \text{SK}) \in G^4 \times \{0,1\}^* \times \{0,1\}^* \times \{0,1\}^k$ and simulates a random oracle in the usual way except for queries of the form $(\hat{Z}_1, \hat{Z}_2, X, Y, \mathcal{C}, \mathcal{B})$ and $(\hat{Z}_1, \hat{Z}_2, Y, X, \mathcal{B}, \mathcal{C})$. When $(\hat{Z}_1, \hat{Z}_2, X, Y, \mathcal{C}, \mathcal{B})$ (resp. $(\hat{Z}_1, \hat{Z}_2, Y, X, \mathcal{B}, \mathcal{C})$) is queried, $\mathcal{S}$ does one of the following.
  1. If $(\hat{Z}_1, \hat{Z}_2, X, Y, \mathcal{C}, \mathcal{B}, \text{SK})$ (resp. $(\hat{Z}_1, \hat{Z}_2, Y, X, \mathcal{B}, \mathcal{C}, \text{SK})) \in H^{\text{list}}$ for some SK, then $\mathcal{S}$ returns SK to $\mathcal{M}$.
  2. Otherwise, $\mathcal{S}$ checks if there exists $(\mathcal{B}, \mathcal{C}, X, Y, \text{SK})$ (resp. $(\mathcal{B}, \mathcal{C}, Y, X, \text{SK})$) $\in R^{\text{list}}$ such that $\text{ddh}_g(XC_1, YB_1, \hat{Z}_1) = 1$ and $\text{ddh}_g(XC_2, YB_2, \hat{Z}_2) = 1$. If such a pair exists, $\mathcal{S}$ returns SK from $R^{\text{list}}$, and stores the new tuple $(\hat{Z}_1, \hat{Z}_2, X, Y, \mathcal{C}, \mathcal{B}, \text{SK})$ (resp. $(\hat{Z}_1, \hat{Z}_2, Y, X, \mathcal{B}, \mathcal{C}, \text{SK})$) in $H^{\text{list}}$.
  3. If neither of the above two cases hold, then $\mathcal{S}$ chooses $\text{SK} \in \{0,1\}^k$ at random, returns it to $\mathcal{M}$ and stores the new tuple $(\hat{Z}_1, \hat{Z}_2, X, Y, \mathcal{C}, \mathcal{B}, \text{SK})$ (resp. $(\hat{Z}_1, \hat{Z}_2, Y, X, \mathcal{B}, \mathcal{C}, \text{SK})$) in $H^{\text{list}}$.

- **SessionKeyReveal**$(\mathcal{B}, \mathcal{C}, X, Y)$ or **SessionKeyReveal**$(\mathcal{B}, \mathcal{C}, Y, X)$: $\mathcal{S}$ maintains an initially empty list $R^{\text{list}}$ with entries of the form $(\text{pid}, \overline{\text{pid}}, W, W', \text{SK}) \in \{0,1\}^* \times \{0,1\}^* \times G^2 \times \{0,1\}^k$. When **SessionKeyReveal**$(\mathcal{B}, \mathcal{C}, X, Y)$ (resp. $(\mathcal{B}, \mathcal{C}, Y, X)$) is queried, $\mathcal{S}$ does one of the following.
  1. If there is no session with identifier $(\mathcal{B}, \mathcal{C}, X, Y)$ (resp. $(\mathcal{B}, \mathcal{C}, Y, X)$), the query is aborted.
  2. If $(\mathcal{B}, \mathcal{C}, X, Y, \text{SK})$ (resp. $(\mathcal{B}, \mathcal{C}, Y, X, \text{SK})) \in R^{\text{list}}$ for some SK, $\mathcal{S}$ returns SK to $\mathcal{M}$.
  3. Otherwise, go through $H^{\text{list}}$ to find $(\hat{Z}_1, \hat{Z}_2, X, Y, \mathcal{C}, \mathcal{B}, \text{SK})$ (resp. $(\hat{Z}_1, \hat{Z}_2, Y, X, \mathcal{B}, \mathcal{C}, \text{SK})$) satisfying $\text{ddh}_g(XC_1, YB_1, \hat{Z}_1) = 1$ and $\text{ddh}_g(XC_2, YB_2, \hat{Z}_2) = 1$. If such a pair exists, $\mathcal{S}$ returns SK, and stores the new tuple $(\mathcal{B}, \mathcal{C}, X, Y, \text{SK})$ (resp. $(\mathcal{B}, \mathcal{C}, Y, X, \text{SK})$) in $R^{\text{list}}$.
  4. If none of the above three cases hold, then $\mathcal{S}$ chooses $\text{SK} \in \{0,1\}^k$ at random, returns it to $\mathcal{M}$ and stores the new tuple $(\mathcal{B}, \mathcal{C}, X, Y, \text{SK})$ (resp. $(\mathcal{B}, \mathcal{C}, Y, X, \text{SK})$) in $R^{\text{list}}$.

- **EphemeralKeyReveal**$(\cdot)$: $\mathcal{S}$ responds to the query faithfully.

- **StaticKeyReveal**$(\mathcal{B})$ or **EstablishParty**$(\mathcal{B})$: $\mathcal{S}$ aborts.

- **Test**(sid): If sid $\neq$ sid$^*$, $\mathcal{S}$ aborts. Otherwise, $\mathcal{S}$ randomly chooses $\zeta \in \{0,1\}^k$ and returns it to the adversary $\mathcal{M}$.

Provided that event $E1_a$ occurs and $\mathcal{M}$ selects the session sid$^*$ as the test session with peer $\mathcal{B}$, the simulation does not fail; let $Y$ denote the test session incoming ephemeral public key. If $\mathcal{M}$ is successful with non-negligible probability it must have queried $H$ with inputs $\hat{Z}_1 = (YB_1)^{x^*+a_1}$ and $\hat{Z}_2 = (YB_2)^{x^*+a_2}$, where $x^* \equiv \text{dl}_g(U) \bmod q$, because $\mathcal{S}$ sets the ephemeral public key $X^*$ of sid$^*$ as $U$.

To solve the CDH instance, $S$ checks if there is an $H$ query made by $M$ of the form $(Z_1, Z_2, U, Y, A, B)$, such that $\mathrm{ddh}_g(UA_1, YB_1, Z_1) = 1$ and $\mathrm{ddh}_g(UA_2, YB_2, Z_2) = 1$. If such an H query exists, $S$ computes[3] $Z_1^* = Z_1/(YB_1)^{a_1}$ and $Z_2^* = Z_2/(YB_2)^{a_2}$. If $Z_1, Z_2$ are correct, then since $B_1 = V$ and $\mathrm{dl}_g(B_2) \equiv r \cdot \mathrm{dl}_g(B_1) \bmod q$ we have,

$$Z_1^*/Z_2^* = (B_1/B_2)^x = U^{\mathrm{dl}_g(B_1) - \mathrm{dl}_g(B_2)}.$$

Therefore, by computing $\left(Z_1^*/Z_2^*\right)^{1/(1-r)}$, $S$ can find $U^{\mathrm{dl}_g(B_1)} = \mathrm{dh}_g(U, V)$.

With probability at least $\frac{1}{s(k)n(k)}$, the test session is $\mathrm{sid}^*$ with peer $B$. Thus, the advantage of $S$ is

$$\mathrm{Adv}^{\mathrm{GDH}}(S) \geq \frac{1}{s(k)n(k)} \Pr[\mathrm{E1_a}]. \tag{5}$$

**Analysis of $\mathrm{E1_b}$.** $S$ prepares $n(k)$ honest parties, selects two distinct parties, say $A$ and $B$, and assigns $A$'s and $B$'s static public keys as $A_1 = U, A_2 = U^s$ and $B_1 = V, B_2 = V^r$, respectively, where $r$ and $s$ are random elements of $Z_q$. The remaining $n(k) - 2$ parties are assigned random static and private key pairs. If $M$ activates sessions owned by any honest party except $A$ and $B$, then $S$ follows the protocol description. The parties $A$ and $B$ are simulated as in the case $\mathrm{E1_a}$.

If $M$ selected the session $\mathrm{sid}^*$ as the test session with owner $A$ and peer $B$, this simulation does not fail provided that the event $\mathrm{E1_b}$ occurs. If $M$ is successful with non-negligible probability, it must have queried $H$ with inputs of the form $Z_1 = (YB_1)^{x+\mathrm{dl}_g(A_1)}$, $Z_2 = (YB_2)^{x+\mathrm{dl}_g(A_2)}$. To solve CDH, $S$ checks if there is an $H$ query made by $M$ of the form $(Z_1, Z_2, X, Y, A, B)$, such that $\mathrm{ddh}_g(XA_1, YB_1, Z_1) = 1$ and $\mathrm{ddh}_g(XA_2, YB_2, Z_2) = 1$. If such an H query exists, $S$ computes $Z_1^* = Z_1/(YB_1)^x$, $Z_2^* = Z_2/(YB_2)^x$. Since $(Z_2^*)^{1/s} = ((YB_2)^{\mathrm{dl}_g(A_2)})^{1/s} = (YB_2)^{\mathrm{dl}_g(A_1)}$,

$$Z_1^*/(Z_2^*)^{1/s} = A_1^{\mathrm{dl}_g(B_1) - \mathrm{dl}_g(B_2)}.$$

Therefore, from $\left(Z_1^*/(Z_2^*)^{1/s}\right)^{1/(1-r)}$, $S$ can find $A_1^{\mathrm{dl}_g(B_1)} = \mathrm{dh}_g(U, V)$.

With probability at least $\frac{1}{n(k)^2}$, $M$ will select a test session with owner and peer $A$ and $B$, respectively. Thus the advantage of $S$ is

$$\mathrm{Adv}^{\mathrm{GDH}}(S) \geq \frac{1}{n(k)^2} \Pr[\mathrm{E1_b}]. \tag{6}$$

**Analysis of $\mathrm{E2_a}$.** $S$ prepares $n(k)$ honest parties, and assigns random static public and private key pairs for these parties. $S$ also chooses two session $\mathrm{sid}^*, \overline{\mathrm{sid}}^*$. Let $A$ be the owner of $\mathrm{sid}^*$ and $B$ owner of $\overline{\mathrm{sid}}^*$. $S$ sets the ephemeral public key

---

[3] Note that the computation requires the knowledge of $a_1$ and $a_2$, and therefore it must be the case that $A \neq B$.

of sid* to be $U$ and of $\overline{\text{sid}^*}$ to be $V$. Hence $\mathcal{S}$'s simulation for $\mathcal{M}$ can fail only if $\mathcal{M}$ issues EphemeralKeyReveal against sid* or $\overline{\text{sid}^*}$.

Provided that $\mathcal{M}$ selects the session sid* as the test session with owner $\mathcal{A}$ and peer $\mathcal{B}$ and $\overline{\text{sid}^*}$ as its matching session, and event E2$_a$ occurs, then the simulation does not fail. If $\mathcal{M}$ is successful with non-negligible probability it must have queried $H$ with $Z_1 = (YB_1)^{\text{dl}_g(U)+a_1}$, $Z_2 = (YB_2)^{\text{dl}_g(U)+a_2}$. To solve the CDH instance, $\mathcal{S}$ checks if there is an $H$ query $(Z_1, Z_2, U, V, \mathcal{A}, \mathcal{B})$, such that $\text{ddh}_g(UA_1, VB_1, Z_1) = 1$ and $\text{ddh}_g(UA_2, VB_2, Z_2) = 1$. If such an H query exists, $\mathcal{S}$ computes $\text{dh}_g(U, V)$ by computing $Z_1/(U^{b_1}V^{a_1}A_1^{b_1})$.

With probability $\frac{1}{s(k)^2}$, $\mathcal{M}$ selects sid* as the test session and $\overline{\text{sid}^*}$ as its matching session. Thus, the advantage of $\mathcal{S}$ is

$$\text{Adv}^{\text{GDH}}(\mathcal{S}) \geq \frac{1}{s(k)^2} \Pr[\text{E2}_a]. \tag{7}$$

**Analysis of E2$_b$, E2$_c$ and E2$_d$.** For event E2$_b$, E2$_c$, E2$_d$, $\mathcal{S}$'s simulation is similar to E1$_b$, E1$_a$, E1$_a$, respectively. We omit the details and provide only the conclusion:

$$\text{Adv}^{\text{GDH}}(\mathcal{S}) \geq \frac{1}{n(k)^2} \Pr[\text{E2}_b] \tag{8}$$

$$\text{Adv}^{\text{GDH}}(\mathcal{S}) \geq \frac{1}{s(k)n(k)} \Pr[\text{E2}_c] \tag{9}$$

$$\text{Adv}^{\text{GDH}}(\mathcal{S}) \geq \frac{1}{s(k)n(k)} \Pr[\text{E2}_d]. \tag{10}$$

Combining equations (5), (6), (7), (8), (9), and (10), the advantage of $\mathcal{S}$ is

$$\text{Adv}^{\text{GDH}}(\mathcal{S}) \geq \max\left\{ \frac{1}{s(k)n(k)} \Pr[\text{E1}_a], \frac{1}{n(k)^2} \Pr[\text{E1}_b], \frac{1}{s(k)^2} \Pr[\text{E2}_a], \right.$$
$$\left. \frac{1}{n(k)^2} \Pr[\text{E2}_b], \frac{1}{s(k)n(k)} \Pr[\text{E2}_c], \frac{1}{s(k)n(k)} \Pr[\text{E2}_d] \right\}.$$

Since $\Pr[\text{A3}]$ is non-negligible, from (3), (4), at least one of $\Pr[\text{E1}_a], \cdots, \Pr[\text{E2}_d]$ is non-negligible, and therefore $\text{Adv}^{\text{GDH}}(\mathcal{S})$ is non-negligible. During the simulation, $\mathcal{S}$ performs group exponentiations, queries the DDH oracle, and simulates $H$. All of these take polynomially bounded time because a group exponentiation takes time $\mathcal{O}(k)$ and $t(k), n(k), s(k), h(k)$ are polynomial in $k$. Therefore, the running time of $\mathcal{S}$ is polynomially bounded. Hence, $\mathcal{S}$ is a polynomial-time algorithm that solves the GDH problem in $G$ with non-negligible probability, which contradicts the assumed security of GDH problem in $G$. This completes the argument.

# 5   Protocol 2

## 5.1   Protocol 2 Description

Protocol 2 is similar to Protocol 1 and follows below. The difference between the two protocols is that Protocol 2 computes two additional shared secrets. In the description, $\mathcal{A}$ is the session initiator and $\mathcal{B}$ session responder.

1. $\mathcal{A}$ chooses at random an ephemeral private key $x \in \mathbf{Z}_q^\times$, computes the ephemeral public key $X = g^x$ and sends $(\mathcal{B}, \mathcal{A}, X)$ to $\mathcal{B}$.

2. Upon receiving $(\mathcal{B}, \mathcal{A}, X)$, $\mathcal{B}$ verifies that $X \in G^\times$. If so, $\mathcal{B}$ chooses at random an ephemeral private key $y \in \mathbf{Z}_q^\times$, computes the ephemeral public key $Y = g^y$. After computing the shared secrets $Z_1 = (XA_1)^{y+b_1}$, $Z_2 = (XA_1)^{y+b_2}$, $Z_3 = (XA_2)^{y+b_1}$, $Z_4 = (XA_2)^{y+b_2}$, the session key $\mathrm{SK} = H(Z_1, Z_2, Z_3, Z_4, X, Y, \mathcal{A}, \mathcal{B})$ and sending $(\mathcal{A}, \mathcal{B}, X, Y)$ to $\mathcal{A}$, $\mathcal{B}$ completes the session with session key SK.

3. Upon receiving $(\mathcal{A}, \mathcal{B}, X, Y)$, $\mathcal{A}$ checks if he owns a session with identifier $\mathrm{sid} = (\mathcal{A}, \mathcal{B}, X, \times)$. If so, $\mathcal{A}$ verifies $Y \in G^\times$ and computes $Z_1 = (YB_1)^{x+a_1}$, $Z_2 = (YB_2)^{x+a_1}$, $Z_3 = (YB_1)^{x+a_2}$, $Z_4 = (YB_2)^{x+a_2}$ and completes the session $\mathrm{sid} = (\mathcal{A}, \mathcal{B}, X, Y)$ with session key $\mathrm{SK} = H(Z_1, Z_2, Z_3, Z_4, X, Y, \mathcal{A}, \mathcal{B})$.

Both parties compute the same $Z_1 = g^{(x+a_1)(y+b_1)}$, $Z_2 = g^{(x+a_1)(y+b_2)}$, $Z_3 = g^{(x+a_2)(y+b_1)}$, $Z_4 = g^{(x+a_2)(y+b_2)}$ and therefore compute the same session key SK.

## 5.2   Security Proof

**Theorem 3.** *If the CDH assumption for $G$ holds and $H$ is a random oracle, then the Protocol 2 is eCK-secure.*

*Proof.* The security proof of Protocol 2 is similar to that of Protocol 1; only the differences are explained here. Let $\mathcal{M}$ be a polynomially bounded adversary against Protocol 2, that runs in time $t(k)$, activates at most $n(k)$ honest parties, at most $s(k)$ sessions and makes at most $h(k)$ queries to the oracle $H$, where $t(k)$, $n(k)$, $s(k)$ and $h(k)$ are polynomially bounded in $k$. Assume also that $\mathcal{M}$ succeeds with non-negligible advantage. As the case of Protocol 1, the adversary has only three ways to distinguish a session key of a test session from a random string: guess, key replication or forging attack. Since $H$ is a random oracle guessing and key replication occur only with negligible probability.

We use the same events and notation as in the security proof of Protocol 1. In event A3, $\mathcal{M}$ computes $Z_1$, $Z_2$, $Z_3$ and $Z_4$ used in the test session and queries $H$ with $(Z_1, Z_2, Z_3, Z_4, X, Y, \mathcal{A}, \mathcal{B})$. As in the security proof of Protocol 1 we show how to construct a CDH solver $\mathcal{S}$.

In the $\mathcal{S}$'s simulations of environment of $\mathcal{M}$, the most important point is to maintain consistency between $H$ and $\mathtt{SessionKeyReveal}$ queries when $\mathcal{S}$ does not know static private key of the honest party that is activated. Such situations occur when $S$ embeds the CDH instance into the honest party's static public key. So, if $\mathcal{M}$ queries $H$ with $(\hat{Z}_1, \hat{Z}_2, \hat{Z}_3, \hat{Z}_4, X, Y, \mathcal{C}, \mathcal{B})$ or $(\hat{Z}_1, \hat{Z}_2, \hat{Z}_3, \hat{Z}_4, Y, X, \mathcal{B}, \mathcal{C})$, then $S$ has to be able to check the correctness of $\hat{Z}_1, \hat{Z}_2, \hat{Z}_3, \hat{Z}_4$.

We now explain how $S$ maintains the consistency. Let $\mathcal{B}$ be an honest party whose static public key is $B_1 = V$, $B_2 = g^s/V^r$, where $s$ and $r$ are randomly selected from $\mathbf{Z}_q$ by $S$. Let $\mathcal{C}$ be a party (not necessarily an honest one) whose static public key is $C_1, C_2$. When $\mathcal{M}$ queries $H$ with $(\hat{Z}_1, \hat{Z}_2, \hat{Z}_3, \hat{Z}_4, X, Y, \mathcal{C}, \mathcal{B})$ or $(\hat{Z}_1, \hat{Z}_2, \hat{Z}_3, \hat{Z}_4, Y, X, \mathcal{B}, \mathcal{C})$, we may assume that there is a session with identifier $(\mathcal{B}, \mathcal{C}, X, Y)$ or $(\mathcal{B}, \mathcal{C}, Y, X)$. Otherwise, it is sufficient for $S$ to return a random string to $\mathcal{M}$. Suppose there is a session with identifier $(\mathcal{B}, \mathcal{C}, X, Y)$, since $\mathcal{B}$ is honest, $Y$ is generated by $S$, so $\mathrm{dl}_g(Y)$ is known to $S$, who can compute

$$\bar{Z}_1 = \hat{Z}_1/(XC_1)^y, \bar{Z}_2 = \hat{Z}_2/(XC_1)^y, \bar{Z}_3 = \hat{Z}_3/(XC_2)^y, \bar{Z}_4 = \hat{Z}_4/(XC_2)^y$$

The values $\hat{Z}_1, \hat{Z}_2, \hat{Z}_3, \hat{Z}_4$ are generated according to the protocol if and only if $\bar{Z}_1 = (XC_1)^{\mathrm{dl}_g(B_1)}$, $\bar{Z}_2 = (XC_1)^{\mathrm{dl}_g(B_2)}$, $\bar{Z}_3 = (XC_2)^{\mathrm{dl}_g(B_1)}$ and $\bar{Z}_4 = (XC_2)^{\mathrm{dl}_g(B_2)}$. The algorithm $S$ can check if $\hat{Z}_1, \hat{Z}_2, \hat{Z}_3$ and $\hat{Z}_4$ are generated according to the protocol specifications by verifying

$$\bar{Z}_1^r \bar{Z}_2 = (XC_1)^s, \bar{Z}_3^r \bar{Z}_4 = (XC_2)^s;$$

the verification holds with probability at least $\left(1 - \frac{1}{q}\right)^2$ when $r, s$ are randomly choosen from $\mathbf{Z}_q^\times$ (see Theorem 1). When there is a session with identifier $(\mathcal{B}, \mathcal{C}, Y, X)$, similar verification can be performed. In this case, $\bar{Z}_1 = \hat{Z}_1/(XC_1)^y$, $\bar{Z}_2 = \hat{Z}_2/(XC_2)^y$, $\bar{Z}_3 = \hat{Z}_3/(XC_1)^y$, $\bar{Z}_4 = \hat{Z}_4/(XC_2)^y$ and $S$ checks if $\bar{Z}_1^r \bar{Z}_3 = (XC_1)^s$ and $\bar{Z}_2^r \bar{Z}_4 = (XC_2)^s$.

To complete the security proof, an explanation of how to embed and solve CDH instance in the cases El$_a$, El$_b$, E2$_a$, E2$_b$, E2$_c$ and E2$_d$ is still needed.

**El$_a$ case.** Suppose that the test session is $(\mathcal{A}, \mathcal{B}, X, Y)$, where $\mathcal{A} \neq \mathcal{B}$, $X = U$, and party $\mathcal{B}$'s static public key is $B_1 = V, B_2 = g^s/V^r$ with randomly choosen $r, s \in \mathbf{Z}_q^\times$. In the event El$_a$, the ephemeral public key $Y$ is controlled by $\mathcal{M}$. If $\mathcal{M}$ is successful with non-negligible probability, it must have queried $H$ with inputs of the form $Z_1 = (YB_1)^{\mathrm{dl}_g(U)+a_1}$, $Z_2 = (YB_2)^{\mathrm{dl}_g(U)+a_1}$, $Z_3 = (YB_1)^{\mathrm{dl}_g(U)+a_2}$ and $Z_4 = (YB_2)^{\mathrm{dl}_g(U)+a_2}$. From these values, $S$ can compute $Z_1^* = Z_1/(YB_1)^{a_1}, Z_2^* = Z_2/(YB_2)^{a_1}$; note that

$$Z_1^*/Z_2^* = U^{\mathrm{dl}_g(B_1)-\mathrm{dl}_g(B_2)} = U^{(1+r)\mathrm{dl}_g(B_1)-s}$$

because $r\mathrm{dl}_g(B_1) + \mathrm{dl}_g(B_2) \equiv s \bmod q$. Therefore, from $\left((Z_1^*/Z_2^*) \cdot U^s\right)^{1/(1+r)}$, $S$ can compute $U^{\mathrm{dl}_g(B_1)} = \mathrm{dh}_g(U, V)$. With probability at least $\frac{1}{s(k)n(k)}$, $U$ is the test session outgoing ephemeral public key and $\mathcal{B}$ is the test session peer. Since the probability that some trapdoor test yields an incorrect answer is at most $2h(k)/q$, the advantage of $S$ is

$$\mathrm{Adv}^{\mathrm{CDH}}(S) \geq \frac{1}{s(k)n(k)} \Pr[\mathrm{El}_a] - \frac{2h(k)}{q}. \tag{11}$$

**E1$_b$ case.** Suppose that the test session is $(\mathcal{A}, \mathcal{B}, X, Y)$, where $\mathcal{A} \neq \mathcal{B}$ and $\mathcal{A}$'s static public key is $A_1 = U, A_2 = g^{s'}/U^{r'}$ and $\mathcal{B}$'s static public key is $B_1 = V, B_2 = g^s/V^r$ with randomly choosen $r, s, r', s' \in \mathbf{Z}_q^\times$. In the event E1$_b$, $Y$ is controlled by $\mathcal{M}$, but $\mathcal{S}$ selects $X$ and so $\mathcal{S}$ knows $\mathrm{dl}_g(X)$. If $\mathcal{M}$ is successful with non-negligible probability, it must have queried $H$ with inputs of the form $Z_1 = (YB_1)^{\mathrm{dl}_g(U)+\mathrm{dl}_g(A_1)}$, $Z_2 = (YB_2)^{\mathrm{dl}_g(U)+\mathrm{dl}_g(A_1)}$, $Z_3 = (YB_1)^{\mathrm{dl}_g(U)+\mathrm{dl}_g(A_2)}$ and $Z_4 = (YB_2)^{\mathrm{dl}_g(U)+\mathrm{dl}_g(A_2)}$. From these values, $\mathcal{S}$ can compute $Z_1^* = Z_1/(YB_1)^x, Z_2^* = Z_2/(YB_2)^x$; note that

$$Z_1^*/Z_2^* = A_1^{\mathrm{dl}_g(B_1)-\mathrm{dl}_g(B_2)} = A_1^{(1+r)\mathrm{dl}_g(B_1)-s}$$

Therefore, from $\left((Z_1^*/Z_2^*) \cdot A_1^s\right)^{1/(1+r)}$, $\mathcal{S}$ can compute $A_1^{\mathrm{dl}_g(B_1)} = \mathrm{dh}_g(U, V)$. With probability at least $\frac{1}{n(k)^2}$, the test session peers are $\mathcal{A}$ and $\mathcal{B}$, and hence the advantage of $\mathcal{S}$ is

$$\mathrm{Adv}^{\mathrm{CDH}}(\mathcal{S}) \geq \frac{1}{n(k)^2}\,\Pr[\text{E1}_b] - \frac{2h(k)}{q}. \tag{12}$$

**E2$_a$ case.** Suppose that the test session and its matching sessions are $(\mathcal{A}, \mathcal{B}, X, Y)$ and $(\mathcal{B}, \mathcal{A}, X, Y)$, respectively, where $X = U$ and $Y = V$ (the case where $X = V$ and $Y = U$ is similar). The simulator $\mathcal{S}$ knows the static private key of all honest parties including $\mathcal{A}$ and $\mathcal{B}$. If $\mathcal{M}$ is successful with non-negligible probability, it must have queried $H$ with inputs of the form $Z_1 = (YB_1)^{\mathrm{dl}_g(U)+a_1}$, $Z_2 = (YB_2)^{\mathrm{dl}_g(U)+a_1}$, $Z_3 = (YB_1)^{\mathrm{dl}_g(U)+a_2}$ and $Z_4 = (YB_2)^{\mathrm{dl}_g(U)+a_2}$. From these, $\mathcal{S}$ can obtain $\mathrm{dh}_g(U, V)$ by computing $Z_1/(U^{b_1}V^{a_1}A_1^{b_1})$. With probability at least $\frac{1}{s(k)^2}$, the test session has ephemeral public keys $U$ and $V$, and hence the advantage of $\mathcal{S}$ is

$$\mathrm{Adv}^{\mathrm{CDH}}(\mathcal{S}) \geq \frac{1}{s(k)^2}\,\Pr[\text{E2}_a]. \tag{13}$$

**E2$_b$, E2$_c$, E2$_d$ cases.** For cases E2$_b$, E2$_c$ and E2$_d$, the arguments are similar to E1$_b$, E1$_a$, and E1$_a$, respectively; therefore

$$\mathrm{Adv}^{\mathrm{CDH}}(\mathcal{S}) \geq \frac{1}{n(k)^2}\,\Pr[\text{E2}_b] - \frac{2h(k)}{q} \tag{14}$$

$$\mathrm{Adv}^{\mathrm{CDH}}(\mathcal{S}) \geq \frac{1}{s(k)n(k)}\,\Pr[\text{E2}_c] - \frac{2h(k)}{q} \tag{15}$$

$$\mathrm{Adv}^{\mathrm{CDH}}(\mathcal{S}) \geq \frac{1}{s(k)n(k)}\,\Pr[\text{E2}_d] - \frac{2h(k)}{q} \tag{16}$$

Combining equations (11), (12), (13), (14), (15), and (16), the advantage of $\mathcal{S}$ is

$$\mathrm{Adv}^{\mathrm{CDH}}(\mathcal{S}) \geq \max\left\{ \frac{1}{s(k)n(k)}\,\Pr[\text{E1}_a], \frac{1}{n(k)^2}\,\Pr[\text{E1}_b], \frac{1}{s(k)^2}\,\Pr[\text{E2}_a], \right.$$
$$\left. \frac{1}{n(k)^2}\,\Pr[\text{E2}_b], \frac{1}{s(k)n(k)}\,\Pr[\text{E2}_c], \frac{1}{s(k)n(k)}\,\Pr[\text{E2}_d]\right\} - \frac{2h(k)}{q}.$$

As the security proof of Protocol 1, if $\mathrm{Adv}^{\mathrm{AKE}}_{\mathrm{Protocol}\ 2}(\mathcal{M})$ is non-negligible, then $\Pr[\mathrm{A3}]$ is also non-negligible and thus at least one of $\Pr[\mathrm{E1_a}], \ldots, \Pr[\mathrm{E2_d}]$ is non-negligible. Therefore, $\mathrm{Adv}^{\mathrm{CDH}}(\mathcal{S})$ is non-negligible. Moreover, during the simulation, $\mathcal{S}$ performs group exponentiations and simulates $H$, all of which take polynomially bounded in $k$ time . Thus, the running time of $\mathcal{S}$ is bounded by a polynomial in $k$ time. Therefore, $\mathcal{S}$ is a polynomial-time algorithm that solves the CDH problem in $G$ with non-negligible advantage, which contradicts the hardness of the CDH problem in $G$. This concludes the argument.

*Remark 1.* In the security argument of Protocol 1 and Protocol 2, for simplicity we do not allow the test session to be of the form $(\mathcal{A}, \mathcal{B}, X, Y)$, where $\mathcal{A} = \mathcal{B}$. However, if we allow the session of the form $(\mathcal{A}, \mathcal{A}, X, Y)$, then the arguments can be modified to solve the Square computational Diffie-Hellman (SCDH) problem. The SCDH problem is given $X \in G$, compute $X^{\mathrm{dl}_g(X)^2}$. More precisely, in Protocol 1 this case is reduced to solve SCDH problem given DDH oracle, and in Protocol 2 reduced to solve SCDH problem. Also, note that CDH problem is equivalent to SCDH problem in prime order cyclic group $G$, see [2].

# 6   Comparison

In this section, we compare our protocols with other related PKI-based two-pass AKE protocols in terms of underlying assumption, computational efficiency and security model. In Table 1 number of exponentiation in $G$, number of static public keys in terms of group elements and number of ephemeral public key in terms of group elements are denoted by E, sPK and ePK, respectively. All protocols are eCK secure except for HMQV, which is a modification of MQV [13]. It is secure in a modified CK [8] model and has additional security properties like resistance to KCI attack, wPFS, and resistance to LEP under GDH and knowledge of exponent assumptions (KEA1) [3].

When comparing computational efficiency, we do not take into account public-key validation, which is a necessary procedure to prevent potential leakage of private information similar to invalid-curve attacks [1] and small subgroup attacks [14]; see also [19,21].

Table 1 presents the naive group exponentiations count; the numbers in parentheses reflect exponentiations using speedup techniques from [18, §2.3] and [20, Alg. 14.88]. The reduced numbers follow from: (i) HMQV, CMQV, and Okamoto's protocol can use simultaneous exponentiation [20, Alg. 14.88]; and (ii) NAXOS, NAXOS+, Huang-Cao protocol, and Protocol 2 have the same base and can save time when applying Right-to-Left binary method. More precisely, in our Protocol 2, from the point of view of protocol initiator, $Z_1, Z_3$ and $Z_2, Z_4$ have the same base $YB_1$ and $YB_2$, respectively. Thus, when applying Right-to-Left binary method the value $(YB_1)^{2^i}$ (resp. $(YB_2)^{2^i}$) can be reused for $Z_1, Z_3$ (resp. $Z_2, Z_4$). Similar arguments apply to NAXOS, NAXOS+ and Huang-Cao's protocol.

Okamoto's protocol is secure in the standard model, but the proof depends on a rather strong assumption of the existence of $\pi$PRF family. In the security

**Table 1.** Protocol Comparison

| Protocol | Computation | Security Model | Assumption | NAXOS approach | Num. of sPK/ePK |
|----------|-------------|----------------|------------|----------------|------------------|
| Okamoto [22] | 8E (4.14E) | eCK | $\pi$PRF, DDH, Standard | O | 2/3 |
| HMQV [12] | 2.5E (2.17E) | CK, wPFS, KCI, LEP | KEA1, GDH, RO | × | 1/1 |
| CMQV [25] | 3E (2.17E) | eCK | GDH, RO | O | 1/1 |
| NAXOS [15] | 4E (3.17E) | eCK | GDH, RO | O | 1/1 |
| NETS [17] | 3E | eCK | GDH, RO | O | 1/1 |
| SMEN$^-$ [26] | 6E (2.46E) | eCK | GDH, RO | × | 2/2 |
| Protocol 1 | 3E | eCK | GDH, RO | × | 2/1 |
| NAXOS+ [16] | 5E (3.34E) | eCK | CDH, RO | O | 1/1 |
| Huang-Cao [11] | 5E (4.17E) | eCK | CDH, RO | O | 2/1 |
| Protocol 2 | 5E (3.34E) | eCK | CDH, RO | × | 2/1 |

proof of HMQV and CMQV, the reduction argument is less tight since the Forking Lemma [24] is essential for the arguments. In comparison, the rest of the protocols in Table 1, including Protocol 1 and Protocol 2, have tighter security reductions and do not use the Forking Lemma.

**No NAXOS' approach.** As shown in Table 1, Protocol 1 has the same characteristic as NETS and Protocol 2 has the same characteristic as NAXOS+ in computation efficiency, security model, and underlying assumption. The difference is that our protocols dispenses with NAXOS' approach, at the expense of an additional group element in the static key. SMEN$^-$ also has features similar to Protocol 1: it is eCK-secure in the random oracle model under the GDH assumption, does not use NAXOS' approach and a static public key is a pair of group elements. It achieves better computational performance (2.46 vs 3 exponentiations), but requires that the an ephemeral key constitutes of two group elements. Therefore it provides a trade-off between computation and communication efficiencies.

We showed that it is possible to construct eCK-secure AKE protocols without using NAXOS' approach, so our protocols are secure even when the discrete logarithm of the ephemeral public key is revealed. As pointed out in [26], protocols that do not rely on NAXOS' approach decrease the risk of leaking the static private key in comparison with protocols that ustilize the NAXOS' approach. This feature makes protocols like ours, SMEN$^-$ and HMQV more practical.

Another advantage of our protocols is the use of single random oracle as opposed to two for HMQV and CMQV. The random oracle is needed for the session key derivation, which is typical way to attain indistinguishability in random oracle model. As pointed in [7], although protocols secure in the random oracle model produce assurance for the scheme's correctness, there may remain some fear since concrete hash function instantiations differ from a truly random function. In the sense of minimal reliance on random oracles, our protocols and SMEN⁻ are the best among protocols in Table 1.

# 7   Conclusion

The extended Canetti-Krawczyk (eCK) definition introduced by LaMacchia, Lauter and Mityagin is a strong security model for authenticated key exchange. This paper presented two eCK-secure AKE protocols without using NAXOS' approach. As a result, our protocols provide strong security assurances without compromising too much on efficiency. In addition, we minimized the reliance on the random oracle for the security argument and were able to utilize the trap-door test to assume only computational assumptions.

# References

1. Antipa, A., Brown, D., Menezes, A., Struik, R., Vanstone, S.: Validation of elliptic curve public keys. In: Desmedt, Y.G. (ed.) PKC 2003. LNCS, vol. 2567, pp. 211–223. Springer, Heidelberg (2002)
2. Bao, F., Deng, R.H., Zhu, H.: Variations of diffie-hellman problem. In: Qing, S., Gollmann, D., Zhou, J. (eds.) ICICS 2003. LNCS, vol. 2836, pp. 301–312. Springer, Heidelberg (2003)
3. Bellare, M., Palacio, A.: The knowledge-of-exponent assumptions and 3-round zero-knowledge protocols. In: Franklin, M. (ed.) CRYPTO 2004. LNCS, vol. 3152, pp. 273–289. Springer, Heidelberg (2004)
4. Bellare, M., Pointcheval, D., Rogaway, P.: Authenticated key exchange secure against dictionary attacks. In: Preneel, B. (ed.) EUROCRYPT 2000. LNCS, vol. 1807, pp. 139–155. Springer, Heidelberg (2001)
5. Bellare, M., Rogaway, P.: Entity authentication and key distribution. In: Stinson, D.R. (ed.) CRYPTO 1993. LNCS, vol. 773, pp. 110–125. Springer, Heidelberg (1993)
6. Bellare, M., Rogaway, P.: Provably secure session key distribution: the three party case. In: STOC 1995, pp. 57–66 (1995)
7. Bellare, M., Rogaway, P.: Minimizing the use of random oracles in authenticated encryption schemes. In: Han, Y., Quing, S. (eds.) ICICS 1997. LNCS, vol. 1334, pp. 1–16. Springer, Heidelberg (1997)
8. Canetti, R., Krawczyk, H.: Analysis of key-exchange protocols and their use for building secure channels. In: Pfitzmann, B. (ed.) EUROCRYPT 2001. LNCS, vol. 2045, pp. 453–474. Springer, Heidelberg (2001)
9. Cash, D., Kiltz, E., Shoup, V.: The twin diffie-hellman problem and applications. In: Smart, N.P. (ed.) EUROCRYPT 2008. LNCS, vol. 4965, pp. 127–145. Springer, Heidelberg (2008)
10. Diffie, W., Hellman, H.: New directions in cryptography. IEEE transactions of Information Theory 22(6), 644–654 (1976)
11. Huang, H., Cao, Z.: Strongly secure authenticated key exchange protocol based on computational Diffie-Hellman problem. In: Inscrypt 2008 (2008)

12. Krawczyk, H.: HMQV: A high-performance secure diffie-hellman protocol. In: Shoup, V. (ed.) CRYPTO 2005. LNCS, vol. 3621, pp. 546–566. Springer, Heidelberg (2005)
13. Law, L., Menezes, A., Qu, M., Solinas, J., Vanstone, S.: An efficient protocol for authenticated key agreement. Designs, Codes and Cryptography 28, 119–134 (2003)
14. Lim, C.H., Lee, P.J.: A key recovery attack on discrete log-based schemes using a prime order subgroup. In: Kaliski Jr., B.S. (ed.) CRYPTO 1997. LNCS, vol. 1294, pp. 249–263. Springer, Heidelberg (1994)
15. LaMacchia, B.A., Lauter, K., Mityagin, A.: Stronger security of authenticated key exchange. In: Susilo, W., Liu, J.K., Mu, Y. (eds.) ProvSec 2007. LNCS, vol. 4784, pp. 1–16. Springer, Heidelberg (2007)
16. Lee, J., Park, J.: Authenticated key exchange secure under the computational Diffie-Hellman assumption, http://eprint.iacr.org/2008/344
17. Lee, J., Park, C.: An efficient key exchange protocol with a tight security reduction, http://eprint.iacr.org/2008/345
18. M'Raïhi, D., Naccache, D.: Batch exponentiation: a fast DLP-based signature generation strategy. In: CCS 1996: Proceedings of the 3rd ACM conference on Computer and communications security, pp. 58–61 (1993)
19. Menezes, A.: Another look at HMQV. Journal of Mathematical Cryptology 1(1), 47–64 (2007)
20. Menezes, A., van Oorschot, P., Vanstone, S.: Handbook of applied cryptography, Florida, USA. CRC Press, Boca Raton (1997)
21. Menezes, A., Ustaoglu, B.: On the importance of public-key validation in the MQV and HMQV key agreement protocols. In: Barua, R., Lange, T. (eds.) INDOCRYPT 2006. LNCS, vol. 4329, pp. 133–147. Springer, Heidelberg (2006)
22. Okamoto, T.: Authenticated key exchange and key encapsulation in the standard model. In: Kurosawa, K. (ed.) ASIACRYPT 2007. LNCS, vol. 4833, pp. 474–484. Springer, Heidelberg (2007)
23. Okamoto, T., Pointcheval, D.: The Gap-Problems: A new class of problems for the security of cryptographic schemes. In: Kim, K.-c. (ed.) PKC 2001. LNCS, vol. 1992, pp. 104–118. Springer, Heidelberg (2001)
24. Pointcheval, D., Stern, J.: Security Arguments for Digital Signatures and Blind Signatures. J. of Cryptology 13(3), 361–396 (2000)
25. Ustaoğlu, B.: Obtaining a secure and efficient key agreement protocol for (H)MQV and NAXOS. Designs, Codes and Cryptography 46(3), 329–342 (2008), http://eprint.iacr.org/2007/123
26. Wu, J., Ustaoğlu, B.: Efficient Key Exchange with Tight Security Reduction, Technical Report CACR 2009-23, University of Waterloo (2009), http://www.cacr.math.uwaterloo.ca/techreports/2009/cacr2009-23.pdf

# ID-Based Group Password-Authenticated
# Key Exchange

Xun Yi[1], Raylin Tso[2], and Eiji Okamoto[3]

[1] School of Engineering and Science, Victoria University
Melbourne, Victoria 8001, Australia
Xun.Yi@vu.edu.au
[2] Department of Computer Science, National Chengchi University
Taipei 11605, Taiwan
raylin@cs.nccu.edu.tw
[3] Department of Risk Engineering, University of Tsukuba
Tsukuba, Ibaraki, 305-8573, Japan
okamoto@risk.tsukuba.ac.jp

**Abstract.** Password-authenticated key exchange (PAKE) protocols are designed to be secure even when the secret key used for authentication is a human-memorable password. In this paper, we consider PAKE protocols in the group scenario, in which a group of clients, each of them shares his password with an "honest but curious" server, intend to establish a common secret key (i.e., a group key) with the help of the server. In this setting, the key established is known to the clients only and no one else, including the server. Each client needs to remember the password only while the server keeps passwords in addition to private keys related to its identity. Towards our goal, we present a compiler that transforms any group key exchange (KE) protocol which is secure against a passive eavesdropping to a group PAKE which is secure against an active adversary who controls all communications in the network. This compiler is built on a group KE protocol, an identity-based encryption (IBE) scheme, and an identity-based signature (IBS) scheme. It adds only two rounds and $O(1)$ communication (per client) to the original group KE protocol. As long as the underlying group KE protocol, IBE scheme and an IBS scheme have provable security without random oracles, the group PAKE constructed by our compiler can be proven to be secure without random oracles.

**Keywords:** Password-authenticated key exchange, group key agreement, protocol compiler, common reference model.

## 1 Introduction

Popularity of group-oriented applications and protocols is currently on the increase and, as a result, group communication is taking place in many different settings, from network layer multicasting to application layer tele- and video-conferencing. Securing group communication makes demands of protocols for

T. Takagi and M. Mambo (Eds.): IWSEC 2009, LNCS 5824, pp. 192–211, 2009.

group authenticated key exchange (AKE), which allows a group of users communicating over an insecure public network to establish a common secret key (i.e., a group key) and furthermore to be guaranteed that they are indeed sharing this key with each other.

Protocols for 2-party AKE has been extensively investigated in [36,15,37,13,11,32,33,34]. A number of works have considered extending the 2-party Diffie-Hellman protocol [36] to the multi-party setting [43,57,29,58,10,50,51]. Among them, the works of Ingemarsson et al. [43], Burmester and Desmedt [29], and Steiner et al. [58] may be the most well-known. They are merely key exchange (KE) protocols, intended to be secure against a passive adversary only. However, AKE protocols aim to be secure against more powerful adversaries, who - in addition to eavesdropping - control all communications in the network. A number of initial protocols for group AKE were suggested in [44,19,7,8,59]. But none of these works have rigorous security proofs in a well-defined model.

Bresson et al. [22,23,24] were the first to define a formal model of security for group AKE and give the first provably secure protocols for this setting. Their model was built on the earlier work of Bellare and Rogaway in the two-party setting [12,13,11] and their protocols were based on the work of Steiner et al. [58], which requires $O(n)$ rounds to establish a key among $n$ users, and therefore not scalable. A constant-round group AKE with a security proof in the random oracle model was given in [20], but it was shown to be insecure in [56].

Katz and Yung [48] were the first to give scalable protocol for group AKE along with a rigorous proof of security in the standard model. They also presented the first efficient compiler that transforms any group KE protocols secure against a passive eavesdropping to authenticated protocols by signing message flows. Their compiler adds only one round to the original protocol. However, this compiler requires each user to have a pair of public and private keys for digital signature. The (high-entropy) private key is not human-memorable and needs additional cryptographic devices to store it.

Bellovin and Merritt [14] were the first to consider AKE based on (low-entropy) password only and introduced a series of so-called "encrypted key exchange" (EKE) protocols for two-party AKE. A password-based AKE (i.e., PAKE) has to be immune to the dictionary attack, in which an adversary exhaustively tries all possible passwords from a dictionary in order to determine the correct one. Even though these attacks are not very effective in the case of high-entropy keys, they can be very damaging when the secret key is a password since the attacker has a non-negligible chance of winning. Dictionary attacks are usually divided into two categories: offline and online dictionary attacks.

Formal models of security for two-party PAKE were firstly given independently by Bellare, Pointcheval and Rogaway [11], and Boyko, MacKenzie, Patel and Swaminathan [21] in 2000. Since then, protocols for two-party PAKE have been continuously proposed and proven to be secure in either the random oracle model (e.g.,[26,27,3,4,5]) or the standard model (e.g., [40,46,45]).

Bresson et al. [25,28] were the first to adapt a group KE protocol to the password-based scenario. As the original protocol, the first group PAKE protocol was not scalable and practical for large groups. In addition, their security proof required ideal models. Recently, a number of constant-round group PAKE have been proposed in the literature by Abdalla et al. [2,6], by Bohli et al. [16], and by Kim, Lee and Lee [49]. All of these constructions are built on the Burmester-Desmedt protocol [29,31] and are rather efficient. Among them, the works of Abdalla et al. [6] and Bohli et al. [16] enjoy security proofs in the standard model.

Most of existing group PAKE protocols assume that users of a group share the same password, e.g., [25,28,2,6]. In the scenarios where a user wants to participate in many groups, the number of passwords that he would need to remember would be linear in the number of possible groups. In order to cut down the number of passwords that a user has to remember, a couple of group PAKE protocols [3,4,52] assume that each user shares his own password with a server, which helps users of a group with establishment of a common secret key (i.e., a group key). The server is assumed to behave in an "honest but curious" manner (i.e., the server may attempt to learn the group key only by passive eavesdropping) and the group key is required to be private to the server. Note that key distribution protocols usually do not achieve this property. The setting with different passwords seems to be more practical in the real world than the setting with the same password.

More recently, Abdalla et al. [1] presented a protocol compiler that transforms any two-party AKE into a group AKE with two more rounds of communication. Their idea is inspired by the construction of Burmester and Desmedt [29], where the trick of constructing a group key from pairwise agreed keys among users of a group was firstly introduced. In particular, applying this compiler to a two-party PAKE protocol yields a group PAKE protocol. The primary motivation of this compiler was the two-party setting. As implied in [48], a compiler tailored from the group setting scales better than the compiler from two-party setting. This leads a question, is there any protocol compiler that transforms any group KE protocol directly to a group PAKE protocol?

**Contribution.** To the best of our knowledge, there has not yet been any protocol compiler that can transform any group KE protocol directly into a group PAKE protocol at present. In this paper, we present such a compiler on the basis of the "state-of-the-art" identity-based cryptosystem, a public-key cryptosystem in which an arbitrary string (e.g., user identity) can be used as the public key.

We assume that clients of a group, each of them shares his own password with an "honest but curious" server, intend to establish a common secret key (i.e., a group key) with the help of the server, where the key established is required to be known to the clients only and no one else, including the server.

Note that our setting for PAKE is, in fact, the extension of the three-party PAKE setting suggested in [3], where two clients do not share a password between themselves but only with a "honest but curious" server, which helps with establishing a session key between them, but gains no information on the value of that session key. For more details of the "honest but curious" server, we can refer to the work of Abdalla et al. in [3].

Our compiler employs any group KE protocol secure against passive eavesdropping, any identity-based encryption scheme (IBE) with chosen-ciphertext security and any identity-based signature scheme (IBS) with existential unforgeability.

The **basic idea** of our compiler is that users of a group firstly run the group KE protocol to establish a group key without any help of the server, and then the server helps users of the group with mutual authentication and key confirmation by the shared passwords (protected with the IBE scheme), and finally each user authenticates the server, along with partnered users and the established key during the group KE, by the IBS scheme.

To analyze the security of our compiler, we put forth a formal model of security for ID-based PAKE in the group setting, by embedding Boneh et al.'s ID-based model [17][18] into the group PAKE model given by Bresson et al. in [25,28] and improved by Abdalla et al. [1].

Our model assumes that all users and servers refer to the common public parameters including the public key of a Private Key Generator (commonly used in ID-based model). Thus, our model is between the Halevi-Krawczyk model [42] (where each user needs to keep the public key of each server or to authenticate it on the basis of a public key certificate and the public key of a certificate authority) and the Katz-Ostrovsky-Yung model [48] (where all users and servers refer the common public parameters only). Different from the Halevi-Krawczyk model, our model is ID-based, where the public key of a server is its identity (which is meaningful, like an e-mail address, and easy to remember and keep) and public key authentication is unnecessary. Thus, the Public Key Infrastructure (PKI) is not needed in our model. Similar to the Katz-Ostrovsky-Yung model, our model includes the public key of a parameter generator in the common public parameters. Although the Katz-Ostrovsky-Yung model assumes that the public parameter generator uses random numbers as the public key of Cramer-Shoup cryptosystem [35], the generator can, in fact, choose the private key at first and then compute the public key without being detected. Furthermore, if the private key corresponding to the public key in the common public parameters is compromised, both the Katz-Ostrovsky-Yung protocol and our protocol have to reset.

We provide a rigorous proof of security for our compiler. Our compiler does not rely on the random oracle model as long as the underlying primitives themselves do not rely on it. For example, by using Burmester-Desmedt group KE protocol [29], Gentry IBE scheme [39], Paterson-Schuldt IBS scheme [54], our compiler can construct a group PAKE with provable security in the standard model.

**Organization.** In Section 2, we introduce a new model for ID-based group PAKE. In Section 3, we present a new ID-based group PAKE compiler. After that, in Section 3, the brief security proof for our protocol is described. We conclude this paper in Section 4. In addition, we describe the underlying cryptographic primitives to build our group PAKE in Appendix A.

## 2    Definitions

A formal model of security for group PAKE was firstly given by Bresson et al. in [25,26] (based on Bellare et al.'s formal model for 2-party PAKE [12]), and improved by Abdalla et al. in [1].

Boneh and Franklin were the first to define chosen ciphertext security for IBE under chosen identity attack [17,18]. In this section, we put forward a new model of security for ID-based group PAKE, on the basis of definitions given by Bresson et al., Abdalla et al. and Boneh et al.

**Participants, Initialization and Passwords.** An ID-based group PAKE protocol involves three kinds of participants: (1) A set of clients (denoted as Client); (2) A set of servers (denoted as Server), which behave in an honest but curious manner; (3) A Private Key Generator (PKG), which generates public parameters and corresponding private keys for servers, and behaves in an honest but curious manner as well. We assume that ClientServerPair is the set of pairs of the client and the server, who share a password. In addition, User = Client $\bigcup$ Server and Client $\bigcap$ Server = $\emptyset$.

Prior to any execution of the protocol, we assume that an initialization phase occurs. During initialization, PKG generates public parameters for the protocol, which are available to all participants, and issues private keys for each server. The private keys are related to the identity of the server (which is public, meaningful, like an e-mail address, and easy to remember or keep). For any pair $(A, S) \in$ ClientServerPair, the client $A$ and the server $S$ are assumed to share the same password $\mathsf{pw}_A^S$. We assume that the client $A$ chooses $\mathsf{pw}_A^S$ independently and uniformly at random from a "dictionary" $\mathcal{D} = \{\mathsf{pw}_1, \mathsf{pw}_2, \cdots, \mathsf{pw}_N\}$ of size $N$, where $N$ is a fixed constant which is independent of the security parameter. The client then stores his password $\mathsf{pw}_A^S$ at the server $S$ for authentication, and remembers or keeps the identity of $S$ for identity-based encryption.

After initialization, a server can be still added to the system as long as it obtains its private key related to its identity from PKG. A client can join the system once he shares his password with a server.

**Execution of the Protocol.** In the real world, a protocol determines how users behave in response to input from their environments. In the formal model, these inputs are provided by the adversary. Each user is assumed to be able to execute the protocol multiple times (possibly concurrently) with different partners. This is modeled by allowing each user to have unlimited number of instances with which to execute the protocol. We denote instance $i$ of user $U$ as $U^i$. A given instance may be used only once. The adversary is given oracle access to these different instances. Furthermore, each instance maintains (local) state which is updated during the course of the experiment. In particular, each instance $U^i$ has associated with it the following variables, initialized as NULL or FALSE (as appropriate) during the initialization phase.

- $\mathsf{sid}_U^i$ and $\mathsf{pid}_U^i$ are variables (initialized as NULL) denoting the session identity and partner identity for an instance, respectively. The session identity $\mathsf{sid}_U^i$ is simply a way to keep track of the different executions of a particular user $U$. The partner identity $\text{pid}_U^i$ is the set of user instances with whom $U^i$ believes it is interacting to establish a session key (including $U^i$ itself).

- $\text{acc}_U^i$ and $\text{term}_U^i$ are boolean variables (initialized as FALSE) denoting if a given instance has been accepted or terminated, respectively. Termination means that the given instance has done receiving and sending messages, acceptance indicates successful termination. In our case, acceptance means that the instance is sure that a group key has been established, thus, when an instance $U^i$ accepts, $\text{sid}_U^i$ and $\text{pid}_U^i$ are no longer NULL.
- $\text{used}_U^i$ is a boolean variable (initialized as FALSE) denoting whether an instance has begun executing the protocol. This is a formalism which will ensure each instance is used only once.
- $\text{state}_U^i$ (initialized as NULL) records any state necessary for execution of the protocol by a user instance $U^i$.
- $\text{sk}_A^i$ is a variable (initialized as NULL) denoting the session key for a client instance $A^i$. Computation of the session key is, of course, the ultimate goal of the protocol. When $A^i$ accepts (i.e., $\text{acc}_A^i = \text{TRUE}$), $\text{sk}_A^i$ is no longer NULL.

The adversary $\mathcal{A}$ is assumed to have complete control over all communications in the network and the adversary's interaction with the users (more specifically, with various instances) or PKG is modeled via access to oracles which we describe now. The state of an instance may be updated during an oracle call, and the oracle's output may depend upon the relevant instance. The oracle types are as follows:

- Execute$(A_1^{i_1}, A_2^{i_2}, \cdots, A_n^{i_n}, S^j)$ – If $A_\ell^{i_\ell}$ and $S^j$ have not yet been used (where $A_\ell \in \text{Client}$, $S \in \text{Server}$, $(A_\ell, S) \in \text{ClientServerPair}$, $\ell = 1, 2, \cdots, n$), this oracle executes the protocol among these instances and outputs the transcript of this execution. This oracle call represents passive eavesdropping of a protocol execution. In addition to the transcript, the adversary receives the values of sid, pid, acc, and term for all instances, at each step of protocol execution.
- Send$(U^i, M)$ – This sends message $M$ to instance $U^i$. Assuming $\text{term}_U^i = \text{FALSE}$, this instance runs according to the protocol specification, updating state as appropriate. The output of $U^i$ (i.e., the message sent by the instance) is given to the adversary, who receives the updated values of $\text{sid}_U^i$, $\text{pid}_U^i$, $\text{acc}_U^i$, and $\text{term}_U^i$. This oracle call models the active attack to a protocol.
- KeyGen$(\text{PKG}, S)$ – This sends the identity of the server $S$ to PKG, which generates private keys $d_S$ corresponding to the identity of $S$ and forwards it to the adversary. This oracle models possible compromising of a server due to, for example, hacking into the server. This implies that all passwords stored in the server are disclosed as well.
- Corrupt$(A)$ – This query allows the adversary to learn the passwords of the client $A$, which models the possibility of subverting a client by, for example, witnessing a user type in his password, or installing a "Trojan horse" on his machine. This implies that all passwords held by $A$ are disclosed.

- Reveal($A^i$) – This outputs the current value of session key $\mathsf{sk}_A^i$ for a client instance if $\mathsf{acc}_A^i$ = TRUE. This oracle call models possible leakage of session keys due to, for example, improper erasure of session keys after use, or cryptanalysis.
- Test($A^i$) – This oracle does not model any real-world capability of the adversary, but is instead used to define security of the session key of client instance $A^i$. If $\mathsf{acc}_A^i$ = TRUE and $\mathsf{sk}_A^i \neq$ NULL, a random bit $b$ is generated. If $b = 0$, the adversary is given $\mathsf{sk}_A^i$, and if $b = 1$ the adversary is given a random session key. The adversary is allowed a single Test query, at any time during its execution.

A passive adversary is given access to the Execute, KeyGen, Reveal, Corrupt, and Test oracles, while an active adversary is additionally given access to the Send oracles. We assume that all servers and the PKG behave in a honest but curious manner. We can imagine a server or the PKG as a passive adversary who have already queried a KeyGen oracle to retrieve the server's private keys and all passwords stored in it. In addition, we assume that all servers and the PKG have no access to any form of Send oracles. In the definition of Execute and Send oracles, we reasonably require that $A_1, A_2, \cdots, A_n$ share different passwords with the same server $S$.

**Partnering.** We say that client instances $A^i$ and $B^j$ are partnered if (1) $\mathsf{pid}_A^i =$ $\mathsf{pid}_B^j \neq$ NULL; (2) $\mathsf{sid}_A^i = \mathsf{sid}_B^j \neq$ NULL; (3) $\mathsf{sk}_A^i = \mathsf{sk}_B^j \neq$ NULL; and (4) $\mathsf{acc}_A^i = \mathsf{acc}_B^i$ = TRUE.

**Correctness.** To be viable, an authenticated group key exchange protocol must satisfy the following notion of correctness: At the presence of both passive and active adversaries, for any two client instances $A^i$ and $B^j$, if $\mathsf{sid}_A^i = \mathsf{sid}_B^j \neq$ NULL and $\mathsf{acc}_A^i = \mathsf{acc}_B^j$ = TRUE, then it must be the case that $\mathsf{sk}_A^i = \mathsf{sk}_B^j \neq$ NULL (i.e., they conclude with the same session key) and $\mathsf{pid}_A^i = \mathsf{pid}_B^j \neq$ NULL (i.e., they conclude with the same group).

**Freshness.** Informally, the adversary succeeds if it can guess the bit $b$ used by a Test oracle. Before formally defining the adversary's success, we must first define a notion of freshness. A client instance $A^i$ is fresh unless one of the following is true at the conclusion of the experiment, namely, at some point,

- The adversary queried Reveal($A^i$) or Reveal($B^j$) with the client instances $A^i$ and $B^j$ being partnered.
- The adversary queried KeyGen(PKG, $S$) where there exists a server instance $S^j \in \mathsf{pid}_A^i$, before a query of the form Send($U^\ell, M$), where $U^\ell \in \mathsf{pid}_A^i$, has taken place, for some message $M$ (or identities).
- The adversary queried Corrupt($A$) or Corrupt($B$) where there is a client instance $B^j \in \mathsf{pid}_A^i$, before a query of the form Send($U^\ell, M$), where $U^\ell \in \mathsf{pid}_A^i$, has taken place, for some message $M$ (or identities).

Note that a passive adversary (e.g., the server or the PKG) has no access to any Send oracles. Therefore, a client instance is fresh to a passive adversary as long as the first event did not happen.

The adversary is thought to succeed only if its Test query is made to a fresh instance. Note that this is necessary for any reasonable definition of security, otherwise, the adversary could always succeed, e.g., submitting a Test query for an instance for which it had already submitted a Reveal query.

**Advantage of the adversary.** We say an adversary $\mathcal{A}$ succeeds if it makes a single query $\mathsf{Test}(A^i)$ to a fresh client instance $A^i$, with $\mathsf{acc}_A^i = \mathsf{TRUE}$ at the time of this query, and outputs a single bit $b'$ with $b' = b$ (recall that $b$ is the bit chosen by the Test oracle). We denote this event by Succ. The advantage of adversary $\mathcal{A}$ in attacking protocol $P$ is a function in the security parameter $k$, defined as

$$\mathsf{Adv}_{\mathcal{A}}^P(k) = 2 \cdot \mathsf{Pr}_{\mathcal{A}}^P[\mathsf{Succ}] - 1$$

where the probability is taken over the random coins used by the adversary and the random coins used during the course of the experiment (including the initialization phase). It remains to define what we mean by a secure protocol. Note that a probabilistic polynomial-time (PPT) adversary can always succeed by trying all passwords one-by-one in an online impersonation attack. This is possible since the size of the password dictionary is constant. Informally, a protocol is secure if this is the best an adversary can do. Formally, an instance $U^i$ represents an online attack if both the following are true at the time of the Test query: (1) at some point, the adversary queried $\mathsf{Send}(U^i, *)$, and (2) at some point, the adversary queried $\mathsf{Reveal}(A^j)$ or $\mathsf{Test}(A^j)$, where the client instance $A^j \in \mathsf{pid}_U^i$. In particular, instances with which the adversary interacts via Execute, KeyGen, Reveal and Corrupt queries are not counted as online attacks. The number of online attacks represents a bound on the number of passwords the adversary could have tested in an online fashion.

**Definition 1.** Protocol $P$ is a secure protocol for password-authenticated key exchange if, for all dictionary size $N$ and for all PPT adversaries $\mathcal{A}$ making at most $Q(k)$ online attacks, there exists a negligible function $\varepsilon(\cdot)$ such that

$$\mathsf{Adv}_{\mathcal{A}}^P(k) \leq Q(k)/N + \varepsilon(k)$$

The above definition ensures that the adversary can (essentially) do no better than guess a single password during each online attack. Calls to the Execute, KeyGen, Reveal and Corrupt oracles, which are not included in $Q(k)$, are of no help to the adversary in breaking the security of the protocol.

**Forward secrecy.** We follow the definition of forward secrecy from [47,1] and consider the weak corrupt model of [12]. An adversary can corrupt a client (i.e., retrieving his password via Corrupt query) or corrupt a server(i.e., retrieving both its private key and all passwords stored in it via KeyGen query). After that, as long as the adversary does not query Send or Reveal oracles, he can still make a Test query on a client instance. If such queries do not give the adversary any information about previous agreed session keys, forward secrecy is achieved.

**Key privacy with respect to the server.** The notion of key privacy respect to the server was introduced in the three-party setting [3] to capture the idea where the session key shared between two client instances should only be known to these two instances and no one else, including the server, who behaves in an honest but curious manner. In our model, a server or the PKG can be imagined as an adversary who has already queried a KeyGen oracle but never queries Send oracle. If such queries do not give the server any information about the session key, key privacy with respect to the server is achieved. In fact, forward secrecy implies key privacy with respect to the server.

## 3 An Efficient Compiler for Group PAKE

### 3.1 Description of the Compiler

In this section, we present an efficient compiler transforming any group KE protocol $P$ to a group PAKE protocol $P'$. Following the communication model given in [48], we assume that every message is sent - via point-to-point links - to every user of the group taking part in the execution of the protocol $P$, in other word, $A_i$ sends each message to all users in the group. For simplicity, we refer to this as "broadcasting message", but stress that we do not assume a broadcast channel and, in particular, an active adversary can deliver different messages to different users of the group or refuse to deliver a message to some of participants.

---

**Round 0** (Group Key Exchange $(P)$)

    Clients $A_\ell, \ell = 1, 2, \cdots, n$

        $\mathsf{pid}_{A_\ell} \leftarrow (A_1, A_2, \cdots, A_n)$

        $(\mathsf{sid}_{A_1}^P | \mathsf{sk}_{A_1}^P, \mathsf{sid}_{A_2}^P | \mathsf{sk}_{A_2}^P, \cdots, \mathsf{sid}_{A_n}^P | \mathsf{sk}_{A_n}^P) \leftarrow \mathsf{Execute}^P(A_1, A_2, \cdots, A_n)$

**Round 1** (Client Authentication)

    Client $A_\ell, \ell \in \{1, 2, \cdots, n\}$, $\mathsf{pid}_{A_\ell} \leftarrow \mathsf{pid}_{A_\ell} \cup \{S\}$, $\mathsf{sid}_{A_\ell} \leftarrow h(g^{\mathsf{sk}_{A_\ell}^P} | \mathsf{sid}_{A_\ell}^P)$

        $\mathsf{Auth}_\ell \leftarrow \mathsf{E}_{\mathsf{ID}_S}[H(\mathsf{sid}_{A_\ell} | \mathsf{pid}_{A_\ell} | \mathsf{pw}_{A_\ell}^S)]$

        $\{S\} \Leftarrow \mathsf{msg}_{A_\ell} = A_\ell | \mathsf{sid}_{A_\ell} | \mathsf{Auth}_\ell$

    Server $S$, $\mathsf{pid}_S \leftarrow (A_1, A_2, \cdots, A_n, S)$, $\mathsf{sid}_S \leftarrow \mathsf{sid}_{A_1}$

        If $\exists \ell$ such that $\mathsf{D}_{\mathsf{ds}}[\mathsf{Auth}_\ell] \neq H(\mathsf{sid}_S | \mathsf{pid}_S | \mathsf{pw}_{A_\ell}^S)$, then return $\bot$

**Round 2** (Server Authentication)

    Server $S$

        $\mathsf{Auth}_S \leftarrow \mathsf{S}_{d_S'}[\mathsf{pid}_S | \mathsf{sid}_S]$

        $\{A_1, A_2, \cdots, A_n\} \Leftarrow \mathsf{msg}_S = S | \mathsf{Auth}_S$

    Client $A_\ell, \ell = 1, 2, \cdots, n$

        If $\mathsf{V}_{\mathsf{ID}_S}[\mathsf{pid}_{A_\ell} | \mathsf{sid}_{A_\ell}, \mathsf{Auth}_S] \neq 1$, then return $\bot$

        Else accept $\leftarrow$ TRUE, $\mathsf{sk}_{A_\ell}^{P'} \leftarrow g^{\mathsf{sk}_{A_\ell}^P}{}^2$

---

**Fig. 1.** ID-based group PAKE protocol $P'$

Given a group KE protocol $P$, our compiler constructs a group PAKE protocol $P'$ as shown in Fig. 1, in which $n$ clients $A_1, A_2, \cdots, A_n$ (in lexicographic order) establish a common authenticated secret key (i.e., a group key) with the help of a server $S$.

A completely formal specification of the group PAKE protocol will appear in Section 4, where we give a brief proof of security for the protocol in the security model described in Section 2.

We present the protocol by describing initialization and execution. In our protocol, the cryptographic building blocks include a group KE protocol, an IBE scheme and an IBS scheme, which are described in Appendix A. We assume that the group KE protocol requires neither public nor private keys. Otherwise, clients needs to remember their private keys besides passwords. This contradicts with our model, where clients needs to remember their passwords only. We let $k$ be the security parameter given to the setup algorithm.

**Initialization.** Given a security parameter $k \in \mathbb{Z}^*$, the initialization includes:

*Parameter Generation*: On input $k$, (1) PKG runs $\mathsf{Setup}^P$ of the group KE protocol $P$ to generate system parameters, denoted as $\mathsf{params}^P$; (2) PKG runs $\mathsf{Setup}^E$ of the IBE scheme to generate public system parameters for the IBE scheme, denoted as $\mathsf{params}^E$, and the secret $\mathsf{master\text{-}key}^E$ for itself; (3) PKG runs $\mathsf{Setup}^S$ of the IBS scheme to generate public system parameters for the IBS scheme, denoted as $\mathsf{params}^S$, and the secret $\mathsf{master\text{-}key}^S$ for itself; In addition, PKG chooses two hash functions $H : \{0,1\}^* \to \mathcal{M}$ (where $\mathcal{M}$ is the plaintext space of IBE) and $h : \{0,1\}^* \to \{0,1\}^\lambda$ from a collision-resistant hash family, and a large cyclic group $G$ with a prime order $q$ and a generator $g$. We assume that group keys established by the group KE protocol $P$ fall into $\mathbb{Z}_q^*$. The public system parameters for the protocol $P'$ is $\mathsf{params} = \{H, h, G, q, g\} \bigcup \mathsf{params}^{P,E,S}$ and the secret $(\mathsf{master\text{-}key}^E, \mathsf{master\text{-}key}^S)$ known only to PKG.

*Key Generation*: On input the identity $\mathsf{ID}_S$ of a server $S \in \mathsf{Server}$, $\mathsf{params}$, and $(\mathsf{master\text{-}key}^E, \mathsf{master\text{-}key}^S)$, PKG runs $\mathsf{Extract}^E$ of the IBE scheme and sets the decryption key of $S$ to be $\mathsf{d}_S$, and runs $\mathsf{Extract}^S$ of the IBS scheme and sets the signing key of $S$ to be $\mathsf{d}_S'$.

*Password Generation*: On input $(A, S) \in \mathsf{ClientServerPair}$, a string $\mathsf{pw}_A^S$, the password, is uniformly drawn from the dictionary $\mathsf{Password} = \{\mathsf{pw}_1, \mathsf{pw}_2, \cdots, \mathsf{pw}_N\}$, and shared by $A$ and $S$. We implicitly assume that $N < q$, which will certainly be true in practice.

**Protocol Execution.** A group of clients $A_1, A_2, \cdots, A_n$ (in lexicographic order), each of them shares a password $\mathsf{pw}_{A_\ell}^S$ with a server $S$ ($\ell = 1, 2, \cdots, n$), run the protocol to establish a common secret key (i.e., a group key) via $S$. At first, they run the group KE protocol $P$ and each client $A_\ell$ derives the initial group key $\mathsf{sk}_{A_\ell}^P$. In addition, let $\mathsf{sid}_{A_\ell}^P$ be the (ordered) concatenation of all messages sent and received by the client $A_\ell$.

Note that the clients may not be authentic and the initial group key derived by different clients in the same session may not be equal. Next, mutual authentication and key confirmation run as follows.

Each client $A_\ell$ computes $\mathsf{sid}_{A_\ell} = h(g^{\mathsf{sk}^P_{A_\ell}}|\mathsf{sid}^P_{A_\ell})$ and encrypts $H(\mathsf{sid}_{A_\ell}|\mathsf{pid}_{A_\ell}|\mathsf{pw}^S_{A_\ell})$ on the basis of the identity $\mathsf{ID}_S$ of the server, where $\mathsf{pid}_{A_\ell} = (A_1, A_2, \cdots, A_n, S)$. The encryption result is denoted as $\mathsf{Auth}_\ell$. Then $A_\ell$ submits $\mathsf{msg}_{A_\ell} = A_\ell|\mathsf{sid}_{A_\ell}|\mathsf{Auth}_\ell$ to the server $S$.

Upon receiving all messages $\mathsf{msg}_{A_\ell}$ ($\ell = 1, 2, \cdots, n$), the server $S$ lets $\mathsf{sid}_S = \mathsf{sid}_{A_1}, \mathsf{pid}_S = (A_1, A_2, \cdots, A_n, S)$ and decrypts the ciphertexts with its decryption key $\mathsf{d}_S$, and verifies whether

$$\mathsf{D}_{\mathsf{d}_S}[\mathsf{Auth}_\ell] = H(\mathsf{sid}_S|\mathsf{pid}_S|\mathsf{pw}^S_{A_\ell}) \tag{1}$$

If equation (1) holds for $\ell = 1, 2, \cdots, n$, $S$ generates a signature $\mathsf{Auth}_S = \mathsf{S}_{\mathsf{d}'_S}[\mathsf{pid}_S|\mathsf{sid}_S]$ with its signing key $\mathsf{d}'_S$ and then broadcasts $\mathsf{msg}_S = S|\mathsf{Auth}_S$.

Upon receiving $\mathsf{msg}_S$, each client $A_\ell$ verifies if

$$\mathsf{V}_{\mathsf{ID}_S}[\mathsf{pid}_{A_\ell}|\mathsf{sid}_{A_\ell}, \mathsf{Auth}_S] = 1 \tag{2}$$

If equation (2) holds, $A_\ell$ computes the final authenticated group key, that is, $\mathsf{sk}^{P'}_{A_\ell} = g^{\mathsf{sk}^P_{A_\ell}{}^2}$.

### 3.2 Correctness, Explicit Authentication, Trust Model and Efficiency

**Correctness.** At the presence of both passive and active adversaries, for any two clients $A_i$ and $A_j$, if $\mathsf{sid}_{A_i} = \mathsf{sid}_{A_j} \neq \mathsf{NULL}$, i.e., $h(g^{\mathsf{sk}^P_{A_i}}|\mathsf{sid}^P_{A_i}) = h(g^{\mathsf{sk}^P_{A_j}}|\mathsf{sid}^P_{A_j})$. Because $h$ is a collision-resistant hash function, we have $g^{\mathsf{sk}^P_{A_i}} = g^{\mathsf{sk}^P_{A_j}}$. Thus, $\mathsf{sk}^P_{A_i} = \mathsf{sk}^P_{A_j}$ and then $g^{\mathsf{sk}^P_{A_i}{}^2} = g^{\mathsf{sk}^P_{A_j}{}^2}$, i.e., $\mathsf{sk}^{P'}_{A_i} = \mathsf{sk}^{P'}_{A_j}$; If $\mathsf{acc}_{A_i} = \mathsf{acc}_{A_j} = \mathsf{TRUE}$, the signature of the server on $\mathsf{pid}_S|\mathsf{sid}_S$ ($= \mathsf{pid}_{A_i}|\mathsf{sid}_{A_i} = \mathsf{pid}_{A_j}|\mathsf{sid}_{A_j}$) ensures that $\mathsf{pid}_{A_i} = \mathsf{pid}_{A_j}$. Thus, our protocol meets correctness.

**Explicit authentication.** By verifying equation (1) which involves the password $\mathsf{pw}^S_{A_\ell}$, the partner identity $\mathsf{pid}_S$ and the initial group key $\mathsf{sk}^P_{A_\ell}$ for $\ell = 1, 2, \cdots, n$, the server $S$ can make sure the authenticity of each client $A_\ell$ and the agreement of the same initial group key. By verifying equation (2) which involves the signature of the server, each client $A_\ell$ is convinced of the authenticity of the server $S$, other partners and the initial group key. If both equations (1) and (2) hold for $\ell = 1, 2, \cdots, n$, all clients are legitimate, the initial group key is genuine and thus the final group key $g^{\mathsf{sk}^P_{A_\ell}{}^2}$ is authentic. This shows that the group PAKE protocol $P'$ achieves explicit authentication, that is, when $\mathsf{acc}_{A_i} = \mathsf{TRUE}$, the client $A_i$ knows that its intended partners have successfully computed a matching session key (i.e, a group key).

**Trust model.** The protocol compiler for group PAKE given by Abdalla et al. [1] is applicable where each user of the group is honest. If two adjacent users are dishonest, they can conspire to include one (or several) impersonating attacker(s) between them, while other users are unaware of this attack. Our compiler assumes that there exist "honest but curious" servers, which are trusted to authenticate users of the group, but may perform passive attacks on the protocol to retrieve the group key. In terms of trust management, we believe that our compiler is more practical than Abdalla et al.'s compiler.

**Efficiency consideration.** The efficiency of our group PAKE protocol depends on performance of the underlying group KE protocol, IBE and IBS schemes. Only two rounds are added to the original group KE protocol $P$. In these two rounds, each client sends out one message and receives one message only. This compiler adds only $O(1)$ communication (per client) to the original group KE protocol. If our compiler employs Burmester-Desmedt group key exchange protocol, our group PAKE protocol has 4 rounds only. The communication cost of each client is $O(2n)$ bits, where $n$ is the number of clients. If Abdalla et al.'s compiler employs KOY 2-PAKE protocol [46] and constructs the commitment scheme with Cramer-Shoup public key encryption scheme [35], their group PAKE protocol has 5 rounds. The communication cost of each user is $O(6n)$ bits. In this sense, we believe that our compiler is more efficient than Abdalla et al.'s compiler. Note that we take into account cryptographic blocks with provable security in the standard model only.

## 4  Proof of Security

First of all, we provide a formal specification of the group PAKE protocol by specifying the initialization phase and the oracles to which the adversary has access, as shown in Fig. 2–4.

During the initialization phase for security parameter $k$, algorithm Initialize generates params $= \{H, h, G, q, g\} \bigcup$ params$^P \bigcup$ params$^E \bigcup$ params$^S$ and the secret (master-key$^E$, master-key$^S$) at first. Furthermore, the sets Client, Server, and ClientServerPair are determined. Passwords for clients are chosen at random, and then stored at corresponding servers.

The description of the Execute oracle matches the high-level protocol described in Fig. 1, but additional details (for example, the updating of state information)

---

Initialize($1^k$)

(params$^{P,E,S}$, master-key$^{E,S}$) $\xleftarrow{R}$ Setup$^{P,E,S}(1^k)$

(Client, Server, ClientServerPair) $\xleftarrow{R}$ UserGen($1^k$)

$(G, q, g) \xleftarrow{R}$ GGen($1^k$), $\{H, h\} \xleftarrow{R}$ CRHF($1^k$)

For each $i \in \{1, 2, \cdots\}$ and each $U \in$ User

    acc$_U^i$ $\leftarrow$ term$_U^i$ $\leftarrow$ used$_U^i$ $\leftarrow$ FALSE, sid$_U^i$ $\leftarrow$ pid$_U^i$ $\leftarrow$ sk$_U^i$ $\leftarrow$ NULL

For each $S \in$ Server, d$_S$, d$_S'$ $\leftarrow$ Extract$^{E,S}$(ID$_S$, params$^{E,S}$, master-key$^{E,S}$)

For each $(A, S) \in$ ClientServerPair, pw$_A^S$ $\xleftarrow{R}$ $\{$pw$_1$, pw$_2$, $\cdots$, pw$_N\}$

Return Client, Server, ClientServerPair, $H, h, G, q, g$, params$^{P,E,S}$

**Fig. 2.** Specification of the initialize

---

$\mathsf{Execute}(A_1^{i_1}, \cdots, A_n^{i_n}, S^j)$, where $A_\ell \in \mathsf{Client}, S \in \mathsf{Server}$

    If $(\exists \ell$ such that $(A_\ell, S) \notin \mathsf{ClientServerPair} \vee \mathsf{used}_{A_\ell}^{i_\ell}) \vee \mathsf{used}_S^j$, return $\bot$

    $\mathsf{used}_{A_\ell}^{i_\ell} \leftarrow \mathsf{used}_S^j \leftarrow \mathsf{TRUE}, \mathsf{pid}_{A_\ell}^{i_\ell} \leftarrow \mathsf{pid}_S^j \leftarrow \{A_1^{i_1}, \cdots, A_n^{i_n}, S^j\}, \ell = 1, 2, \cdots, n$

    $(\mathsf{sid}_{A_1}^P | \mathsf{sk}_{A_1}^P, \mathsf{sid}_{A_2}^P | \mathsf{sk}_{A_2}^P, \cdots, \mathsf{sid}_{A_n}^P | \mathsf{sk}_{A_n}^P) \leftarrow \mathsf{Execute}^P(A_1^{i_1}, A_2^{i_2}, \cdots, A_n^{i_n})$

    $\mathsf{sid}_{A_\ell}^{i_\ell} \leftarrow h(g^{\mathsf{sk}_{A_\ell}^P} | \mathsf{sid}_{A_\ell}^P), \mathsf{Auth}_\ell \leftarrow \mathsf{E}_{\mathsf{ID}_S}[H(\mathsf{sid}_{A_\ell}^{i_\ell} | \mathsf{pid}_{A_\ell}^{i_\ell} | \mathsf{pw}_{A_\ell}^S)]$

    $\mathsf{msg}_{A_\ell} \leftarrow A_\ell^{i_\ell} | \mathsf{sid}_{A_\ell}^{i_\ell} | \mathsf{Auth}_\ell, \ell = 1, 2, \cdots, n$

    $\mathsf{sid}_S^j \leftarrow \mathsf{sid}_{A_1}^{i_1}, \mathsf{Auth}_S \leftarrow \mathsf{S}_{d_S'}[\mathsf{pid}_S^j | \mathsf{sid}_S^j], \mathsf{msg}_S \leftarrow S^j | \mathsf{Auth}_S$

    $\mathsf{acc}_{A_\ell}^{i_\ell} \leftarrow \mathsf{term}_{A_\ell}^{i_\ell} \leftarrow \mathsf{acc}_S^j \leftarrow \mathsf{term}_S^j \leftarrow \mathsf{TRUE}, \mathsf{sk}_{A_\ell}^{i_\ell} \leftarrow g^{\mathsf{sk}_{A_\ell}^P{}^2}, \ell = 1, 2, \cdots, n$

    Return $\mathsf{status}_{A_1}^{i_1}, \cdots, \mathsf{status}_{A_n}^{i_n}, \mathsf{status}_S^j$

$\mathsf{KeyGen}(\mathsf{PKG}, S)$

    Return $d_S, d_S'$ and $\mathsf{pw}_A^S$ for any $A$

$\mathsf{Corrupt}(A)$                              $\mathsf{Reveal}(A^i)$

    Return $\mathsf{pw}_A^S$ for any $S$             Return $\mathsf{sk}_A^i$

$\mathsf{Test}(A^i)$

    $b \xleftarrow{R} \{0, 1\}, \mathsf{sk}' \xleftarrow{R} G$. If $b = 1$ return $\mathsf{sk}'$ else return $\mathsf{sk}_A^i$

---

**Fig. 3.** Specification of the Execute, KeyGen, Corrupt, Reveal, Test oracles

are included. We let $\mathsf{status}_U^i$ denote the vector of values $(\mathsf{sid}_U^i, \mathsf{pid}_U^i, \mathsf{acc}_U^i, \mathsf{term}_U^i)$ associated with instance $U^i$.

Given an adversary $\mathcal{A}$, we imagine a simulator that runs the protocol for $\mathcal{A}$. More preciously, the simulator begins by running algorithm $\mathsf{Initialize}(1^k)$ (which includes choosing passwords for clients) and giving the public output of the algorithm to $\mathcal{A}$.

When $\mathcal{A}$ queries an oracle, the simulator also responds by executing the appropriate algorithm. The simulator also records all state information defined during the course of the experiment.

In particular, when the adversary completes its execution and outputs a bit $b'$, the simulator can tell whether the adversary succeeds by checking whether (1) a single Test query was made, for some client instance $U^i$; (2) $\mathsf{acc}_U^i$ was true at the time of Test query; (3) instance $U^i$ is fresh; and (4) $b' = b$. Success of the adversary is denoted by event Succ. For any experiment $P'$ we define

$$\mathsf{Adv}_{\mathcal{A}}^{P'}(k) = 2 \cdot \mathsf{Pr}_{\mathcal{A}}^{P'}[\mathsf{Succ}] - 1$$

Based on the model described in Section 2, we have

**Theorem 1.** Assume that (1) the group KE protocol is secure against passive eavesdropping; (2) the IBE scheme is secure against the chosen-ciphertext attack; (3) the IBS scheme is existential unforgeability under the chosen-message attack; (4) the squaring decisional Diffie-Hellman (SDDH) problem is hard over a cyclic group $G$ with a prime order $q$ and a generator $g$; (5) CRHF is a collision-resistant hash family; then the protocol $P'$ described in Fig. 1 is a secure group PAKE protocol.

---

$\mathsf{Send}_0(A_\ell^{i_\ell}, (A_1^{i_1}, \cdots, A_n^{i_n}))$

    If $\mathsf{used}_{A_\ell}^{i_\ell}$, return $\perp$

    $\mathsf{used}_{A_\ell}^{i_\ell} \leftarrow \mathsf{TRUE}$

    . . . . . . . . .

$\mathsf{Send}_0'(A_\ell^{i_\ell}, S^j)$

    If $\neg\mathsf{used}_{A_\ell}^{i_\ell} \vee (A_\ell, S) \notin \mathsf{ClientServerPair} \vee \mathsf{term}_{A_\ell}^{i_\ell}$, return $\perp$

    $\mathsf{pid}_{A_\ell}^{i_\ell} \leftarrow \{A_1^{i_1}, \cdots, A_n^{i_n}, S^j\}, \mathsf{sid}_{A_\ell}^{i_\ell} \leftarrow h(g^{\mathsf{sk}_{A_\ell}^P} | \mathsf{sid}_{A_\ell}^{i_\ell})$

    $\mathsf{Auth}_\ell \leftarrow \mathsf{E}_{\mathsf{ID}_S}[H(\mathsf{sid}_{A_\ell}^{i_\ell} | \mathsf{pid}_{A_\ell}^{i_\ell} | \mathsf{pw}_{A_\ell}^S)]$

    $\mathsf{MsgOut} \leftarrow A_\ell^{i_\ell} | \mathsf{sid}_{A_\ell}^{i_\ell} | \mathsf{Auth}_\ell, \mathsf{state}_{A_\ell}^{i_\ell} \leftarrow (\mathsf{pid}_{A_\ell}^{i_\ell}, \mathsf{sk}_{A_\ell}^P, \mathsf{MsgOut})$

    Return $\mathsf{status}_{A_\ell}^{i_\ell}$

$\mathsf{Send}_1'(S^j, (A_\ell^{i_\ell} | \mathsf{sid}_{A_\ell}^{i_\ell} | \mathsf{Auth}_\ell)_{\ell=1,2,\cdots,n})$

    If $(\exists \ell$ such that $(A_\ell, S) \notin \mathsf{ClientServerPair}) \vee \mathsf{used}_S^j$, return $\perp$

    $\mathsf{used}_S^j \leftarrow \mathsf{TRUE}, \mathsf{pid}_S^j \leftarrow \{A_1^{i_1}, A_2^{i_2}, \cdots, A_n^{i_n}, S^j\}, \mathsf{sid}_S^j \leftarrow \mathsf{sid}_{A_1}^{i_1}$

    If $\exists \ell$ such that $\mathsf{D}_{d_S}[\mathsf{Auth}_\ell] \neq H(\mathsf{sid}_S^j | \mathsf{pid}_S^j | \mathsf{pw}_{A_\ell}^S)$, reject and return $\mathsf{status}_S^j$

    $\mathsf{Auth}_S \leftarrow \mathsf{S}_{d_S'}[\mathsf{pid}_S^j | \mathsf{sid}_S^j], \mathsf{acc}_S^j \leftarrow \mathsf{term}_S^j \leftarrow \mathsf{TRUE}, \mathsf{MsgOut} \leftarrow S^j | \mathsf{Auth}_S$

    Return $\mathsf{status}_S^j$

$\mathsf{Send}_2'(A_\ell^{i_\ell}, S^j | \mathsf{Auth}_S)$

    $\mathsf{state}_{A_\ell}^{i_\ell} \leftarrow (\mathsf{pid}_{A_\ell}^{i_\ell}, \mathsf{sk}_{A_\ell}^P, \mathsf{FirstMsgOut})$

    If $\neg\mathsf{used}_{A_\ell}^{i_\ell} \vee \mathsf{term}_{A_\ell}^{i_\ell} \vee (S^j \notin \mathsf{pid}_{A_\ell}^{i_\ell})$, return $\perp$

    If $\mathsf{V}_{\mathsf{ID}_S}[\mathsf{pid}_{A_\ell}^{i_\ell} | \mathsf{sid}_{A_\ell}^{i_\ell}, \mathsf{Auth}_S] \neq 1$, reject and return $\mathsf{status}_{A_\ell}^{i_\ell}$

    $\mathsf{acc}_{A_\ell}^{i_\ell} \leftarrow \mathsf{term}_{A_\ell}^{i_\ell} \leftarrow \mathsf{TRUE}, \mathsf{sk}_{A_\ell}^{i_\ell} \leftarrow g^{\mathsf{sk}_{A_\ell}^P \, 2}$

    Return $\mathsf{status}_{A_\ell}^{i_\ell}$

---

**Fig. 4.** Specification of the Send oracles

We follow the methods of the security proofs given in [48,46] to prove the security of our compiler without random oracles. The detail proof of Theorem 1 can be provided upon request.

Note: The squaring decisional Diffie-Hellman (SDDH) problem is detailed in Appendix A.

## 5   Conclusion

In this paper, we present an efficient compiler to transform any group KE protocol to a group PAKE protocol from identity-based cryptosystem. In addition, we can provide a rigorous proof of security for our compiler. As long as our group PAKE protocol is built on a group KE protocol, and IBE and IBS schemes with provable security without random oracles, it can be proven to be secure without random oracles.

# References

1. Abdalla, M., Bohli, J.-M., González Vasco, M.I., Steinwandt, R. (Password) authenticated key establishment: From 2-party to group. In: Vadhan, S.P. (ed.) TCC 2007. LNCS, vol. 4392, pp. 499–514. Springer, Heidelberg (2007)

2. Abdalla, M., Bresson, E., Chevassut, O., Pointcheval, D.: Password-based group key exchange in a constant number of rounds. In: Yung, M., Dodis, Y., Kiayias, A., Malkin, T.G. (eds.) PKC 2006. LNCS, vol. 3958, pp. 427–442. Springer, Heidelberg (2006)

3. Abdalla, M., Fouque, P.-A., Pointcheval, D.: Password-based authenticated key exchange in the three-party setting. In: Vaudenay, S. (ed.) PKC 2005. LNCS, vol. 3386, pp. 65–84. Springer, Heidelberg (2005)

4. Abdalla, M., Fouque, P.A., Pointcheval, D.: Password-based authenticated key exchange in the three-party setting. In: IEE Proceedings in Information Security, vol. 153(1), pp. 27–39 (2006)

5. Abdalla, M., Pointcheval, D.: Simple password-based encrypted key exchange protocols. In: Menezes, A. (ed.) CT-RSA 2005. LNCS, vol. 3376, pp. 191–208. Springer, Heidelberg (2005)

6. Abdalla, M., Pointcheval, D.: A scalable password-based group key exchange protocol in the standard model. In: Lai, X., Chen, K. (eds.) ASIACRYPT 2006. LNCS, vol. 4284, pp. 332–347. Springer, Heidelberg (2006)

7. Ateniese, G., Steiner, M., Tsudik, G.: Authenticated group key agreement and friends. In: Proc. CCS 1998, pp. 17–26 (1998)

8. Ateniese, G., Steiner, M., Tsudik, G.: New multi-party authentication services and key agreement protocol. IEEE Journal on Selected Areas in Communications 4(18), 628–639 (2000)

9. Bao, F., Deng, R.H., Zhu, H.: Variations of diffie-hellman problem. In: Qing, S., Gollmann, D., Zhou, J. (eds.) ICICS 2003. LNCS, vol. 2836, pp. 301–312. Springer, Heidelberg (2003)

10. Becker, C., Wille, U.: Communication complexity of group key distribution. In: Proc. CCS 1998, pp. 1–6 (1998)

11. Bellare, M., Canetti, R., Krawczyk, H.: A modular approach to the design and analysis of authentication and key exchange protocol. In: Proc. 30th Annual ACM Symposium on Theory of Computing, pp. 419–428 (1998)

12. Bellare, M., Pointcheval, D., Rogaway, P.: Authenticated key exchange secure against dictionary attacks. In: Preneel, B. (ed.) EUROCRYPT 2000. LNCS, vol. 1807, pp. 139–155. Springer, Heidelberg (2000)

13. Bellare, M., Rogaway, P.: Entity authentication and key distribution. In: Stinson, D.R. (ed.) CRYPTO 1993. LNCS, vol. 773, pp. 232–249. Springer, Heidelberg (1993)

14. Bellovin, S.M., Merritt, M.: Encrypted key exchange: Password-based protocol secure against dictionary attack. In: Proc. 1992 IEEE Symposium on Research in Security and Privacy, May 1992, pp. 72–84 (1992)

15. Bird, R., Gopal, I., Herzberg, A., Janson, P., Kutten, S., Molva, R., Yung, M.: Systematic design of two-party authentication protocols. IEEE Journal on Selected Areas in Communications 11(5), 679–693 (1993)

16. Bohli, J.M., Vasco, M.I.G., Steinwandt, R.: Password-authenticated constant-round group key establishment with a common reference string. Cryptology ePrint Archive, Report 2006/214 (2006), http://eprint.iacr.org/

17. Boneh, D., Franklin, M.: Identity-based encryption from the weil pairing. In: Kilian, J. (ed.) CRYPTO 2001. LNCS, vol. 2139, pp. 213–229. Springer, Heidelberg (2001)
18. Boneh, D., Franklin, M.: Identity based encryption from the Weil pairing. SIAM Journal of Computing 32(3), 586–615 (2003)
19. Boyd, C.: On key agreement and conference key agreement. In: Mu, Y., Pieprzyk, J.P., Varadharajan, V. (eds.) ACISP 1997. LNCS, vol. 1270, pp. 294–302. Springer, Heidelberg (1997)
20. Boyd, C., Nieto, J.M.G.: Round-optimal contributory conference key agreement. In: Desmedt, Y.G. (ed.) PKC 2003. LNCS, vol. 2567, pp. 161–174. Springer, Heidelberg (2003)
21. Boyko, V., MacKenzie, P.D., Patel, S.: Provably secure password-authenticated key exchange using diffie-hellman. In: Preneel, B. (ed.) EUROCRYPT 2000. LNCS, vol. 1807, pp. 156–171. Springer, Heidelberg (2000)
22. Bresson, E., Chevassut, O., Pointcheval, D.: Provably authenticated group diffie-hellman key exchange - the dynamic case. In: Boyd, C. (ed.) ASIACRYPT 2001. LNCS, vol. 2248, pp. 290–309. Springer, Heidelberg (2001)
23. Bresson, E., Chevassut, O., Pointcheval, D., Quisquater, J.J.: Provably authenti-cated group Diffie-Hellman key exchange. In: Proc. CCS 2001, pp. 255–264 (2001)
24. Bresson, E., Chevassut, O., Pointcheval, D.: Dynamic group diffie-hellman key ex-change under standard assumptions. In: Knudsen, L.R. (ed.) EUROCRYPT 2002. LNCS, vol. 2332, pp. 321–336. Springer, Heidelberg (2002)
25. Bresson, E., Chevassut, O., Pointcheval, D.: Group diffie-hellman key exchange secure against dictionary attacks. In: Zheng, Y. (ed.) ASIACRYPT 2002. LNCS, vol. 2501, pp. 497–514. Springer, Heidelberg (2002)
26. Bresson, E., Chevassut, O., Pointcheval, D.: Security proofs for an efficient password-based key exchange. In: Proc. CCS 2003, pp. 241–250 (2003)
27. Bresson, E., Chevassut, O., Pointcheval, D.: New security results on encrypted key exchange. In: Bao, F., Deng, R., Zhou, J. (eds.) PKC 2004. LNCS, vol. 2947, pp. 145–158. Springer, Heidelberg (2004)
28. Bresson, E., Chevassut, O., Pointcheval, D.: A security solution for IEEE 802.11s ad-hoc mode: password-authentication and group-Diffie-Hellman key exchange. In-ternational Journal of Wireless and Mobile Computing 2(1), 4–13 (2007)
29. Burmester, M., Desmedt, Y.G.: A secure and efficient conference key distribution system. In: De Santis, A. (ed.) EUROCRYPT 1994. LNCS, vol. 950, pp. 275–286. Springer, Heidelberg (1995)
30. Burmester, M., Desmedt, Y.G., Seberry, J.: Equitable key escrow with limited time span. In: Ohta, K., Pei, D. (eds.) ASIACRYPT 1998. LNCS, vol. 1514, pp. 380–391. Springer, Heidelberg (1998)
31. Burmester, M., Desmedt, Y.: A secure and scalable group key exchange system. Information Processing Letters 94(3), 137–143 (2005)
32. Canetti, R., Krawczyk, H.: Key-exchange protocols and their use for building secure channels. In: Proc. Eurocrypt 2001, pp. 453–474 (2001)
33. Canetti, R., Krawczyk, H.: Universally composable notions of key exchange and secure channels. In: Knudsen, L.R. (ed.) EUROCRYPT 2002. LNCS, vol. 2332, pp. 337–351. Springer, Heidelberg (2002)
34. Canetti, R., Krawczyk, H.: Security analysis of iKE's signature-based key-exchange protocol. In: Yung, M. (ed.) CRYPTO 2002. LNCS, vol. 2442, pp. 143–161. Springer, Heidelberg (2002)
35. Cramer, R., Shoup, V.: A practical public key cryptosystem provably secure against adaptive chosen ciphertext attack. In: Krawczyk, H. (ed.) CRYPTO 1998. LNCS, vol. 1462, pp. 13–25. Springer, Heidelberg (1998)

36. Diffie, W., Hellman, M.: New directions in cryptography. IEEE Transactions on Information Theory 32(2), 644–654 (1976)
37. Diffie, W., van Oorschot, P., Wiener, M.: Authentication and authenticated key exchange. Designs, Codes, and Cryptography 2(2), 107–125 (1992)
38. Galindo, D., Herranz, J., Kiltz, E.: On the generic construction of identity-based signatures with additional properties. In: Lai, X., Chen, K. (eds.) ASIACRYPT 2006. LNCS, vol. 4284, pp. 178–193. Springer, Heidelberg (2006)
39. Gentry, C.: Practical identity-based encryption without random oracles. In: Vaudenay, S. (ed.) EUROCRYPT 2006. LNCS, vol. 4004, pp. 445–464. Springer, Heidelberg (2006)
40. Goldreich, O., Lindell, Y.: Session-key generation using human passwords only. In: Kilian, J. (ed.) CRYPTO 2001. LNCS, vol. 2139, pp. 408–432. Springer, Heidelberg (2001)
41. Goldwasser, S., Micali, S., Rivest, R.: A digital signature scheme secure against adaptive chosen-message attack. SIAM J. Computing 17(2), 281–308 (1988)
42. Halevi, S., Krawczyk, H.: Public-key cryptography and password protocols. ACM Transactions on Information and System Security 2(3), 230–268 (1999)
43. Ingemarsson, I., Tang, D.T., Wong, C.K.: A conference key distribution system. IEEE Transactions on Information Theory 28(5), 714–720 (1982)
44. Just, M., Vaudenay, S.: Authenticated multi-party key agreement. In: Proc. Asiacrypt 1996, pp. 36–49 (1996)
45. Jiang, S., Gong, G.: Password based key exchange with mutual authentication. In: Handschuh, H., Hasan, M.A. (eds.) SAC 2004. LNCS, vol. 3357, pp. 267–279. Springer, Heidelberg (2004)
46. Katz, J., Ostrovsky, R., Yung, M.: Efficient password-authenticated key exchange using human-memorable passwords. In: Pfitzmann, B. (ed.) EUROCRYPT 2001. LNCS, vol. 2045, pp. 475–494. Springer, Heidelberg (2001)
47. Katz, J., Ostrovsky, R., Yung, M.: Forward secrecy in password-only key exchange protocols. In: Cimato, S., Galdi, C., Persiano, G. (eds.) SCN 2002. LNCS, vol. 2576, pp. 29–44. Springer, Heidelberg (2003)
48. Katz, J., Yung, M.: Scalable protocols for authenticated group key exchange. In: Boneh, D. (ed.) CRYPTO 2003. LNCS, vol. 2729, pp. 110–125. Springer, Heidelberg (2003)
49. Kim, H.-J., Lee, S.-M., Lee, D.-H.: Constant-round authenticated group key exchange for dynamic groups. In: Lee, P.J. (ed.) ASIACRYPT 2004. LNCS, vol. 3329, pp. 245–259. Springer, Heidelberg (2004)
50. Kim, Y., Perig, A., Tsudik, G.: Simper and fault-tolerant key agreement for dynamic collaborative groups. In: Proc. CCS 2000, pp. 235–244 (2000)
51. Kim, Y., Perrig, A., Tsudik, G.: Communication-efficient group key agreement. In: Proc. IFIP TC11 16th Annual Working Conference on Information Security (IFIP/SEC), pp. 229–244 (2001)
52. Kown, J.O., Jeong, I.R., Sakurai, K., Lee, D.H.: Password-authenticated multi-party key exchange with different passwords. Cryptology ePrint Archive, Report 2006/476, http://eprint.iacr.org
53. Maurer, U.M., Wolf, S.: Diffie-hellman oracles. In: Koblitz, N. (ed.) CRYPTO 1996. LNCS, vol. 1109, pp. 268–282. Springer, Heidelberg (1996)
54. Paterson, K.G., Schuldt, J.C.N.: Efficient identity-based signatures secure in the standard model. In: Batten, L.M., Safavi-Naini, R. (eds.) ACISP 2006. LNCS, vol. 4058, pp. 207–222. Springer, Heidelberg (2006)
55. Patel, S.: Number-theoretic attack on secure password scheme. In: Proc. IEEE Symposium on Research in Security and Privacy, pp. 236–247 (1997)

56. Choo, K.-K.R., Boyd, C., Hitchcock, Y.: Errors in computational complexity proofs for protocols. In: Roy, B. (ed.) ASIACRYPT 2005. LNCS, vol. 3788, pp. 624–643. Springer, Heidelberg (2005)
57. Steer, D.G., Strawczynski, L., Diffie, W., Wiener, M.: A secure audio teleconference system. In: Goldwasser, S. (ed.) CRYPTO 1988. LNCS, vol. 403, pp. 520–528. Springer, Heidelberg (1998)
58. Steiner, M., Tsudik, G., Widner, M.: Key agreement in dynamic peer groups. IEEE Transactions on Parallel and Distributed Systems 11(8), 769–780 (2000)
59. Tzeng, W.-G.: A practical and secure fault-tolerant conference-key agreement protocol. In: Imai, H., Zheng, Y. (eds.) PKC 2000. LNCS, vol. 1751, pp. 1–13. Springer, Heidelberg (2000)
60. Waters, B.: Efficient identity-based encryption without random oracles. In: Cramer, R. (ed.) EUROCRYPT 2005. LNCS, vol. 3494, pp. 114–127. Springer, Heidelberg (2005)

# 6 Appendix A: Cryptographic Building Blocks

## 6.1 Group Key Exchange

A group key exchange (KE) protocols allow users of a group communicating over an insecure public network to establish a common secret key (i.e., a group key), where the shared secret key is derived by two or more users as a function of the information contributed by, or associated with, each of these, (ideally) such that no user can predetermine the resulting key. They are intended to be secure against the passive adversary only. A passive adversary is given access to the Execute, Reveal, and Test oracles as defined in Section 2. In the definition of Execute oracle, we reasonably require that different executions yield different group session keys.

We say a passive adversary $\mathcal{A}$ succeeds if it makes a single query $\mathsf{Test}(A^i)$ to a fresh instance $A^i$ (i.e., no Reveal oracle is queried to $A^i$ and his partnered instances), and outputs a single bit $b'$ with $b' = b$ (recall that $b$ is the bit chosen by the Test oracle). We denote this event by Succ. The advantage of a passive adversary $\mathcal{A}$ in attacking a group KE protocol $P$ is a function in the security parameter $k$, defined as $\mathsf{Adv}_{\mathcal{A}}^{P}(k) = 2 \cdot \mathrm{Pr}_{\mathcal{A}}^{P}[\mathsf{Succ}] - 1$.

A group KE protocol $P$ is secure against passive eavesdropping if no polynomial bounded adversary $\mathcal{A}$ has a non-negligible advantage in attacking it.

The group KE protocols proposed by Ingemarsson et al. [43], Burmester and Desmedt [29], and Steiner et al. [58] may be the most well-known. Among them, Burmester-Desmedt protocol has been shown to be secure against passive eavesdropping in the standard model by Katz and Yung [48].

## 6.2 Identity-Based Encryption

An identity-based encryption (IBE) scheme is specified by four randomized algorithms: Setup, Extract, Encrypt, Decrypt as follows.

– Setup: On input a security parameter $k$, it returns params (public system parameters) and master-key (known only to the "Private Key Generator").

- Extract: On inputs params, master-key and a public identity ID $\in \{0,1\}^*$, it returns a private key $d_{\text{ID}}$.
- Encrypt: On inputs params, ID, and a message $M \in \mathcal{M}$ (the plaintext space), it returns a ciphertext $C \in \mathcal{C}$ (the ciphertext space).
- Decryption: On inputs params, $C \in \mathcal{C}$, and a private key $d_{\text{ID}}$, it returns $M \in \mathcal{M}$.

Chosen ciphertext security is the standard acceptable notion of security for a public key encryption scheme. An IBE scheme is semantically secure against the adaptive chosen ciphertext attack if no polynomial bounded adversary $\mathcal{A}$ has a non-negligible advantage against the challenger in the following game:

- *Initialize*: The challenger runs the Setup algorithm, gives params to the adversary, but keeps the master-key to itself.
- *Phase* 1: The adversary adaptively asks a number of different queries $q_1, q_2, \cdots, q_m$, where $q_i$ is either Extract($\text{ID}_i$) or Decrypt($\text{ID}_i, C_i$).
- *Challenge*: Once the adversary decides that Phase 1 is over, it outputs a pair of equal length plaintexts $(M_0, M_1)$ and an identity ID on which it wishes to be challenged, where ID must not appear in Phase 1. The challenger picks a random bit $b \in \{0,1\}$ and sends $C = $ Encrypt($\text{ID}, M_b$) as the challenge to the adversary.
- *Phase* 2: The adversary issues more queries $q_{m+1}, q_{m+2}, \cdots, q_n$ adaptively as in Phase 1, except that the adversary may not request a private key for ID or the decryption of $(\text{ID}, C)$.
- *Guess*: Finally, the adversary outputs a guess $b' \in \{0,1\}$ and wins the game if $b' = b$.

We define the adversary $\mathcal{A}$'s advantage in attacking the IBE scheme as a function of the security parameter $k$, $\text{Adv}_{\mathcal{A}}^E(k) = |\text{Pr}_{\mathcal{A}}^E[b' = b] - 1/2|$, where the probability is over the random bits used by the challenger and the adversary. The most efficient identity-based encryption schemes are currently based on bilinear pairings on elliptic curves, such as the Weil or Tate pairings. Boneh and Franklin [17,18] were the first to give an IBE scheme from Weil pairing and prove it to be adaptive chosen-ciphertext security in the random oracle model. More recently, several new IBE schemes from pairing (e.g., [60][39]) were proposed and proven to be adaptive chosen-ciphertext security in the standard model. A common feature of the latest IBE schemes is that the plaintext space is a cyclic group of prime order.

## 6.3   Identity-Based Signature

An identity-based signature (IBS) scheme can be described by four algorithms Setup, Extract, Sign, Verify as follows.

- Setup: On input a security parameter $k$, it returns params (public system parameters) and master-key (known only to the "Private Key Generator").

- Extract: Given params, master-key and a public identity ID $\in \{0,1\}^*$, it returns a private key $d_{\text{ID}}$.
- Sign: Given a message $M$, params, ID and a private key $d_{\text{ID}}$, it generates a signature $\sigma$ of the user (with identity ID) on $M$.
- Verify: Given a signature $\sigma$, a message $M$, and params, ID, it outputs accept if $\sigma$ is a valid signature of the user (with identity ID) on $M$, and outputs reject otherwise.

An IBS scheme is existential unforgeability under the chosen message attack [41] if no polynomial bounded adversary $\mathcal{A}$ has a non-negligible advantage against the challenger in the following game:

- *Initialize*: The challenger runs the Setup algorithm, gives params to the adversary, but keeps the master-key to itself.
- *Queries*: The adversary adaptively asks a number of different queries $q_1, q_2, \cdots, q_m$, where $q_i$ is either Extract($\text{ID}_i$) or Sign($\text{ID}_i, M$).
- *Forgery*: Once the adversary decides that queries are over, it outputs a message $M'$, an identity $\text{ID}'$ and a string $\sigma'$. The adversary succeeds (denoted as Succ) if Verify($\text{ID}', M', \sigma'$) = 1, where $\text{ID}'$ cannot appear in Extract queries and $(\text{ID}', M')$ cannot appear in Sign queries.

We define the adversary $\mathcal{A}$'s advantage in attacking the IBS scheme as a function of the security parameter $k$, $\mathsf{Adv}_{\mathcal{A}}^S(k) = \mathsf{Pr}_{\mathcal{A}}^S[\mathsf{Succ}]$, where the probability is over the random bits used by the challenger and the adversary.

A generic approach to construct IBS schemes is to use an ordinary (i.e., non-identity-based) signature scheme and simply attach a certificate containing the public key of the signer to the signature [38]. An IBS scheme with provable security in the standard model was given by Paterson and Schuldt in [54].

## 6.4 Squaring Decisional Diffie-Hellman Problem

The squaring computational Diffie-Hellman (SCDH) problem in a cyclic group $G$ with a prime order $q$ and a generator $g$ is: Given $g, g^a$ where $a$ is randomly chosen from $\mathbb{Z}_q^*$, determine $g^{a^2}$. The problem is as hard as Diffie-Hellman problem [53,30,9].

The squaring decisional Diffie-Hellman (SDDH) problem in a cyclic group $G$ with a prime order $q$ and a generator $g$ is to distinguish between two distributions $(g, g^a, g^{a^2})$ and $(g, g^a, z)$, where $a$ is randomly chosen from $\mathbb{Z}_q^*$ and $z$ is randomly chosen from $G$. This problem is not harder than the decisional DH problem, but it is believed that this problem can still be hard, that is, we can assume that the advantage of any PPT algorithm $\mathcal{A}$ that outputs $b \in \{0,1\}$ in solving the SDDH problem is negligible, namely,

$$|Pr[\mathcal{A}(g, g^a, g^{a^2}) = 0] - Pr[\mathcal{A}(g, g^a, z) = 0]|$$

is negligible, where the probability is over the random choice of $a$ in $\mathbb{Z}_q^*$ and $z$ in $G$, and the random bits consumed by $\mathcal{A}$.

# A Proposal of Efficient Remote Biometric Authentication Protocol

Taiki Sakashita[1], Yoichi Shibata[2], Takumi Yamamoto[2], Kenta Takahashi[3], Wakaha Ogata[4], Hiroaki Kikuchi[5], and Masakatsu Nishigaki[2]

[1] Graduate School of Systems and Information Engineering, University of Tsukuba, 1-1-1, Tenoudai Tsukuba science city, Ibaraki 305-0006, Japan
sakashita@cipher.risk.tsukuba.ac.jp
[2] Graduate School of Science and Technology, Shizuoka University, 3-5-1 Johoku, Hamamatsu-shi, Naka-ku, Shizuoka-ken, 432-8011, Japan
f5745037@ipc.shizuoka.ac.jp, nisigaki@inf.shizuoka.ac.jp
[3] Hitachi, Ltd., System Development, Lab., 292, Yoshida-cho, Totsuka-ku, Yokohama-shi, Kanagawa, 244-0817, Japan
kenta.takahashi.bw@hitachi.com
[4] Graduate School of Innovation Management, Tokyo Institute of Technology, 2-12-1 O-okayama, Meguro-ku, Tokyo, 152-8552, Japan
wakaha@mot.titech.ac.jp
[5] School of Information Technology and Electronics, Tokai University, 1117 Kitakaname, Hiratsuka, Kanagawa, 259-1292, Japan
kikn@tokai.ac.jp

**Abstract.** ZeroBio has been proposed for a secure biometric authentication over the network by conducting secret computing between prover and verifier. The existing ZeroBio are based on zero-knowledge proof that a committed number lies in an interval, or on oblivious neural network evaluation. The purpose of ZeroBio is to give verifier a mean to authenticate provers with perfectly concealing provers' biometric information from verifier. However, these methods need high computational complexity and heavy network traffic. In this paper, we propose another type of ZeroBio protocol that can accomplish remote biometric authentication with lower computational complexity and lighter network traffic by tolerating small decline of security level.

**Keywords:** biometrics, authentication, zero knowledge interactive proof, secret computing.

## 1 Introduction

Recently, biometric authentication has been applied to our daily life, and its application range and usage amount have kept growing. In contrast to conventional authentication with password or security token, biometric authentication has an advantage that they don't suffer from forgetting password and loss of token. However, it is needed for biometric authentication to store prover's biometric information to verifier as a template. Since biometric information is unique and

T. Takagi and M. Mambo (Eds.): IWSEC 2009, LNCS 5824, pp. 212–227, 2009.

unchangeable over the life time of the individual, it could be a serious problem of privacy if the prover's biometric information and/or templates are compromised. To cope with the leakage of biometric information from the prover's side, the use of biometric information which will not remain and can not be lifted (e.g., veins of the finger or the palm) is recommended. On the other hand, the protection of the templates stored in verifier's side may be more serious. Particularly, when biometric authentication is carried out over the network, verifiers are not always trusted (e.g., phishing site) and giving biometric information as it is to verifiers is not considered to be secure. Therefore protecting biometric templates is an essential issue.

To solve this problem, Ratha et al. introduced the concept of cancelable biometrics in which biometric information in transformed form is stored and verifies it in transformed space [1], and proposed an image block transformation and a minutia nonlinear transformation. Cambier et al. also proposed a method transforming the iris date by rotating and distorting [2]. Hirata et al. proposed a transformation for two-dimensional image matching based biometrics [3]. Cancelable biometrics makes it possible to (i) protect biometric information by storing it in transformed form as a template and (ii) update the template by alternating the transforming function, or the random numbers used in the transforming function. However, there is a concern in cancelable biometrics that the matching score (the difference between biometric information presented at the authentication phase and the template) is not concealed from the verifier, which could be a potential vulnerability such as hill-climbing attack [4].

Nagai et al. proposed the concept of asymmetric biometric authentication, or ZeroBio, where information stored by prover and verifier are asymmetric [5]. They show an authentication method with neural networks that can authenticate prover through zero knowledge interactive proof (ZKIP) without revealing prover's biometric information even to the verifier. Ogata et al. also proposed another ZeroBio which is based on ZKIP to prove that difference between prover's biometric information and stored template is sufficiently small [6]. Both methods above can perfectly conceal provers'biometric information from verifier, but they also have shortcomings that they need high computational complexity and heavy network traffic. Therefore in this paper, we propose a different type of ZeroBio with lower computational complexity and lighter network traffic by tolerating small decline of security level. Our proposed method calculates the difference between the presented biometric information and the enrolled biometric information with secret computing based on the encryption function with a property of homomorphism. Then the significance of the difference is checked secretly and efficiently by using blinded decryption and hash function.

The remainder of this paper is organized as follow. In Section 2, we discuss remote biometric authentication model. In Section 3, we describe related works. In Section 4, we propose an asymmetric biometric authentication protocol based on secure computation, blinded decryption and hash function. In Section 5, we discuss security evaluation, and show our method has superior in computationalcomplexity and network traffic compared to other asymmetric biometric authentication presented in Section 3. In Section 6, we show an improvement to our protocol. Finally, we conclude our study in Section 7.

## 2   Remote Biometric Authentication Models

Remote biometric authentication model is classified into server (verifier) authentication model and client (prover) authentication model according to where templates are stored. Templates for all clients are managed centrally by a server for the server authentication model, while the template for each client is stored individually in client's smart card for the client authentication model. Although the client authentication model has an advantage of lower privacy concern, it is reported that information stored in a smart card can be revealed with good accuracy by side-channel attack [7]. Therefore this paper targets and discusses the server authentication model.

One of the biggest issues in the server authentication model is privacy. Obviously, it is not desirable in a sense of privacy to store and/or present biometric information to server without encryption. In this paper, we propose a remote biometric authentication method which can verify the authenticity of biometric information by conducting secret computing between prover and verifier. Our proposed method requires clients to have a smart card to carry helper information such as an encryption key to conceal biometric information itself from server. Note that it is impossible to derive biometric information from the helper information stored in the smart card.

## 3   Related Works

### 3.1   Cancelable Biometrics

In cancelable biometrics proposed in [2,3], the biometric information is masked by a random number, and then, the masked information is stored in server as a template. For security reason, the random number used for masking is needed to have a certain level of entropy, and to be stored in a smart card carried by authorized user. Biometric information presented at the authentication phase is also masked by the same random number, and compared with the template (biometric information masked by the random number). Therefore it is important to select proper masking methods appropriate for the comparison of target biometric information.

These methods mask the template by a random number, and thus no biometric information will leak out even if the templates are compromised. Also, in these methods no information except for the random number is stored in a smart card, so biometric information will not leak out even if the smart card is stolen. However, these methods allow server to compute the difference between masked biometric information presented at the authentication phase and the masked template to verify the authenticity of presented biometric information. Therefore, the server can get information of the difference of two biometric information.

## 3.2   ZeroBio Proposed by Nagai et al.

Nagai et al. proposed a method that can prove the authenticity of user's biometric information while perfectly concealing the biometric information by using oblivious neural networks evaluation [5]. We call the method Nagai scheme.

At enrollment phase, user trains his/her neural network with a set of feature extracted from his/her own biometric information and a set of feature for other users. Throughout the training, the weights of neural network are adjusted so that the neural network can output 1 for authorized user's biometrics information and 0 for unauthorized user's biometric information. After training, the weights of the output layer $\overline{w_j}$ and the commitments of weights of hidden layer $Com(w_{ij})$ in the neural network are enrolled.

At authentication phase, user is authenticated if the user can prove by zero knowledge interactive proof (ZKIP) that the neural network outputs 1 when his/her biometric information are inputted to the neural network without revealing his/her private biometric information. Note that the input biometric features are not exactly identical to that used to train the neural network. The variations will be absorbed by the property that neural networks can accept similar inputs.

## 3.3   ZeroBio Proposed by Ogata et al.

In cancelable biometrics, biometric information is masked by random number to generate template, while Fuzisaki-Okamoto commitment [8] is used for masking in Ogata et al's method [6]. We call the method Ogata scheme.

At enrollment phase, authorized user computes $E = Com(x, r)$, commitment of biometric information $x$, and stores it in server as a template. Then, random number $r$ is stored in the user's smart card. From the characteristic of commitment, biometric information will not leak out from the template.

At authentication phase, user computes $E' = Com(x', r')$, commitment of presented biometric information $x'$, and transmits it to the server. The server can calculate the commitment of $x - x'$ by secret computing. Then, the user conducts zero knowledge interactive proof protocol (ZKIP) which proves "difference between two committed biometric information is sufficiently small"

Note that the enrolled biometric information $x$ is not stored in the authorized user's smart card. This means that the authorized user can not calculate the difference between $x$ and $x'$ in the authentication phase. Therefore, in Ogata scheme, the authorized user generates $2\theta + 1$ estimated values $\tilde{x} \in \{x', x' \pm 1, x' \pm 2, \ldots, x' \pm \theta\}$ from the presented biometric information $x'$, and uses $\tilde{x} - x'$ instead $x - x'$ when proving the difference between $x$ (committed in $E$) and $x'$ (committed in $E'$) calculated by the server is in the (small) interval $[-\theta, \theta]$ using "ZKIP for proving interval." In other words, ZKIP for proving interval composes of $2\theta + 1$ proofs. The server accepts authentication if at least one of $2\theta + 1$ proofs is accepted.

# 4 Proposed Method

## 4.1 Elemental Technique

Proposed method uses the (slightly modified) ElGamal encryption which has homomorphism to encrypt biometric information.

Let $p$ be a large prime and $g$ be a primitive element of $Z_p^*$. The user chooses a random integer $s$ from $1 \le s \le p - 1$ as a secret key, which is kept secret. Then the user computes $y = g^s$ in $Z_p^*$. Public key of the user is $y$, $p$ and $g$.

The ciphertext $Enc(x)$ of biometric information $x$ is computed as $Enc(x) = (g^r, g^x \cdot y^r) = (G, M) \pmod{p}$. Here, $r \in Z_p$ is a random number. The decryption is done by $g^x = M/G^s \pmod{p}$.

It is important to note that the encryption function has a property of homomorphism. For two ciphertexts $Enc(x_1) = (G_1, M_1)$ and $Enc(x_2) = (G_2, M_2)$, let $Enc(x_1) \cdot Enc(x_2)$ be defined as $(G_1 \times G_2, M_1 \times M_2)$. Then we have $Enc(x_1) \cdot Enc(x_2) = Enc(x_1 + x_2)$. Similarly, we have $Enc(x_1)/Enc(x_2) = (G_1/G_2, M_1/M_2) = Enc(x_1 - x_2)$.

In this way, anyone can compute a ciphertext of difference between two biometric information $x_1$ and $x_2$ without decrypting $Enc(x_1)$ nor $Enc(x_2)$.

## 4.2 Outline

We propose an asymmetric biometric authentication which can be executed with lower computational complexity and lighter network traffic than these Nagai scheme and Ogata scheme.

Our method consists of enrollment phase and authentication phase. Authentic biometric information is encrypted and submitted to the server at the enrollment phase. At the authentication phase, the user encrypts his/her biometric information and sends it to the server. The server computes a ciphertext of difference between enrolled biometric information and presented biometric information using secret computing based on homomorphism of the encryption function. Then the server multiplies the ciphertext by a blind constant and sends it back to the user. The user proves to the server that the decryption of the blinded ciphertext (difference of two biometric information) is smaller than the threshold without disclosing the decryption to the verifier. In this paper, for simplifying explanation, we assume that difference between biometric information is formularized by absolute value of difference.

The outline of the proposed method is shown in Fig. 1.

## 4.3 Authentication Method

Authorized user and server share the following common parameters: prime number $p$, primitive root $g \in Z_p^*$, hash function $Hash()$, threshold $\theta$, set of possible difference $\Delta = \{0, \pm 1, \pm 2, \cdots, \pm \theta\}$. If difference between two biometric information is in $\Delta$, then two biometric information are considered to be sufficiently close. Every calculations in the protocol are computed in $Z_p^*$.

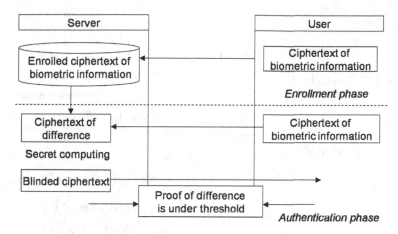

**Fig. 1.** Outline of our proposed method

## Enrollment Phase

**Step 1-1:** Authorized user chooses random integers $k, r \in Z_p$ ($k \neq 0$).

**Step 1-2:** The user generates secret key $s$ of ElGamal encryption and corresponding public key $y = g^s$.

**Step 1-3:** The user puts his/her authentic biometric sample to the biometric reader to obtain biometric information $x$, and computes the ciphertext $(t_1, t_2) = (g^r, g^{kx} \cdot y^r)$. Note that the user encrypts not the biometric information $x$ but $kx$. The reason why $kx$ is encrypted will be explained in Sec. 5.1.

**Step 1-4:** The user transmits y and $(t_1, t_2)$ to the server.

**Step 1-5:** The server stores y and $(t_1, t_2)$ together with the user ID, while the user stores $s, y, k$ in his/her smart card.

## Authentication Phase

**Step 2-1:** A user chooses random integer $r' \in Z_p$.

**Step 2-2:** The user puts his/her biometric sample to the biometric reader to obtain biometric information $x'$ . Then, the user retrieves $s, y, k$ from his/her smart card, and computes the ciphertext $(t_1', t_2') = (g^{r'}, g^{kx'} \cdot y^{r'})$.

**Step 2-3:** The user transmits $(t_1', t_2')$ to the server.

**Step 2-4:** The server chooses random integers $z, \alpha \in Z_p$ as blind factors. Then the server computes $(w_1, w_2) = (g^z t_1 / t_1', \alpha y^z t_2 / t'_2)$ and sends back it to the user. Note that $(w_1, w_2)$, the encrypted difference of $(t_1, t_2)$ and $(t_1', t_2')$, is concealed from the user by $z$ and $R$.

**Step 2-5:** The user decrypts $(w_1, w_2)$ with secret key s to obtain $m = \alpha \cdot g^{k(x-x')}$.

**Step 2-6:** The user chooses a random number $u \in Z_p$ as a blind factor. Then the user computes
$\Gamma = \{Hash(u \| m \cdot g^0), Hash(u \| m \cdot g^{\pm k}), \ldots, Hash(u \| m \cdot g^{\pm k\theta})\}$ and transmits $\Gamma$ and $u$ to the server, where '$\|$' denotes concatenation. Here,

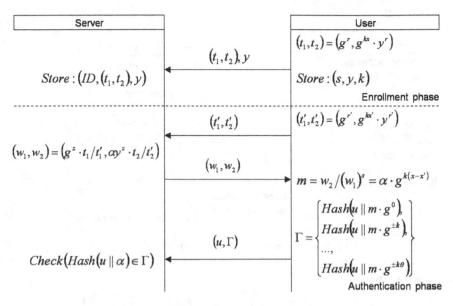

**Fig. 2.** Proposed protocol

the order of elements of $\Gamma$ is permuted before transmitting. The reason why the hashing and permutation are needed will be explained in Sec.5.1.

**Step 2-7:** The server computes $Hash(u\|\alpha)$. The server authenticates the user if $Hash(u\|\alpha) \in \Gamma$ is satisfied. If $x - x' \in \Delta$, then there exists $d \in \Delta$ such that $(x - x') + d = 0$. That is why, the server can understand that the presented biometric information $x'$ is sufficiently close to the enrolled biometric information $x$ if there exists $d \in \Delta$ such that $m \cdot g^{kd} = \alpha$.

Fig. 2 illustrates the above protocol.

# 5  Property of Proposed Protocol

## 5.1  Remarks

The proposed protocol uses some techniques to prevent attack. In this section, we explain how our techniques work.

**Necessity of Hash Function.** In Step 2-6 in the authentication phase, every elements of $\Gamma$ are hashed. If they were not hashed, then the server could abuse the authentication protocol as a decryption machine in the following way.

Assume that the server has a ciphertext $(w_1, w_2)$ and wants to know the plaintext. Then the protocol would be the followings: The server sends $(w_1, w_2)$ back to the user in Step 2-4. The user decrypts $(w_1, w_2)$ to obtain plaintext $m$ in Step 2-5, and generate $u \in Z_p$ to compute
$\Gamma = \{(u\| m \cdot g^0), (u\| m \cdot g^{\pm k}), \ldots, (u\| m \cdot g^{\pm k\theta})\}$ in Step 2-6.

In this case, all the values $\{\ldots, m \cdot g^{-2k}, m \cdot g^{-k}, m \cdot g^{k}, m \cdot g^{2k}, \ldots\}$ are disclosed to the server since $\Gamma$ and $u$ are transmitted to the server in Step 2-6. Here, the server knows a "knowledge about $\Gamma$" that one of the elements of $\Gamma$ is $m(= m \cdot g^0)$ and $\Gamma$ forms $\{\ldots, u \| m \cdot g^{-2k}, u \| m \cdot g^{-k}, u \| m \cdot g^{k}, u \| m \cdot g^{2k}, \ldots\}$. Such knowledge helps the server to decide which one in $\Gamma$ is $m$, even if the order of elements is permuted.

When the value of each element in $\Gamma$ is not disclosed, the server can't deduce $m$ even if the server knows the "knowledge about $\Gamma$." Thus, this attack can be prevented by hashing each element in $\Gamma$, in this case, server no longer treat the user as decryption machine.

**Necessity of permutation of elements of $\Gamma$.** In Step 2-6 in the authentication phase, the elements of $\Gamma$ are permuted and then transmitted to the server. If elements of $\Gamma$ were not permuted, then the server could derive the difference between the enrolled biometric information and the presented biometric information $x - x'$ in the following way.

Assume that the $l$th element of $\Gamma$ is equal to $Hash\,(u \| \alpha)$. This means that $Hash(\,u \| \alpha \cdot g^{k(x-x')} \cdot g^{kl}) = Hash(\,u \| \alpha)$, i.e., $x - x' + l = 0$. Therefore the server can derive $x - x'$.

This is caused by the fact that the server can deduce the preimage of the hashed value from the order of elements of $\Gamma$. Therefore, this attack can be prevented by the permutation of elements of $\Gamma$ in every authentication.

**Necessity of $k$.** In Step 1-3 in the enrollment phase and Step 2-2 in the authentication phase, the user encrypts not the biometric information $x$ or $x'$, but $kx$ or $kx'$. If ciphertext of $x$ or $x'$ were used, then the server could derive the difference between the enrolled biometric information and the presented biometric information $x - x'$ in the following way.

Assume that we do not use $k$, that is, $k = 1$ in our protocol. In this case, the elements in $\Gamma$ transmitted from the user to the server in Step 2-6 are $\left\{ Hash\left( u \| \alpha \cdot g^{(x-x')\pm 0} \right), Hash\left( u \| \alpha \cdot g^{(x-x')\pm 1} \right), \ldots, Hash\left( u \| \alpha \cdot g^{(x-x')\pm \theta} \right) \right\}$. Here, the server who knows $g$, $\alpha$ and $u$ could try to compute $\left\{ Hash\left( u \| \alpha \cdot g^{(x-x')\pm 0} \right), Hash\left( u \| \alpha \cdot g^{(x-x')\pm 1} \right), \ldots, Hash\left( u \| \alpha \cdot g^{(x-x')\pm \theta} \right) \right\}$ by guessing $x - x'$. This means that the server can know the guess is correct when the server's calculation is identical to $\Gamma$ transmitted from the user.

This attack is caused by the fact that the server also can compute the elements of $\Gamma$. Therefore, this attack can be prevented by introducing a random number $k$ which is secret from the server.

## 5.2   Security

In this section, we evaluate the security of our proposed protocol. Here we first define the attack model to derive security requirements for biometric authentication system, and then confirm that proposed protocol satisfies these requirements.

**Table 1.** List of attacks

|  | acquisition of biometric information | Impersonation |
|---|---|---|
| server hijacking | Attack1 | not avoidable |
| theft of smart card | Attack2 | Attack3 |
| wiretapping of communication line | subset of Attack1 | Attack4 |

## Attack model and requirements for biometric authentication system

Attack model can be divided into attacker's objectives and means of attack.

**Attacker's objectives** : One of the biggest attacker's objectives is "impersonatio"of a certain system itself. Also, attackers try "acquisition of biometric information"of authorized users in a certain system to use them for further frauds such as impersonation of the other system or trace of the users.

**Means of attack** : We consider that attackers can attack the server, the authorized user, or the communication line. The first type of attack is a kind of "server hijacking."If an attacker succeeds in hijacking a server, the attacker can access all information in the server. Note that hijack means impersonation of the server administrator (or, maybe cheating by the server administrator). So, impersonation has no meaning for hijackers. The second type of attack is done by "theft of a smart card."We assume that the attacker can extract the information stored in the smart card that he/she steals. The third type of attack is "wiretapping of communication line."In remote authentication protocols, every information transmitted in the communication line are received or generated by the server. Therefore, if an authentication system can protect biometric information from the server hijackers, the system is robust also against the acquisition of biometric information by the wiretapping of communication line.

The combination of attacker's objectives and means of attack indicates us that we have to consider security against 4 types of attacks showed in Table1. Here, we assume that more than one of the above attacks are not conducted by attackers at the same time. Note that the security analysis described here is a kind of informal analysis. For instance, if the server is malicious, the attacker (server) who get the information stored in the smart card will be able to impersonate. Therefore, to be precise, the formal security analysis should be conducted.

From Table1, biometric authentication system has to satisfy following requirements.

**Requirement 1** (against attack 1) : The server can not obtain any information about biometric information of authorized users from the enrolled data and/or through authentication protocol.

**Requirement 2** (against attack 2) : Anyone can not derive any information about biometric information from data stored in a smart card.

**Requirement 3** (against attack 3) : Even if attacker gets a smart card of an authorized user, it is impossible to impersonate the user without knowing biometric information sufficiently close to the enrolled biometric information.

**Requirement 4** (against attack 4) : Even if attacker uses information obtained by wiretapping the communication line, it is impossible to impersonate anyone.

**Security Evaluation.** We show the proposed protocol in Section 4 satisfies the above requirements.

**Requirement 1.** Information obtained by the server through protocol are only ciphertexts of biometric information and hash values of difference between biometric information concatenated with a random number.

The server does not have a secret key. Also, the server can not abuse the authentication protocol as a decryption machine, as described in Sec.5.1. Therefore the server can not decrypt any ciphertext. In addition, the server can not estimate the preimage of hash values because of onewayness of the hash function.

Therefore, even if an attacker can hijack the server, the attacker can not obtain information about biometric information.

**Requirement 2.** Information stored in a smart card is only secret key $s$ and random number $k$. Therefore it is impossible for an attacker to obtain information about biometric information by theft of a smart card.

**Requirement 3.** An attacker with a user's smart card can retrieve the user's secret key $s$ and random number $k$. However, we can show that even if an attacker can obtain a smart card, the attacker can not succeed impersonation without knowing the user's biometric information:

To succeed in impersonating, the attacker has to transmit to the server a set of hash values $\Gamma$ which contains $Hash\,(u||\alpha)$ in Step 2-6. This means that the attacker is required to guess $\alpha$ with high probability. This is, however, proved to be impossible, as explained as explained below.

The attacker can present an arbitrary data $\hat{x}$ to the server, instead of the attacker's biometric information, since the attacker knows the secret key. That is, the attacker encrypts $\hat{x}$ to obtain the ciphertext $(t'_1, t'_2)$, and transmits it to the server in Step 2-3. In this case, $(w_1, w_2)$ calculated by the server using $(t_1, t_2)$ and $(t'_1, t'_2)$ in Step 2-4 is a ciphertext of $\alpha \cdot g^{k(x-\hat{x})}$. Therefore, after receiving $(w_1, w_2)$, all information the attacker knows is $\left(k, \hat{x}, \alpha \cdot g^{k(x-\hat{x})}\right)$. To guess the value $R$ from $\left(k, \hat{x}, \alpha \cdot g^{k(x-\hat{x})}\right)$, it is necessary for the attacker to know $x$ or $x - \hat{x}$ with high probability. This means that the attacker who succeeds impersonation can estimate the user's biometric information $x$ with high probability before the start of the protocol. - Q.E.D.-

More preciously, if the attacker could only get the amount of the difference $x - \hat{x}$, the attacker can calculate $R$ without knowing the user's biometric information $x$ itself. In practical sense, however, we can understand that this is not a critical issue, since the attacker who knows $x - \hat{x}$ is almost equivalent to the attacker who knows $x$.

**Table 2.** Security comparison

|  | Traditional | Cancelable Biometrics | Proposed method |
|---|---|---|---|
| Requirement1 | Not satisfied | Partially Satisfied | Satisfied |
| Requirement2 | — (1) | Satisfied | Satisfied |
| Requirement3 | — (1) | Satisfied | Satisfied |
| Requirement4 | Not satisfied | Not satisfied | Satisfied |
| Update of Template | Not satisfied | Satisfied | Satisfied |

[1] Traditional biometric authentication does not utilize a smart card.

**Requirement 4.** An attacker can retransmit $(t'_1, t'_2)$ that an authorized user transmitted in Step 2-3. However, the server generates different random numbers $z$, $\alpha$ each time to compute $(w_1, w_2)$ in Step 2-4, therefore the attacker without knowledge of the secret key $s$ can not decrypt $(w_1, w_2)$, and thus impersonation will fail.

Finally we compare security issues of our protocol with the traditional biometric authentication protocol and the cancelable biometric authentication protocol. Table 2 shows the result of comparison.

Cancelable biometrics do not fully satisfy Requirement 1, because difference between the enrolled biometric information and the presented biometric information is leaked out to the server hijacker. Also, Requirement 4 is not satisfied, because it is possible to succeed replay attack by retransmitting the information derived from wiretapping of the communication line.

On the other hand, our protocol as well as Nagai scheme and Ogata scheme satisfies all requirements. However, as described in Requirement 3, our protocol will allow an attacker who knows the amount of the difference $x - \hat{x}$ to impersonate an authorized user without knowing the user's biometric information $x$. In practical sense, the attacker who knows $x - \hat{x}$ is almost equivalent to the attacker who knows $x$. So, we can understand that this is not a critical problem. But, it is small decline of security level compared to Nagai scheme and Ogata scheme. We will give an improvement of our protocol against this issue in Sec.6.

## 5.3  Comparison of Efficiency

Here, we compare the efficiency of our protocol with other ZeroBio protocols such as Nagai scheme and Ogata scheme presented in Section 3.

We compare computational complexity by the number of exponentiation operation needed for one authentication phase, and network traffic by the number of data transmitted during one authentication phase. Ogata et al. improved their result in [9] by storing additional information in a smart card to reduce both computational complexity and network traffic without declining any security. However, as the same improvement as [9] can be applied also to our protocol, we compare here Ogata scheme and our scheme without utilizing the improvement proposed in [9].

**Table 3.** Comparison of proposed protocol and other ZeroBio protocol

|  |  | Nagai scheme | Ogata scheme | Our work |
|---|---|---|---|---|
| Netwrok traffic | user | $6\ell$ $L\_p$ | $(40\theta+21)L\_p$ | $(2\theta+1)L\_h+3L\_p$ |
|  | server | $2\ell$ $L\_p$ | $(4\theta+2)L\_p$ | $2L\_p$ |
| Computational complexity | user | $5\ell$ +1 | $40\theta+22$ | $2\theta+4$ |
|  | server | $5\ell$ | $36\theta+18$ | 2 |

Let $L\_p$ be the size of the transmitted data packets (typically, $L\_p = 1024$ bits) and $L\_h$ be the length of a hash value (typically, $L\_h = 160$ bits). Let $\ell$ be the number of hidden layer unit in neural network. And $\theta$ be a security parameter used in Ogata scheme and our scheme to define the authentic interval $[-\theta,\ \theta]$ for the difference between biometric information. Then, we can summarize the estimates of computational complexity and network traffic needed for each protocol in Table 3.

We first compare our protocol with Nagai scheme. Although the biometric information fed to neural network is $n$-dimensional vector in Nagai scheme, we assume $n = 1$ here for simplicity of estimation. We can see from Table 3 that computational complexity and network traffic are proportional to the number of hidden layer unit $\ell$. As $\ell$ and $\theta$ are different parameter, we can not directly compare with Nagai scheme. However Nagai scheme at least needs additional computational cost to train the weight of the connection in the neural network.

Next, we compare our protocol with Ogata scheme. Our protocol achieves improvement in both computational complexity and network traffic needed for the server and the user. For the user, our protocol needs only $1/20$ of computational complexity and network traffic needed for Ogata scheme. For the server, our protocol needs $1/(18\theta + 9)$ of computational complexity, and $1/(2\theta + 1)$ of network traffic needed for Ogata scheme. Therefore, we can confirm that our protocol achieves the performance improvement compared to Nagai scheme and Ogata scheme.

## 6   Improvement of Our Protocol

In the security evaluation with respect to Requirement 3 in Section 5.2, we described that if an attacker knows $x - \hat{x}$, the attacker can impersonate without knowing the enrolled biometric information $x$. This means that even if $\hat{x}$ is not close to $x$, an attacker who presents an arbitrary data $\hat{x}$ will be authenticated in the case that the attacker knows the difference $x - \hat{x}$. In practical sense, we can understand that this is not a critical issue, since the attacker who knows $x - \hat{x}$ is almost equivalent to the attacker who knows $x$. However, it is more preferable if our protocol can prove that the user indeed possesses $x'$ such that sufficiently close to the enrolled biometric information $x$. Therefore, in this section, we try to improve our protocol.

More concretely, the user transmits every ciphertext of integers $d \in \Delta$ at the enrolled phase. The server generates random bit $b$ at the authentication phase. If $b = 0$, then the server transmits the ciphertext of $\alpha d$ to the user and checks the reply from the user satisfies $Hash\,(u||\alpha) \in \Gamma$ to confirm that the user compute with the proper $d$. If $b = 1$, the regular authentication phase (namely, the Authentication Phase described in Section 4.3) is conducted. Note that the procedures for the user are the same regardless of whether $b$ is 1 or 0.

Detailed explanation of our improved protocol is described as follow.

## 6.1 Authentication Method

### Enrollment phase

**Step 3-1:** Authorized user chooses random integers $k, r \in Z_p$ ($k \neq 0$). In addition, the user chooses random integers $r[d] \in Z_p$ for each $d \in \Delta$, where $r[d]$ is used for encrypting each $d$ in Step 3-4.

**Step 3-2:** The user generates secret key $s$ of ElGamal encryption and corresponding public key $y = g^s$.

**Step 3-3:** The user puts his/her authentic biometric sample to the biometric reader to obtain biometric information $x$, and computes the ciphertext $(t_1, t_2) = (g^r, g^{kx} \cdot y^r)$.

**Step 3-4:** The user computes $E(\Delta) = \{(g^{r[d]}, g^{kd} \cdot y^{r[d]})|d \in \Delta\}$, the set of ciphertexts of $kd$ for all $d \in \Delta$.

**Step 3-5:** The user transmits $y$, $(t_1, t_2)$ and $E(\Delta)$. Note that the elements of $E(\Delta)$ should be permuted before sending to server. Otherwise, attackers may guess the relationship between ciphertexts and plaintexts from the order of elements of $E(\Delta)$.

**Step 3-6:** The server stores $y$, $(t_1, t_2)$ and $E(\Delta)$ together with the user ID, while the user stores $s, y, k$ in his/her smart card.

### Authentication phase

**Step 4-1:** A user chooses random integer $r' \in Z_p$.

**Step 4-2:** The user puts his/her biometric sample to the biometric reader to obtain biometric information $x'$. Then, the user retrieves $s, y, k$ from his/her smart card, and computes the ciphertext $(t_1', t_2') = (g^{r'}, g^{kx'} \cdot y^{r'})$.

**Step 4-3:** The user transmits $(t_1', t_2')$ to the server. Step 4-4 to Step 4-8 are independently conducted $L$ times at the same time.

**Step 4-4:** The server generates random bit $b$. If $b = 0$, then, the server randomly chooses $z, \alpha \in Z_p$ and $(e_1, e_2) \in E(\Delta)$ as blind factors, and transmits $(w_1, w_2) = (e_1 g^z, e_2 \alpha y^z)$ to the user. If $b = 1$, then the server randomly chooses $z, \alpha \in Z_p$ as blind factors, and transmits $(w_1, w_2) = (g^z t_1/t_1', \alpha y^z t_2/t_2')$ to the user.

**Step 4-5:** The user decrypts $(w_1, w_2)$ with secret key $s$ to obtain $m = \alpha \cdot g^{k(x-x')}$.

**Step 4-7:** The user chooses a random number $u \in Z_p$ as a blind factor. Then the user computes $\Gamma = \{Hash\,(u||m \cdot g^{kd})\,|d \in \Delta\}$, and transmits $\Gamma$ and $u$ to the server. Here, the order of elements of $\Gamma$ is permuted before transmitting.

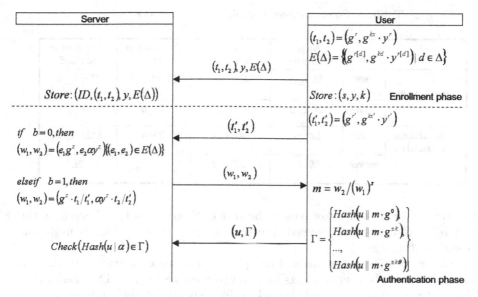

**Fig. 3.** Protocol with higher security

**Step 4-8:** The server computes $Hash\,(u||\alpha)$, then checks whether it satisfies $Hash\,(u||\alpha) \in \Gamma$.

**Step 4-9:** If Step 4-8 is always true, then the user is authenticated.

We illustrate the above protocol in Figure 3.

### 6.2 Discussion

In our regular protocol shown in Sec.4, $(t'_1, t'_2)$ does not have to be a ciphertext of $kx'$ where $x'$ is sufficiently close to $x$. We first show that in our improved protocol, the user (or attacker) is not authenticated with high probability if $x'$ is not close to $x$.

Assume that $(t'_1, t'_2)$ is a ciphertext of $k\hat{x}$ generated by an attacker in Step 4-2, where $x - \hat{x}$ is not small enough and the attacker knows the amount of $x - \hat{x}$. In the case of $b = 1$, Step 4-4 to Step 4-8 are the same as the regular authentication phase. Therefore, the attacker can impersonate using the knowledge of the difference $x - \hat{x}$. More concretely, the attacker generates $Hash\,(u||\alpha)$ by calculating $Hash\,(u||m \cdot g^{kd})$ with $d = -(x - \hat{x})$, mixes it into $\Gamma$, and transmits $\Gamma$ to the server in Step 4-7.

On the other hand, if $b = 0$, the attacker has to calculating $Hash\,(u||m \cdot g^{kd})$ with every $d \in \Delta$ to compute $\Gamma$ in Step 4-7 so that the attacker can obtain $\Gamma$ which includes $Hash\,(u||\alpha)$ in it.

That is, to succeed impersonation, the attacker needs to use $d = -(x - \hat{x})$ for $b = 1$ and $d \in \Delta$ for $b = 0$ when calculating $Hash\,(u||m \cdot g^{kd})$, However $(w_1, w_2)$ transmitted from the server in Step 4-4 is concealed by the random number $R$, and the attacker has no way to know the value $b$. This means that

Table 4. Computational complexity and network traffic

| | | Nagai scheme | Ogata scheme | Proposed in section4 | Proposed in section5 |
|---|---|---|---|---|---|
| Netwrok traffic | user | $6\ell$ $L\_p$ | $(40\theta+21)L\_p$ | $(2\theta+1)L\_h$ $+3L\_p$ | $(2+i)L\_p$ $+ (2\theta+1)iL\_h$ |
| | server | $2\ell$ $L\_p$ | $(4\theta+2)L\_p$ | $2L\_p$ | $2iL\_p$ |
| Computational complexity | user | $5\ell$ $+1$ | $40\theta+22$ | $2\theta+4$ | $L(2\theta+2)+2$ |
| | server | $5$ $\ell$ | $36\theta+18$ | $2$ | $2L$ |

the probability that attacker passes the test of Step 2-8 is $1/2$. Therefore, the probability that attacker succeeds impersonation is $(1/2)^i$, which is negligible for sufficiently large $i$.

Next, we discuss computational complexity and network traffic. In the improved protocol, the user conducts Step 4-4 to Step 4-8 $i$ times. This means that computational complexity and network traffic depend not only on $\theta$ but also on security parameter $i$. There is the tradeoff between security and computational complexity and network traffic. Therefore it is important to set proper $i$ which satisfies the required security level.

Table 4 shows the estimate of network traffic and computational complexity needed for our protocol, where $L\_p$, $L\_h$, $\ell$ and are the same definition as used in Table 3. We can find that the improvement in the security level of our protocol is accompanied by an increase in its computational complexity and network traffic.

# 7    Conclusion

In this paper, we proposed a secure remote biometric authentication system which has a certain level of resistance against impersonation and biometric information disclosure. We also compared our method with other asymmetric biometric authentication, and found that our method achieves the asymmetric biometric authentication with comparatively smaller computational complexity and network traffic.

# References

1. Ratha, N.K., Connell, J.H., Bolle, R.M.: Enhancing Security and Privacy in Biometrics-based Authentication Systems. IBM Systems Journal 40(3) (2001)
2. Cambier, J.L., Cahn von Seelen, U., Glass, R., Moore, R., Scott, I., Braithwaite, M., Daugman, J.: Application-Specific Biometric Templates. In: IEEE Workshop on Automatic Identification Advanced Technologies, Tarrytown, NY, March 14-15, pp. 167–171 (2002)
3. Hirata, S., Takahashi, K.: Cancelable Biometrics with Perfect Secrecy for Correlation-based Matching. In: Tistarelli, M., Nixon, M.S. (eds.) ICB 2009. LNCS, vol. 5558, pp. 875–885. Springer, Heidelberg (2009)

4. Hill, C.J.: Risk of masquerade arising from the storage of biometrics, Bachelor thesis, Dept. of CS, Australian National University (2002)
5. Nagai, K., Kikuchi, H., Ogata, W., Nishigaki, M.: ZeroBio - Evaluation and Development of Asymmetric Fingerprint Authentication System Using Oblivious Neural Network Evaluation Protocol. In: Proceedings of 2007 International Conference on Availability, Reliability and Security, pp. 1155–1159 (2007)
6. Ogata, W., Kikuchi, H., Nishigaki, M.: Zero-knowledge interactive proofs for proving nearness of biometrics and its application. In: Symposium on Information Theory and its Applications, SITA2006, pp. 319–322 (2006)(in Japanese)
7. Paul, K., Joshua, J., Benjamin, J.: Differential Power Analysis. In: Wiener, M. (ed.) CRYPTO 1999. LNCS, vol. 1666, pp. 388–397. Springer, Heidelberg (1999)
8. Fujisaki, E., Okamoto, T.: Statistical Zero-Knowledge Protocols to Prove Modular Polynomial Relations. In: Kaliski Jr., B.S. (ed.) CRYPTO 1997. LNCS, vol. 1294, pp. 413–430. Springer, Heidelberg (1997)
9. Ogata, W., Kikuchi, H., Nishigaki, M.: Improvement of the biometric authentication system using ZKIP. In: Symposium on Information Theory and its Applications, SITA2007, pp. 689–693 (2007)(in Japanese)

# Author Index